WILD IRELAND

A TRAVELLER'S GUIDE

BRENDAN LEHANE

WITH PHOTOGRAPHS BY
MARC SCHLOSSMAN

INTERLINK BOOKS
An imprint of Interlink Publishing Group, Inc.
NEW YORK

First American edition published 2000 by
INTERLINK BOOKS
An imprint of Interlink Publishing Group, Inc.
99 Seventh Avenue • Brooklyn, New York 11215 and
46 Crosby Street • Northampton, Massachusetts 01060

Copyright © 1995, 2000 Sheldrake Holdings Ltd
Main text copyright © Brendan Lehane 1995, 2000

Library of Congress Cataloging-in-Publication Data
Lehane, Brendan
   Wild Ireland: a traveller's guide / by Brendan Lehane.
   p. cm. – (Wild Guides)
   Originally published: San Francisco: Sierra Club
   Books, 1995
   Includes bibliographical references (p.)
   ISBN 1-56656-363-1
   1. Natural history–Ireland–Guidebooks. 2. Natural
   areas–Ireland–Guidebooks. 3. Ireland–Guidebooks.
   I. Title. II. Wild guides (Interlink Books)
   QH143.L43 2000
   508.415–dc21   99-087775

Printed in Hong Kong

Front cover: A winding, rock-lined creek leads down to
Lough Tay from Sally Gap, in the heart of the Wicklow
Mountains.

EDITOR: SIMON RIGGE
Art Direction: Ivor Claydon
Map Eitor: Malcolm Day
Senior Editorial Assistants: Jennie Matthew, Robin
Titchener
Editorial Assistants: Richard Blake-James, Giles Clare,
Charles Dietz, Marie Fanget, Vincent Guerin, Ingrid
Karikari, Chrisoula Petridis, Daniele Pittimo, Suzanne
Scott, Sarah West
Line Illustrations: Syd Lewis
Production Assistant: Anja Kusber
Typesetting: Cameron Typesetting
Maps: Arcadia Consultants
Index: Indexing Specialists

To order or request our complete catalog,
please call us at **1-800-238-LINK** or write to:
Interlink Publishing
46 Crosby Street • Northampton, MA 01060
E-mail: info@interlinkbooks.com
Website: www.interlinkbooks.com

THE AUTHOR

BRENDAN LEHANE comes from an old Irish
family and has lived for long periods in Ireland.
He has written, among other books, *The Companion Guide to Ireland, Dublin, The Compleat
Flea, Natural History,* an introduction for children, *The Power of Plants,* a survey of the influences of plants on human life, and *The Quest of
Three Abbots,* a view of life and spirituality during the golden age of Irish Christianity. He has
travelled in Africa, America, the Middle East
and continental Europe, and has written articles
for the *Telegraph Magazine* and many other publications. In 1999 he was elected a Fellow of the
Royal Society of Literature.

THE PHOTOGRAPHER

MARC SCHLOSSMAN contributes to many
national newspapers and magazines in his native
United States and in Britain, including *The Independent, Harper's and Queen* and *BBC Wildlife
Magazine.* In his travels he has climbed Mount
Kilimanjaro, lived with headhunters in the jungle
of the Philippines and canoed into the North-
West Territories. His love of Ireland takes him

there as often as possible. He travelled 7,000
miles, walked, climbed, camped on location and
got soaked and chilled photographing the landscape of Ireland for this book.

THE GENERAL EDITOR

DOUGLAS BOTTING has travelled to Brazil,
South Yemen, the Sahara, Arctic Siberia and to
many European wild places. His travel books include *One Chilly Siberian Morning, Wilderness
Europe* and *Rio de Janeiro.* He has recently written the authorized biography of the author and
conservationist, Gerald Durrell.

CONSULTANTS

JOHN BURTON is a natural history and
wildlife conservation writer and consultant. Formerly secretary of the Fauna and Flora Preserva-
tion Society, he is the co-founder with Douglas
Botting of the Wild Guides series.

ELEANOR MAYES is an ecological consultant.
She works in ecological research and survey, as
well as in conservation policy, and provides planning and management advice.

CONTENTS

ABOUT THE SERIES

What would the world be, once bereft
Of wet and of wilderness? Let them be
  left,
O let them be left, wildness and wet;
Long live the weeds and the wilderness
  yet.
Gerard Manley Hopkins: Inversnaid

These books are about those embattled refuges of wildness and wet, the wild places of Europe. But where, in this most densely populated sub-continent, do we find a truly wild place?

Ever since our Cro-Magnon ancestors began their forays into the virgin forests of Europe 40,000 years ago, the land and its creatures have been in retreat before *Homo sapiens*. Forests have been cleared, marshes drained and rivers straightened. Even some of those landscapes that appear primordial are in fact the result of human activity. Heather-covered moorland in North Yorkshire and parched Andalusian desert have this in common: both were once covered by great forests which ancient settlers knocked flat.

What then remains that can be called wild? There are still a few areas in Europe that are untouched by man – places generally so unwelcoming either in terrain or in climate that man has not wanted to touch them at all – and these are indisputably wild.

For some people, wildness suggests conflict with nature: a wild place is a part of the planet so savage and desolate that you risk your life whenever you venture into it. This is in part true but would limit the eligible places to the most impenetrable bog or highest mountain tops in the worst winter weather – a rather restricted view. Another much broader definition considers a wild place to be a part of the planet where living things can find a natural refuge from the influence of modern industrial society. By this definition a wild place is for wildlife as well as that portmanteau figure referred to in these pages as the wild traveller: the hillwalker, backpacker, bird-watcher, nature lover, explorer, nomad, loner, mystic, masochist, *aficionado* of the great outdoors, or permutations of all these things.

This is the definition we have observed in selecting the wild places described in these books. Choosing them has not been easy. Even so, we hope the criterion has proved rigid enough to exclude purely pretty (though popular) countryside, and flexible enough to include the greener and gentler wild places, of great natural historical interest perhaps, as well as the starker, more savage ones where the wild explorers come into their own.

These are not guide-books in the conventional sense, for to describe every neck of the woods and twist of the trail throughout Europe would require a library of volumes. Nor are these books addressed to the technical specialist – the caver, diver, rock climber or cross-country skier; the orchid-hunter, lepidopterist or beetle-maniac – for such experts will have data of their own. They are books intended for the great outdoor traveller – including the expert outside his own field of expertise (the orchid-hunter in a cave, the diver on a mountain top) – who wishes to scrutinize the range of wild places on offer in Europe, to learn a little more about them and to set about exploring them off the beaten track.

One of the greatest consolations in the preparation of these books has been to find that after 40,000 years of hunting, clearing, draining and ploughing, Cro-Magnon and their descendants have left so much of Europe that can still be defined as wild.

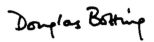

WILD IRELAND: AN INTRODUCTION

Nothing sudden triggered the race. A hefty mantle of ice, which had cloaked most of Ireland and the rest of northern Europe for millennia and made the living of any life beneath it more or less impossible, began during a new wave of warmth to melt. From southerly latitudes opportunist organisms began creeping, swimming, flying, drifting, blowing, walking and trundling in. They crossed the dry land which would in due course become the English Channel and some colonized Britain-to-be. A good many more went on to cross the dry land already beginning to be covered by what would be known as the Irish Sea and St George's Channel. Beginning 10,000 years ago, the period of melting lasted about 2,000 years, causing the sea to rise more than 300 feet (100 metres) – though part of this increased depth was due to a sinking of the floor of the Irish Sea. Many plants and creatures won this race to arrive before the last of the Irish-British land bridges flooded, but in species-counts, Britain, with only one water-barrier between it and Europe, did considerably better.

When all that could do so had settled down, Ireland had not much more than two-thirds the number of Britain's wild plants and insects, about four-fifths of the birds, a third of the amphibians and a quarter of the reptiles. Britain, moreover, is not, relatively speaking, well off. In terms of vascular plants, for example, Ireland today has 815 native species; Britain 1,172. But France, whence many of them came, has 3,500.

Not all this can be put down to Ireland's early insularity. Birds fly thousands of miles, some seeds float similar distances without harm, others are carried by flying birds. Many animals swim. There are indeed wild plants in Ireland which do not grow in Britain at all and come from sources much further off. The truth is that, compared with other countries, Ireland was short of habitats as well. Absence of mountains as high as Scotland's, of England's chalk downs and lowland heaths meant that many British plants, birds and animals, even if they had made it to Ireland, would have found no home there. When humans moved in and flexed their muscles, they tamed – because it was so tameable – a much larger proportion of the land than was the case in most other countries. Limited in size, habitats and species, Ireland might seem a poor bet for those in search of wilderness.

In fact, it is one of the world's more beautiful countries: a land of greens and purples and dramatic shapes and contours under a changing canopy of blue and white, blown in from the Atlantic. With a third of the area of Great Britain it contains no more than a fourteenth of the population. It does, it is true, spread its people more thinly and widely than Britain (Irish country people preferring the homestead to the village). But there are few places outside towns where numbers become oppressive, except perhaps in summer and on well-trodden tourist paths. Old tradition has for generations made it possible for travellers to walk almost anywhere (though a fencing frenzy financed by Europe is curtailing this privilege). Ireland's size makes it easy to get anywhere, except to islands in bad weather. Mountain and moorland come cheek by jowl with lush river valley, lowland bog, steep cliffs and broad sandy beaches. Ireland lies athwart important bird-routes, providing wonderful seasonal spectacles of the migrations of (in particular) sea-birds and waders, and the frequent occurrence of rarities blown off their familiar routes, as well as the continual viewing of its native birds.

Ireland is rich in unexpected sites of wildness, often too small for detailed treatment in this book but fascinating all the same. Wildness of course begins as soon as humans turn their backs. Ants, mice, moths and other wildlife advance from the sidelines. A minute spider swings in like Tarzan on a rope of gossamer. Wildness pullulates under our eyes. In a mysteriously cheap Dublin flat many years ago I was to be so vexed by fleas that I turned to studying them as a therapy – *tout comprendre c'est tout pardonner* – and in due course published a book on them. In our towns, foxes scavenge among the garbage bags and peregrines nest on towers. Huge flocks of pied wagtails spend winter nights on bare trees in the middle of Dublin's central thoroughfare. A naturalist could keep busy well within city limits.

Unless they had a pressing reason for doing otherwise, the Irish have generally left redundant buildings to rot and corners of old fields and demesnes to grow and teem and tangle according to nature's way. They have let hedges grow fat at the expense of pasture. They have left disused canals to breed their own aquatic populations; ancient barns and monasteries and churches and bridges and Anglo-Irish mansions to drape themselves in ivy and offer homes to innumerable owls, swallows, bats, squirrels, frogs, toads, fungi and lichens.

I use the past tense here not because these things are no longer true but because they are less true than they used to be. At a time when most people acknowledge that a stop has to be put to the poisoning and squandering of natural resources, the Irish – with the help of the EU – seem to be squandering, polluting, fouling, spraying, ripping up and hacking back more than ever before. You see miles of hedges cut with disfiguring mechanical cutters (often at a season when birds are nesting inside them), prematurely bare and savagely ruined choirs, where evicted birds have no more cause to sing; you see barbed-wire fences where once all could roam freely; you see mile upon mile of flat muddy rock from which ten feet of peat, the accumulation of up to ten thousand years, has been gradually lifted. Less harmful but quite out of keeping with the spirit of the wild, it is necessary to mention the doings of the Irish equivalent of the Indian baboo, the normally deskbound functionary who cannot see a blade of grass without wishing to attach an explanatory label to it. There seems at times to be hardly a hill or lake or

pass or valley they have not ringed by with signposts – 'The Tain Trail', 'The Comeraghs Drive', 'Sarsfield's Route' – so much so that you find yourself choosing roads bare of these baubles, not so much to escape the signs as to find out what exceptional qualities can cause a route to be left without them.

I have to be very careful in saying all this. There is a strong tendency among writers about the country to thrash Ireland for doing things other countries have been doing with impunity for years. Ireland for some reason brings out the old-fashioned parent or pedagogue in the people of other nations. You can fancy you hear them saying – perhaps you can even hear yourself saying – very late and quite without penitence, 'Don't do as I did, foolish child. Do as I say.'

The truth is that Ireland's record, while not stainless, is considerably better than those of Britain and other European countries. Ireland may be small, but it is still quite big enough to offer huge and magical tracts that have escaped so far the hand of polluter and bureaucrat. There are the mountains, many of them (especially in the South-West) wild enough to pose problems to the most experienced climber, even if they may have quite easy alternative routes to the top. There are inland ranges and inland lakes and rivers, some of which have retained the rugged air of wilderness. Most of all, there is the west coast, the startling, varied sequence of sliced mountain, lone islands, long façades of spume-splashed cliff, bird-packed stacks, snaking promontories and stiletto inlets, golden strands, blue lagoons, deep, clear, rocky bays – and an ancient people who have graduated from the harshest buffets of climate and history to become as friendly and kind and hospitable as any on earth.

THE KEY TO IRELAND'S WILD PLACES

THE SHAPE OF THE WILD

Ireland consists of a generally flat, limestone-floored interior, rimmed disjointedly by mountains or lesser uplands. The mountains in Donegal, Mayo and north-west Galway go back to the so-called Caledonian orogeny (or mountain-birth) of some 400 million years ago, whose south-west to north-east foldings and upthrusts also created the Highlands of Scotland. Some of the central ridges of these mountains consist of granite. The ranges in the southern part of the country are predominantly formed of old red sandstone and tend to lie in an east-west direction. They resulted from the Hercynian orogeny, which erupted about 300 million years ago, and created over to the east what have become the Harz mountains of Germany. The long peninsulas in the west of Counties Kerry and Cork are also of sandstone. The Wicklow mountains of the south-east, another huge granite outcrop hemmed by durable metamorphic rocks, came about through the upheavals of 500 million years ago. In the north-east the Mourne mountains are another, far more recent, granite intrusion, dating from about 65 million years ago, the end of the age of dinosaurs.

Limestone is not confined to the low-level midlands where it underlies the great but diminished bogs and the lush pastures of Ireland's richest dairy farms. It also rises up to form grass-topped mountains in Sligo and Leitrim; distinctive rock overhangs, dramatic cliffs and gorges in Fermanagh and Cavan; and the uncanny landscape of the Burren in County Clare.

All these things happened while Ireland drifted wherever the tectonic plates of which she forms part took her: from near the Antarctic, where all the world's land masses were once concentrated, over the Equator (with long periods of submergence and a time of division which carried one half of the country hundreds of miles from the other and back again), to her present location a little closer to the North Pole than to the Equator. This is 99 per cent of Ireland's history. In the most recent moments of geological time – a million or so years ago – came the Ice Age, which periodically covered parts or all of the country in a mile or more of ice. An instant ago came humans.

The movement of ice wore down rock, scraped rough surfaces smooth, dug out valleys and blocked them with stony litter so that many became lakes. People removed the forests that sprang up when the ice receded, turned land to pasture and crops, dug away much of the peat that came after the tree-felling, drained marshes, dammed rivers, and made reservoirs, towns, highways.

WILD HABITATS

All of these stages in their varied ways provided homes, temporary or permanent, for all kinds of flora and fauna. Many of the species of the past have disappeared for ever, such as the great auk and giant Irish deer (*Cervus giganteus*). Others like the hippopotamus and elephant have moved to more sympathetic climates. Plenty remain and most of them survive in habitats which still qualify as wild.

The coast: the battle between land and sea is at its most relentless on the west coast, where Atlantic might is flung, most days and most nights, and with real if imperceptible effect, at massive cliff-faces like those of Slieve League, Croaghaun and Moher, or the toppling defences at the ends of the peninsulas of Cork and Kerry. Most of the rest of the coast is rocky, too, but lower-lying, less stark and bluff: rock coves, rock stacks, rock islands. More kinds of bird inhabit the coastal features of Ireland than any comparable habitat. Where rivers meet the sea there are, in many cases, deep broad estuaries, emptying and filling with the tides, fringed with mud-flats, sand-dunes or salt marshes and attracting thousands of wading birds and wildfowl. Seaside pastures such as the Wexford Slobs are used by wintering geese, swans and ducks, sometimes in flocks of many thousands, making some of the most impressive spectacles Ireland has to offer.

Mountain and bogs: most of Ireland's raised bogs have been lost to peat exploitation but a handful remain, mostly as nature reserves. However, together with the coast, the highlands occupy the greater part of Ireland's wild places and most, on their upper levels, are covered by blanket bog, which developed after the Ice Age. The plants supported by the bog must be acid-lovers, either needing a minimum of minerals or able to supplement the soil's meagre supply.

7

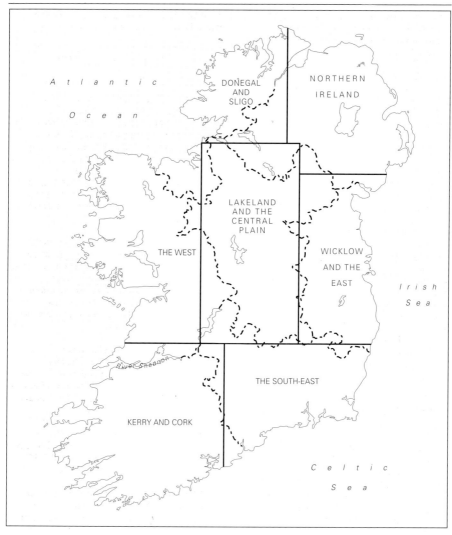

Inland waters: with its miles of coastline, its tracery of rivers, its ubiquitous lakes, its marshes, callows, canals, lagoons, rias and heavy rainfall, Ireland is a watery fief. On her own, nature did not overload these waters with fish. Freshwater natives are few in number. Since the Ice Age, which killed off all previous species, only migrant fish – salmon, sea trout, shad, smelt – and stickleback and lamprey were able to occupy the lakes and rivers. A surviving curiosity is the char, usually found in and close to the Arctic. A similar Arctic species is the pollan, found in Lough Neagh and in the lower Shannon.

Birds that eat them follow the fish but many more settle on rivers and lakes to graze or eat the seeds of the underwater and waterside vegetation – reeds, spike-rushes, pondweeds, mare's tail grasses and several kinds of algae – or excavate wet mud and pasture for invertebrates. Some choose this habitat as protection from predators. The heron is a solemn, still presence in almost all freshwater habitats. Lough Neagh, the country's biggest lake, and Lough Corrib are the most important Irish lakes for birds, mainly because they are quite shallow. They attract huge numbers of duck and other waterfowl.

Low-lying riverside pastures which regularly flood in winter are known in Ireland as callows. Thousands of birds take advantage of the safety afforded by the floodwaters in winter and early spring. Callows are found on the Shannon river, on the River Suck in County Roscommon and on the River Blackwater in County Waterford. Turloughs or karst lakes provide protection for curlews, lapwings, some golden plovers and other waders and wildfowl.

Woodlands: the broadleaf forests, primarily of native oak, but including also native elm, ash, yew, hazel, birch, rowan, willow and alder which once covered most of the country have been reduced to patches and pockets by massive clearances. Irrepressible sycamore, beech, horse-chestnut and the one deciduous conifer, larch, are all introductions of recent centuries.

Woodland animals may include grey and red squirrels, pine martens, foxes, badgers, and in the fewer places where they occur, fallow, sika, red and red-sika hybrid deer. By far the largest number of woodland birds - up to 85 per cent according to surveys - are robin, wren, blue tit, coal tit, chaffinch and goldcrest, the country's smallest bird, common in conifer woods as well as broadleaf. Treecreeper, jay, sparrowhawk, kestrel, woodcock, pheasant, chiffchaff, blackcap, song thrush and wood pigeon are also found.

PROTECTED WILD PLACES

National parks in the Irish Republic, as in most other countries but not in Britain, are entirely state-owned. There is therefore no clash between the interests of visitors and those of resident farmers and landowners. It means, however, that the space occupied by such parks is small, less than half a per cent of the country's area. The five existing national parks are Glenveagh National Park, Co. Donegal; Connemara National Park, Co. Galway; Killarney National Park, Co. Kerry; Wicklow Mountains National Park; and Burren National Park, Co. Clare.

Natural Heritage Areas at present being designated, following a new survey, will cover much more of the country: some five to seven per cent. They are equivalent to Sites of Special Scientific Interest (SSSI) in Northern Ireland and in Britain.

Northern Ireland contains no national parks but does have officially designated Areas of Outstanding Natural Beauty, SSSIs, National Trust land and reserves and the island's only World Heritage Site, the Giant's Causeway.

TO THE READER

Organization: Each chapter is divided into exploration zones containing a narrative description, followed by a fact-pack which gives practical information backed up with postal, e-mail and web-site addresses, telephone and fax numbers and lists of maps and further reading. This hybrid arrangement avoids cluttering the author's personal narrative with tedious guide-book detail, but at the same time ensures that you can find practical references instantly when you want them.

Eagle symbols: the eagle symbols used in this book indicate the wildness of the exploration zone to which they refer. This scale is based on a number of factors, including remoteness, ruggedness, spaciousness, uniqueness, wildlife interest, natural beauty and the author's subjective reactions. Three eagles is the highest rating, no eagles the lowest.

Maps: the Bord Fáilte Map of Ireland, 1:600,000, covers both the Republic and Northern Ireland and is useful for initial route planning and orientation. Once you get closer to an exploration zone you will need the Ordnance Survey of Ireland (OSI) Discovery Series 1:50,000 maps or the Ordnance Survey of Northern Ireland (OSNI) Discoverer Series 1:50,000 maps listed in each fact-pack. Contact the OSI and OSNI (see USEFUL ADDRESSES, page 216) for map sales and stockists.

Updating: while everything possible has been done to ensure the accuracy of the facts in this book, information does become outdated. For this reason we would welcome readers' comments and corrections for incorporation in subsequent editions. Please write to The Editor, Wild Guides, Sheldrake Press, 188 Cavendish Road, London SW12 0DA, or send an e-mail to: mail@sheldrakepress.demon.co.uk.

Non-liability: both author and publishers have gone to great pains to point out the hazards that may confront the traveller in certain places described in *Wild Ireland*. We cannot under any circumstances accept any liability for any mishap, loss or injury sustained by any person venturing into any of the wild places listed in this book.

CHAPTER 1

Donegal and Sligo

Malin Head, a scatter of rock at the north end of Ireland, is better than most places to start pursuing Irish wildness. Wildness is what its name, location and character suggest. Europe stops here. Northward, across a thousand-mile gap of bleak ocean, lies the Arctic. The ghostly green of the northern lights is sometimes seen from these shores. Anyone who has heard years of shipping forecasts in Ireland or Britain knows of the frequency of Malin's gale-force 9s or storm-force 11s. The cliffs to its right and left glower out their resistance to the worst that north and north-westerly wind, tide, sleet and hail can do. It takes a lot of getting to, whatever means are employed. As wildness goes these days, Malin and the miles of mountain and moor and rock promontory that are its neighbours well deserve the epithet.

You can see this untamed landscape, dramatically, from an ancient elevated structure south of the peninsula and just five miles (eight kilometres) north-west of the city of Derry. The Grianan (pronounced greenan; it means 'sun-place') of Aileach is a restored circular stone royal palace, with much myth attached. It offers a telling preview of substantial parts of Counties Donegal, Derry and Tyrone. To the north is clearly seen Inishowen's great mass, and left of that, every bay and inlet of winding Lough Swilly, which the Fanad peninsula separates from Mulroy Bay and Sheephaven. To complete a circuit of the closer landmarks you can cast your

Sunset falls over Loughros Point on the Donegal coast. To the north lies Dawros Head, to the south the dramatic mass of the Slieve League peninsula and to the west, America.

eye around anti-clockwise until, after the basalt bluff of Binevenagh across to the east and the simple, shapely outline of Lough Foyle, you come back to Inishowen again. Further to the west a receding series of domed, coned and elongated outlines takes the view almost to the limits of this north-western corner of Ireland, to the west and south of Donegal and the nearer heights of Counties Sligo and Leitrim.

For me, and many others I think, this coastline of Donegal was once the most romantically wild of all. You thought of the battered galleons of the Armada, the great rebel Gaels sailing away from all their dreams, or Wolfe Tone cutting his throat when his last great hope turned to despair. Thirty years ago, neither nature nor man had done much to mar the setting of these pictures. Eagles and wolves had gone since Tone's time, it is true, but most of the rest would have at least looked unchanged. In recent years, however, something has happened which has removed the essentially wild personality from large tracts of land and coast.

Anyone looking for the wildness of Ireland nowadays has to adopt an attitude to bungalows. Their presence here is as intrusive as it is anywhere in the country, and although I never thought I should use the remotest coast of Donegal to discuss a rampant rash of bourgeois construction, it now seems the most sensible place. I shall look very hard for balance.

I used to think a symbol of Ireland was the explosive bush. If you walked close to almost any tangle of briar, bramble, thorn, furze or broom, in almost any field, on almost any summery day, your approach triggered a buzzing firework of insect life: flies, bluebottles, greenbottles, bugs, ladybirds, cardinal beetles took off in all directions – a wonderful precipitation of colourful motley. Years before, England had the same thing, but stripping fields for monoculture crops or grasses did for it there, and many parts of Ireland have gone the same way since. But there are still yards and in some places acres of these knotty shrubs, left because farmers like them or cannot be bothered to smooth the bumps or clear the stones or claim the soil they occupy.

One of Ireland's major crops must, in consequence, be the blackberry, and I must have removed tons of the fruit myself. I have seldom seen anyone else picking it. The Irish like blackberries, for sure, said my Irish cousin years ago. They will buy tins of blackberries with pleasure. They will buy frozen blackberries with delight. But they will not pick blackberries. Picking blackberries is what their grandparents or great-grandparents had to do to stay alive, and they would sooner avoid that association.

I say all this to stress that until recent years the country Irish were forced and accustomed to concentrate on necessities, and to work hard and long to acquire them. It was not a life – least of all in the barren west – that offered much time for refinements. It is difficult now to recall how hard life was in the west only thirty and forty years ago. There was no tourism, and farming offered no more than subsistence. All the young went to England or America. For the rare visitor, such as myself, it was very picturesque and appealing: there were thatched hovels and courteous peasants with leathery skins and charming turns of phrase, and transport by horse and cart, and fortunes under mattresses from mistrust of banks, and much porter and poteen and smiles and nasal song and the music of fiddles and some noisy drunkenness. A few people still spoke as they speak in the plays of Synge, who after all got some of his dialogue from listening to kitchen girls through the cracks in the floor of his rented room on Aran. For all the hardship, human life seemed congruous with nature.

But it is, and would have been then had one bothered to ask, perfectly clear that the peasants themselves did not think so. Those who could do so with ease escaped. Islanders gladly left lovely islands in which scraping a living took a heavy toll on health and time. They gladly forgot the Gaelic language that tied them to these harsh ways. But many of them could barely afford to do so. On the mainland too, life was a struggle.

Quite suddenly, the things the Irish coveted in Britain and the USA became available to them at home. Huge investments in tourism paid off. The European Common Market brought a range of subsidies, skills and opportunities that could not have been dreamt of ten years before. There were jobs, grants, buoyancy. To hell, the collective voice of western Ireland might have said, to hell with your blackberries. From now on we buy them in syrup, in cans. To the devil, they said, with your Donegal thatched cottages, that you came to admire and patronize for a couple of weeks and never had to live in. They were damp and dark and cramped and dirty. We hated them. We wanted spreading bungalows with glowing white walls and pedimented porticoes as in *Dallas* and *Dynasty*. We wanted big picture windows with views over the sea and the cliffs; wall-to-wall carpeting and central heating and swishing curtains with fancy pelmets; satellite television, fitted kitchens, en-suite bathrooms and lavatories, car ports, patios, balustrade boundaries and lions and pineapples on the piers of our garden gates. And now we can have them, and by Jesus, Mary and Joseph we will, say

what you dare. And our old houses can rot and go to the devil.

In an amazingly short span of years the bungalows were there. Revisiting parts of the west coast after long intervals, I got the impression that it had all happened, slyly, while my back was turned, as in a game of grandmother's footsteps. There is no other option but to see the inhabitants' point. Some of them can be rather touchy on the matter. If you say, 'Yes, but is it not a pity to abandon perfectly sound and agreeable two-storey houses to the winds?' they may sense the opposition they have heard often enough before, and bristle slightly. If you mention that the many new bungalows in Northern Ireland are at least subject to stringent planning laws, and kept in clusters rather than spread piecemeal about the most conspicuous eminences of the landscape, they will think you have gone far enough and their eyes may start to narrow. They may suggest that you would prefer to see them back in their cabins, ten to a room and the pig in with them, and a hole in the roof to let the smoke out. Or that you would have objected, twelve centuries ago, to the mass construction of the so-called beehive huts for monks on the Kerry promontories, claiming they spoilt the view (I probably should have done). The houses are there, occupied, giving deep satisfaction. Mr Jack FitzSimons, author of *Bungalow Bliss*, which for years outsold the Bible and provided plans for hundreds of such homes, made his fortune amid the grateful thanks of his fellow countrymen. In a decade the country underwent the greatest change of its whole existence. And bungalows did not bring the tourist numbers down.

It is what they have done to the nebulous ideal of wildness which is our concern here. You trudge round a windswept cape to be confronted by a pyramid pattern of bungalows. Like fairy lights, glossy white bungalows shine over the former desolation of a broad peat bog. There are bungalows beside the quiet meanders of tree-lined stream, or on the shores of a lake that is otherwise the private haunt of birds and fish. But they are not everywhere. They are most numerous on the west coast, a large proportion serving as holiday cottages, to let or not as the case may be. A lot of Donegal's bungalows are owned and used by citizens of Northern Ireland. Inland is relatively – but not entirely – free of them. Mountains are mercifully spared, and there are mighty tracts of unspoilt wilderness. Above a certain height, bungalows, like trees, do not flourish. We may soon be talking of the bungalow line. Otherwise they can spring on you anywhere, without warning. I recommend a bungalow blindspot, a knack of looking past, over or around them without actually noticing. So far it has eluded me.

I have put the worst of it. I believe it needed saying, but it is certainly not the last word on this or indeed any part of modern Ireland. Small it may be by comparison with its neighbours, but Ireland could sustain a lot more blemishes without losing its beauties, or its wildness. Up and down the north-west and west coasts are those wild habitats which draw huge numbers of sea-birds to breed every spring and summer: mile upon mile of cliff for the auks and others who lay and guard their solitary eggs against all perils and dangers; countless sea-girt rocks and islands whose grazing attracts vast numbers of wintering geese; broad mud-flats for long-legged, long-billed waders; cliff-top grasslands for puffins and nocturnal shearwaters. Ireland's abundance is not in numbers of species but in the numbers of individuals within a species – including spectacular breeds like gannets – which fill the available spaces.

Not only the coast teems with wildlife. Donegal's interior – Errigal and Muckish and other mountains, the deer-stocked parklands of Glenveagh, the Poisoned Glen, Lough Dunlewy and the rest – is as dramatic as anywhere in Ireland: primevally beautiful. Further south, in County Sligo, are the picturesque mountain formations of Ben Bulben, the stunning waterscapes of Glencar and Glenade, and the wealth of plants their limestone substrate induces. And not a bungalow in sight.

ST PATRICK

Most places associated with St Patrick, Ireland's patron saint, are in the northern half of the country, although most information about him is rather vague. He was born in Britain, perhaps Wales, perhaps Cumberland, possibly Dunbartonshire. A piratic Irish chief – ancestor of the O'Neill family – kidnapped him and he was put to work as a shepherd. A few years after escaping (to England or the continent) he saw visions calling him back to Ireland and he went in 429, or 430 or 431. He was not the first Christian or missionary, but he was clearly very successful. In other countries of Europe the establishment of Christianity took much longer and cost martyrs' lives. Ireland took to it readily.

Patrick generated more stories than most. On the summit of Croagh Patrick, where he was spending Lent, he exiled all snakes from the country. He explained the idea of the Trinity by means of a three-leafed flower, the so-called shamrock, and thereby converted a king. When he died, in 461, at Saul, near Downpatrick in County Down, the country was more or less converted. The day of his death was 17 March, St Patrick's Day, since then the most important date in the Irish calendar.

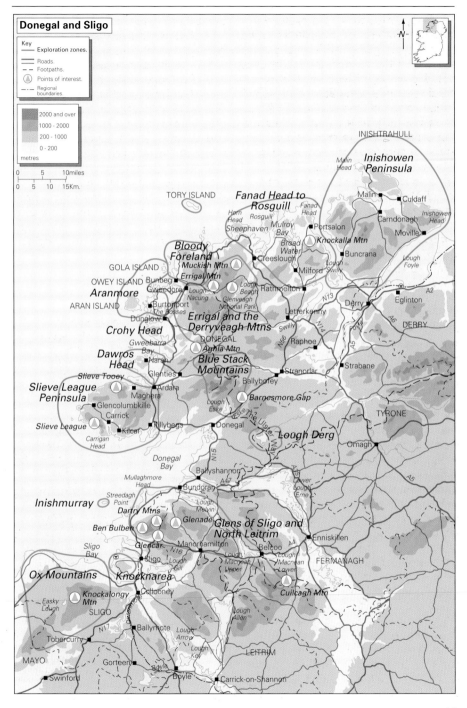

Donegal and Sligo

Key
— Exploration zones.
═ Roads.
- - Footpaths.
Ⓐ Points of interest.
-·-· Regional boundaries.

2000 and over
1000 - 2000
200 - 1000
0 - 200
metres

0   5   10miles
0   5   10   15Km.

-N-

INISHTRAHULL

Inishowen Peninsula

TORY ISLAND
Fanad Head to Rosguill
Malin Head
Malin
Culdaff
Horn Head
Fanad Head
Rosguill
Sheephaven
Mulroy Bay
Portsalon
Carndonagh
Inishowen Head
Broad Water
Knockalla Mtn
Moville
Bloody Foreland
Creeslough
Buncrana
Lough Foyle
GOLA ISLAND
Muckish Mtn
Milford
Lough Swilly
OWEY ISLAND
Bunbeg
Errigal Mtn
Gweedore
Lough Beagh
Rathmelton
N13
Derry
A2
Eglinton
Aranmore
Lough Nacung
Glenveagh National Park
Letterkenny
DERRY
ARAN ISLAND
Burtonport
The Rosses
Dunglow
Errigal and the Derryveagh Mtns
Swilly
Raphoe
N14
N15
Strabane
TYRONE
Crohy Head
DONEGAL
Aghla Mtn
Dawros Head
Gweebarra Bay
Naran
Blue Stack Mountains
Ballybofey
Stranorlar
Slieve Tooey
Glenties
Barnesmore Gap
Slieve League Peninsula
Maghera
Ardara
Lough Eske
Eske
The Ulster Way
Lough Derg
Omagh
Glencolumbkille
Carrick
Rillybegs
Donegal
Slieve League
Kilcar
Lough Derg
Carrigan Head
Donegal Bay
Lough Derg
Inishmurray
Mullaghmore Head
Ballyshannon
A47
Lower Lough Erne
A5
Streedagh Point
Bundoran
Dartry Mtns
Lough Melvin
N15
Glenade
Glens of Sligo and North Leitrim
Enniskillen
Ben Bulben
Glenade
Belcoo
A4
FERMANAGH
Sligo Bay
Glencar
Manorhamilton
Lough Macnean Upper
Lough Macnean Lower
Ox Mountains
Gleniff
N16
Knocknarea
Sligo
Lough Gill
Cuilcagh Mtn
Easky Lough
Knockalongy Mtn
Collooney
Lough Allen
SLIGO
N17
Ballymote
Lough Arrow
Tobercurry
Lough Key
LEITRIM
MAYO
Gorteen
Boyle
Swinford
Carrick-on-Shannon

CHAPTER 1: DONEGAL AND SLIGO

GETTING THERE

By air: regular flights from the UK, major European cities and North America go to Belfast, Dublin and Shannon airports. All the airports have useful web-sites: www.belfastairport.com, www.dublinairport.com and www.shannonairport.com. For further details see pp184 and 197. British Airways fly from Manchester and Glasgow to Derry, T: (0845) 722 2111 (UK), www.britishairways.com; Aer Arann flies from Dublin to Donegal and Sligo and from Shannon to Sligo, T: (01) 814 5240, www. aerarann.ie.

By sea: Stena Line, T: (0870) 570 7070 (UK), www.stenaline.com, and Irish Ferries, T: (0870) 517 1717 (UK), www.irishferries.ie, operate from Holyhead to Dublin and Dun Laoghaire. Stena also crosses from Stranraer to Belfast. P&O runs from Larne to Cairnryan, T: (0870) 242 4777, www.poef.com, and Norse Irish Ferries from Liverpool to Belfast, T: (028) 9077 9090, www.Norse-Irish-Ferries.co.uk.

By car: traffic is not permitted on any but the authorized border crossings marked on road maps. If you are hiring a car in the Republic, ask whether the insurance covers you for Northern Ireland and vice versa; you may have to pay an extra premium. No extra payment is necessary for UK-registered cars driven in Northern Ireland.

By rail: Iarnrod Eireann runs 3 trains daily from Dublin (Connolly) to Sligo, T: (01) 836 6222, www.irishrail.ie. Northern Ireland Railways run 7 services daily (fewer at weekends) from Belfast (Central) to Derry, T: (028) 9089 9411, www.translink.co.uk.

By bus: Bus Eireann operates regular services from Dublin to Sligo, Donegal Town and Letterkenny. Express services also run from Donegal Town to Derry and Enniskillen, T: (01) 836 6111, www.buseireann.ie.

WHERE TO STAY

The Irish Tourist Board (Bord Fáilte) produces yearly guides to approved hotels, B&Bs, Irish homes, hostels and caravan (vacation-home) and camping parks. Local BF offices operate a nationwide accommodation reservation service for a nominal booking charge.

ACTIVITIES

Walking: access to some of the coastal paths can be difficult. A good map and compass are essential when walking in Irish mountains. The National Way-marked Ways Committee, Dept of Tourism, Sport & Recreation, Frederick Buildings, South Frederick Street, Dublin 2, T: (01) 662 1444, gives useful information as does BF's *Walking Ireland* booklet. See also *Walking Ireland* (Lonely Planet, 1999). The Donegal section of the Ulster Way stretches from Pettigo to Gortahawk on the north coast. See *The Ulster Way* by Paddy Dillon (O'Brien Press, 1999). The 30-mile (48-km) Leitrim Way offers dramatic views of lake and mountain. For route details contact Leitrim County Council, Carrick-on-Shannon, T: (078) 20005.

Cycling: routes cross mountain ranges at up to 864 ft (270 m) as well as following the rugged coastline. Contact Walking/Cycling Ireland, Mespil House, Sussex Road, Dublin 4, T: (01) 668 8278. BF Information Sheet 14G, *Cycling Atlantic Coast & Donegal Highlands*, suggests routes and bike-hire outlets. Details are also given in North Tourism's *Hiking and Biking Guide*.

Riding: for riding centres in the area see the BF *Equestrian Holidays Ireland* brochure and the North West Tourism's *Saddle-Up Equestrian Guide*. Contact BF, see below.

Climbing: the Derryveagh mountains in Co. Donegal offer some of the finest rock climbing in Ireland. Climbing in Co. Sligo is mostly on limestone. Contact BF or the Association for Adventure Sports and Mountaineering Council of Ireland, House of Sport, Longmile Rd, Dublin 12, www.mountaineering.ie, T: (01) 450 7376.

Fishing: Ireland's north-west is renowned for freshwater and sea fishing. The BF publishes information on species, seasons, equipment and regulations in its booklets *Game Angling*, *Coarse Angling* and *Sea Angling*.

Watersports: yacht charters are available on the north-west coast. Contact the Irish Sailing Association, 3 Park Road, Dun Laoghaire, Co. Dublin, T: (01) 280 0239. The north-west coast offers some of the world's most challenging surfing with equipment available for hire at selected resorts. Contact Zoe Lally, of the Irish Surfing Association, T: (096) 49020.

FURTHER INFORMATION

Tourist offices: the region's main office is in Sligo at Aras Reddan, Temple Street, T: (071) 61201, www.ireland-northwest.travel.ie. It is open all year, as is the Letterkenny tourist office, T: (074) 21160. There are other seasonal offices in Donegal, T: (073) 21148; Bundoran, T: (072) 41350; Dunglow, T: (075) 21297; and Carrick-on-Shannon, T: (078) 20170.

FURTHER READING

Walk Guide West of Ireland by Whilde and Simms (Gill & Macmillan, 1999).

Inishowen Peninsula

Rugged country of mountain and blanket bog edged by tall cliffs and sweeps of sandy beach. The road round it is known, from its length (in miles), as the 'Inishowen 100'

This fist of mountain, bog, cliff and rock, thrusting so far seaward that its northernmost headland, Malin, is also the northern extremity of Ireland, clung on more obstinately than other parts to its link with Britain. The last land-bridge to unite the two islands at the end of the Ice Age probably ran from Inishowen to Jura, Islay and the western Grampians. There were other bridges between the east coast and Wales, but they did not survive quite as long.

Across these bridges, as the ice receded and the land warmed, animals, birds and plants returned, by the multifarious methods they have evolved. But access was of limited duration. Melting ice gradually raised the sea-level. This in turn submerged the land-bridges. By perhaps 9,000 years ago most of the forms of wildlife that characterize Ireland today were in position. Only those species which wind, waves, birds or humans would bring in, deliberately or otherwise, were still absent.

In historical times the peninsula has been known not for international links but for remote inaccessibility, barely affected by the insistent claims of tourism. The transatlantic liners which called in the late 19th century at Moville, on the east coast, were simply removing suffering surplus population to America. Like the earlier flight of the earls – a bowing out of the scene by rebel leaders at the end of the reign of Elizabeth I, which took place from the opposite shore of Lough Swilly across to the west – it was a one-way traffic.

Inishowen was O'Neill territory from earliest times. O'Neills built the Grianan of Aileach, the massive circular stone fort which, heavily restored in the 19th century, still commands all approaches to the peninsula, from Inch island to Derry. This was a family of lasting influence. Niall of the Nine Hostages, its founder, was a pirate-prince among whose captives, taken on raiding trips to Wales, was the youthful Patrick, patron-saint-to-be. Niall's successors became high kings of Ireland (a title of little meaning but high prestige), and the clan thrives to this day, rich in lands and titles. As recently as the 1960s it produced a prime minister of Northern Ireland.

Some towns on the east side offer what is still called good crack (by which the Irish mean nothing more sinister than good talk and high spirits) to young people driving out from Derry at evenings and weekends, but for the most part this tapering wedge of land is desolate and scantily peopled. The highest peak is that of Slieve Snaght (2,019 feet/615 metres), centrally placed south-west of Carndonagh, the area's main market town. The mountain can be climbed without excessive exertion from the road running along its south-eastern perimeter. There are fine views from the top, of Lough Swilly and the Donegal Mountains to the west, and Lough Foyle, Antrim and even the Scottish coast to the east.

The most picturesque scenes are along the west and north coasts, with their bays and beaches. Here are the great headland bluffs of Malin Head, Glengad Head and Inishowen Head. North of Buncrana the road nearest the coast makes for Dunree Head, then turns right up the bleak Owenerk valley to the Gap of Mamore. On either side the heathery terrain rises to heights (Croaghcarragh, 1,250 feet/381 metres; and Mamore Hill, 1,361 feet/415 metres) from which the alternations of promontory and inlet along the crenellated coast of Donegal show up wonderfully, the more so in afternoon or early evening light.

There are good walks along the ridge from the Gap, south-west into the Urris Hills or north-eastward towards Raghtin More. Good walking is also to be had between Malin Head and Glengad Head. Around Malin, for all its exposure to Arctic storms and western breakers, the country is quite gently contoured, while the coast itself is rich in beaches, but as you move eastward the ground rises to successions of cliff, with labyrinthine tracks and deep chasms. Malin is an important staging post for birds migrating southward in the autumn, when north-westerly winds bring sooty shearwaters, Leach's petrels and Sabine's gulls in large quantities, and a long list of rarities over the years. A few miles south, the broad mud-flats of Trawbreaga Bay and adjoining meadows and dunes of Doagh Island attract large populations of geese, ducks and waders. Winter brings flocks of brent and barnacle geese. In summer there are at least three kinds of tern – common, Arctic and little – laying their eggs without defence (but with effectively camouflaged shells) on the pebbles of beaches. Eiders are to be seen all the year round.

BEFORE YOU GO
Maps: OSI Discovery Series, map Nos 1 and 3.

GETTING THERE
By car: from Letterkenny take the N13 (north-west) to the R239, which leads to the R238; 20 miles (35 km) on, the R241 takes you to Inishowen Head and the R242 to Malin Head.
By bus: Lough Swilly Buses run 4 services a day from Derry, stopping at Muff, Carndonagh and Strove, with a reduced service on Sun, T: (028) 7126 2017 (UK).

WHERE TO STAY
Hotels: there are plenty to choose from in the area.
B&Bs: try the Norris family farm in Tremone, T: (077) 67121; Molly's Brae at Carndonagh, T: (077) 74137; Culdaff House, Culdaff, T: (077) 79103; or Suzanne McFeely, Moville, T: (077) 82529. The Inishowen Tourism Society publishes an accommodation guide for the area, T: (077) 74933, e-mail: info@inishowen.com.
Youth hostels: there are 2 hostels on the Malin Head peninsula: Sandrock Holiday Hostel, T: (077) 70289, and Malin Head Hostel, T: (077) 70309.
Outdoor living: camping is available at the Moville Holiday Hostel, Moville, T: (077) 82378, e-mail: scanavas@iol.ie.

ACTIVITIES
Walking/Cycling: Homefield Walking & Cycling Centre specializes in cycling and walking holidays in Donegal and Sligo, T: (072) 41288 www.surfers-paradise.com/gateway/courses/homelang.htm.
Riding: the Lenamore Stables in Muff offer hacking and trekking, T: (077) 84022.
Fishing: you can fish from the shore at Moville for pollack, wrasse and mackerel. Lough Foyle provides cod, dogfish, pollack, coalfish, ray, ling, tope and haddock. Contact Foyle, Carlingford and Irish Lights Commission, T: (028) 7134 2100, e-mail: loughs @dnet.co.uk.
Bird-watching: Lough Swilly has large autumn arrivals of whooper swan, wintering greylag geese and other migrants, best seen between Buncrana and the southern end of the lough.

FURTHER INFORMATION
Tourist offices: call Inishowen Tourism at Carndonagh, T: (077) 74933. BF offices are in Derry, T: (028) 7136 9501 (UK), and Letterkenny, T: (074) 21160, both open all year.

A newcomer to Ireland in 1911, the fulmar, an elegant glider with a strong but superficial similarity to a gull, now nests all round the Irish coast, generally on narrow ledges set in sheer cliffs.

Fanad Head to Rosguill

Sandy beaches like this one, hidden in a deep cove beneath Raghtin More, decorate the rugged west coast of the Inishowen Peninsula. The nearest town is Ballyliffin.

These peninsulas confine their heights inland. Seaward, they share mild contours and their rims are low, sandy and sinuous, punctured by the dents and penetrations of long, angular bays

From the heights above Lough Swilly you can snatch a visual geography lesson before engaging with County Donegal's northern coastline. What shows up best is the jigsaw of land and water of which the lough and the inlets to its left are part, a pattern of islands, a layout of lagoons and dunes, white foam-fringes, brown-purple heather, chequerboards of pasture and marsh and clusters of hill and low mountains spread out beneath a huge sky, not necessarily blue, nor always recognizably a sky at all, but for most of the year a lively expanse of white-blue variations. In Ireland, there is more to be had from remembering to look at the sky than in most other countries.

The Donegal coast is holiday country for Irish northern and southern. In this part of the county, the contortions and curlicues of the coast mean there are innumerable separate sandy beaches, often with sand-dunes and machair grassland on the landward side, and it is still quite possible to have one to oneself, even in the summer. But it is no longer possible, as it was a few years ago, to (almost) guarantee it. The dilemma is one that recurs constantly down the west coast: wilds may cease to be wild when overrun by tourists, but many of them revert when the tourists leave. If we are set on seeing wild country, and have to come in peak holiday times, do we simply avoid the parts we should hurry to if they were unpeopled? Or go, and make the best of it? There are certainly places which it would be silly – so it seems to me – to miss.

Along the western shore of Lough Swilly, north of Rathmelton (sometimes spelt, as it is pronounced, Ramelton), are a number of nice old fishing villages and quays, rich in

19

history. The rocks on the seashore are strewn with seaweeds and shells by the million from minuscule to mussel-sized, the latter tight-shut when the tide is out and presumably edible. Oystercatchers pick and peck among them, and a curlew flies by with its musical gargle. There is a good walk on this peninsula, from end to end of Knockalla Mountain, set amid miles of gently undulating bog. This knobbly ridge is known as the Devil's Backbone, though to me it suggests a knuckleduster. At its north-eastern end, Saldanha Head gives spectacular views over Lough Swilly, the golden sands of Ballymastocker Bay and the bulky humps of Inishowen over the water.

It would be sad to miss Mulroy Bay with its pretty bony and angular islands, some of them covered in conifers. The whole area has good, changing bird populations; ducks and swans are in evidence here all the year round, and the elegant Sandwich tern breeds on the islands. But the fish farms strike a discordant note of human interference.

After Fanad Head you need to go 14 miles (23 kilometres) inland before you can start on your way to the sprawling sandy headland of Rosguill, and to go thence to Horn Head requires a detour of similar distance around Sheephaven, which unfortunately is seldom seen because the road is set well back. Horn Head is a grand sight, though it would be a great deal grander from the sea, for the north-facing 600-foot (180-metre) cliffs hold at times, and especially in winter, impressive numbers of kittiwake, guillemot and razorbill – some four thousand of each – and many other sea-birds.

A narrow lane, lengthened in recent years to include a circuit of Croaghnamaddy, takes the driver close to a concrete viewing post. All habitations and pasture have been left behind, but not human activity. Turf is cut here and some of the local young, I imagine, use the abundant stones to form large names, nicknames and obscenities visible for hundreds of yards. All the same, these cannot detract from the intense drama of the place, with diminishing promontories, besieged by white foam, receding into the distance right and left. Out to sea, to the north, lies Inishtrahull, an island formed of Ireland's oldest rock, Lewisian gneiss, and a breeding ground for eider duck.

BEFORE YOU GO
Maps: OSI Discovery Series, map No. 2.

GETTING THERE
By car: Grianan of Aileach is to the left of the N13 just over the border from Derry. For the Fanad peninsula, follow the N13 to Letterkenny, then the R245 to Rathmelton. The R245 leads to the R246 which runs up the western side of the peninsula and the R247 up the eastern side. The Fanad Scenic Drive is signposted.
By bus: Lough Swilly buses operate 2 daily services to Portsalon and Tawny, T: (074) 22863. Gallagher's run a mini-bus once a day to Rosguill from Downings, T: (074) 37037.

WHERE TO STAY
B&Bs: in Rathmelton, contact

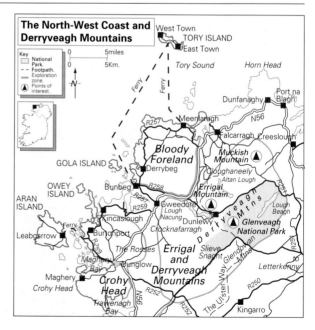

Mrs Campbell, T: (074) 51243, or Mrs Corry, T: (074) 51055.
Youth hostels: the Tra na Rosann on the Rosguill peninsula is Ireland's most northerly hostel, T: (074) 55374, and is open all year.

FURTHER INFORMATION
Tourist office: Letterkenny BF, T: (074) 21160.

Bloody Foreland

The north-western corner of Donegal is a scrawny, stony land bounded by a rocky coast

It is not the colour of Atlantic sunsets that gives Ireland's north-west corner its name, Bloody Foreland, though there are days when you might think it was. A red mineral has at some geological period stained the bands of quartzite inlaid among the granite, and the effect can be a blood-red glow. It is a place to inspire awe: the hill running down to the rocky coast and the sea, and over the horizon Iceland, Greenland, and the land – so people once believed – of perpetual youth. It produced poignant legends. While you grew not a day older during your stay, the world you had left went on as before; and if you returned and touched ground, you acquired all the years you had till then deferred. The poet and warrior Oisin (pronounced Usheen) rode there over the waves with his lover; but on returning for a visit, dismounted and found his skin wrinkled, his beard long and grey, his back bent. Worse, the pagan life he had known and loved was being ousted by the mission of St Patrick. Before dying, he made a nice

heathen attack on the new pieties, and Patrick in particular.

When I came here a generation ago, this kind of thing worked a magic on me. I loved the Irish way of identifying mythical sites: the mountain-top beds slept in by eloping Dermot and Grania, the fields of great battles and, a few miles over the sea from here to the north, Tory Island, home of Balor the giant, a glance from whose single eye killed those it fell on, till his grandson pressed a red-hot iron into the eye and finished him. There was the magic of the view as well. Standing on the hill slope and looking down the west coast you saw – and still see – a succession of lateral lines, made up of tongues of land, elongated islands and islets, shingle spits, strip after strip of white foam in fidgetty motion, and the intervening bands of grey sea. But you cannot any longer entirely lose yourself in contemplation of natural grandeur, for on the landward side there has been a huge and amorphous burgeoning of bungalows. Had Oisin delayed his return to now, I think he might have accelerated death by cutting his throat. Balor might have put his one eye out voluntarily.
Before you go *Maps:* OSI Discovery Series, map No. 1. *Guide-books: Great Walks: Ireland* by David Herman (Cassell, 1991).
Getting there *By car:* from Letterkenny follow the N56. After Gortahawk take the R257 along the coast to Bloody Foreland. *By bus:* Feda O'Donnell Coaches run daily services from Gweedore to Letterkenny, T: (075) 48114. McGinley's operate services between Annagary, Gweedore and Dublin, T: (074) 35201. Lough Swilly buses stop at Dunfanaghy, T: (074) 22863.

Where to stay *Hotels:* try the Foreland Heights Hotel, Bloody Foreland, T: (075) 31785. *Youth hostels:* Corcreggan Mill near Dunfanaghy, T: (074) 34609, e-mail: brendanr@tinet.ie; the Shamrock Lodge Hostel, Falcarragh, T: (074) 35859; and Ballyconnell House, T: (074) 35363.
Activities *Bird-watching:* the area is home to various sea-birds including puffins, kittiwakes and guillemots.
Further information *Tourist office:* nearest BF office is in Letterkenny, T: (074) 21160.

Aranmore

Off-shore islands of north-western Donegal, including the largest, Aranmore or Aran Island, as well as Tory Island and a scatter of other cartographic pinpricks

The boat from Bunbeg sails north at scheduled times, weather allowing, to Tory Island, which with its two villages and native artists is perhaps the most thriving, if bare and windswept, of Ireland's off-shore islands. Along this north-western stretch of the Donegal coast, a boat can deliver delights. It opens up views of long winding inlets, which become sculptured mudscapes at low tide and are thronged with sea-birds at all times. Out to sea it allows you to explore a straggling archipelago of islands great and small, some occupied and cropped by sheep, some lone and rocky and seemingly forgotten. On an ocean-facing sandy beach, of which there are hundreds, you can believe yourself deserted by mankind, though grey seals may keep you company.

The Rosses, opening out to the south of Bunbeg, is a low-lying mainland area, six or seven miles across, of heath and grass, spattered with farms and rocks and more than a hundred lakes. From Burtonport, on its western edge, boats cross regularly to Aran Island, winding first among a jigsaw of smaller islands. (Aran Island is sometimes called Aranmore, not to be confused with the more famous Aran Islands off County Galway, the largest of which, since *mor* means big, is also called Aranmore.) The high ground of this island, which rises to 750 ft (229 m), is composed of quartzite, hard enough to survive the originally overlaid granite which climate has worn away. Aranmore, too, has long sandy beaches and fine cliffs in the north-west where sea-birds breed, and also mountain lakes and good climbs. The thousand people living on it tend to keep themselves, their cars and shops near the east side, where the quay is.

Before you go *Maps:* OSI Discovery Series, map No. 1.

Getting there *By sea:* Tory Island is accessible by boats in summer from Bunbeg, T: (074) 31991, and Magheraroarty, T: (074) 35061. Less frequent services operate from Meenlaragh and Port na Blagh. The 20-min ferry service from Burtonport to Aranmore operates all year round, with more frequent services in summer, T: (075) 21532. *By car:* N56 and R257 pass close to all departure ports for Tory Island. For Burtonport turn off the N56 at Dunglow and take the R259.

Where to stay *Hotels and*

B&Bs: Hotel Ostan Thoraigh, T: (074) 35920, Duffy's B&B, T: (074) 35136, both on Tory Island. The Glen Hotel on Aranmore, T: (075) 20505, is open only in summer. *Youth hostels:* Greene's Hostel, Dunglow, T: (075) 21943/21021; Shamrock Lodge, Falcarragh, T: (074) 35192/35859.

Further information *Tourist office:* Dunglow BF office, T: (075) 21297.

Crohy Head

A bulbous projection into Gweebarra Bay, the peninsula hides dramatic lakes and tough climbs in its hinterland, but is prodigal with marvellous sea views from its peripheral road

Here is a quartzite peninsula, bulking up over the widespread granite of the area. Discounting bumps and appendages, it is about 3 miles (5 km) across, and Croaghegly, something south of centre, reaches 808 ft (246 m). Aware of its scenic splendours, the tourist board has caused the road which used to end at a hamlet halfway round, to continue and complete the circuit.

Maghery Bay, at the north of the promontory's seaward side, is prized by geologists for the variety of its rocks. More obvious to the layman are the mats of kelp (*Laminaria*), known locally as sea rods, which are strewn over the sandy beaches, especially after rough weather (when strong

From Horn Head, with its dizzying drops to rock and ocean, you can look back across Sheep Haven to Rinnafaghla Point and Rosguill with its promontory tapering to Melmore Head (upper left).

currents can make these beaches dangerous). Its ruddy, bull-pizzle stems often remind me of classical serpents and bring out my Laocoon complex. They are collected in huge numbers and dried over fences and walls for months before being sent to Greenock in Scotland to be manufactured into an antibiotic.

Grandeur is higher up. You leave the nicely scruffy village of Maghery and climb steeply. Crohy Head discloses good views of the series of headlands to the north, the Dawros peninsula just to the south, and of Aghla and the Blue Stack Mountains, away to the southeast across a pretty inlet of Gweebarra Bay. Heady permutations of the marine panorama are to be had during steep walks and climbs over the blanket bog of Croaghegly.

Before you go *Maps:* OSI Discovery Series, map Nos 1 and 10.

Getting there *By car:* from Dunglow take the minor road to Maghery Bay. *By bus:* Lough Swilly buses run to Dunglow from Letterkenny, T: (074) 22863.

Where to stay: An Oige hostel, Crohy Head, T: (075) 21950, and limited B&B in Maghery.

Further information *Tourist Office:* Dunglow BF, T: (075) 21297.

Dawros Head

Unlike the promontories to north and south, Dawros is a gentle expanse of hills and lakes, its deeply indented shoreline providing sandy coves and beaches and long ranks of cliff

Robert Lloyd Praeger is the patron saint of Irish naturalists. He lived from 1865 to 1953 and distinguished himself as botanist, geologist and archaeologist: a polymath in an age that still tolerated them. He knew all the scholars of his day – it was an age when that too was possible, in a country the size of Ireland – and was always going on missions of discovery with them. He loved the outdoors and even in old age never missed the chance, when tramping over the countryside, of bathing in pond, lake or river. He makes hikers of our own time seem namby-pamby, never seeming to let safety considerations, as of mist on mountains or soft patches of bog or rough seas, discourage him.

If he wanted to get somewhere he strode off (or cycled in extremes; cars he loathed) and usually got there, an hour or eighteen later, soaking wet, utterly cheerful, and full of some unexpected plant he had encountered up the mountain. He wrote, apart from more scientific work, a memoir of travels in Ireland called *The Way that I Went*, which has never been bettered, even by one of Ireland's latter-day great geologists, Frank Mitchell, who in a gesture of homage called his own memoirs *The Way that I Followed*. In fact, almost everyone who has written since Praeger's time about the Irish outdoors has pillaged his work, and I am no exception. He had a soft spot for the Dawros, with its rather subtle attractions. 'Not lofty,' he wrote, 'but full of little heathery hills and lakes, with a sandy or cliffy shore – a particularly attractive area.'

Attractive it is, though its appeal is not as dramatic or stupefying as that of the Slieve League a few miles to the south. No mountains are to be found here, but there are a few nice cliffs, some good long sandy beaches (at Naran and Rosbeg), quite a few lakes, birds, rocks and inspiring antiquity. Off Naran, on the north coast, is Inishkeel. The name means 'narrow island', and so it is at high tide, but it is joined to the mainland at low tide by an exposed reef of sand. It has the ruins of two churches on it, and the memory of a 6th-century monastic retreat founded by St Conall Caol, in whose honour there is an annual May pilgrimage. Other ancient remains are scattered over the promontory: a huge unrestored round fort of stone from the 9th century, built on a lough island; a 20-ft (6-m) dolmen; cairns, crosses and other survivors. Every so often along this farthest coastline, north and west, there are signs

Several species of the seaweed *Laminaria*, known as kelp, are collected, as they have been for centuries, when the ebbing tide exposes them. Once dried, kelp can be used in various medical and culinary preparations. Nowadays it is exported to Scotland for factory processing.

of human activity, dating from two, five, even – as the discovery of mesolithic remains under peat testifies – ten thousand years ago. Usually we know peoples so distant from ourselves only through their pots, weapons, knives and needles; as if we ourselves were to be identified aeons from now only by the salvaged contents of a branch of Woolworths.

There is one other element here, which always mystifies and awes me: the force that drew them to the edge of a world which was not, as far as we can tell, crowded, to subsist on the begrudged gifts of rock and air and hostile sea, and on beliefs and aspirations we shall never know. Would we recognize this force, from traces left in our myths and religions, or would we have to admit the existence of wholly alien sentiments in people who were, give or take a gene, our own flesh and blood?

There are far more ancient remains. Among the gnarled hummocks, bumps, hollows, lynchets and sullen black cattle lies an untidy sprinkling of granite core-stones, remains of an outflow from inland Donegal. Contrary to reputation, granite (often permeated by cracks which admit water and chemicals in solution) can break down easily. Faultless cubes are often left, which in time are worn into the spheres we see here.

Before you go *Maps:* OSI Discovery Series, map No. 10.
Getting there *By car:* road near Dawros Head to Naran, Portnoo and Rosbeg branches off R261. **Where to stay** *B&B:* An Geata Glas, Ardara, T: (075) 41546. *Youth hostel:* Campbell's Holiday Hostel, Glenties, T: (075) 51491.
Further information *Tourist office:* BF, Dunglow, T: (075) 21297.

Slieve League Peninsula

A massive promontory whose interior pattern of mountain and glen is upstaged by the dramas of the coastline

Seen from a distance, as it is from many angles, the Slieve League peninsula (the peninsula of which the heights of the Slieve League occupy the south-western seaboard) is of a deeply satisfactory shape: an utterly enormous hump or mound or hedgehog or guinea pig or upturned hulk or bisected egg. Somebody has perhaps worked out how many Empire State Buildings or *Titanics* or tankers of Guinness would fit into it but, whatever the number, there are few places which give me such a sense of mass and solidity. It has other distinctions. It is 30 miles (48 kilometres) long and at its widest, 12 miles (19 kilometres). Round most of its edge it falls from a height straight, or steeply, down to the sea. Most of its summits range from 1,000 to 1,500 feet (300 to 500 metres) with the highest, Slieve League, 1,970 feet (600 metres). In half a dozen places, hardly more, estuaries of the tumbling rivers which drain its plateau give access to boats.

Glencolumbkille on the west side of the peninsula and Carrick and Kilcar on the south are substantial villages, but elsewhere the population is a thin smattering. Most of the hamlets formed at river mouths are abandoned; distance, gradient and the tightly winding approach roads priced contact with the outside world too high.

Slieve Tooey is the northerly summit of the peninsula. You can drive to Maghera, at sea-level to its east, or Port or Glencolumbkille to its west, and walk part of the way along a rudimentary and treacherous sheep-path close to its cliff edges, with exhilarating views of coastal Donegal and the Atlantic.

A close relative and often associate of the jackdaw, the chough confines itself chiefly to the rockiest, ruggedest cliffs, headlands and islands of the West.

Seekonk
Public Library

25

Ten o'clock on a raw, windy morning, and a fisherman is out in his boat (*previous page*), a mere speck beneath the southern flank of the Slieve League Peninsula. To the east, across the inlet, lie Muckros Head and the inner reaches of Donegal Bay.

Below you are vertiginous drops (down which less than a century ago nerveless natives were lowered on ropes to collect sweet grass), fanciful and contorted rock shapes, knife-edge ridges from one pinnacle to another, rocky bays and spindly rock stacks. There are loughs inland and rather poignant descents to the lonely habitations.

For all its magnificence the north is out-classed. The southern seaward face of the peninsula where Slieve League looms over the shore is one of the grandest sights in Ireland. Not many years ago you had to go to sea to appreciate it, but now a spiralling road takes you up the south-eastern spur beside Carrigan Head to a tarmac park where you can admire the view from inside a car. The only time I used this facility (and after looking furtively all round in case of human company), I moved my car back from where I had first parked it to a more sheltered spot. I have never known such wind. I pictured an exceptional gust followed by an encapsulated fall to the rocks below. Soon after this I was hypnotized by the nearby movements of gulls, choughs and jackdaws, who seemed to have discovered the perfect distraction for such weather. Looking down 1,500 feet from where I stood, tethered to posts by both

IRISH PLACE NAMES

English place-name element (Irish-language source or equivalent), *meaning*

agha, augh (achadh), *field*
ard (ard), *high place, hill*
ass (eas), *waterfall*
ath, augh (ath), *ford*
ballagh (bealach), *pass*
bally (baile), *townland*
bar (barr), *top*
barna (bearna), *gap*
bawn (ban), *white*
beagh (veagh), *birch tree*
beg (beag), *small*
bel (beal), *river mouth, ford*
ben, ban (beann), *peak*
bo, mo (bo), *cow*
boher (bothar), *road*
bohreen (botharin), *little road or track, originally for cows*
boola, boley (buaile), *summer hill-settlement*
brack (breac), *speckled*
cahir (cathair), *stone fort*
cairn (carn), *pile of stones*
cappagh (ceapach), *tillage plot*
carrig, carrick (carraig), *rock, stone enclosure*
carrow (ceathramhadh), *quarter of land*
cashel (caiseal), *ring-fort*
clare (clar), *expanse of land, plain*
clogh (cloch), *stone, stone place or building*
cloghan (clochan), *stone hut,*

beehive hut
cloon, clon (cluain), *meadow*
cor (corr), *round hill*
cork (corcaigh), *marsh*
coum (com), *corrie*
croagh (cruach), *steep hill*
darrig (dearg), *red*
derry (doire), *oak wood*
donagh (domhnach), *church, especially an early one*
doon (dun), *promontory or conspicuous fort*
drum (droim), *ridge*
duff, doo (dubh), *black*
eask, esk (eisc), *cliff, rock gully*
emlagh (imeallach), *marginal land*
faha (faiche), *lawn*
fin (fion), *white, clear*
freagh (fraoch), *heather*
glash (glas), *stream*
glass (glas), *green*
glen (gleann), *valley*
gort (gort), *tillage field*
green (grianan), *sunny place*
gwee (gaoith), *wind*
illaun (oilean), *island*
inish, inch (inis), *island*
inver (inbhear), *river mouth*
ken (ceann), *headland*
kill (cill), *church*
knock (cnoc), *hill*
kyle (coill), *wood, grove*
lack (leac), *flagstone*
lackan (leaca, leacan), *hillside*
lag, leg, lig, lug (lug, lag), *hollow*

law (lagh), *hill*
lea (liath), *grey*
lis (lios), *ring fort*
lough (loch), *lake*
mace, mas (mas), *thigh, low hill*
magha (macha), *cattle-field*
maghera (machaire), *plain*
maum (mam), *pass*
mweel (maol), *bare hill*
money (muine), *grove*
more (mor), *big*
mullagh (mullach), *summit*
oughter (uachter), *upper*
ow, owen (abha, abhainn), *river*
poll, pool (poll), *hole*
rath (raith), *ring fort*
reen, ring (rinn), *point, headland*
roe (rua, ruadh), *red*
ros, ross (ros), *headland*
scarriff (scairbh), *ford*
see (suidh), *seat*
shan (sean), *old*
shee (sidh), *fairy hill*
skellig (sceilig), *rock*
sker, skerry (sceir), *rock, reef*
slee (slidhe), *road, track*
slieve (sliabh), *mountain, mountain range*
tagh, ty (teach), *house*
tave (taobh), *hillside*
teer, tir, tyr (tir), *land*
temple (teampall), *church*
tor (tor), *tall rock*
tra, tray (traigh), *strand, beach*
tubber (tobar), *well*
tully, tulla (tulach), *low hill*

hands, I saw them begin to rise, one by one, from a point close to the sea. Their ascent brought them close to me and then high above, above me and the land – all in one vertical rise. They paused for seconds, and began a slow but accelerating swoop towards the sea on the far side of the headland, behind me. This must have been more than half a mile. Approaching the water they levelled off, swerved round and glided towards the start-point, completing an aerobatic triangle. It was mesmerizing, but one thing surprised me more than any other. Such was their mastery of their element, I do not believe they ever moved their wings by more than a few adjusting degrees.

This was, however, the side-show. Behind the birds and in front of me, placed as I was on my raised wing as in a theatre box, stretched a two-mile wall of 2,000-foot (600-metre) cliff, ranged above little bays with narrow stone beaches and a sea of deep blue growing paler as it approached the land. The

grain, faults, knots and jointings of the cliffs made me think of a gnarled old log split open, but as the sun appeared and hid in turns, far more showed up. All over the place, among projecting rocks and vertical patches of grass and sprawls of grey scree were areas of glinting pigmentation, like much used and smudged palettes. One would comprise shades of red ochre and terra-cotta and raw sienna – a spectrum of reds and browns – while another changed from deep grey through cobalt to white, and another from pale sulphurous yellow to green and coppery verdigris.

From various angles Slieve League can be climbed, none of them presenting great difficulty, although on one approach there is an (avoidable) two-foot shelf with a steep drop beside it known as One Man's Path. I must climb it one day, but if, as before, time makes me choose between the view from it and that sweeping seaward view of it, I shall again choose the latter.

BEFORE YOU GO
Maps: OSI Discovery Series, map No. 10.
Guide-books: *Walk Guide West of Ireland* by Tony Whilde and Patrick Simms (Gill &

Macmillan, 1999).

GETTING THERE
By car: N56 from Donegal and Glenties goes to Killybegs. From there take R263 along

the coast to Slieve League and Malin Beg.
By bus: a Donegal–Glencolumbkille bus stops at Kilcar and Carrick, T: (074) 21309.

WHERE TO STAY
B&Bs: there are places in Glencolumbkille and Killybegs.
Youth hostels: the Derrylahan Independent Hostel is in Kilcar, T: (073) 38079.

ACTIVITIES
Walking: the coastal path from Teelin along One Man's Path offers spectacular views.
Climbing: there are good cliff climbs at Malin Beg. Contact The Mountaineering Council of Ireland, T: (01) 450 9845.
Fishing: the Glen river has good trout fishing. Contact Frank O'Donnell, T: (073) 39231.

FURTHER INFORMATION
Tourist offices: BF office in Letterkenny is open all year, T: (074) 21160.

South-West Donegal

Key
- - Footpath.
Exploration zone.
▲ Points of interest.

-N-

0   5miles
0   5Km.

Gweebarra Bay
Portnoo
Naran
N56
Dawros Head
Maas
Stone Fort
Bonny Glen Wood
R250
Loughros More Bay
R263
Loughros Point
Lough Machugh
N56
Port Hill
Slievetooey
Crockund
Lough Nalugraman
Ardara
Glengesh Pass
Forest
Glen Head
Common Mtn
Mulmosog Mtn
R262
Rocky Point
Glencolumbkille
R263
Glen River
Mulnanaff
N56
Slieve League Peninsula
Malin Beg
Carrick
Milltown
Slieve League
Killybegs
N56
Kilcar
Dunkineely
Carrigan Head
Teelin
R263
Muckros Head
Drumanoo Head
Doorin Point
INISHDUFF
St John's Point

Errigal and the Derryveagh Mountains

The central fastness of County Donegal, an area richly varied in scenery and wildlife at every level, from the waters of Dunlewy and Nacung to the dominating quartzite cone of Errigal; includes Glenveagh National Park

To understand the work of geologists, I have sometimes imagined a madman going berserk in a room. He pushes tables over, throws down other bits of furniture, hauls books off shelves and rips them apart, turns on taps, opens windows to smash porcelain, empties files, heaves the carpet off the floor and dumps it among the debris. That is to represent the effects of geological time, the eruptions, earthquakes, ice, weather and so on over 2,500 million years. The geologist must now examine the nature of everything in the room and the way it lies and has been damaged. He must deduce from all this its original position and state; and when, and by what route, however violent and precipitate, it arrived where it is. If I am right, then Donegal imposes special demands. Reading Donegal calls out for the Sherlock Holmes of geologists.

No other part of Ireland has experienced such seismic surges, tugs, stretchings and tumblings. Its deepest foundations have been rolled over by subterranean power, subjected to inconceivable heat and covered for hundreds of thousands of years by moving, mile-thick carpets of ice. The earth's crust has been sliced in two and then sliced again and again, and the sliced parts have slid miles out of their original alignment. All this has left a landscape of unique form and variety: a seaboard riddled with indentation

Above Poisoned Glen in the Derryveagh Mountains a small lake lies tranquilly between two marshy ridges. This secret eyrie may be reached by 45 minutes of long, squelchy walking from the nearby minor road (R254), itself deserted.

and hemmed by islands; and behind, a wall of mountain, an interior of chasms, lakes, vertiginous heights, boulder-strewn valleys and broad heathery plateaux, which for many people make Donegal the most beautiful county in Ireland.

What is most noticeable is the south-west to north-east orientation of the central features. The county is bisected by a long tear-fault that includes Glenveagh and the Owenbeagh river, and from either side of which rise parallel mountain ranges of granite. The part of the county to the north-west of this line, including most of the spectacular coastline, is virtually islanded by the divide, connected only by main roads close to the sea at either end. The mountains are an extension of the Caledonian ranges in Scotland, and were formed with them, around 400 million years ago, during the Lower Palaeozoic. The cause of this phase of orogeny, or mountain formation, was the eastward movement of what is now North America across the so-called Proto-Atlantic ocean towards Europe, squeezing deep strata of rock until they folded upward into mountain ranges. The same movement created America's Appalachian Mountains, and also the Scottish

Flowering cotton grasses catch the evening sun on the slopes near Poisoned Glen.

Herds of red deer, the only indigenous Irish deer (other species having been introduced in Norman and later times), occur in Glenveagh, County Donegal, Killarney National Park and the Wicklow Mountains.

Highlands, which accounts for the frequent comparison of Donegal with the Highlands.

Errigal mountain is 2,466 feet high (752 metres). It has twin pointed conical tops but from west and south only one can be seen, which makes Errigal look like the perfect mountain-shaped mountain, and renders it recognizable from any angle. In any wanderings round Donegal its unmistakable shape keeps reappearing from behind trees or other mountains or hills. The climb, if the height is no deterrent, is an easy one. The summit really is pointed, with scarcely room for a person to lie down. The view, with every feature of north-west Ireland laid out below, is one of the best in the world. A narrow ridge, without room for two people to pass, leads to the second summit, and a filling of any gaps in the previous view.

Apart from the distant vistas of coast and sea and mountain range, there is a fine view of the surrounding hinterland. South-west are two adjoining lakes, Nacung and Dunlewy. The long line of the granite Derryveagh Mountains, with Slieve Snaght and Dooish especially prominent, blocks the horizon south-east. Errigal's northern slope

dips down dangerously – owing to the quantities of loose scree – into the long cold forbidding crescent of Altan Lough, from whose further shore rise directly the two Aghlas, More and Beg.

The whole region offers some wonderful walks and climbs and sights. People walk from Muckish to Errigal in a day, taking in the Aghla peaks. Eastward and out of sight behind the Derryveaghs is Glenveagh Castle, a romantic Victorian reconstruction of an imagined medieval fortress – all towers and arrow-slits and battlements and lacking only a distressed and captive damsel – given to the nation a few years ago by the American owner. With the castle went gardens (a triumph of refinement in a hostile setting), a huge railed-in red-deer park and the rest of a colossal estate, over three miles long, which has now become the Glenveagh National Park and includes much of what we can see. At the centre of the region is Lough Beagh, scoured out of the granite by a glacier during the last Ice Age. Its steep granite walls, pendant streams and waterfalls and overhanging mountains covered in blanket bog make it an awesome sight.

A hundred years ago, golden eagles nested here but they have not been seen since. Gulls, peregrines, ravens and ring ouzels nest on high rocky shelves, curlews and red grouse on the floor of the moorland. There are a few sleek red-throated divers and goosanders nesting on the lakes, and a large variety of woodcock and smaller birds can be found in the oak woods among the hills.

From the main road below Errigal (the R251) a lane curls down past a ruined Protestant church and round the lake to the little village of Dunlewy. From here a path leads south-east, along a small stream, into the mountains. The valley is U-shaped with a broad floor between steep slopes, which reveals its glacial origins; for the infinitely slow sweep of the receding glacier gouged out channels of this shape.

Three miles on, deep down among a brotherhood of huge, shadowy, round-shouldered mountains, lies the Poisoned Glen, an awesome, marshy place but very beautiful and intriguing. The name is thought to derive from the former presence of Irish spurge (*Euphorbia hyberna*), still known in east Donegal, south-east Galway and Cork and Kerry, whose poisonous sap might have contaminated the water. Smooth walls of pink granite tower above, often glinting with recent rain water, but there are kinder gradients to the east. One of the finest walks in Donegal takes you up from here, over the Ballaghgeeha Gap to the Owenbeagh valley, and down through the heather, with glimpses of red deer, to the romantic castle of Glenveagh.

BEFORE YOU GO
Maps: OSI Discovery Series, map Nos 1, 2 and 6.

GETTING THERE
By car: take the N56 north from Letterkenny. Beyond Kilmacrenan take the R255 (west) until it meets the R251. Follow this past the Derryveagh Mountains to the left and Errigal mountain to the right. At the Glenveagh National Park, cars must be left at the entrance, but a free bus takes you to the visitor centre.
By bus: Bus Eireann services from Derry, Dublin and Sligo stop in Letterkenny, T: (074) 21309. Local bus services are operated by McGeehan's, T: (075) 46101, and the Lough Swilly Bus Company, Letterkenny, T: (074) 22863.

WHERE TO STAY
Hotels: Castle Grove Country House is in Letterkenny, T: (074) 51118, and there are others in Bunbeg, including the Sea View Hotel, T: (075) 31159, e-mail: boylec@iol.ie.
B&Bs: Mrs Lee's B&B is in Letterkenny, T: (074) 22529; and Mrs Boyle's near Churchill, T: (074) 37167. Fern House is in Kilmacrenan, T: (074) 39218; and Loch Na Toohey in Creeslough, T: (074) 38061. North West Tourism publishes its own guide to self-catering (vacation-home) accommodation in the area. To obtain a copy contact the local Bord Fáilte office (see below). **Youth hostels:** An Oige runs the Errigal Hostel at Dunlewy, T: (075) 31180. The independent Manse Hostel is on the High Road, Letterkenny, T: (074) 25238. Both are open all year.

ACTIVITIES
Walking: there are trails through the Derryveagh Mountains (including a section of the Ulster Way) and from Glenveagh National Park and Muckish mountain to Errigal mountain. You can lose your bearings quite easily in the forested areas of the national park so marked trails have been laid out. Guided nature and hill walks are available in the park in summer, and you will have the chance of seeing the largest herd of red deer in Ireland. The visitor centre has an audio-visual exhibition about the park and Glenveagh Castle, open Easter–end Oct, 10.30 am–6.30 pm, T: (074) 37088/37090.
Cycling: there are routes through the Glenveagh National Park starting from the visitor centre. Bikes can be hired from Church Street Cycles in Letterkenny, T: (074) 26204.
Riding: contact the Dunlewy Riding Stables, T: (086) 846 7509.
Climbing: the Garton Outdoor Education Centre, Garton, Churchill, Letterkenny, runs week-long climbing courses, T: (074) 37032/37254.
Fishing: both Gweedore and Glenveagh lakes have good trout fishing. Contact the Northern Regional Fisheries Board in Ballyshannon for details, T: (072) 51435.

FURTHER INFORMATION
Tourist office: the BF office in Letterkenny is open all year, T: (074) 21160.

Blue Stack Mountains

A neglected range of rounded mountains, webbed with good walks, hanging above the scenic splendours of Lough Eske

From the town of Donegal, tucked firmly into the north-eastern corner of Donegal Bay, the broad and fertile valley of the River Eske rises on a gentle incline to the pretty, tree-lined expanse of Lough Eske. At the lake, the battlemented tower of a ruined 19th-century castle peers over a dense cushioning of conifers; islands and tiny islets, the bigger among them supporting a gorse bush or thorn tree, decorate the water, which is home to swans and grebes. Beyond the kempt green foothills whose scattered upright evergreens suggest Tuscany is a broad backdrop of granite mountains.

Those north of Lough Eske are the Blue Stack Mountains, rising over the heather of the lower slopes to 2,219 ft (676 m). To the east the range culminates in Barnesmore (1,491 ft/454 m), isolated on the far side of the Lowerymore river and the road (and formerly the railway) from Donegal town where they pass through the spectacular Barnesmore Gap. The name is one of those many tautologies generated by the mixing of languages: Barnesmore means

33

big gap, so Barnesmore Gap repeats itself, as – elsewhere – do River Avon and Combe Vale. Shining walls of pink granite, stained by feldspar and polished by the infinitely slow passage of ice, rise a thousand feet either side of the pass.

Too close to the dramas of the coast, the Blue Stack have not detained many visitors, and inhabitants have always been few, except for the highwaymen who preyed on travellers through the gap well into the 19th century. On the lower land to north and east the uniform spread of mountain bog has a loneliness and desolation in it. But the heights offer good walking – much of it tough going, and without tracks – with fine views displaying the picturesque and intriguing effects of the last Ice Age. There are interesting plants: ferns usually associated with the south of the country, and the whorled caraway (*Carum verticillatum*), which has chosen to grace a very few select locations in Ireland.

During the Ice Age, a glacier seems to have centred on Lough Eske and moved across the mountains, scouring deep grooves and *roches moutonnées* (solid masses of rock, their long backs smoothed to an upward slope, the hinder end left rough and shaggy), depositing erratic boulders and gouging out huge basins which have now become in many cases rather formidable, sunless, north- or east-facing mountain tarns with tall sheer crescents of rock as backdrops. A walk which starts and finishes at the rough road beside the upper Reelan river to the north of the range and takes in the five peaks over 2,000 ft (600 m) high, passes all these features and more. There are granite crags where eagles once nested, lattices of stream and cataract, fragments of a

Sunderland aircraft which crashed in 1944, and Lough Belshade pocketed among sheer cliffs.

A stratum that underlies every inch of Ireland but eludes the most diligent geologist is that of myth and legend. Plenty are concealed hereabouts: of Aonghus Og, a god who fell in love with a maiden in his dreams, learned that she lived in the form of a swan on this lake and was promised she would be his if he picked her out from a flock of 150. He did, naturally, and took her away to bliss in his palace by the Boyne. There is, too, a crock of gold within the lough. As tends to be the case, it is guarded; in this instance by a ferocious black cat. I am not sure whether it or the temperature of the water affords the greater deterrent.

Before you go *Maps:* OSI Discovery Series, map Nos 10 and 11.

Guide-books: The Ulster Way by Paddy Dillon (O'Brien Press, 1999) and *Ulster Walk Guide* by Richard Rogers (Gill & Macmillan, 1991).

Getting there *By car:* the R250 (south-west) from Letterkenny passes Aghla mountain. From Glenties the R253 runs north of the Blue Stack Mountains to Ballybofey. From there the N15 (south) goes through the Barnesmore Gap and past Lough Eske. *By bus:* Bus Eireann run services from Donegal to Letterkenny, via Lough Eske, and from Donegal to Glenties, via Killybegs, T: (074) 21309. McGeehan's run buses to Killybegs and Glenties from Dublin, T: (075) 46150.

Where to stay *Hotels and B&Bs:* Mrs McGowan, T: (073) 21523, St Ernans House Hotel, T: (073) 21065, e-mail: sainternans@tinet.ie, Bried McGinty, T: (073) 23300, are all in Donegal; Ardnamona, T: (073) 22650, e-mail: ardnamon@

tempoweb.com, and Mrs Noreen McGinty, T: (073) 22029, are both at Lough Eske. *Youth hostels:* independent hostels in Donegal are The Cliffview Hotel Hostel, T: (073) 21684, e-mail: cliffview@tinet.ie, and Donegal Town Independent Hostel, T: (073) 22805.

Activities *Walking:* the Co. Donegal extension of the Ulster Way takes in the east shore of Lough Eske and the east end of the Blue Stack Mountains. *Fishing:* salmon in the River Finn. *Riding:* the Finn Farm Hostel, T: (074) 32261.

Further information *Tourist offices:* BF in Donegal Town, open Apr–Sept, T: (073) 21148; year-round office in Letterkenny, T: (074) 21160.

Lough Derg

Lake known for pilgrims and a reputed path to purgatory

Praeger calls it the 'dreariest of Donegal waters' and it has not improved since his time, though the land about has been altered by the large-scale planting of conifers, set amid miles of almost featureless black bog. Lough Derg has about 25 islands, one of which is made top-heavy by an ugly and amorphous range of buildings rimming a basilica of 1930. Hell on earth, you could call it; and in the opinion of perhaps

On the north side of Glencar Lake, between Sligo and Manorhamilton, a beautiful, mossy, ferny glen provides the setting for Yeats's Waterfall. The poet is buried at Drumcliff churchyard, beneath the peak of nearby Ben Bulben.

millions you would be near the mark. Since the Middle Ages this island, called Station Island, and another called Saint's Island further to the north, have been visited by innumerable pilgrims intent on earning those visions of purgatory and hell which were vouchsafed to St Patrick when he came here for a retreat during the 5th century. He sat in a cave on Saint's Island and saw a succession of the punishments delivered to the wicked after death, and got a glimpse of the entrance to paradise.

All this was described in a 12th-century account, since when people have flocked here in large numbers every summer, prepared to undergo various mortifications and deprivations for a number of days (two in our time). Authorities from popes to English governments have tried to suppress the whole thing. Despite or perhaps because of this it thrives now as never before. A new transit area beside the quay on the mainland, possessing every conceivable facility, has been completed recently.

Station Island (which refers to the Stations of the Cross) is open only to bona fide pilgrims. For those who do not cross the water the options are limited. The surrounds are flat, monotonous, cheerless and without colour, unless you consider conifer plantations a refreshment. There is a reasonable walk on the east side which takes in the hills of Crokkinagoe and Grousehall, some two miles (three km) away. From the first of these, you can see the islands and the basilica, and, in the distance, the peaks of Tyrone and Donegal. Ferry boats ply the lake continually during the pilgrimage season from 1 June to 15 August.

There are temperaments for which drear melancholy and dour wilderness have a certain appeal. I urge you to check yours is one of them before making the detour.
Before you go *Maps:* OSI Discovery Series, map No. 11. *Guide-books: The Ulster Way* by P. Dillon (O'Brien Press, 1999) and *Ulster Walk Guide* by Richard Rogers (Gill & Macmillan, 1991).
Getting there *By car:* the R233 goes right up to the lake car park.

By bus: Bus Eireann operate a summer-only service from Sligo to Lough Derg, stopping in Pettigo. During the pilgrim season in the summer a special service operates from Dublin each day, T: (01) 836 6111.
Where to stay *B&Bs:* there are 2 places in Pettigo: Mrs McVeigh, T: (072) 61565, and Mrs O'Shea, T: (072) 61535. Self-catering (vacation-home) accommodation is also available. Mr Gallagher rents out an apartment for 3, T: (072) 61511, and Mr Campbell a house for 8, T: (028) 8224 4025 (Northern Ireland).
Access: anyone over the age of 14 can travel to Station Island and join the other pilgrims by obtaining a pass.
Activities *Walking:* the Donegal extension of the 435-mile (700-km) Ulster Way, a waymarked route, passes Lough Derg on its way to the north coast. Contact Ordnance Survey in Belfast, T: (028) 9025 5755.
Fishing: Lough Derg provides fine brown-trout fishing, mayfly time only. Contact the Northern Regional Fisheries Board, Ballyshannon, T: (072) 51435.
Further information *Tourist office:* BF in Bundoran is open June–Sept, T: (072) 41350.

Glens of Sligo and North Leitrim

A region rich in wild glens, plateau-capped mountains with concave sides, water cascading and water at rest in long wood-edged lakes

Fifteen miles (24 kilometres) east of Sligo town lies the little town of Manorhamilton, impressively sited at the hub of a wheel of mountains whose five spokes are formed by valleys and glens radiating outwards. To the north-west is the chunky sector, bounded by Glencar and Glenade, which ends in the strange formations of Ben Bulben, famous for its shape and beauty, its plant-life, its myths and the remains of Yeats in a graveyard at its feet. Northward rises the peak of Crocknagapple and other pinnacles ending in the broad, fish-rich span of Lough Melvin. North-east is Dough mountain, south-east an area of highlands pocked with little lakes, and west-south-west, between the Ben Bulben range and the valley of the Bonet river, is Benbo and a further lean line of peaks, dropping sharply towards Sligo. South of here, between the main heights and the north bank of Lough Gill, there lies a fascinating little area of lakes and minor peaks which is known as the Doons.

These ranges boast almost every outline a mountain is capable of taking: cone, basin, ridge, bun, loaf. I do not know why it should seem remarkable when something made by nature resembles something made by man, as if nature would ever bother itself with imitating art, or need to be congratulated on getting it right. Nature's designs – eye, ear, orchid, humming bird, crystal, whirligig beetle, oak tree – are cleverer than the cleverest of ours. Nevertheless I think it is true that part of the appeal of this area comes from the almost unnatural, the positively man-made look of it: the semi-abstract impression (depending on angle of view) of a colony of Saracen castles, tiered cakes, table tops, high-heeled shoes or, in the case of the ridge north-east of Ben Bulben, a particularly vicious-looking rotary blade for gouging holes out of something very hard. It is an area of geological freaks but there is nothing in the least ugly about it. Quite the contrary. In my opinion this is one of the most beautiful and intriguing parts of Ireland.

The region owes its nature to the earth's stirrings 350 million years ago, when a warm sea covered this part of the globe. The expended shells of minuscule animals floated down and laid a thick foundation of carboniferous limestone over its bed. Sand was swept in and, under the sea's weight, compacted first into sandstone and shales, then into millstone grit. When the sea retreated, the subsequent growth of plants led to the formation of coal. Now weather began its work. Rivers formed and their channels were readily deepened because all the rock they cut through was of this sedimentary kind and relatively soft. Much more recently, the ice scoured through, rounding the channels into the present-day shapes of the glens. The high plateaux, whose vertical substructures stand out so starkly, were left, and remain, grandly distinct.

Judging from the number of their burial chambers and other memorials surviving in elevated places, our Stone Age ancestors saw grandeur here too, but where we reach for kitchen comparisons, they saw perhaps spiritual meaning and significance. The place became imbued with legend, more it seems than other parts of Ireland, which has everywhere been fertile in myth-making. One of the greatest of these tales reaches its climax here, on the summit of Ben Bulben. Dermot, a beautiful youth who had eloped years before with a girl, Grania, destined for the ageing hero Finn, comes with Finn to hunt a magic wild boar. Dermot kills it, but not before it has lethally gored him. As he lies dying, Finn gloats over him, refuses to use his healing powers, and lets the water Dermot craves slip through his fingers.

The two star glens, Glencar and Glenade, seem to crack the hills asunder to disclose an enchantment of long lakes fringed with trees, thick woods, waterfalls. At the north edge the many-islanded Lough Melvin rests the eye with its vast flatness. To the east, straddling the national border, are Loughs Macnean (Upper and Lower), with Cuilcagh mountain and its descending line of caves, made easily accessible at Marble Arch, rising to the south of the lower lake. In the south of the region there is Lough Gill, a contrast: its steep wooded sides sometimes too forbidding for the epithet pretty, a touch Scottish with its castles and rocks and innate romance. And there, a mile above the eastern end of the lake, rise the Doons.

They are smaller than the surrounding mountains, these flattish-topped, vertical-collared remnants of marine reefs pressed

Giant of the crow family, the all-black, thick-billed raven is often seen among mountains or coastal cliffs: a strong flier and skilled aeronaut, keen on aerial tumbles or flying on its side for long stretches.

From the south Ben Bulben reveals the sawn-off tip of its massive peak, celebrated by Yeats in the epitaph he wrote for himself, describing his resting place 'Under bare Ben Bulben's head'.

into a lasting firmness by the regular wash of currents, and surviving long after less densely packed rock around them was eroded away. They stand up like prows from the slopes and valleys about them, and for my money offer some of the most rewarding walks: crisp, quite tough, with amazing views. High on the ascent, with a doon or two below and another, bigger one to overcome, you can look across a broad sweep of valley, hear a sheep's bleat or cough or a raven's churr come from the other side with the clarity of a bell, gaze over to the opposite hillside with its greens, browns, gaps of grey rock and wavy contours, and view the giant doodles worked unconsciously by men cutting peat in the past. 'I'd niver notice it. I suppose I was cradled to it,' a farmer down below said, curiously canvassing my opinion (which is patchy and covered with rust) of Churchill and Chamberlain, rather than talk of the land which is his life. Up here,

though above the world, there is something Parnassian, with every ridge revealing some splendid picture of mountain, lake, wood or broad panorama.

There are orchids, violets, daisies, primroses among the heather and grasses of these hills and mountains, but there are rarities too. Alpines, usually found on north-facing cliffs and surviving here from the time the ice left, include the very rare, pretty, white-flowered fringed sandwort (*Arenaria ciliata*), Arctic saxifrage (*Saxifraga nivalis*) with its spherical cluster of flowers held high over a whorl of basal leaves, and chickweed-leaved willowherb (*Epilobium alsinifolium*), an inconspicuous creeper.

Cast a cold eye
On life, on death
Horseman, pass by.

W. B. Yeats, 'Under Ben Bulben'
(the epitaph on his grave at Drumcliff,
beside the mountain)

Maps: OSI Discovery Series, map No. 16.
Guide-books: *The Leitrim Way* (Leitrim County Council, 1992), *The North Leitrim Glens* by David Herman (Cordee, 1993).

GETTING THERE
By car: take the N16 (east) from Sligo to Manorhamilton, passing Glencar lake and forest on the way. From Manorhamilton take the R280 (north-west) towards Bundoran, skirting the shore of Lough Glenade. Turn right at Kinlough on to the R281, shadowing the south side of Lough Melvin. For Ben Bulben, take the N15 (north) from Sligo. Several small tracks run from this road to the mountain. The R286 (south-east) from Sligo passes north of Lough Gill.
By rail: 3 services run each day from Dublin (Connolly) to Sligo, T: (01) 836 6222.
By bus: Bus Eireann, T: (071) 60066, in conjunction with Ulsterbus, T: (028) 9033 3000 (NI), operate a service between Sligo, Manorhamilton and Enniskillen. Regular Bus Eireann services run each day from Sligo, Derry, Dublin and Galway to Bundoran. Feda O'Donnell operate a service from Crolly to Galway, stopping at Bundoran, T: (075) 48114.

WHERE TO STAY
Hotels and B&Bs: Mrs McPartland is in Manorhamilton, T: (072) 55018; Mrs Fergus at Tullan Strand, Bundoran, T: (072) 41287; Bridie Flannery, T: (072) 41705, and Bernie Dillon, T: (072) 42357, are in Bundoran. Urlar House is in Drumcliffe, T: (071) 63110. There is a wider selection in Sligo, including the Innisfree Hotel on the High Street, T: (071) 42074, and the Clarence Hotel on Wine Street,

T: (071) 42211, e-mail: clarencehotel@tinet.ie.
Youth hostels: the independent Leitrim Lakes Hostel is at Kiltyclogher, open Apr–Oct, T: (072) 54044; Homefield Hostel is in Bundoran, open all year, T: (072) 41288.
Outdoor living: the Dartry View CCP, just outside Bundoran, is open Easter–Sept, T: (072) 41794; or try Lakeside CCP, Ballyshannon, T: (072) 52822, or Greenlands CCP, Rosses Point, T: (071) 77113/45618.

ACTIVITIES
Walking: the 45-mile (72-km) Leitrim Way, a waymarked route, starts in Manorhamilton and heads south-east to Drumshanbo, joining up with the Cavan Way. Contact Leitrim County Council, Governor House, Carrick-on-Shannon, Co. Leitrim, T: (078) 20005.
Cycling: BF suggest a 32-mile (51-km) circular route from Bundoran taking in Lough Melvin. Ask the local BF office for leaflet No. 149.
Riding: the Horse Holiday Farm in Grange organizes treks along the Sligo and Donegal trails, or by the sea, T: (071) 66152, e-mail: hhf@tinet.ie. The Stracomer Silver Strand Equestrian Centre is based in Bundoran, T: (072) 41288, e-mail: homefield@indigo.ie.
Caving: for pot-holing, contact Gortatole Outdoor Education Centre, T: (028) 6634 8888.
Fishing: salmon and brown-trout fishing is available at Lough Melvin. The Lough Melvin Trout Wet-Fly International takes place 17–19 June. Contact Jim Dillon of the Kinlough and District Anglers' Association, T: (072) 42357.

FURTHER INFORMATION
Tourist offices: there is a BF office in Bundoran, T: (072) 41350, open June–mid-Sept.

The Sligo office, T: (071) 61201, and a private office in Manorhamilton, T: (072) 41288 /55833, are open all year.

Knocknarea

A cairn-capped hill west of Sligo town, on a promontory bisecting Sligo Bay and seen from five counties

Twenty-five years ago I bought a day-return railway ticket for me and my bicycle from Dublin, where I was writing a book, to Sligo. The book was about the early Celtic Church in Ireland, and one day I felt an overwhelming desire to visit the mountain-top grave of one of the characters, Queen Maeve. Her remains are supposed to lie under the 40,000 tons of stones that form a cairn, visible on a good day all over the county of Sligo and beyond, on the broad flat surface of Knocknarea.

From the station in Sligo town I cycled the five or six miles to the foot of the hill, hid the bike under a bush, and climbed, admiring the wonderful views over sea and land. I considered the unscrupulous monarch whose jealousy and greed led (in legend, anyway) to a desperate and tragic war between Ulster and her own Connacht, and whose remains, now shared this mountain-top with me alone. She is one of those many historical figures who have taken on the attributes of a mythical namesake – a figure which in this case has given us the personage of Queen Mab. The grave has never been excavated – and an old tradition that visitors carry up a stone to add to the cairn makes it all the time more difficult to contemplate. Such chastity in a remarkable tomb is rare, and adds to the awe of the place.

I came down again after a couple of hours or so. A man approached.

'We saw ye hidin' yer bike,' he said. Was he, I wondered, going to warn me to be more careful, or complain that I had not asked permission? His house, it seemed, was a hundred yards or so away.

'We saw ye,' he went on, 'and now ye're sure to be needin' a cup of tea.'

That was true. He led me to his cottage. Inside, his wife stood beside a table laid with plates of potatoes, Limerick ham, boiled eggs, salad, trifle, bread, cheese and a quart-sized pot of tea. I almost cried with pleasure. In addition I heard more about Maeve than I have heard or read ever since.

I cannot guide you to the cottage. When I went back after twenty years I was not sure which it had been, or whether it had been replaced by a new one, and inquiries failed to find my benefactors. But I can recommend the climb, the view, and epics of Irish myth in which Maeve figures.

Before you go *Maps:* OSI Discovery Series, map No. 25.

Getting there *By car:* the R282 from Sligo goes right round Knocknarea mountain and cairn. *By rail:* regular trains to Sligo from Dublin (Connolly), see p39.

By bus: Sligo is well served by Bus Eireann routes from Belfast, Dublin and Derry, T: (071) 60066.

Where to stay *Hotels and B&Bs:* places in Sligo and Strandhill. Try the Innisfree Hotel, T: (071) 42014.

Youth hostels: 2 independents in Sligo, the White House, T: (071) 45160, and the Eden Hill, T: (071) 43204. *Outdoor living:*

camping at Strandhill, T: (071) 68120.

Activities: apart from walking up Knocknarea to see the grave of Queen Maeve, you can enjoy good beaches and see important prehistoric remains at Carrowmore.

Further information *Tourist office:* BF office in Sligo, T: (071) 61201, is open all year.

Inishmurray

A low, flat, wind-swept, now deserted island in the middle of Donegal Bay, rich in ancient remains, wintering geese and breeding sea-birds

One kind of wildness – the ferocity of weather and the bleak animosity of land or sea – is usually avoided these days. More often than not, we stay indoors. This was an option closed to the torn remnants of the Spanish Armada when, having rounded the north of Scotland from east to west, seeing one after another of their vessels swallowed up, three frigates in the vicinity of Inishmurray, off the north-west coast of Sligo, were pounded by storms on to the opposite strand at Streedagh. Next day 1,100 bodies were counted.

Until 1948 Inishmurray was inhabited by a community of a hundred or so who knew a way of avoiding such catastrophe. Three drops of water from a particular island well sprinkled on the sea always ensured a calm crossing. They had other ways and rituals that sound strange or wonderful to us. Turning certain stones widdershins ensured the success of a curse; clockwise, of a

blessing. They could cure disease by water and faith. They buried their men in one graveyard, their women in another far apart. But for nearly half a century now, such practices have been discontinued. The island is left to its wealth of ancient ruins – many of them from a monastery first founded in the 5th century by Muiredach, a follower of St Patrick – and to the birds which were doubtless there before humans came.

In winter, barnacle geese – distinguished from the rapidly proliferating Canada geese by their shorter neck, white face and grey rather than brown plumage – fly in from their breeding grounds in Greenland and elsewhere in the Arctic Circle to graze on the two hundred or so acres of the island, the majority of which is bog. In spring it becomes the breeding ground for some gulls, the Arctic tern, which may have spent the winter in Antarctica, eiders – easily recognized by their white upper and dark lower plumage – and storm petrels, traditionally known to sailors as Mother Carey's chickens. The petrels' eerie calls may be heard from their rabbit-hole nests at night, but they are unlikely to be seen in the vicinity since they pass the day on and over the sea.

True to ancient belief, the first chronicler of the Anglo-Norman invasion of Ireland, Giraldus Cambrensis, thought that barnacle geese were born from logs of fir lying in sea-water. Other cultures have them growing on trees. Until they were strong enough, Giraldus asserted, they clung by their beaks to seaweed attached to the logs. For these birds, mating had no connection with procreation. So close were they to the life of the sea that they could be eaten, according to a useful Irish tradition, on fast days.

Today the weather is still as wild as it ever was, and the low flat terrain is short on defence and shelter. The land is poor – the former inhabitants' income came from fish – and access is no simple matter. Antiquities and bird life can, however, be rewarding. The best hope of a lift across is at Rosses Point or Mullaghmore, on the mainland 4 miles (6 km) away.

Before you go *Maps:* OSI Discovery Series, map No. 16.

Getting there *By sea:* no regular boat service, but trips can be arranged from Mullaghmore through Lomax Boats, T: (071) 66124. At least 6 people are needed to make the crossing economical. **Where to stay:** there is no accommodation on the island, but there is a large selection in Sligo and Bundoran. **Further information** *Tourist offices:* BF office in Sligo, T: (071) 61201, open all year, and seasonal office in Bundoran, T: (072) 41350.

Ox Mountains

A long granite ridge of wood and moorland with an isolated lake, tying County Mayo to Sligo

People are rather patronizing about the Ox Mountains, a long low wall (rising at its highest point, Knockalongy, to 1,786 ft/544 m) which almost divides Counties Mayo and Sligo, and which can seem from some angles and a fair distance to be short on features and character, especially in comparison with the sculpted peaks of north Sligo and north Leitrim. The Ox Mountains are a quite different affair: much

older (consisting of igneous and metamorphic rocks, mainly granite and gneiss, built up by the great Caledonian upheavals 400 to 500 million years ago), much harder, and of much gentler outline. But they are rich in the remains of ancient cultures. Cairns and other megalithic monuments abound. Probes of the peat have revealed well-developed field systems worked much later by Bronze Age people. Fossil forests under the peat also show that the blanket bog which covers much of the range and extends over most of the neighbouring county of Mayo has increased at the expense of widespread conifer forests. One of the commoner ancient plants was the rhododendron. This too was to die out. Spreads of rhododendron seen now in the middle and west of Ireland come from the re-introduction of the plant in the 18th century.

The centre of the range, not spectacular, still has the appeal of the big, broad, strong and self-assured. The glen that cuts across the middle and contains Easky Lough, though dully afforested in the foothills, rises slowly about the banks of the Owenaher. Higher up, there are scatterings of massive, Attic rockiness, then the mile-long shallow basin of rock-fringed lake where the only sounds are the lapping of water, the wind and an occasional bleat. (Sheep, of an impressively fearless kind, are everywhere.) It feels like the world's summit, or the roof of Tibet. I have seen lakes like this in Iceland, which leads me to expect to hear, though I have never heard nor found evidence that others have, the carrying calls of the great northern diver or whooper swan. The nearest I can get is the common gull, which nests around the edge of the lake and bravely swoops to

frighten away human intruders, and the pert and ubiquitous common sandpiper.

Near the mountains' eastern end, and west of Collooney, gneiss rock gives way to quartzite, whose hardness here and elsewhere means that it often stays stubbornly upright when later rock accretions have been worn off its surface by wind, ice and water. The result is a silhouette unlike that of the rest of the range – a knobbly dinosaur-back which stands out vividly as a landmark and supplies more varied walks than other parts.

Before you go *Maps:* OSI Discovery Series, map Nos 24 and 25.

Getting there *By car:* from Sligo take the N4 (south) to Collooney and then the N17 to Tobercurry. Turn right here on to the R294 which crosses the Ox Mountains. The R297 skirts the north coast and can be reached from the N59 a few miles east of Ballina or Dromore West. *By rail:* services between Dublin (Connolly) and Sligo run every day. T: (01) 836 6222. *By bus:* Bus Eireann run services between Sligo and Ballina, T: (01) 836 6111. Treacy's also run a daily service from Ballina to Sligo, T: (096) 70968. **Where to stay** *Hotels and B&Bs:* plenty in Sligo and Ballina. Mrs Kennedy's is in Tobercurry, T: (071) 85268; the Markree Castle at Collooney, T: (071) 67800. *Youth hostel:* nearest is the independent White House Hostel in Sligo, T: (071) 45160. *Outdoor living:* camping on the north coast at Eastky, T: (096) 49001, and Enniscrone, T: (096) 36132. **Activities** *Cycling:* bikes may be hired from Gerry's Cycle Centre, Ballina, T: (096) 70455. **Further information** *Tourist office:* seasonal BF in Ballina, T: (096) 70848, and year-round in Sligo, T: (071) 61201.

CHAPTER 2

The West

A bout 600 million years ago, almost all lands and continents were clustered far to the south of the Equator. North America (as it would in time become), distantly detached from South America, looked as if it had keeled over clockwise, its present east coast facing south. Between that coast and the South Pole lay the British Isles, a quarter turn clockwise from their present orientation. The sea bounded on the north by North America and on the south by Britain, known as the Iapetus Ocean, contained an east–west line of islands which would become a number of different things. They and the two land masses were the more prominent features of two huge plates of earth-crust – there are seven major ones today – floating on the molten magma of which the earth's interior consists.

These two were moving inexorably together and, at the incomprehensibly drawn-out pace of geological time, they eventually collided in what would seem to us impossibly slow motion – a yard or metre or two a year. Nevertheless the effect of their clash was cataclysmic. One end of the American plate slowly, imperceptibly, nudged, scraped, and was eventually forced under the European plate. All prominent features, including the intervening islands, were now squeezed (I imagine) in a prolonged sequence of searings, crashings and seethings, creating mountains, valleys and every other conceivable physical feature, as well as heat and steam clouds like those from nuclear

The north shore of the lake at Delphi supports rich woodland, a rarity in the highlands of south Mayo. Not unlike its Parnassian namesake, it is hemmed in by rocky mountains, with the shoulder of Ben Creggan thrusting in from the right and the Sheefry Hills rising steeply in the background.

explosions. After a hundred or so million years the clash was about complete. The islands had been changed into the prominences, some of which after eras of erosion by weather would become the central range of Connemara (the Twelve Bens), the Maumturk Mountains to the east and several of the peaks of County Mayo to the north, all quartzite-hearted and consequently resistant to the depredations of climate.

Other, lesser ranges – Joyce Country, the Partry Mountains – were at the same time pushed up from surrounding sedimentary rocks, which had been fused by heat into schists and marbles. The recipe for the delicate pairings of green and black in Connemara marble is to be found in the infernal convulsions of this era. But the heat generated by these movements moved downwards too. Far below the earth's surface it melted solid rock into a magma which burst up and spread over the south of Connemara (the broad coastal strip) in the form of an uneven but never very high blanket of granite.

Still united, the American and Eurasian plates were all the time floating northward, away from the original cluster around the South Pole. Three hundred million years ago Connemara and the rest of Ireland were covered by sea: a warm sea because the part of the sea-bed destined to become Ireland was at that time passing over the Equator. A rich sediment of tiny marine shells coated Ireland with the carboniferous limestone which still underlies the major part of the country. For the most part, though, it has been washed off the Galway highlands.

Something under 200 million years ago, the two plates began to separate again. The division, after what had occurred, could not tidily replicate what went before. Bits from each plate stuck to the other. As it happens, half of modern Ireland – the half that includes Ulster, Louth, Sligo, Mayo and much of Galway and the northern midlands – having been part of the western, American continent, clinging to what is now Newfoundland, stayed this time with the European. The join seems to have occurred along a rough line from Clogher Head in County Louth to Connemara. (It might be tempting to read political significance into these changes – to try to see allegiance in alignment – but they predated humans and all human aspirations by rather too long a period for that.)

The greatest geological dramas in the formation of this part of Ireland were over. There was some volcanic activity to follow in the last 60 million years, the so-called Tertiary age. Doon Hill, beside Bunowen Bay on the way to Slyne Head, comprises a volcanic plug, a bolt of lava that cooled within the core and was in due course partially exposed by erosion. The Ice Ages changed much, but in the manner of a plastic surgeon, modifying and altering features without breaking the underlying mould. There are mountain lakes in carved-out corries, scree-hung valleys, slopes of rock scraped smooth, moraines, eskers, a colony of drumlins and here and there erratic boulders left by ice in its several comings and goings.

Plants moved in as the ice receded. Dwarf birch and hawthorn served as curtain raisers until oak and pine established themselves over large areas. Then man came, as thorough and nihilistic as the ice itself. To get land for animals and crops he felled and burned trees on an Amazonian scale. The fires he lit, and the many which began naturally, created charcoal. Charcoal clogged the soil, making it more or less impervious, a process assisted by the leaching of minerals through the soil to form a compacted layer below. Rain fell and lay on the surface. Plants lived and died and sank into the acid, increasingly airless water, which greatly slowed down their decomposition. Bog was being created, and as it took hold it curtailed the number of plants able to survive. The only trees to come from the bog are the stumps and boles of those ancient oaks and pines which preceded it. Connemara – mountain and coast – is for the most part singularly bare of trees, though there are entrancing exceptions to the rule.

For want of forests, of course, modern man has been destroying the peat that developed slowly in the bog, not just in Connemara but over much of the country. Burning it in his grate made little impact, but selling it to bulk out the soil in suburban gardens in other parts of the world, and to be converted to energy in power stations, and leaving nothing much in its place, has gravely changed large parts of the West, not least the bleak boggy wilderness of north-western Mayo known as the Barony of Erris. Equally jarring change has come from the conifer plantations that here and there spread a dull green domestic velvet over the former grand desolation of moorland.

Yet the West and the South-West of Ireland retain between them by far the largest share of the country's wildness. For most visitors, the West is not the easiest part of the country to reach. You arrive on the east coast or the south, and wherever you start and however you travel, getting to Counties Clare and Galway and Mayo loses you at least half a day, unless you arrange to fly to Knock, Shannon or Farranfore. But if wildness does not take some getting to, it is hardly worth the name.

Remoteness, though, is a relative word, and it is not at all what it used to be. Not long ago I stayed at an inn in the north of County Mayo, and imagined what it would have been like at the beginning of the 20th century. Getting away once darkness fell would have been unthinkable. You would have been thrown on the company and hospitality and catering skills of the innkeeper, his wife and a handful of local peasants, and bad weather would have kept you here for days. Your companions' conversation would have been limited in scope to their experience, mostly local. But I dare say everything about it would have been memorable. As it was, when I was there, the television dominated the bar. Locals asked for international-sounding things like Bacardi and tequila with Coke, and talked about cars and sex. I had telephone conversations with people hundreds of miles away in Ireland or England. If I had had the right sort of computer I could probably have linked up with the Library of Congress catalogue in Washington, DC.

Then I walked out into the twilight air. It was a sepia print of a view: sepia moorland all about, low sepia hills, breaking now and again to show vees of sepia sea, and behind me mountains too dark to be called anything but black shadows against a deep-violet sky. The only sound was of regularly spaced stonechats, uttering their indignation at (I suppose) my presence at this time of night. It was easy to forget the world I knew; but nonetheless a pity not to know it was utterly out of reach, as it would have been from an uninhabited offshore island.

To reach wildness a bit of getting away is always necessary, from the town, perhaps, or simply from the road. In the parts of the West that are best to see and walk in, there are singularly few of either. In Erris you can walk all day and cross only one road. The Twelve Bens, the central glory of Connemara, are surrounded by a respectable road, but only one or two single-lane tracks lead into their central precinct. Coastal Connemara has easier road access and a great many people to take advantage of it. Few, however, go to the uninhabited islands; to get to these involves a deal with a fisherman which might cost dear. The Burren draws crowds in cars and coaches, and in season they clog the roads, especially at places the brochures make much of. Leave them behind, trust to two feet, and humanity becomes a memory. It is still amazingly true that two districts of world fame – Connemara and the Burren – can, in great part, be so free of people.

The component areas of the West are, in the Irish way, very different in character. Elsewhere you would have to travel hundreds of miles to cover such a range of landscapes. The Burren is a pavement of stone wherein every dip and crack and crevice capable of carrying a teaspoon of soil supports plants of kinds that draw botanists from all over the world. In central Connemara and to its east, brotherhoods of mountains rise in conclaves, challenging the climber and botanist to scramble up their hunched shoulders. Salmon breed in the rivers that start in tumbles down their sides, and there are broad fish-rich lakes in the dells of Joyce Country and the Partry Mountains. Connemara's periphery is a belt of flat-lands sequinned with small lakes and hemmed by sea. There are festoons of spring flowers here, and many that are rare and far from their normal homes: America or Spain. A botanist's Mecca, the author Robert Lloyd Praeger called the country near Roundstone. A hedonist's too, he might have added. And then, a few miles away, are the monotone bog-lands of Mayo, and a few miles further still, the wild cliffs of Achill, a fist of resistance held out to the battering Atlantic.

GETTING THERE

By air: Dublin and Shannon are the main international airports, with incoming flights from major European cities and North America. Contact Aer Lingus in Dublin, T (01) 886 8888, www.aerlingus.ie, for details, or visit the airports' web-sites, www.dublin airport.com or www.shannon airport.com. Internal flights from Dublin to Shannon, Galway and Sligo are also operated by Aer Lingus. Aer Arann fly from Dublin to Sligo and from Inveran to all 3 Aran Islands, T: (01) 814 5240 or (091) 593034/593054.

By sea: there are no ferry services to the west coast, but Swansea Cork Ferries, T: (01792) 456116 (UK), www.swansea-cork.ie, sail to Cork from Swansea 4 days a week in the off-peak season and 6 times a week in summer (including an overnight crossing). Stena Sealink, T: (0870) 570 7070 (UK), www.stena line.com, and Irish Ferries, T: (0870) 517 1717 (UK), www.irish ferries.ie, operate services to the east coast from UK ports such as Stranraer, Holyhead, Fishguard, Pembroke and Swansea. Regular ferries go from Galway, T: (091) 567283, and Rossaveal, T: (091) 568903, to the Aran Islands.

By car: main roads link all ports of entry with Galway and other major towns in the West. One advantage of sailing overnight to Cork is that it allows a full day for the drive.

By rail: from Dublin (Heuston), Iarnrod Eireann operate 3 services a day to Ballina and Westport, 5 to Galway and 10 to Limerick. Contact Iarnrod Eireann, T: (01) 836 6222, www.irishrail.ie.

By bus: from Dublin there are 3 Expressway services a day to Ballina, and 13 to both Galway and Limerick. Contact Bus Eireann, T: (01) 836 6111, www.buseireann.ie.

WHERE TO STAY

There is no shortage of campsites, B&Bs, hostels, hotels and self-catering (vacation-home) accommodation in this part of Ireland. Bord Fáilte publishes accommodation guides which list approved places to stay. Hostels run by the Irish YHA, An Oige, require membership, T: (01) 830 4555, www.ireland yha.org. The Independent Holiday Hostels of Ireland are privately owned and require no membership card, T: (01) 836

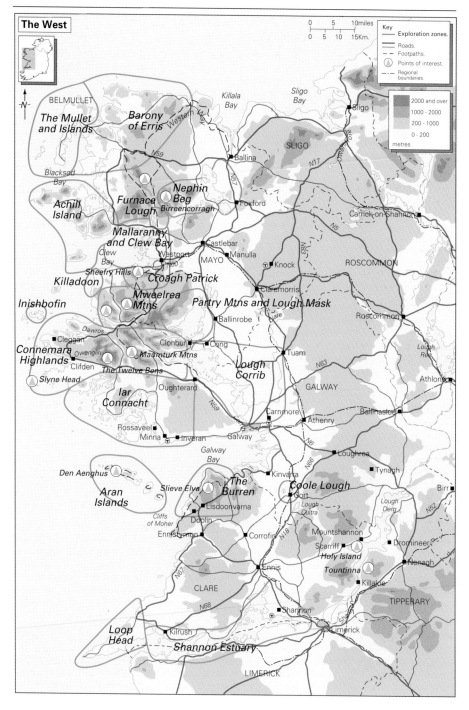

The West

0   5   10miles
0 5 10 15Km.

Key
— Exploration zones.
═ Roads.
--- Footpaths.
⓵ Points of interest.
─ ─ Regional boundaries.

2000 and over
1000 - 2000
200 - 1000
0 - 200
metres

-N-

BELMULLET

The Mullet and Islands

Barony of Erris

Western Way

Killala Bay

Sligo Bay

Sligo

Ballina

N59

SLIGO

N17

Carrick-on-Shannon

Blacksod Bay

Achill Island

Furnace Lough

Nephin Beg
Birreencorragh

Foxford

N5

N61

Mallaranny and Clew Bay

Clew Bay

Castlebar

Manulla

Knock

ROSCOMMON

Westport

N60

MAYO

Sheefry Hills

Killadoon

Croagh Patrick

Claremorris

Mweelrea Mtns

Partry Mtns and Lough Mask

Roscommon

Inishbofin

Ballinrobe

Clare

Cleggan

Dawros

Clonbur

Cong

Tuam

Lough Ree

Connemara Highlands

Owenglin

Clifden

Maumturk Mtns

Lough Corrib

N63

GALWAY

Athlone

Slyne Head

The Twelve Bens

Oughterard

Iar Connacht

N59

Carnmore

Athenry

Ballinasloe

Rossaveel

Minna

Inveran

Galway

N6

N66

Loughrea

Tynagh

Galway Bay

Den Aenghus

Aran Islands

Slieve Elva

The Burren

Kinvarra

Coole Lough

Gort

Lough Cultra

Birr

Lough Derg

N52

Cliffs of Moher

Lisdoonvarna

Doolin

Corrofin

N18

Mountshannon

Dromineer

Ennistymon

Scarriff

Holy Island

Nenagh

N67

Ennis

Tountinna

CLARE

Killaloe

N68

Shannon

TIPPERARY

Loop Head

Kilrush

Shannon

Limerick

Shannon Estuary

LIMERICK

47

4700, www.hostels-ireland.com. Camping and caravanning (mobile-home) details are available from Irish Caravan and Camping Council, PO Box 443, Dublin 2, www.camping-ireland.ie.

ACTIVITIES

Walking: the Western Way is a 140-mile (225-km) waymarked route divided into 7 stages, varying from about 10 miles (16 km) to 40 miles (65 km). Starting from Oughterard the way skirts Lough Corrib, cuts through and then curves round to the west of the Maumturk Mountains, continues north along the east side of the Sheefry range, through the mountains and moors of the Barony of Erris in Co. Mayo, finishing in the Ox Mountains. See *The Western Way* by J. McDermott and R. Chapman (Mayo County Council, 1993). **Cycling:** 3 lengthy circular routes in the region are recommended by BF. The plains of

Galway and Mayo are the least demanding while Connemara and Killary are more rugged. The Mountains of Mayo route, with its breathtaking cliff scenery, is the longest at 194 miles (312 km). Mayo Leisure Cycling arrange a variety of cycling holidays, T: (094) 25220, e-mail: cyclingm@anu.ie. **Riding:** contact Willie Leahy at The Connemara/Coast Trails & Aille Cross Trails, Aille Cross, Loughrea, Co. Galway, T: (091) 841216, or The Ashford Equestrian Centre at Cong, T: (092) 46024/46507.
Climbing: Ben Corr in the Twelve Bens has a quartzite crag with good routes up to 1,000 ft (300 m) which provide choices for climbers of different standards. Maumtrasna in the Partry Mountains has shorter, easier climbs on sandstone.
Fishing: salmon rivers include the Bundorragha, Clare, Corrib, Dawros, Erris and Owenglin. Loughs Feeagh and Furnace have salmon. Lough

Corrib has brown trout and salmon. Lough Mask is better known for its trout. Grasshopper Cottage on Lough Corrib offers accommodation and fly-fishing for wild brown trout, open Mar–Oct, T: (092) 48165. Contact the Western Regional Fisheries Board, T: (091) 563118, e-mail: wrfb@iol.ie. **Watersports:** Little Killary Adventure Centre, T: (095) 43411, offers activities including sailing and wind-surfing. The Ringville Sailing Club, T: (091) 794527, is just east of Galway.

FURTHER INFORMATION
Tourist offices: the main BF office is in Galway, T: (091) 563081. Accommodation can be booked by e-mail: booking @western-tourism.ie. There is another year-round BF office in Westport, T: (098) 25711.

FURTHER READING
Walk Guide West of Ireland by T. Whilde and P. Simms (Gill & Macmillan, 1999).

Barony of Erris

A fretted coastline of cliffs and some fishing harbours, and inland the vast unpeopled peatlands of north Mayo

Mayo is as wild a county as Ireland possesses: a big county which imprints itself on the visitor's mind as a carpet of bog interrupted by some stately mountains and contained within a coastline of frenzied indentations and a quite uncountable number of islands. Among the hard acid terrain of the interior there are in fact some rich alkaline lands, most of them once colonized by the Anglo-Irish, who could usually tell good soil from bad. These lands tend to be around Killala Bay, Lough Conn and Lough Mask, and east of Clew Bay between Westport and Newport. One of the great

Ascendancy houses that has found its feet as a tourist draw in modern times is Westport House, home of the Browne family, marquesses of Sligo, of whom twelve generations have lived here since Tudor times. Another family possessing lands in the county for four centuries is the Binghams, earls of Lucan. The last earl disappeared after the murder of his children's nanny in London several years ago, and is generally assumed to be dead. But as long as there was serious doubt, I have been told, tenants on his lands around Castlebar decided without overmuch distress that it would be inappropriate to pay rent to his heir and best to pay nobody. This could, of course, be groundless gossip.

The less kempt demesnes of the old Anglo-Irish landlords are often places where a certain wildness can be found. The Irish people are not inclined to gut or clear away deserted buildings. Ruins of all kinds – defensive, ecclesiastical, domestic – remain from all the eras of Irish history. Beside the shell of some 18th-century or earlier mansion, abandoned or burnt by accident or design, there will often be woods and an uncontrolled growth of shrubbery and weeds replacing what was garden or decorative parkland. Such areas may well have become unofficial nature reserves, havens for birds, ringing with morning and evening song. All such lands are private. Many are jealously guarded by a rump of the landlord family who may in some cases be carrying on their lives in an unrecognizably intact corner of a house which is otherwise ruinous. Care and courtesy are called for in what can be a rewarding approach.

St Patrick, calling a blessing on Ireland from the summit of Croagh Patrick, is traditionally supposed to have missed out Mayo's more characteristic surface: the blanket bog of the great Barony of Erris in the north and the Nephin Beg range along the southern edge, in parts heavily planted with monotonous forestry trees. You would not explore it for richness of scenery or flora or fauna – though the familiar little Pickwickian stonechat, with its buff chest and white collar, light cheep followed by cicada's churr, is a common attraction, as is the graceful wheatear – visiting for the summer – with its mottled shawl and white rump. Golden plover, snipe, woodcock, merlin and the amphibious dipper are pleasing to see but not to be counted on. The red grouse is uncommon and clever at camouflage. The expansive brown or purple of the bog, with mountains of like colours as backdrop, is less scenery than tone, or mood; something not to comment on or describe but to feel one's way into a kind of communion with. According to taste and temperament, you can be serenely in tune with the landscape or bored out of your mind.

Where bored, I suggest you home in and narrow the focus. The bog was not daubed by an impressionist, to be loved or not for its general depiction. It was painted lovingly by an early Flemish or Italian artist, disclosing more and more precise detail to the inquisitive eye. The Wildlife Service's Knockmoyle Sheskin nature reserve in the middle of the Barony of Erris is an excellent place to put this claim to the test. (You are advised not to go without a qualified guide because of the danger of walking into a hollow, pond or swallow-hole.)

It is, simply, a well-maintained 3,000 acres (1,200 hectares) of blanket bog, endowed by nature with streams, pools, wet hollows and so-called flush areas rich in minerals and supporting their own tally of plants, including birch and willow trees. What man has done to much of the surrounding bog – a third afforested by means of European Union money; substantial parts mechanically removed for fuel or to bulk out the flower-beds of millions of suburban gardens; part chomped up for drainage schemes – has been prohibited here for good.

You can identify bog grasses, rushes, mosses, red worm-like liverworts, bogbean, crowberry, ling and bell heather and many others, discerning the soils they like and companions they choose. You can see a sinister threesome of bog plants reversing nature's normal procedure of animal eating plant. The sundew traps the unwary insect with glue-tipped red tentacles rising from its whorl of reddish leaves. It folds them over and slowly squeezes and digests nutrient juices from the cadaver. The yellow-green leaves of the butterwort ooze adhesive, trap and dissolve their prey, while the aquatic Greater bladderwort (*Utricularia vulgaris*) wafts hair-triggers from its roots in the water. When touched, the hairs open up a small round bladder whose interior vacuum sucks in the victim. The flowers of all three

The strikingly spotted, furry-bodied emperor moth lives among the heather, which provides its food during June and July. The male can detect a female well over a mile away.

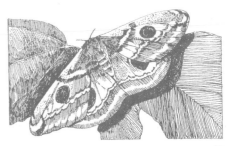

carnivores wave innocently atop leafless stems, while the carnage is conducted by leaves below.

The north coast is as different as can be from this insulating bog; here the landscape is clearly more specific and variegated, but wild too, and awesome in high winds and racing clouds. Much of it consists of cliffs, the grandest being Benwee Head in the county's north-west corner, but this is only visible in full splendour from the sea. (There are, of course, stupendous views from its summit.) There is a good walk from close to Porturlin harbour eastward to Belderg, after which the road runs along and sometimes almost next to the coast. The distinct trio of small islands known as the Stags of Broad Haven are a couple of miles out to sea. About halfway along the 10 or 11 miles (16 kilometres) of the walk, cliff-top positions give views of the island of Illanmastir where two thousand pairs of puffins nest and breed, one of the more important Irish colonies. With unquestionable wisdom, the Irish Wildbird Conservancy bars access, but no harm is done by a distant scrutiny with binoculars. The second, eastern half of the walk, with a couple of sweeping descents and the steep climb to Glinsk, is more dramatic than the first.

BEFORE YOU GO

Maps: OSI Discovery Series, map Nos 22, 23, 30 and 31.

Guide-books: *West of Ireland Walk Guides: The Western Way* by Joe McDermott and Robert Chapman (Mayo County Council, 1993); and *The Bangor Trail Map Guide* (Mayo County Council, 1992).

GETTING THERE

By car: take the N59 from Ballina to Bangor, or shadow the north coast by following the R314 from Ballina to Barnatra.
By rail: Iarnrod Eireann run 3 services a day from Dublin (Heuston) to Ballina, T: (01) 836 6222.
By bus: a Bus Eireann service runs from Ballina to Blacksod Point, stopping at Belmullet, T: (096) 71800. Treacy's, T: (096) 22563, run to Ballina from Sligo, and Barton Transport, T: (01) 628 6026, from Dublin.

WHERE TO STAY

Hotels and B&Bs: there are quite a few B&Bs on the main

From the cliffs beneath Croaghaun, Achill Island's second highest peak, knife-edge ridges continue north-west for nearly two miles (3 km) before tailing off beyond Little Saddle to the digital extremity of Achill Head.

---

road approaching Belmullet, and plenty of hotels, guesthouses and B&Bs scattered about, though there is a huge almost unpeopled area in the south of the barony. Mrs Geraghty's B&B is on the Belmullet peninsula, T: (097) 85741. In Belmullet itself are Mrs Tallott, T: (097) 81294; Mrs Maguire-Murphy, T/F: (097) 81195, e-mail: dromcaoin@clubi.ie; and Mrs Horan, T: (097) 81321. Mrs Cosgrove is in Bangor Erris village, T: (097) 83494; and Mrs Murphy has a B&B in Belderrig, on the R314 west of Ballycastle, T/F: (096) 43148.
Youth hostel: the independent Kilcommon Lodge Hostel, Pullathomas, is north of Carrowmore lake near Carrowteige, T: (097) 84621.
Outdoor living: Hiney's campsite is 2 km from Lough Conn, open Mar–Oct, T: (096) 31262/31348.

ACTIVITIES

Walking: the Dun Caochain Cliff walk between Belderg and Carrowteige, passing Porturlin harbour on the way, is a wonderful 25-mile (40-km) route along cliffy coast, one of the best in the country. Part of the County Mayo stretch of the Western Way crosses the Barony of Erris, as it sweeps north from Newport to Ballina, past Ballycastle and Killala. Note, however, that the walks across the moorland and mountains can stray miles from habitation and should not be undertaken lightly or alone. The circular Bangor Trail (26 miles/42 km) also makes for good walking. For full route details contact BF or the Mayo County Council, The Mall, Castlebar, T: (094) 24444.
Fishing: the River Oweniny is one of several good salmon rivers in the area. Contact the Western Regional Fisheries Board, T: (091) 563118. For sea-angling contact Michael John Mallen in Belmullet, T: (097) 82093.

FURTHER INFORMATION

Tourist offices: there are information points at Ballycastle, T: (096) 43256, and Ballina, T: (096) 70848. Both these offices are open only during the summer. The BF office in Westport, T: (098) 25711, is open all year round.
Ecology: the Knockmoyle-Sheskin Nature Reserve, north of the Bangor–Crossmolina road, is an area of lowland blanket bog with interesting flushes (no tel.). For further details contact National Parks and Wildlife Service, T: (01) 661 3111.

The Mullet and Islands

Peninsula lying between the ocean and Blacksod Bay, with much sandy beach and machair on its western side and, off-shore, a number of uninhabited islands

The Mullet, a long thin peninsula hanging north to south from the mainland at Belmullet, has a rocky north-west coast with wintering and breeding bird-life. Nearby, areas of machair grassland and marsh provide the only breeding ground in Ireland for the red-necked phalarope. Most of the peninsula is windswept, treeless and largely cultivated, segmented by barbed wire and scattered with new bungalows. (This was once prime Bingham territory, as several place names suggest.) Further west are a number of islands of many shapes and sizes. On Inishglora, storm petrels nest on the stony beach. Inishkea North and South have been uninhabited since 1927 when storm-damage to the fishing fleet finally killed the traditional way of life. More seals breed here than elsewhere in Ireland, and barnacle geese (some 2,000 pairs) spend the winter, grazing on the rough grasses that proliferate over the windswept flats.

Reaching these and other islands is a matter of negotiating with fishermen, complicated nowadays by insurance considerations. There was no such thought ten, twenty and even fifty years ago, when the author of *The Once and Future King*, T. H. White, took a cottage on the Mullet and sailed from island to island looking for the magic image of St Mac Dara, thrown into the sea in the 18th century by a Catholic priest who believed it was encouraging idolatry.

The search took White to many islands because it had become inlaid with other islanders' accounts and with his own theories about fertility cults and phallic symbols. He did not discover the idol, which may for all I know remain where it was thrown, off St Mac Dara's Island, south Galway. But his inquiries brought him all kinds of knowledge about island beliefs and rituals, faith and religion, about Penal Days murders, about a giant's wife turned into a heron on Inishkea, about where to practise falconry and shoot geese or catch salmon, all of which he enjoyed. One night, on one of the islands, he came face to face with the Devil. It had a wicked face, horns, cloven feet. Of course, it turned out at dawn to be a particularly dark goat, innocently grazing, but the story White tells in his account of this quest, *The Godstone and the Blackymor*, is a wonderful evocation of the richness of life, history and tradition in islands which without such sources yield little of their past and can even seem to be hitherto untrodden by man.

Before you go *Maps:* OSI Discovery Series, map No. 22.
Getting there *By car:* follow the N59 (west) or the longer coast road, the R314 (north then west), from Ballina. Both join

---

THE CHILDREN OF LIR

Lir was the god of the sea (related in myth to Shakespeare's King Lear) and by his first wife had three sons and a daughter. When his wife died he married her younger sister Aoife. She became the classically jealous stepmother. She took the children to Lough Derravaragh in County Longford and ordered a servant to kill them. When he refused she had them pushed into the lough and turned by magic into swans. (Men, women, gods and goddesses were often converted into birds in Irish myths, and birds were, for this reason, frequently protected by a ban on hunting or shooting.)

The swans were fated to spend 300 years of misery on the lake, 300 more on the waters of the Moyle (the icy strait below Fair Head, off the north coast of County Antrim) and a final 300 on the sea by Inishglora, west of the Mullet in County Mayo. Here they were at last restored to human form, only to die and be buried on the island. When he learned what his wife had done, Lir had Aoife turned into a wretched air spirit, to float homeless for the rest of time. The story is known as one of 'the three sorrowful tales of Ireland', a gross underestimate. Celtic gloom recurs constantly in the old literature.

The great Gaels of Ireland
  Are the men whom God made mad;
For all their wars were merry,
  And all their songs were sad.

the R313 which leads straight to Belmullet.
By rail: services run from Dublin (Heuston) to Ballina, T: (01) 836 6222.
By bus: the Bus Eireann service between Blacksod Point and Ballina stops at Belmullet, T: (096) 71800.
Where to stay *B&Bs:* in Belmullet: Mrs Maguire-Murphy, T/F: (097) 81195, and Mrs Reilly, T: (097) 81260. Mrs Geraghty, T: (097) 85741, is on the peninsula. *Youth hostel:* Kilcommon Lodge in Pullathomas, T: (097) 84621.
Activities: for sea-angling along the coast, contact Michael John Mallen in Belmullet, T: (097) 82093.
Further information: McIntyre's Travel in Belmullet, T: (097) 81172.

Nephin Beg

A tall, handsome range of peaks and lakes stretching from the sea at Clew Bay far into the boggy interior of Mayo

You can still stand within the southern half of the Barony of Erris and look to north, south, east and west without seeing any land-surface other than blanket bog. A hundred years ago, and for a hundred years before that, you would have seen people too: bent, undernourished people whose little smoky cabins, home also to any sheep or goats or pigs they were fortunate enough to possess, crowded many of the valleys and lower hillsides. The unmistakable patterns of the so-called lazy beds they constructed are still evident on the most unlikely slopes. But there are no more people. The population which peaked in the

'When the airs is warming, in four months or five, it's then yourself and me should be pacing Neifin in the dews of the night, the times sweet smells do be rising, and you'd see a little, shiny new moon, maybe, sinking on the hills.'

J. M. Synge, The Playboy of the Western World

1840s, just before the great famines, slumped, then rose, teetered at an impossibly high level for the rest of the 19th century and finally drained away to almost nothing in the 20th.

This is the bleakest, barest, most brooding, most haunting countryside in Ireland, occupying about 400 sq miles (1,000 sq km) of plain from the centre of which rises the great Nephin Beg range: Slieve Car, Nephin Beg itself, Birreencorragh and the outlying Nephin, isolated and shapely across the valley of the River Crumpaun. Not that the bog has been left alone by meddling man. In the middle of the plain, north of Nephin Beg, the power station of Bellacorick has devoured miles of peat for the generation of electricity. What is left behind is an earth-scar which will last years. There are big forestry plantations of dull monotone evergreens. Around the base of Nephin Beg, they create quite a barrier to those wishing to climb the mountain.

The bog itself, of course, was probably man's doing, at least in part created by the wholesale tree-fellings carried out by Neolithic settlers. But that seems long enough ago to be sanctioned now as natural, certainly long enough to have attracted its own flora and fauna: black bog rush, bog asphodel, purple moor grass, cross-leaved heath and several other grasses and sedges, mosses and liverworts. Cotton-grass and white-beaked sedge

are staple foods for the Greenland white-fronted geese and also for golden plovers, merlins – the smallest of falcons, precision killers – meadow pipits, skylarks, snipe and many other birds.

The Nephin Beg Mountains are of quartzite, heated to its present obdurate consistency by the same volcanic turbulence that created the Scottish Highlands and the mountains of Donegal. Resistance to erosion has given them a clear, sharp outline, and their silhouettes are impressive from most angles. Closer in, they offer good walks and climbs,

The merlin is found all over Ireland, a small falcon that can fly close to the ground over lowland bog and (in summer) over high mountain with equal facility, snatching small birds from their perches or chasing them with uncannily accurate, twist-and-turn dexterity.

with a number of icy lake-filled corries, tumbling streams and modest waterfalls. From their heights mighty panoramic views open out over the upland plains of Mayo, the distant line of the Ox mountains, Achill island and its massy peaks, Clew Bay with its shoals of drumlins, innumerable islands, the sculpted peaks of Connemara and the unbounded, hemming Atlantic. Robert Lloyd Praeger, considering the bare brown heather of these mountains, found them 'not lonely or depressing but inspiriting. You are thrown at the same time back upon yourself and forward against the mystery and majesty of nature, and you may feel dimly something of your own littleness and your own greatness.' It has to be said, in spite of this, that Tony Whilde and others who know the range well sound less than inspired by

their climbs. There are, moreover, dangers in hiking in parts which can be ten or more miles from the nearest tarred road. Sizeable patches of bright green sphagnum moss may indicate hidden pools, which can give way with dangerous consequences. Although tracks cross the range here and there, it would be rash to make a long lone foray into this territory.

Before you go *Maps:* OSI Discovery Series, map Nos 23, 30 and 31.
Guide-books: The Bangor Trail by Joe McDermott and Robert Chapman (Mayo County Council, 1992) has maps and useful information.
Getting there *By car:* the mountains are circumscribed by roads. The N59 runs north from Westport on the west side and the R317 and R312 on the east. *By rail:* 3 services a day from Dublin (Heuston) stop at Foxford, Castlebar and Ballina,

T: (01) 836 6222. *By bus:* Bus Eireann run 3 services daily to Ballina from Dublin. An Expressway between Ballina and Cork stops at Foxford once a day. The Mon–Sat bus between Dooagh and Cork stops at Pontoon daily, T: (096) 71800.
Where to stay *Hotel and B&B:* try Daly's Hotel, T: (094) 21961, or Mrs Flannelly's B&B, T: (094) 21002, both in Castlebar. *Outdoor living:* Hiney's CCP, Crossmolina, T: (096) 31262/31348; Carrowkeel at Ballyvarry, T: (094) 31264.
Activities *Walking:* the Bangor Trail (26 miles/42 km) and part of the 140-mile (220-km) Western Way cross the Nephins. *Fishing:* Lough Conn is a world-famous brown-trout lake.
Further information *Touirst offices:* the seasonal BF office at Castlebar, T: (094) 21207, and the Heritage Centre, Crossmolina, T: (096) 31809.

Achill Island

A large remote island, its central flat-lands densely inhabited, its coastal periphery rising, especially on the west and south-west, to huge and spectacular walls of cliff

A chill, Ireland's largest island, is only 20 feet (6 metres) away from the mainland. Indeed Ireland and Achill are joined by a bridge. (When the first bridge was constructed in 1888, foxes crossed over and islanders found it necessary to protect their poultry.) To get to this island you have to pass the stony hem of Corraun, a mountain which is all but an island itself, attached to the mainland for a short half-mile or so just to the west of Mallaranny.

West of the Mweelrea Mountains, and south of Killadoon, broad white beaches alternate with massive sand dunes. At low tide, the water's edge on this strand beneath Mweelrea is at least 400 to 500 yds (350–450 m) out from the shoreline.

The southern coast road to Achill has the best views. If you can judge mountains, as they say you can people, by the company they keep, then both Corraun and Achill are sensational. The haze that so often rises off the water of Clew Bay colours each distant plane a slightly different shade of blue, and it is these degrees of distinction, as well as the variety, stature and shapes of the features seen, that makes progress such a pleasure. A slow sweep of the view from Corraun takes in the slant backs of the drumlin islands cluttering Clew Bay, the faded blue of the distant Partry Mountains, the darker cone of Croagh Patrick, the hazily withdrawn Sheefry hills, the huge shadowy wraith of Mweelrea and many other slopes, cones and curves of the Mayo and Galway mountains. Looming from the Atlantic as you round the coast comes the crouching sphinx of Clare Island, paws and head to the right, rising rump and long extended tail to the left. Then the road turns away, up the narrow sound to Achill bridge.

Another reason for enjoying the distant view is that when you come close things may

From the coast below Mweelrea the sea stretches westward, shallow but deepening, to a scatter of islands, a long curving projection of the mainland west of Killary Harbour and 3,000 miles of ocean.

not be all you expected. Achill once personified the deprived west. Before and after the famine too many people tried to live off a frugal crop of oats and potatoes. The exploitation of the one rich resource, fish, was far from thorough, though basking sharks (unfortunately for themselves, perhaps, not aggressive to humans) were netted for their oil, off Keem Bay. Before the famine, at a time when corn was still ground between stones, an Anglican missionary picked on the island to undertake a mass conversion of Catholics to his own faith. He built a settlement for the converts, acquired more than half the island's land and laboured restlessly, providing school, orphanage, printing works at Doogort, and a colony of homes on the slopes behind. Not for the first or last time in Irish history religions confronted each other. The Catholics, put on their mettle, began to match the mission's innovations and slowly recouped their

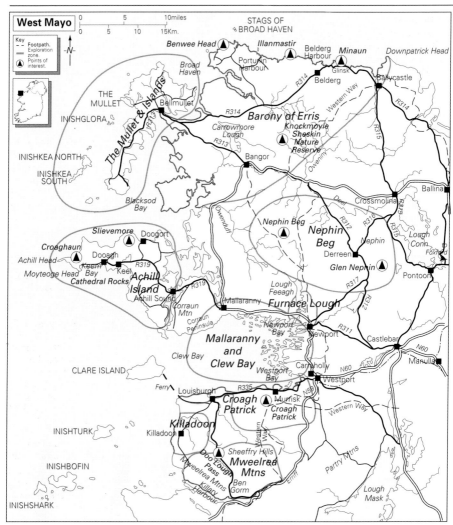

losses. The Anglican colony is now a small ghost town, and philanthropy has turned to commerce. Thus the impression given by the three main centres, Dooagh, Keel and Doogort, is one of brash prosperity. Roads that were almost impassable earlier in the 20th century are smartly tarred. The race on now is to win not souls but tourists. To this end, they have a few magnificent natural assets.

Achill, like much of the rest of west Mayo, consists largely of quartzite and schists, rocks that were chemically converted or baked by the convulsions of 400 to 500 million years ago into a hardness that stubbornly and more successfully than other rocks resists many of the attempts of wind and particularly water to erode it. Sudden, distinctly shaped mountains break from the Achill plain. The west-facing Cathedral Rocks and the nearby Menawn cliffs rise sheer out of the sea on the island's southern edge to a height of 1,500 feet (450 metres) and, when a rich red sun sets over the Atlantic ocean, they reflect its light in a rosy twilight glow of incredible beauty.

Slievemore (2,204 feet/672 metres), on the

north coast above Doogort, is the island's highest summit. The climb from Doogort is quite steep but follows a simple route and provides, of course, dazzling views of coast, mountains, ocean and islands. At the western tip of Achill, beyond Keem Bay, where amethysts produced by chemical action at the time of the great convulsions are often found, the land rises to one of those sights best seen from the sea: the broad face of dramatic cliffs under Croaghaun (2,192 feet/668 metres). But here the landward features are themselves among the finest natural scenes in Ireland. The slant of the land in parts suggests a board, heavily weighted in the middle, that has cracked, so that one of its halves has risen steeply to a great height. Its edge is narrow, even at times sharp, with the supporting cliffs dropping vertically away below. The knife-sharp ridge of the Little Saddle tails off to Achill Head on the western extremity. Among the heady uplands north-east of Croaghaun, a number of lakes appear, one of them, Lough Bunnafreeva, almost teetering on the edge of the cliffs. This whole western range offers a wealth of scenery but also real danger from the precipitous angle of cliffs. The sea eagle, which was described as common in the early 19th century, had gone by the beginning of the 20th. But the rest of the outward views from heights which are not easy to reach are, quite simply, as beautiful and inspiring as any in Ireland.

BEFORE YOU GO
Maps: OSI Discovery Series, map No. 30.
Guide-books: *Achill Island Map Guide* (Bob Kingston, 1988); *Walk Guide West of Ireland* by T. Whilde and P. Simms (Gill & Macmillan, 1999) covers the cliff-top walk which takes in Achill Head and Croaghaun.

GETTING THERE
By car: from Westport follow the N59 (north-west) to Mallaranny, then take the R319 or the minor coast road to Achill Sound.
By rail: 3 services run between Dublin (Heuston) and Westport each day, Mon–Sat, T: (01) 836 6222.
By bus: the Bus Eireann Expressway between Dooagh and Belfast stops at Achill Sound once a day. The local bus between Dooagh and Ballina stops there 5 times a day in summer and 3 times in winter. A local bus also runs from Westport to Achill Sound in summer, T: (096) 71800.

WHERE TO STAY
Hotels and B&Bs: there is quite a large selection on Achill Island, including Mrs Cannon's,

T: (098) 45134, and Mrs Sweeney's, T: (098) 45755, e-mail: achill_island @ hotmail.com. Gray's Guest House is at Doogort, T: (098) 43244. For self-catering (vacation homes) contact BF's reservation service for the west of Ireland, T: (091) 567673.
Youth hostel: The Wayfarer Hostel is at Keel, T: (098) 43266.
Outdoor living: Seal Caves Caravan Park, T: (098) 43262, is on the island's north coast at Doogort. Keel Sandybanks

Camping Park is by the beach, T: (094) 32054/(098) 43211.

ACTIVITIES
Walking: the highest peak is Slievemore and there are magnificent views from the summit. The path to the top can be reached from behind Slievemore village. At the western end of the island, a ridge-back trail runs from Moyteoge Head to Achill Head (see Guidebooks entry above). Other walks on the island are waymarked. Contact Karen Grealis

Up to 30 ft (10 m) long, and one of the world's largest fishes, the basking shark is a resident of Irish as of most temperate seas. Capable of raising itself almost out of the water – it weighs up to four tons – it is harmless to man, surviving on a diet of sieved plankton.

of Achill Tourism for a leaflet,
T: (098) 47353.
Cycling: bikes can be hired
from the Achill Sound Hotel,
T: (098) 45245.
Hang-gliding: there is hang-
gliding from the top of
Menaun.

FURTHER INFORMATION
Tourist offices: Achill Tourism
has an office on the island, T:
(098) 47353.Contact the Achill
Outdoor Education Centre in
Keel for information on wind-
surfing, rock-climbing and
hang-gliding, T: (098) 47253. A
year-round office is in Westport, T: (098) 25711.

With its slates glistening in the
rain, an abandoned cottage adds
a touch of melancholy to the road
leading north from wooded Delphi.
Ahead lie Doo Lough and the
Sheefry Hills.

Furnace Lough

*A small lake in bumpy,
hillocky country, rich in
salmon and home of the
Salmon Research Trust of
Ireland*

Just to the north of the eastern
part of Clew Bay, a narrow
road leads off the main
Newport–Achill road. It takes
you quickly into a charming
little toytown lakeland,
climbing steeply, diving
precipitately, curving round
some rather hectic bends with,
feet away, drops of say 20 ft
(6 m) and enough water at the
bottom to dunk a fair-sized car
in. The land between the lakes
is very rocky, supporting some
bracken, more heather and a
few diminutive trees. Suddenly,

if you take the right turns and
omit the wrong ones, you are at
Burrishoole Fishery, with
Lough Feeagh above, Furnace
Lough below, and the Salmon
Research Agency of Ireland
beside you.
    Anglers come here for fish,
advice, information and various
related services. Germans come
to restock the Rhine, from
which a quarter of a million
salmon might have been fished
a century ago but which by the
1940s contained none. In a
most sportsmanlike manner
salmon continue to come, in
spite of the danger of being
caught in nets at sea, or on the
end of a line, legitimate or
otherwise, in rivers. The
Agency monitors numbers and
condition of salmon
throughout the country, and at
present is carrying out a
programme of restocking the
waters of Connemara. In fact,

all matters relating to salmon (and to a lesser extent trout and sea trout and other game fish) are subjects of the agency's active concern.

In spite of the management, restocking, monitoring and analysis, salmon remain an ingredient of wild Ireland. They follow a hazardous and still mysterious life-cycle, breeding in, and greatly enhancing the value of many Irish rivers. Those of us who do not fish can be well educated by the agency's presentations, displays, aquaria and video, and are welcome to call during the summer months.

Before you go *Maps:* OSI Discovery Series, map No. 31.

Getting there *By car:* the N59 from Westport and Newport runs past the lough. *By rail:* the nearest station is Westport; services run from Dublin (Heuston) 3 times a day. *By*

bus: there are Bus Eireann services to Westport from Galway and Ballina. The Expressway from Westport to Newport passes close to the lake, as does the local bus from Dooagh to Ballina, T: (096) 71800.

Where to stay *B&Bs:* Newport House, T: (098) 41222, Mrs Chambers, T: (098) 41145, or Mrs McGovern, T/F: (098) 41178, all in Newport. *Youth hostel:* the An Oige Traenlur Lodge is above Lough Feeagh, T: (098) 41358.

Activities *Cycling:* bikes can be hired from the Skerdagh Outdoor Centre, T: (098) 41500. *Fishing:* in Newport Mary, T: (098) 41562, and Pat, T: (098) 41265, organize angling trips. Contact the Salmon Research Agency of Ireland for information, T: (098) 41107.

Further information *Tourist office:* BF, Newport, T: (098) 41895, is open in summer.

Wild salmon occur in rivers and lakes throughout Ireland, surviving nets, traps and skilled fly-fishers on their way to spawn in the rivers' upper reaches.

Croagh Patrick

One of the West's most distinctive landmarks, the quartzite peak draws crowds of pilgrims in late July (and other months), offering fabulous views of land, ocean and archipelago

Places which in other countries might be considered wild beyond argument may, in Ireland, be tamed and regulated for human purposes. The bleak islands in Donegal's Lough Derg and the storm-torn summit of Kerry's Mount Brandon were long ago adopted for religious purposes, a cairn or chapel raised on them like a territorial flag, and a regular pilgrimage established. Croagh Patrick (usually called the Reek) is the most famous and popular of such mountains. The path up it has been worn by the passage of millions of feet. All the same, this is not some rural equivalent of the department-store escalator. It is steep, exposed and, towards the top, a little dangerous.

In the past, pilgrims in their thousands climbed by night on the last Sunday of July to celebrate a festival with pre-Christian roots. They carried burning torches; when they reached the top – which consists not of the conical point you are led to expect from below but a half-acre plateau on which stands a small chapel – they walked long penitential circuits on the bare rock on their knees. But these traditions have been discontinued, and the main pilgrimage is officially confined to the daytime; for good or ill the world has lost that annual night spectacle, a line of glimmering light moving upward, whatever the weather, in a harsh, backward (as it quite recently was) and remote territory of mountain and sea. It can still be hard, and, with wind or rain beating in from the Atlantic, seem desolate and hostile. To make it harder, some of the pilgrims still go barefoot.

Croagh Patrick occupies another key place in the story of wild Ireland. St Patrick, in the course of converting the country to Christianity in the 5th century, retired to this mountain, close to the probable site of his boyhood slavery, to spend the forty days and nights of Lent. During this time he summoned, by divine power, all the more noxious and repellent beasts of Ireland to the mountain and persuaded them to drop to their deaths down the sheer southern side. The result being that Ireland to this day has no snakes. Nor, for that matter, does it have any wild cats or moles.

Biologists explain things otherwise. Ireland's animals arrived from Britain after the retreat of the ice by means of a surviving land connection. Some were too slow, or failed to cross for other reasons. Of these some have since been introduced by man, not least those prizes of Lakeland, bream, rudd, pike and possibly perch. The status of frogs is argued about. The frog bones found among prehistoric remains in Sligo could, it seems, belong to animals which slipped through at a much later period. They are thought to have been released at Trinity College at the end of the 17th century. Of toads, only the natterjack exists in Ireland, in County Kerry and a few other places. They were introduced. Ireland possesses only one reptile, the common lizard.

It has not, so far as I know, been suggested that the view from the summit went to the holy man's head, though it would not be surprising if it had. Clew Bay lies below, with its packed school of drumlins appearing to swim out from the inner shore. To the south are the Sheefry Hills and some of the Connemara Bens rearing up behind, while to the north, over the water, are the impressive peaks of Achill, Corraun and the Nephin Beg range. You do not necessarily require Christian convictions to find a spiritual boost here.

Before you go *Maps:* OSI Discovery Series, map Nos 30, 31, 37 and 38.

Getting there *By car:* from Westport take the R395 (west) to Murrisk, which lies below Croagh Patrick.

By rail: services run to Westport from Dublin (Heuston) 3 times a day, T: (01) 836 6222.

By bus: there are plenty of services to Westport. From there a local service runs to Louisburgh, stopping at Murrisk near Croagh Patrick, T: (091) 562 0000.

One of the plants whose tripartite leaves are worn as shamrock on St Patrick's Day, the lesser trefoil is a yellow-flowered relation of clover which grows commonly among grass from May to September.

SHAMROCK

As Irish as a harp, luck or a pint of Guinness, the shamrock is also a mystery. St Patrick is said to have used its leaf to explain the three-in-one, one-in-three nature of the Holy Trinity, and the Irish put it in their buttonholes on 17 March, St Patrick's Day. However, plants displayed in this way may belong to any of several different species and there is no universal agreement on what the correct one might be. The claims of several members of the pea family (*Leguminosae*) are well supported. Fairly equal at the top of the list come white clover (*Trifolium repens*) and lesser yellow trefoil (*Trifolium dubium*), another clover, with small yellow flowers. A hundred years ago a collection of plants used as shamrocks and drawn from several counties produced, in addition to those already mentioned, red clover (*Trifolium pratense*), spotted medick (*Medicago arabica*), black medick (*Medicago lupulina*), watercress (*Nasturtium officinale*), wood sorrel (*Oxalis acetosella*) and several others.

The Irish word *seamrog* means clover, without distinguishing which of the closely related clovers, medicks or trefoils this might be. (A similar Arabic word is said to have the same broad definition.) Its use is not recorded, anyway, earlier than 1571. Seventeenth-century English writers often refer to shamrock as an important part of the Irish diet, and some call it bitter, which is true of wood sorrel but not of the rest. But many such writers were keen to dispossess or eliminate the Irish, and could be wildly inaccurate when holding forth about their nature and ways. To complicate the issue, many Irish claim the shamrock does not flower. It almost certainly does, but not, in all probability, by 17 March. After that date interest in it quickly wanes.

The incentive to pin shamrock down to one species comes from its place as a national emblem, which in turn stems from the link with St Patrick. It is, of course, possible that the saint used several of the plants mentioned, since the leaves of all of them are divided into three and would have served his purpose. However, since the Patrick connection is not mentioned in writing or print before 1727, in spite of numerous lives of the saint having appeared during the previous thousand years, it may be that the account is a late invention. On the other hand, clovers and trefoils had interesting reputations long before Patrick. Four-leafed clover could (and still perhaps can) help you discover treasure. The clubs of playing cards take their design from the trefoil. Pliny, writing in the 1st century AD, says that snakes never go anywhere near trefoils, and that the plant can be used to heal the stings of snakes and scorpions. This account predates Patrick by four centuries but nevertheless leads us straight back to him: the saint is, of course, famous for expelling snakes from Ireland. Possibly his association with the shamrock is thus explained. Specific identification remains impossible, though. Pliny does not help. And if you look closely at Irish buttonholes next 17 March you will doubtless see the mix as before.

In the North, by the way, and with neat Northern irony, the phrase 'shamrock tea' means weak tea. It tastes, the inference is, like tea brewed with no more than three leaves.

Where to stay *Hotels:* in Westport the Clew Bay Hotel, T: (098) 28088, e-mail: clewbay@anu.ie; Olde Railway Hotel, T: (098) 25166, e-mail: railway@anu.ie; and the Central, T: (098) 27257. *B&Bs:* in Westport Mrs Gill, T: (098) 66548, e-mail: seabreeze@tinet.ie; Cedar Lodge, T: (098) 25417, e-mail: mflynn@anu.ie; and Mrs Gavin, Murrisk, T: (098) 64819.

Youth Hostels: in Westport the An Oige hostel, T: (098) 26644/26717; the independent Old Mill Hostel, T: (098) 27045, e-mail: oldmill@iol.ie; and Club Atlantic, T: (098) 26644.
Outdoor living: Parkland CCP, T: (098) 27766; and Old Head Forest CCP, T: (098) 66021, near Louisburgh.
Activities *Cycling:* in Westport

bikes can be hired from the Old Mill Hostel, T: (098) 27045, Breheny Bike Hire, T: (098) 25020, and Sean Salmon, T: (098) 25471. *Fishing:* sea-angling is available in Clew Bay. Contact Mrs Julie Connolly, Monomore, Lodge Road, Westport (no tel.).
Further information *Tourist office:* BF in Westport is open all year, T: (098) 25711.

Killadoon

Leading nowhere in particular, the road down the west of the Barony of Murrisk passes delightful seascapes and broad beaches of white sand

It was a place that invited deep speculation. I sat on a rock and wondered what it would be like to be a meat-eating animal stuck to the floor waiting in vain for animals that you wanted and needed to eat to enter your mouth without compulsion. How would it feel to function best submerged in salt water and spend half your time – half of each day – all but out of water, in the air, and much of the rest of your day tantalizingly pummelled and sluiced, as the tide went in and out, by licks of water from which there was no chance of extracting anything to eat at all. This, it seemed from looking at it, was the essential daily cycle of the small beadlet sea anemone (*Actinia equina*), as it remained in its rock pool assaulted by the flow and ebb of the tide. Some anemones stayed open, the pretty tassels that fringe their dark recesses waving when there was water to wave in. Others closed up and looked like wet conkers, as if they were rather sniffily refusing to join in the waves' game.

There was no limit to the number of things to be looked at in the rock-pools of the Silver Strand near Killadoon. The rock I was on was like a large vessel, 30 yards across, set in a sea of shining white sand. Its surface was pocked with little pools, ranging from a few inches to several feet across. The rock was a grey limestone but it was mostly covered with thin coats and stains of black and yellow lichens, themselves obscured by thousands of barnacles which collectively had the texture of coarse sandpaper. Sprays of seaweed of various kinds, innumerable clusters of small mussels, from bead size to about an inch across, colonies of limpets and many varieties of shellfish filled in almost

The steep southern flank of Mweelrea mountain, valued as a tough hike by climbers, stands bright in the evening sunlight, above the creek of Killary Harbour.

any available space. Terns flew about; a lone razorbill dived repeatedly out at sea. In the pools little fish darted into crevices when any shadow crossed the water.

I imagine anyone could spend the four hours or so that I did in such a scene, under a warm sun, watching the destinies of other beasts and plants played out, naming, identifying, theorizing, glowing with the entertainment and the warmth. Of course, my island in the sand became, as I watched and dreamed, an island in the incoming sea, but this was not to be a case for the air-sea rescue people. It was solved by the removal of shoes and socks, and the rolling-up of trousers and a pleasant paddle across to dry land. The sea almost followed me in, because the sand is very flat and the beach nearly half a mile across.

Silver Strand lies towards the end of a road down the south-west coast of County Mayo, from Louisburgh to a point close to the opening of Killary Harbour, inaccessible here because the mountain drops flush into the water. The day I was there – in May – hardly anyone else was. There are other huge strands along the way – Gobis of warm white sand. On the other side of the road the Mweelrea Mountains appear to present a soft lap into which to climb. North of the beaches is an isolated hotel – of no pretension, and pleasant – at Killadoon.

That evening I walked down to the sea past an inland lake in the middle of which is

Between Doo Lough and Sheefry Wood, a peat cutter digs winter fuel in the time-honoured Irish way, watched by his dog. Extraction on this scale is insignificant beside commercial exploitation of boglands for fertilizer and electricity generation.

a round island perhaps 30 feet (9 metres) across. On it were about 200 breeding terns, their number leavened by a few gulls. Here again, in spite of midges, was entertainment for an hour or two, for the terns had created the atmosphere of a barracks bathroom. Raucous gargles, belches, raspberries and fouler noises are pure tern, and when I went on to the beach there they were – two or three of them – buzzing and harrying me, like yapping terriers, to get me away. It shows the troubadour in me that I cannot reconcile these loudmouths' noisiness with their grace and beauty, like that of swifts made wholly white.

BEFORE YOU GO
Maps: OSI Discovery Series, map No. 37.

GETTING THERE
By car: from Westport follow the R395 (west) to Louisburgh. A minor road runs along the coast from Louisburgh to Killadoon.
By rail: 3 services a day run to Westport from Dublin (Heuston), T: (01) 836 6222.
By bus: a Mon–Sat Bus Eireann service runs from Westport to Louisburgh and Killadoon, twice a day, T: (096) 71800.

WHERE TO STAY
Hotels and B&Bs: the Beach Hotel, T: (098) 68605, and Mrs C. Heneghan's B&B, T: (098) 68730, are both in Killadoon. Mrs Claire Kenny, T: (098) 66289, Mrs Mary Sammin, T: (098) 66484, and Mrs McNamara, T: (098) 66062, have B&Bs in Louisburgh.
 Outdoor living: the Old Head Forest CCP is near Louisburgh, T: (098) 66021.

FURTHER INFORMATION
Tourist office: Westport BF is open all year, T: (098) 25711.

Mallaranny and Clew Bay

The hump-backs of drumlins crowd the eastern end of Clew Bay. Pleasant resorts cling to the land between sea and mountain

There is a Homeric grandeur to this wild west coast. Yet I choose with special affection an unremarkable village, a cosy and *déclassé* resort, stretched along a road too main for comfort, with two supermarkets, two garages and a huge hotel which, when I was last there (and following a change of ownership) was grotesquely empty, the glass in its ground-floor windows painted white, its extensive gardens turning to jungle.

In part, what appeals is nostalgia for an age and its ways; not my own ways, but missed all the same. In part it is what remains. Memory brings back annual family holidays of Irish and English at the Great Southern Hotel, with the railway itself just behind, or in rented houses; nannies and a maid or two brought along with the luggage. There were expeditions to the beach, to Achill, Newport and Westport, but mostly a routine of eating, sleeping, games and bathing, to ease which a causeway had been built for passage from the hotel's ornamental lower gardens, over the extensive flats and dunes left by the ebbing tide, to the bathing beach.

The causeway is there, and the beach, and the dunes and acres of sand, covered twice daily by the tide; and the views across Clew Bay to the flotilla of motionless green porpoises – which are, of course, partly submerged drumlins – facing out to sea from Westport. I do not suppose the birds have changed either. The coastline lurches drunkenly with bays and inlets, and much of the shore is marshy and reedy. There are swans, terns, oystercatchers, ringed plovers, dunlins and the rest; the usual cheery, perky complement of companions for a beach walk. There is a woolly yellow moss that colours patches of sand and dune on which brent geese feed when they arrive for the winter, having

bred and summered on the tundra and estuaries of the Arctic. I have stood on the beach watching, and for bouts of a minute or two being watched by, a seal every time I have been to Mallaranny.

Everything that man did grandly is slowly falling away and decaying or being replaced, if at all, by tat. Perhaps the result is a little advance for nature – certainly trees are moving up the hill behind the hotel. Dissolution, birds, jungle greenery, the distant scrutiny of Croagh Patrick and the rest of its mountain brethren over the bay, and the twice-daily surge and retreat of the tide over the half-mile of almost level sand: all these make the place curiously irresistible for me. It is an enthusiasm in which I expect no support at all.

Before you go *Maps:* OSI Discovery Series, map Nos 30 and 31.

Getting there *By car:* from Westport follow the N59 (north) round Clew Bay to Mallaranny. *By rail:* regular services from Dublin to Westport, T: (01) 836 6222. *By bus:* a local Bus Eireann service from Westport to Achill Sound stops at Mallaranny 3 times a day, T: (096) 71800.

Where to stay *Hotels and B&Bs:* Breezemount B&B, Mullaranny, T: (098) 36145, and the up-market Newport House, Newport, T: (098) 41222. In Westport try Mrs O'Malley, T: (098) 25719. *Youth hostel:* the An Oige Traenlur Lodge is at Lough Feeagh, T: (098) 41358. *Outdoor living:* the Parkland CCP, Westport, T: (098) 27766. There are camp-sites on Achill Island.

Activities *Fishing:* deep-sea angling in Clew Bay.

Further information *Tourist offices:* seasonal BF in Newport, T: (098) 41895; all-year BF in Westport, T: (098) 25711.

Mweelrea Mountains

No roads penetrate the interior of the Mweelrea Mountains, a grand volcanic range marking the southern boundary of County Mayo

The north of County Mayo is to a large (though unfortunately lessening) extent a roadless bog. The south-west of the county is an expansive range of almost roadless mountain. It comprises the Mweelrea Mountains, Sheefry Hills and Ben Gorm, three groups of immense inner beauty, any of which well repays the trouble of climbing. You will not see them otherwise. Distances are, for Ireland, long, and the boggy ground is often wet and always uneven. Care is advised in both the planning and execution of any long-distance walk.

Even the car-bound visitor who crosses this region from north to south will see some enchanting scenes. The road from Louisburgh to Leenaun cuts down between the Mweelreas on the west and the other two groups on the east. The northern part of this road-valley has a great and almost Scottish appeal, recalling the brooding broadness of the west Highland glens. The side of Mweelrea is sheer, much of it rock-grey with runnels and slipways of scree. Chutes of rock must often slide into the long low pouch containing Doo Lough. Steepness on all sides puts a heavy emphasis on falling, descent, precipitation. Gravity becomes a very palpable feature of the landscape.

But just to the south comes the pretty oasis of Delphi,

named early in the 19th century by a young Marquess of Sligo whose lands, based in Westport, included most of this region, and who put a fishing lodge here. Now there is an adventure centre. Still further south, at Bundorragha, the road turns left short of Killary Harbour, a long deep inlet of ten miles by perhaps a half: the sunken channel of the River Erriff, which divides the Sheefry Hills from the Partry Mountains. From the north shore (not accessible by car) one of several routes up Mweelrea begins. You can also start from Delphi or Bundorragha, or indeed anywhere else on the perimeter, though some approaches call for rock-climbing skills. All ways take several hours because of the distances involved. You want to be sure the weather is settled and

that there is time enough and more before dark. Mweelrea is the highest mountain in the province of Connacht, which includes Connemara, and the views from the top are superb. It also has comforting, rather human contours, reminiscent of knees, a hollow chest, a lap.

Before you go *Maps:* OSI Discovery Series, map No. 37.

Getting there *By car:* from Westport follow the R395 (west) to Louisburgh and then south over Doo Lough Pass, to the east of the Mweelrea Mountains.

By rail: the nearest station is Westport, where services run from Dublin 3 times a day, T: (01) 836 6222.

By bus: a Bus Eireann service from Westport to Louisburgh runs 3 times a day in summer, twice a day in winter, T: (096)

71800.

Where to stay *Hotels and B&Bs:* the Delphi Lodge, T: (095) 42222, is a fine hotel whose guests can fish several miles of river and lake. The Lodge also rents out the charming Wren's Cottage. The Ben Gorm Farmhouse B&B overlooks the spectacular Killary Harbour, T: (095) 42205.

Outdoor living: the Old Head Forest CCP is near Louisburgh, T: (098) 66021.

Activities *Climbing:* the Mweelrea Mountains may be climbed from several points close to Killary Harbour and from the R395, both north and south of Doo Lough. *Watersports:* water-skiing, wind-surfing and sea-angling at Clew Bay.

Further information *Tourist office:* BF in Westport, T: (098) 25711, is open all year.

Connemara Highlands

Wild and ancient region of bog and fish-rich river and lake, dominated by the central range of the Twelve Bens and surrounded by a jagged, varied coastline and countless islands of great beauty; includes Connemara National Park

Connemara is mountain, lake and electro-encephalographically ragged coastline. It is quite short on roads, so that a tour by car or bicycle follows one of a limited number of routes. It has marvellous beaches in such plenty that for much of the year it is easy to get one to yourself (though often enough someone fond of company will settle, a few minutes after you do, within yards). Beyond the shore, within and without the many big bays, lies a confetti of islands. In the middle of the region rise the hard, rocky slopes of the Twelve Bens, some bare, some peaty. These are arranged in the form of a mauled starfish with Benbaun rising to 2,395 feet (729 metres) at the hub, and the other

eleven peaks distributed along the five ridges.

As so often in the new Ireland, you can no longer be sure of getting where you want from any point on the road because of the spread of barbed wire across the countryside. Still, you can get on to the Bens from little penetrating lanes and tracks, and there are some good, if taxing, mountain walks and very challenging climbs. Much of the ground is bare rock or stony scree. There are dangerous cliffs but the Bens lack the high lakes that feature attractively in surrounding ranges. At the head of Glen Inagh, according to Tony Whilde, co-author of *The New Irish Walk Guides*, are some of the longest rock climbs in Ireland.

If the uplands are short of lakes the periphery of the Bens is not. In parts it is moated: on the east by wood-fringed Loughs Inagh and Derryclare which divide the Twelve Bens from the Maumturk Mountains and the plum-pudding peak of Knocknahillion, and on the south by the lovely Ballynahinch lake. The MP Richard Martin built his grand home (now a hotel) on the banks of Ballynahinch; he also helped found what later became the Royal Society for the

Prevention of Cruelty to Animals. Martin could boast of being able to walk the thirty miles to Galway without straying from his own land. Kylemore lake lies along the north rim of the Bens, overlooked on its north-western edge by Kylemore Castle, a 19th-century Gothic affair lushly wreathed in rhododendron, fuchsia and good trees. The mountain behind the castle, Doughruagh (1,736 feet/529 metres), offers a steep, circular, bracing walk and fine views of mountain, sea and islands. There are, incidentally, lakes high in this small range in which insects – certain diving beetles, *Dytiscus* species, water-boatmen and others – have lived an isolated life since the Arctic conditions which originally suited them prevailed in post-glacial times.

West of Kylemore two or three miles, and outside the village of Letterfrack, is what is called the Connemara National Park, rather less than ten square miles of land conserved to standards which would ideally apply to the whole region. The inevitable 'centre' shows a film and stages an exhibition which introduce the history and ecology of the area, telling of the eras which followed the

Ice Ages, and of the emergence of the flora and fauna to be found there. It also delves into the origins and growth of peat, shows the bird and plant life dependant on it, and the few scattered parts of our planet in which it is to be found. In Ireland, we learn, during the 20th century, more than 80 per cent of the peat, which has been five thousand years in the making, has been destroyed.

Out of doors there is a choice of nature trails, the higher of which may be extended to a climb up Diamond Hill (1,460 feet/445 metres). A useful guide points out the kind of birds, animals and plants which may be seen here and, of course, in the region at large. A feature which might puzzle travellers new to the West, and which, once understood, brings the historical past closer than any other survival, is the series of faintly separated vertical ridges running along the bases, and sometimes higher levels, of hillsides. These bear the quite unjustified name of 'lazy beds'. I do not know of ghosts more evocative than these faint ridge-and-furrow sites where hard-driven cabin-dwellers of one and two and more centuries ago, on slopes far too steep for anyone today to think of

BOG TYPES

Raised bogs and blanket bogs are the two main types of bog in Ireland. Raised bogs are characteristic of the central lowlands. They develop in former lakes, where underlying marl impedes drainage. Fen plants such as grasses, sedges, rushes and reeds fill the marshy lake bed and decompose, forming fen peat. Sphagnum mosses grow on top of this layer, and in turn decompose into sphagnum peat. Sphagnum is able to live on rain water and can therefore continue to grow well above the level of the underlay and its contained ground water. A bog will contain several different kinds of sphagnum moss, some of which prefer dips and wet places, while others form mounds known as hummocks. Two mosses in particular turn red in the autumn, creating what are known as red bogs. Ling heather commonly grows on the moss bed.

Round-leaved sundew, cranberry and bog rosemary will also be found.

Blanket bogs are widespread among the mountains of the West. They form where rainfall is so high and frequent (45 to 50 in/c. 1,200 mm a year) that peat can develop without the marshy conditions that promote the formation of raised bogs. Various sedges and grasses and other plants – bog cotton, black bog rush, purple moor-grass, bogbean, cross-leaved heath, and certain liverworts and mosses – form peat immediately above the soil or rock and spread over huge areas of plain and mountainside. Blanket bogs are the most widespread kind of terrain in large parts of Galway, Mayo and Donegal. Bilberry and crowberry are found at the higher levels. Like raised bogs, blanket bogs are broken up by pools, streams and sphagnum hummocks.

cultivating, grew their daily food. The ridges were built up of soil, seaweed, sand, peat and manure for the growing of the staple potatoes and oats. The furrows in between afforded drainage. Here, preserved like old scars on the surface of the land, are the historic work place and larder of the Irish peasant.

Across the way, over the broad curve of Glen Inagh and its lakes, the sprightly wraith of Robert Lloyd Praeger strides across the boggy uplands of the Maumturk Mountains, also composed in the main of hard-wearing quartzite. 'A traverse of the whole ridge from Maam Cross to Leenane', Praeger wrote in *The Way That I Went*, 'provides a glorious day's walking, but the main interest will lie not in the hills themselves but in the striking and varied scenery on either hand. I followed that route one mellow October day, and shall not soon forget the lovely tints on hill and bog.' A day's walking it certainly is – 14 or so uneven miles (22 kilometres) and climbs totalling 7,000 feet (2,133 metres) or more – and mere mortals following in Praeger's steps in October might find, if the going on the bog were specially soggy, that they were pressing uncomfortably close to sundown after a start soon after dawn. More often than not during the walk they will be several miles from the nearest road. From the heights, of course, there are dazzling views of local lakes and neighbouring mountains framing the distant sea and islands in various dispositions.

Leenane consists of a long line of houses, shops, pubs, purveyors of bed and breakfast and a big centre whose educational theme – put across in films and displays – is sheep and wool. The air is thickly commercial: full of foreign cars, Gaelic muzak and the untiring, humour-drained smiles of natives doing nicely. Beside the town is the eastern end of Killary harbour, a lovely ten-mile inlet of sea. It is also, looked at the other way, the drowned valley of the River Erriff, which drops picturesquely over its final falls a couple of miles away at Aasleagh. Here, in season, salmon fresh from Greenland waters are to be seen hurling themselves upward in their passage to upstream breeding grounds.

On a coast pocked by inlets, Killary is the one which can be truly described as a fjord: a valley of sea-water deeper than the sea-floor beyond and divided from it by a substantial underwater bar – the heap of moraine swept down by an ancient glacier. It goes down to 80 feet (24 metres) in mid-channel and has in the past accommodated fleets. Nowadays farmed mussels are more familiar than warships. It has greater distinction than the right to a Norwegian name, for it is both beautiful and in large part free of people. Apart from the road that flanks Killary at its eastern end, there is a track along the southern shore and nothing at all along most of the northern, which rises steeply out of the water and hardly pauses till it reaches the summit of Mweelrea, 2,688 feet (819 metres) above. Walking is not in fact difficult along this stretch, and it is the base for one of the popular ascents of the mountain. But the rarity of people enhances the chance of seeing wildlife. The philosopher Ludwig Wittgenstein, who spent long periods here late in life, escaping what he saw as the petty pother of university existence, found seagulls settled on his shoulders if he stood in silent meditation. So at least claimed his colleague Bertrand Russell. The shore also offers one of the better Irish opportunities to see otters.

Connemara is mountainy and flat in about equal measures, and the flatness tends to be close to the chaotic doodles of the coastline. North-west of Clifden (a pretty little Georgian town) the terrain has a bumpiness with a certain aesthetic appeal, but it must have been a cruel life that depended on fields where the stone count seems sometimes to exceed the number of grass blades. With Europe's intervention, though, quality of land and the status of its farmers no longer tally. There are big cars and bright white bungalows here to match those among the deep green pastures of Kildare.

South of Clifden a curious broad plain of blanket bog and lake, mixed in almost equal proportions and peppered with rocks, is overseen by the neat cone of Errisbeg (987 feet/300 metres). The area is full of natural curiosities. Pipewort (*Eriocaulon aquaticum*) grows at the edges of lakes: a long thin stem with white button-flowers at the top and a whorl of long thin leaves – underwater – at the bottom. It is found abundantly hereabouts, less so in other parts of western Ireland, here and there in the Hebrides, and in vast quantities in America. The idea that it was brought in by human agency (the first aeroplane to cross the Atlantic, for instance, which has been commemorated by a wing of stone north of Ballyconneely) is scotched by pollen evidence that it was here 6,000 years ago. Also found here are the insectivorous oblong-leaved sundew (*Drosera intumedia*), and bog pondweed (*Potamogeton polygoni-folius*). Several other rarities are well described by Praeger, and by Tony Whilde in his exhaustive *Natural History of Connemara*. Connemara's wealth of orchids include the early purple, the spotted, the pyramidal, the green-winged (holding out here far better than in other parts of the country) and, in one or two restricted areas, the dense flowered.

There are good beaches along the coast, none better than the sheltered, west-facing Dog's Bay with its mile-long curve of white sand. Behind the bay is a substantial spit of sand broadening into a flat granite island. The sand of the bay is not all sand in the normal sense of sea-bed and surrounding rocks ground to minuscule grains. Some of Dog's Bay consists of *foraminifera* carried up by currents from the sea-bed to which they sank, after a brief lifetime as single-celled organisms contained within casings of shell. The shells are composed of calcium carbonate secreted by the organisms themselves or of granules of rock they have attached to themselves by an exuded glue. If you walked across the beach you might guess from the feel of each step that this was a different strand. You need a lens to appreciate the full difference. The shells are superbly decorative spirals, some flat, some round, many patterned by what look like pin-pricks. Different organisms have gone to make the so-called coral strands of Mannin Bay and other spots. They are not coral, which is of animal origin, but the petrified remains of old seaweed.

In summer, on mountain and moorland, the trim, bold, buff-chested wheatear is seldom far away, fearlessly chattering its varied calls and song from flight or perch. Occurring on coasts too, it nests in holes in rock or wall.

BEFORE YOU GO

Maps: OSI Discovery Series, map Nos 37, 38, 44 and 45.

Guide-books: *Insider's Guide to Connemara, Galway and the Burren* by T. Fitzpatrick and T. Whilde (Gill & Macmillan, 1992); *The Mountains of Connemara* by J. Lynam (Folding Landscapes, 1988).

GETTING THERE

By car: from Westport go south on N59, which runs right down to Clifden through Leenaun and the Connemara Highlands. From Galway, follow N59 (west) to Clifden, along the south of the Twelve Bens.

By rail: there are 3 trains to Westport and 5 to Galway, Mon–Sat, from Dublin (Heuston), T: (01) 836 6222.

By bus: in the summer a daily Bus Eireann Expressway runs between Westport and Clifden. A service from Galway to Clifden runs several times a day, passing the Maumturk Mountains and the Twelve Bens, T:

(091) 562000.

WHERE TO STAY

Hotels and B&Bs: there are lots of places including the luxurious Ballynahinch Castle, south of the Twelve Bens, T: (095) 31006, e-mail: bhinch@iol.ie; the family-run Sweeney's Oughterard House, T: (091) 552207, e-mail: phiggins@ iol.ie; the Davin Family B&B in Renvyle, next to the Castle, T: (095) 43460; The Quay House in Clifden, T: (095) 21369; and at Moyard, Mrs Conneely's B&B, T: (095) 41171.

Youth hostels: the 3 independent hostels in Clifden are Leo's Hostel, T: (095) 21429; Brookside Hostel, T: (095) 21812; and Clifden Town Hostel, T: (095) 21076. There are An Oige hostel at Ballinafad, just south of the Connemara Highlands, T: (095) 51136, and at Rosroe, north of Connemara, on the site of the cottage where Wittgenstein lived in 1948, T: (095) 43417.

Outdoor living: camp-sites include the Renvyle Beach CCP, T: (095) 43462, and the Connemara CCP at Lettergesh, T: (095) 43406/43527.

ACTIVITIES

Walking: take the Sky Road, signposted to the west of Clifden, for breathtaking views from the cliffs. The Connemara National Park, south of Letterfrack, has marked walks. The entrance to the Park is on the N59 near Letterfrack. The Bens themselves offer dramatic walks and, depending on the season, interesting birds including grouse, Greenland white-fronted geese, plover, snow and corn bunting. The Western Way passes the Maumturk Mountains and other peaks in Connemara. Doughruagh peak behind Kylemore Castle offers a circular walk, which is quite steep in places. Following Praeger's route along the Maumturk Mountains, described in *The Way That I Went*, is a hard day's work and not to be undertaken lightly without good equipment and companions.

Cycling: Mannion's in Clifden, T: (095) 21160, hire out bikes; BF has details of a route from Galway to Clifden, running through the Connemara Highlands.

Riding: Willie Leahy, based in Loughrea, runs The Connemara Coast and Aille Cross Trails, T: (091) 841216.

Fishing: Lough Corrib and the Owenglin river are good for salmon; contact Clifden Anglers for details, T: (095) 21039.

FURTHER INFORMATION

Tourist offices: BF in Westport is open all year, T: (098) 25711, and a seasonal office is in Clifden, T: (095) 21163.

Park office: Connemara National Park, T: (095) 41006/41054.

THE WESTERN WAY

OSI Discovery Series, map Nos 37 and 38.

Starting where County Sligo abuts County Mayo on the central ridge of the Ox Mountains, the Western Way takes the walker west to Ballina, then northward and close to the coast of Killala Bay, from where it sweeps round to cross the forests, mountains and desolate peat bogs of the Barony of Erris. This is walking for the stalwart, though there are rewards for those who take time off to study the plants and fauna of the bog. South of the Nephin range, the path continues through wet, flat terrain to Westport, passes close to Croagh Patrick and the steep track familiar to millions of pilgrims, and on through the Sheefry Hills to Leenaun on Killary harbour. The dramatic beauty of this part of the walk is a prelude to a traverse of Connemara by way of the Maumturk Mountains, down Lough Corrib to Oughterard. All told, the walk covers some 140 miles (220 kilometres). Those who plan to trek from beginning to end should be sure to have good information on places to stay (if they are not camping) and to buy provisions. There are long, lonely stretches, especially in the region of Erris and Nephin, in north-west County Mayo.

Before you go *Maps:* OSI Discovery Series, map Nos 23, 24, 30, 37, 38, 44, 45. *Guide-books: The Western Way in Connemara* by T. Robinson & J Lynam (Folding Landscapes, 1997); *The Western Way* by J. McDermott and R. Chapman (Mayo County Council, 1993). **Getting there** *By car:* to reach the Ox Mountains, follow the R294 (east) from Ballina through the middle of the range. For Leenaun and Oughterard, follow the N59 (south-west) and then (east) from Westport. *By rail:* 3 services a day run from Dublin to Westport and Ballina, T: (01) 836 6222. *By bus:* in the summer the Westport-Clifden Expressway and the Galway-Clifden service stop at Leenaun. Bus Eireann services go to Ballina from all over Ireland, T: (091) 562000. Treacy's, T: (096) 22563, run a daily service to Ballina from Sligo and Barton Transport, T: (01) 628 6026,

from Dublin.

Where to stay *B&Bs:* are available along the way. Try Ms Forde in Oughterard, T: (091) 552678, Mrs Hopkins in Westport, T: (098) 26436, and Mrs O'Hara in Killala, T: (096) 32023. **Activities** *Walking:* the 140-mile (220-km) Western Way is split into 7 stages: 1, Oughterard to Leenaun (30 miles/48 km); 2, Leenaun to Westport (27 miles/45 km); 3, Westport to Newport (10 miles/16 km); 4, Newport to Ballycastle (41 miles/67 km); 5, Ballycastle to Killala (10 miles/16 km); 6, Killala to Ballina (10 miles/16 km); 7, Ballina to Ox Mountains (12 miles/18 km). Contact Mayo County Council, T: (094) 24444.

Further information *Tourist offices:* BF in Westport, T: (098) 25711, and Oughterard, T: (091) 552808, are open all year. Newport, T: (098) 41895, Ballina, T: (096) 70848, and Killala, T: (096) 32166, are seasonal.

Partry Mountains and Lough Mask

Less known than Connemara, the Partry Mountains are spotted with lakes and penetrated by deep glens on the eastern side, sloping down to the huge wood-lined waters of Lough Mask

In modern usage the name Connemara is only vaguely defined, but it is generally agreed not to stray over the borders of County Galway. Mountains do, though. The highlands of Joyce Country subside into the valley of the Fooey and Lough Nafooey, but start up again, even before the border, to begin the essentially Mayo range of the Partry Mountains. In fact, several peaks are on the Galway side, including the Devil's Mother, a straightforward climb of rather more than 3,000 feet (900 metres), most easily made from the Erriff valley, which gives wonderful views of the lakes below and Croagh Patrick in the distance.

Further east a curious lip of County Galway – remnant perhaps of ancient baronial disputes and ambitions – laps up the mountainside and colonizes a few more summits. Whatever the historic reason for this, the border country is worth a visit. Here you have a region of heights, valleys, cliffs and a lovely long lake, which has still not attracted the tourist in huge numbers. I have driven along Lough Nafooey in summer without passing another car. The road is along one side; on the other the land rises steeply to the heights of Benbeg (1,788 feet/545 metres) and Bencorragh (1,539 feet/469 metres). Close to the water are the vertical stripes of ancient lazy beds (so-called), looking as if made by a comb with wide-apart teeth. Above, the land becomes a

wall of rock. In the north-west, the lough is supplied by a long white waterfall dropping beside angular trees that sprout from the sheer rock. It is a scene an old engraver could have reproduced without need of picturesque additions.

Below and east of Nafooey two long prongs of water from Lough Mask and the intervening upland make delightful scenery. North of them the River Owenbrin (technically a tautology, this; 'owen', like 'avon' means river) has carved a valley in the mountainside which affords a route for tackling the highest of the Partry Mountains, Buckaun (2,046 feet/623 metres). This is not a heroic climb, with about 1,400 feet (425 metres) to ascend from the place at which a car can be left, though there are steep drops beside the topmost ridge. Four mountain

The Irish sky plays a favourite game, allowing shafts of light through moving keyholes in thick cloud to spotlight scenes on the gnarled hills rising from Lough Fee.

Killary Harbour, once a haven for ships of the Royal Navy, is nowadays left mostly to anglers, fish farmers, the odd solitary philosopher and enterprising yachtsmen with a taste for the remote and an eye for the picturesque.

loughs can be taken in. North of the Owenbrin, however, the Partry range becomes lakeless and flat-topped: a dull final fortress before the broad plains of Mayo and east Galway open up a fairly featureless view. Between heights and plains, though, are the most attractive Loughs Carra and Mask, continued to the south by the mighty expanse of Lough Corrib; the three of them making Galway into something approaching an island, with access only through the city of Galway, Cong or the few miles connecting the north of Lough Mask to the sea.

Carra, a shallow lake never more than 30 feet (9 metres) deep, is noted for its bird life. Shooting is prohibited. Up to fifteen hundred mallard and a number of tufted duck breed there. There are wigeon, teal, shoveler and pochard in considerable numbers, and, in winter, some goldeneye. Various gulls breed on the islands. The novelist George Moore, whose ancestral home is on the lake's eastern shore, had – or perhaps merely claimed – a wild side to his life. He was forever bragging about sexual conquests. When guests were gathered he would look at the fireside carpet and sigh, 'Such scenes of passion that rug has witnessed'. Or come back from the front door saying he had just seen off a woman seduced by him in Paris years before, who had come to demand money to educate the resultant child. Yeats and many others consumed hours arguing about the truth or otherwise of Moore's claims. He was a good novelist, and may have been exercising his talents for fiction.

BEFORE YOU GO
Maps: OSI Discovery Series, map Nos 37 and 38.
Guide-books: *Walk Guide West of Ireland* by Tony Whilde and Patrick Simms (Gill & Macmillan, 1999).

GETTING THERE
By car: from Castlebar take the N84 (south) to Ballinrobe, then the R334 to Neale and the R345 (west) to Cong and Clonbur, travelling south down the east side of Lough Mask. To reach Benbeg, Bencorragh and Buckaun, take the R345 (west) and R336 from Clonbur to Leenaun, then the N59 (north) towards Westport. These roads pass close to the peaks, as do the minor access roads on the west side of Lough Mask.
By rail: Claremorris is the nearest station; 3 services run each day from Dublin (Heuston) to Castlebar and Westport, all stopping at Claremorris, T: (01) 836 6222.
By bus: Bus Eireann services from Ballina, Cork, Galway and Castlebar stop at Ballinrobe and Cong. A summer service from Galway stops at Cong and Clonbur daily, T: (091) 562000.

WHERE TO STAY
B&Bs: in Ballinrobe try Flannery's pub, T: (092) 41055/41724, Mrs Kavanagh, T: (092) 41154, or Hazelwood House, T: (092) 41372. In Cong try Mrs Coakly, T: (092) 46060; Ms Gorrman, T:(092) 46103; and Mrs Holian, T: (092) 46403.
Youth hostels: include the An Oige Cunga Fheichin, T: (092) 46089, and the independent Quiet Man Holiday Hostel in Cong, T: (092) 46089, e-mail: quiet.man.cong@iol.ie; and the Courtyard Hostel at Cross, T: (092) 46203, e-mail: dowagh@iol.ie.
Outdoor living: the Cong CCP is open all year, T: (092) 46089.

ACTIVITIES
Walking: good walks go up the Devil's Mother and Benbeg.
Cycling: bikes can be hired from O'Connor's Garage, Main

A diving duck with a rather peaked head, bright golden eyes and, in the case of the male, a large white patch behind the bill, the goldeneye winters in many parts of Ireland, coastal and inland. Some breed in the North.

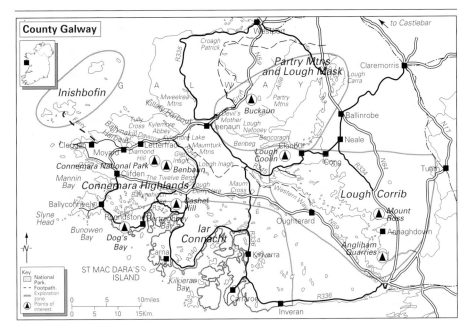

Street, Cong, T: (092) 46008.
Good views are to be had of
Lough Mask and Lough Cor-
rib from the top of Mount
Cable.
Riding: contact Ashford Equestrian Centre, Cong, T: (092)
46024/46507.
Fishing: Lough Mask is a good
brown-trout lake and the World
Cup Brown-Trout Wet-Fly Angling Championship is held
here in late July. Contact John
Nester, 10 Lakelawns,
Ballinrobe, T: (092) 41174, for
more details.
Caving: there are quite a few
caves in the area. Cross the
bridge near Monk's Fishing
House, a mile to the west of
Cong along the R345, for Pigeon Hole, Ballymaglancy Cave
and Teach Aille. Cave maps are
available from all the hostels.

FURTHER INFORMATION
Tourist offices: there are seasonal BFs in Cong, T: (092)
46542, and Ballinrobe, T: (092)
42150. Galway BF is open all
year, T: (091) 563081.

Iar Connacht

*An austere region of granite
rock, dappled with pond,
lake and boggy stretches,
between the north coast of
Galway Bay and the
esteemed fishing grounds
of Lough Corrib*

West of Galway city is a large,
low-lying coastal area of stone
and lake, beach and headland,
with much bog and bare rock.
People living in the region have
always kept to the coast, leaving
the interior uninhabited, and
eked a living from fishing (to
which hidden sandbanks and
currents are hostile), peat (of
which much of the land is now
denuded), making tweed and

growing staple crops on the thin
soil, which they fortify with
dried seaweed. The stone is
granite, extruded through older
rocks as a result of heat
generated by the slow impact of
two tectonic plates, the
American and the European.
But this is granite different in
details of composition from
that which created the Wicklow,
Mourne and Donegal
mountains. Only one peak in
Iar Connacht tops 1,000 ft (304
m). The rock is of a variety
more than usually prone to
erosion. Over hundreds of
millions of years it has worn
low.
  Like all hard, hostile
landscapes, Iar Connacht has a
peculiar gritty beauty to it,
subject to strange variations as
the weather changes, its
thousand lakes reflecting the

Lough Nafooey (*overleaf*) lies in a tuck of mountain within the district
known as Joyce Country, with the slopes of Benbeg rising from its
southern shore, and the vaster, steeper sides of Maumstrasna (left) to
the north.

blue or grey of the sky, heavy rain among the lakes making it seem that the world was made of water. It seems timeless, even now that the new tourism, the new bungalows, the new Brussels budget have made their mark. People still speak Irish, for this is one of the Gaeltacht heartlands, where those who have given up almost everything else traditional hold on to their language and are, of course, encouraged to do so by the prospect of government carrots. Another Irish ghost haunts the area. Patrick Pearse, the poet and schoolteacher who led the Easter Rising of 1916 and was shot after it, had a cottage beside Lough Aroolagh, near the head of Kilkieran Bay. He built a little house here and spent holidays learning Irish and writing. The house, now a memorial to him and open to visitors, is vested by many Irish with a kind of holiness, for they see Pearse as the country's latter-day Messiah.

The fishing which does go on successfully is for lobster and scallops, and there are oyster beds and salmon-farming in Kilkieran Bay. Inland there are the characteristic plants of the bog: bog myrtle, bog asphodel, purple moor grass, which in autumn dyes the landscape, along with heathers and sedges, and the bright illuminations of springtime gorse.

Of sea-birds, there are three kinds of diver and common scoter out in the bay in winter, and terns breed on the islands in summer. Bird life actually gets richer further east at this season, and the sandier, more sheltered coves and creeks of the east coast of Galway bay support abundant populations of wintering duck, geese, waders and gulls.

In the interior of Iar Connacht the vegetation is not such as to support a rich bird life. The modest, graceful meadow pipit can normally be counted on. There may well be cuckoos in evidence in early summer, for they parasitize pipits in these parts. Ravens are around. Red grouse make occasional, and fewer, appearances; they may be victims of the surfeit of sheep and overgrazing of the heather on which they depend. Nobody is going to come here to see rarities, even though they may occur. No, the rarity here is the character of the landscape. Climbing the higher of the hills – Cashel Hill or Errisbeg further over to the west – shows it well, set in a sensational frame of inner Connemara mountains, Atlantic, Aran Islands, and the varied silhouettes of Galway Bay. But of course their dazzle obscures it. Better to walk its roughness and take the reward of a bathe from one of its scatter of sandy beaches.

Before you go *Maps:* OSI Discovery Series, map Nos 37, 38, 44 and 45, and the Connemara Map, 1:63,360, by Folding Landscapes.
Guide-books: The Mountains of Connemara, A Hill Walker's Guide by Tim Robinson, Joss Lynam and Justin May (Roundstone, 1988); and the *Insider's Guide to Connemara, Galway and the Burren* by Trish Fitzpatrick and Tony Whilde (Gill & Macmillan, 1992). There are also relevant sections in *Hill Walkers' Atlantic Ireland* by David Herman (Shanksmare, 1999).

Getting there *By car:* from Galway either follow the N59 (west) towards Clifden or drive along the coast through Spiddal, Screeb, Kilkieran, Toombeola and Roundstone, following the R336, the R340, the R342 and the R341.
By rail: services run from Dublin (Heuston) to Galway 5 times a day, T: (01) 836 6222.
By bus: Bus Eireann services run from Galway to Clifden 6 times a day in summer (twice a day in winter), T: (091) 562000.
Where to stay *Hotels and B&Bs:* there are numerous places in the area, including the pricey Cashel House Hotel, Cashel, T: (095) 31001, www.cashel-house-hotel.com;

Only plants adapted to acidic peat, which is frequently waterlogged and leached thereby of nitrogen and phosphorus, can survive in Ireland's bog-lands. Characteristic varieties include (from left): the bogbean, which thrives in pools; the sundew, augmenting thin rations with insects it traps; sphagnum moss, forming hummocks a few inches high on raised bogs; bog asphodel which can conserve water in its fleshy leaves; and St Dabeoc's heath, a rarity, found only in Galway and Mayo.

Fermoyle Lodge, Costello, T: (091) 786111, www.hidden-ireland.com/fermoyle; Mrs Conneely, T: (091) 593124, in Spiddal; and Mrs McDonagh in Cashel Bay, T: (095) 31054. *Outdoor living:* Carraroe CCP, T: (091) 595266; Spiddal CCP, T: (091) 553372, e-mail: spidpark@gofree.indigo.ie, and Gurteen CCP, Roundstone, T:

(095) 35882/35787. **Activities** *Walking:* there are plenty of good walks and views along all of this wild coastline. Most of the routes follow the R roads mentioned above. *Fishing:* excellent on Lough Corrib. Good salmon rivers include the Owenglin river, just north of Clifden. Contact Danny Goldrick, Western

Regional Fisheries Board, The Weir Lodge, Earl's Island, Galway, T: (091) 563118, e-mail: wrfb@iol.ie. **Further information** *Tourist offices:* there is an information point at Monahan's, Oughterard, T: (091) 552808, and in Clifden a seasonal BF office, T: (095) 21163. Galway BF is open all year, T (091) 563081.

Inishbofin

An inhabited island off the north-west coast of County Galway, a haven of historic remains but wild, windswept and precipitous on its westward side, and host to breeding sea-birds and peregrines

A haircut and the date of Easter put Inishbofin on the map. It was 664 AD. A synod was called at Whitby in Yorkshire to sort out differences in practice between the Roman branch and the Irish or Celtic branch of the British Church. The issues were the style of monks' tonsures and the method of deciding the date of Easter, but it was really two opposing attitudes and dispositions that were being judged. Wilfrid of Canterbury's Rome-trained delegates were cool and dispassionate and had lawyers' skills. Colman of Lindisfarne's Irish, who were certainly wayward in observing Vatican rules, had more fire and feeling. They were both harsher to themselves and more sentimental, not least in their attitude to animals. The Roman case predictably prevailed, and the Irish, who had successfully brought Christianity to Scotland and Northumbria, had to pack up or conform. They chose to go. Thirty English monks accompanied them to Ireland, preferring their way to Wilfrid's. Unfortunately this sad but dignified departure was not the end of the story. Colman brought his monks to Inishbofin and they started to build a monastery, but the English soon complained they were the only ones doing real work. Quarrelling set in, and the

English were moved to Mayo on the mainland to build a new establishment. Nothing but ruins remain today, except, in the opinion of some, an eternal polarity between Irish and English. Ireland, of course, has for centuries been obedient (more or less) to Rome, and it is the English who are now the heretics, but underlying attitudes may remain close to what they were.

Ruins are there to see: of Grania O'Malley's fortifications, perhaps of Cromwell's concentration camp for priests, and the pirate Bosco's castle. Like most of the west, Inishbofin had more happening in the past than the present. Unlike most islands (including Inishark next door) it remains inhabited – by about 250 souls – and a regular ferry service is maintained from mainland Cleggan, famous for its lobsters. Earlier this century the lobster industry was more important than it is today. A French agent lived at Cleggan and boats took off for St Malo with 3,000 Paris-bound lobsters in tanks. In those days, while most lobsters were caught in pots or kreels, baited with lugworms, some were taken by hand – or with an iron hook – from their rock-holes.

With a deeply serrated coastline the island is at most nearly four miles (six kilometres) long. The few hills are low. Cultivation is kept mainly to the south, leaving the rest mainly as stony moorland, from which most of the old peat has been cut away. There is a wonderful broad sandy bay on the east side. It is a good area for walking in, along the coast which is dramatic in parts or on the superfluous abundance of lanes inland. Getting on for 350 plant species grow on the island. Spotted rock-rose (*Tuberaria guttata*) occurs here and in very few other parts of Britain or Ireland; a low, pretty flower with a red dot on each of its five yellow petals. The island is also rich in lichens, of which about 200 kinds have been noted. Hardly any trees or sizeable shrubs grow, but this does not unduly deter birds, which are present in surprising numbers. Among them is the corn bunting (*Emberiza calandra*), an undistinguished little brown bird getting rarer in Ireland. There are fulmars on the rocks, a few choughs and plenty of common terns in summer. Irregular rarities are recorded, but Inishbofin is not a bird-watcher's Mecca. Inishark, over the water, is more so, with its variety of sea-birds and breeding peregrines. To cross to it you have to make your own arrangements. Grey seal breed around both islands. Last time I was there a school of dolphins had appeared close to the harbour on the previous day.

BEFORE YOU GO
Maps: OSI Discovery Series, map No. 37.

GETTING THERE
By sea: boats from Cleggan to the island are operated by King's Ferries, T: (095) 44642/21520, and O'Halloran's, T: (095) 44750/45806.
By car: for Moyard take the N59 (south-west) from Westport or (north-west) from Galway. Then follow the tracks out to Cleggan, from where the ferry leaves for the island.
By rail: services run from Dublin (Heuston) to Westport 3 times a day, T: (01) 836 6222.
By bus: Bus Eireann services run from Westport and Galway to Moyard once a day in the summer (not Sun). A year-round local service from Galway to Moyard runs on Tues and Sat only, T: (091) 562000.

WHERE TO STAY
Hotels and B&Bs: 2 family-run hotels on the island are Day's Hotel, T: (095) 45809, which also hires out bikes, and the Doonmore Hotel, T/F: (095) 45804; Mrs King's B&B is in Cleggan, T: (095) 44688.
Youth hostels: the Inishbofin Island Hostel is open Apr–Nov, T: (095) 45855.
Outdoor living: the nearest camp-sites, at Renvyle on the mainland, are the Connemara CCP, T: (095) 43406, and the Renvyle Beach CCP, T: (095) 43462/43632.

A geometry of stone walls, each stone extracted by hand from the soil that now appears so green and bountiful, recalls an age of want, when too many sought their livelihood from a miserly terrain.

ACTIVITIES
Walking: many of the beaches on the island provide good walks.
Bird-watching: in their appropriate season the birds on Inishbofin include choughs, corn buntings, fulmars and common terns.

FURTHER INFORMATION
Tourist offices: there is a seasonal BF in Clifden, T: (098) 25711, and a year-round office in Galway, T: (091) 563081.

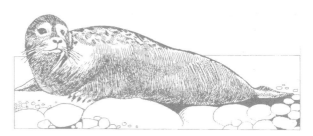

The common seal is seen all round Ireland – often keeping its head above water to observe human life on the shore. It keeps mainly to sandbanks and mud-flats while the grey seal frequents the rockier coastline.

Lough Corrib

Ireland's second largest lake, dotted with drumlin islands and magnetic to anglers, Lough Corrib divides the flat, fertile limestone-based east of County Galway from the barren, romantic west

The neck of land dividing Corrib from Mask was for a long time Guinness territory. The Guinness family occupies a unique place in the Irish social system: native brewers who made good in the 18th century, acquired titles and English (as well as Irish) estates and went to Eton and married into the aristocracy in the 19th and 20th, and yet remain blessedly immune to the taint of landlordism that has seen off so many rich English in the last hundred years. Their product, of course, spreads feelings of well-being and goodwill. So does the record of their benefactions to Ireland, in housing and sport and education and restoring cathedrals and a hundred other fields. My own favourite charity is the Irish Georgian Society which struggles to preserve the best of old architecture all over the country and shamelessly cajoles the wealthy of all nations to make donations for this purpose. A Guinness, Desmond, founded it, made it his life's work and with his own money bought Castletown House in County Kildare, which was for long its pride and joy. Such things make the

glugging of a cream-capped pint of porter an even greater pleasure.

Guinnesses used to own much of the land hereabouts, and a glimpse of the massive mock-Gothic walls and battlements of Ashford Castle, outside Cong, suggests the scale and grandeur of their lives. It is a luxury hotel now with lands running handsomely to the lake's edge. Guinnesses no longer (I imagine) take picnics hence to Lough Coolin on the side of Benlevy, trailed by maids and footmen ready to spread plates holding nine kinds of meat and game on the freshly laundered linen that covered the trestle tables. With fewer encumbrances, perhaps, we can. It is certainly worth making the small effort to reach the top (700 feet/200 metres from the south-east approach) because the views over Lough Corrib – not to mention Lough Mask, Galway Bay, an Aran island and much else besides – are sensational. Framed by the eastern uplands of Joyce Country and the granite hills of Iar Connacht on the west bank and the flat green billiard table of inner Galway on the east, the lough – second biggest in Ireland after Lough Neagh – is spangled with rocks and islands and long thin headlands as it bends one way and another on its 30-mile (50-kilometre) course to Galway city and the sea.

The flatness, granite hills apart, extends for some miles beyond the lake, for the underlying rock here, and on and on continuously through the midlands to Dublin, is limestone of the Carboniferous period, formed from shells and corals of the

79

equatorial sea that covered Ireland 300 million years ago. The ease with which water erodes limestone and the rock's porosity have endowed the lake with varying depths and submarine cave systems and reefs and other irregularities. The porosity was oddly neglected by 19th-century engineers who came during the great famines of the 1840s, with the aim of providing work for men desperate to earn, to join Mask and Corrib by a navigable canal. The excavation was completed and a date set for opening. The upper sluice gates were opened and water poured through. But it did not stay. It quickly drained through the stone and was gone. The four miles of the canal are there – west of Cong – to this day, still perfectly useless.

If the lake is famous for its brown trout, it is not the monopoly of anglers. You can explore it by hired boat and see its more obvious charms from steamers that ply from Cong and Oughterard in season. The shore can be reached by any number of roads and lanes. At Annaghdown, on the south-eastern edge of the lake, are various abbey remains on the site of a monastery founded, it is said, by St Brendan the Navigator, whose claimed discovery of America is discussed on page 99. He died here, full of years, in the arms of his abbess sister. A few miles to the south, at Angliham marble quarries, and a few miles north, at Mount Ross, winter duck populations are easily seen. All year round the lake supports varied if not unusual species of ducks, waders and others, including over 8,000 pochard in early winter, the second biggest flock in Ireland (Lough Neagh has the biggest).

BEFORE YOU GO
Maps: OSI Discovery Series, map No. 45.

GETTING THERE
By sea: the *Corrib Queen* plies the lake every day from Ashford Castle Quay in Cong to Oughterard, T: (092) 46029.
By car: from Galway take the N84 (north) to Headford, then the R334 to Neale to drive up the east side of Lough Corrib, or take the N59 to Oughterard to go up the west side.
By rail: the nearest station is Galway, with 5 services to and from Dublin (Heuston) a day, T: (01) 836 6222.
By bus: a Bus Eireann Expressway from Ballina to Galway runs along the east side of the lough, and a few local buses serve both sides of the lough, T: (01) 836 6111. Nestor Coaches, T: (091) 797144, and Burke Brothers, T: (093) 55416, operate services from Galway.

WHERE TO STAY
Hotels: the 5-star Ashford Castle, once a Guinness-family country house, is just outside Cong, near the lough, T: (092) 46003; alternatively, try the riverside Ryan's Hotel in Cong, T: (092) 46243.
B&Bs: Mrs Morrin's, between Cong and Clonbur, overlooks the lough, T: (092) 46302; Mrs Peirce's B&B is at Cornamona, T: (092) 48165; Mrs Dolly's, T: (091) 552168, and the Costello family B&B, T: (091) 552121 /552146, are at Oughterard.
Youth hostels: there are several hostels open all year in the area. An Oige runs a hostel on the shores of the lough at Cong, T: (092) 46089. There are 3 independents in Galway City: Kinlay House, T: (091) 565244; Great Western House, T: (091) 561139; Barnacles Quay Street House, T: (091) 568644. The Lough Corrib Hostel is in Oughterard, T: (091) 552688, e-mail: hickey@bigfoot.com.
Outdoor living: Hunter's Silver Strand CCP, T: (091) 592040/ (088) 266 1530, is at Barna; Ballyloughane CCP, open Apr–Sept, is at Renmore only 5 mins' drive from Galway City centre, T: (091) 755338/752029; the Cong CCP is open all year, T: (092) 46089.

ACTIVITIES
Walking: north of Oughterard the Western Way runs beside Lough Corrib. See p69.
Cycling: bikes can be hired from Lough Corrib Bike Hire, T: (091) 80194, in Oughterard.
Riding: the Ashford Equestrian Centre at Cong offers instruction, trail and cross-country riding. Fox hunting can be arranged on request, T: (092) 46024/46507.
Caving: there are caves near Cong at the top of Lough Corrib and maps are available from the hostel in Cong, T: (092) 46089.
Fishing: Oughterard is one of Ireland's principal angling centres. The Irish Wet-Fly Masters Open Competition is held here every year. Contact Michael Walsh, Headford and Corrib Anglers' Association, Ower House, Greenfield, Ower PO, Co. Galway. Boats for fishing can be hired in Oughterard from M. Healy, T: (091) 82736, and other local boatmen.

FURTHER INFORMATION
Tourist offices: there is a private tourist office in Cong, T: (091) 46542, open in the summer, and a BF office in Galway, T: (091) 563081, open all year.

Aran Islands

An oblique line of three inhabited islands of solid rock and a few tiny, unpeopled ones, forming a broken continuation of the limestone pavements of the Burren and guarding the entrance to Galway Bay

There was a time when these islands would have been the wildest of all: three massive chunks of limestone obstinacy thrown at the Atlantic, fallen at a distance that takes a boat, depending on weather, one hour or as many as eight; brazening out winds, storms and waves that will eventually, if nothing intervenes, wear, rub, grind and batter them to extinction. Nature made few locations wilder.

Yet they have been inhabited and built on since time beyond knowing. The concentric stone half-rings of Dun Aenghus, hanging over 250-foot (75-metre) cliffs on the seaward side of Inishmore, are one of the most impressive, as well as puzzling, survivals in Europe. There are innumerable remains of monasteries, churches, castles and fortifications on each of the three islands. The modern population, about 1,500, have most of the technology to be found on the mainland. Each island is parcelled into little fields by solid stone walls. The people speak Irish, but English too and everything you have heard or seen on television they are likely to have heard or seen too. They know how to profit from tourists. Unless you arrive on a dark and windy winter's evening, thoughts of wildness are unlikely to enter your head.

The Aran Islands must be mentioned, though, because of their shapes and positions and composition, because only a hundred years ago the wildness of the elements here dictated life, and often enough, death. The formidable, centuries-old struggle to tame them makes an astonishing story. In the distant past, the islands were bare rock, protruding from a submerged line of limestone that ran from the Burren in County Clare far out into the Atlantic. Myths make the line continuous above water, and describe Galway Bay as a contained lake; this may actually have been the case for a time. Nature provided no soil. The soil that makes crops and pasture possible has been created by islanders over the centuries using sand and seaweed from the north-eastern shores, which they spread about after stopping up the deep fissures in the limestone with pebbles and splinters. Field walls and buildings were built mostly from countless loose stones of all sizes churned up and deposited by glaciers. Last time I was there Inishmaan was getting itself a football field. In most places this would mean at most ploughing and rolling a suitable area. Here, though, certain preliminaries were necessary. Six hundred tons of soil had to be imported from the mainland and unloaded within an hour of high tide; at other times the boat could not moor. All the island's fit and young assembled for the task twice a day – about 4 am to start. It still took about a week.

The islands are still among the natural wonders of Ireland. But, like the Giant's Causeway in County Antrim, they have had the wildness combed out of them. Irish is spoken and taught, certainly. Canvas curraghs are still used for conveyance, true. Memory carries glimpses of times when fish were caught and all peat for burning carried from the Galway coast in canvas boats, in all weathers. A rich literature – including plays of John Millington Synge and novels of Liam O'Flaherty – tells of the transition, the battles between tradition and advance, between the old Celtic ways and the new mainland ways – especially those of England and America.

There are plants that like the abundant calcium of limestone, but nothing like as many as in the Burren. There is the fascinating chessboard of field walls and other human constructs. The views are sumptuous: the Atlantic to the west, the Burren and the Moher cliffs to the east, the Twelve Bens north and the hills of Kerry south. But wild? No. The 600 tons of soil imported for the football pitch made a fitting climax to one hundred years of domestication.

A grassy sloping ledge (*overleaf*) provides secluded nesting for a group of puffins, protected on one side by a mighty drop to the sea and on the other by a sheer wall to the cliff-top above.

The Burren

A large, uneven region in the north-west of County Clare, bordering sea on two sides, consisting over much of its surface of huge limestone slabs, and supporting a rich and unusual flora; includes the Burren National Park

Between the scenic prima donnas of Connemara and Kerry lies the quieter, flatter, altogether less dramatic terrain of County Clare. It too has features that attract immediate attention, and coaches regularly pull up for delighted tourists to inspect the jutting headlands of the Cliffs of Moher, the crescent beaches of Kilkee and Liscannor and a wealth of ruined abbeys and castles inland. The Burren is a different matter. It has its coaches disgorging tourists but, on close inspection, many of these are seen to bear an expression of courteous bemusement. A hundred square miles – about ten by ten – of bare rock, relieved only by patches of scrub, a handful of small towns, some ill-drained

fields and a scattering of stone formations evidently constructed by humans at a clumsy stage in their development – all this clearly seems to them a queer taste.

Bernard Shaw in *Back to Methuselah* called this apparent lunar void 'a region of stone-capped hills and granite fields' (wrongly, as it happened, for the Burren is all limestone). Thackeray wondered 'how the deuce' Lord Gort's nearby mansion 'got into the midst of such a desolate country'; the house 'seemed to bore itself there considerably'. Two centuries before, Cromwell's agents found the Burren wanting for different reasons: 'neither water enough to drown a man, nor a tree to hang him, nor soil enough to bury'. Between Neolithic man, who was present in some force, and relatively recent times, hardly anyone has left a good word about it.

The growth of the Burren's popularity is mainly due to the fact that certain Victorian geologists and botanists began to look carefully and closely, and marvelled at what at first they had missed. To understand the Burren's appeal to them it is necessary to go back about 360 million years, when the Burren rock was little more than a collective glint in the eyes – if they had them – of untold millions of brachiopods, corals, molluscs, echinoderms and other creatures formed mainly of calcium carbonate, floating luxuriantly in the warm sea which then covered this part of Ireland. These little animals mated and reproduced, mated and reproduced, and at the end of their mortal span sank to the bottom. Their offspring did the same, and theirs, and theirs, until the strata of their chalky skeletons grew thick on the sea-bed and, along with sand and mud, was compressed by the sea's weight into the limestone rock we see today. Every now and again the earth heaved, the climate changed or a volcano spewed, causing a crack in the accumulation. Each horizontal stratum became clearly marked off from that beneath, and vertical irregularities appeared.

These divisions and faults were compounded in subsequent eras by exposure to the air when the sea flowed away, by the pressure of ice in successive Ice Ages and by erosion caused by tons of running water when the ice melted. The water had effects similar to those produced by lactic acids in the making of some cheeses. The Burren is shot through with holes and cave systems that sometimes stretch for miles. Unlike cheese, however, limestone is porous. Water percolates not only the channels and caverns, but the fabric of the rock, too. Acids in the water continually dissolve particles of rock and imperceptibly reduce the Burren's body.

As the last Ice Age drew to its close, ten or more thousand years ago, plants that were adapted to extreme cold and a very short flowering season – wintergreens, alpine bearberry, the ethereally blue spring gentians, mountain avens and many more – moved into the high areas formerly covered by glaciers. There they were slowly hemmed in by pine forests. They would have remained rarities or possibly died out had not the earliest settlers cut down the forests

---

Stony seaboard, far and foreign,
  Stony hills poured over space,
Stony outcrop of the Burren,
  Stones in every fertile place,
Little fields with boulders dotted,
  Grey-stone shoulders saffron-
    spotted,
Stone-walled cabins thatched with
  reeds,
  Where a Stone Age people
    breeds
The last of Europe's stone age race.

John Betjeman, 'Sunday in Ireland'

---

with the fecklessness of those deforesting the Amazon basin today. Where man cleared, alpine herbaceous plants and creepers extended their range. The Burren puzzle is that, as the climate grew warmer, attracting large numbers of plants from the south, the alpine flora was able to survive as well. A relatively consistent temperature, with the

COUNTRYSIDE HAZARDS

Snakes, poisonous or otherwise, are not established in Ireland, and reports of sightings are rare enough to be discounted. Nor should bulls met in fields be dangerous, though it may be wise to take the view that no bull – not even a happy heifer-haremed Hereford – is entirely pacific. Male deer, during their rutting seasons (around October), have been known to charge, hurt and even kill humans, but only a handful of times a century; all the same, it is wise to avoid coming between a buck and his does.

Leopard amanita (*Amanita pantherina*) is among the more poisonous fungi; common ink-cap (*Coprinus atramentarius*) may be harmful when eaten with alcohol, and the golden rule is to be positively sure the mushroom you intend to eat is a good one, rather than that it is not one of the bad ones. Shellfish caught on the west coast at a time of red tides (a phenomenon occurring once a year or so and not fully understood) may be poisonous, and no responsible caterer would supply them at such a time.

Gulf Stream modifying the extremes of winter and summer, is one reason for this.

The result is an unusual, though not unique, mix of plants generally considered alpine with many more often associated with quite warm climates, like the Mediterranean. It is this unusual combination which makes the Burren botanically enticing, not the rarity of any particular plant. All the orchids to be found here occur in other parts of the British Isles; the presence of 22 separate orchid species, however, is almost unique; from May to July there is always an abundance of these intriguing and ingenious plants.

There is another oddity. The rock naturally attracts lime-loving plants. Yet the humus which develops in dips and clefts from spores, seeds and fruits brought in by the wind and subsequently decomposed, will contain acid constituents, too. As the rain falls (twice as much a year as in Dublin) and soaks into the rock, it dissolves, as we have seen, and leaches away much of the alkaline content. In patches, therefore, a preponderance of acid soil remains. That is why the limey Burren is spattered with ghettoes of acid-loving plants: heathers and ling, St John's wort, bracken and gorse.

When humans arrived, with their cattle and goats, the Burren suited them well.

Bloody cranesbill with its crimson blooms, the free-flowing yellow froth of lady's bedstraw, white chickweed and other flowers throng the richly fertile gaps lying between limestone slabs on the side of Slieve Carran in the Burren.

There was a most agreeable climate, caves in plenty to live in, and near the coast a plentiful diet of oysters, mussels, crabs, lobsters and other fish. Assuming aesthetic tastes were similar to our own, the views would have been delightful: Galway Bay and the Bens of Connemara, the Aran Islands daubed on the sea before a fiery ocean sunset, mountains like lashings of limestone cream poured from a celestial jug. Stock-farming could not have been easier. In the Burren there are no frosts to speak of and grass grows the year round. Water rising through the rock after heavy rain souses the soil with a fertilizing solution of lime. There was no need – there is still no need – to provide either winter shelter or winter hay. To get the best of the grass, the booley system was practised, and continues in modified form: cattle were moved to the high ground in summer and the whole farming family went along too, living in huts and burying butter in the bog to keep it fresh.

Walking or driving in this curious countryside reveals more than rock and plant. Doolin, a pretty fishing village on the west coast, has become through its 'singing pubs' a folk-music Mecca. Lisdoonvarna is famous for arranged marriages. Up to a generation or two ago Irish farmers married late, waiting till they inherited land. When the time came they turned up here, to take the spring-water cure, so they said; but as often as not they returned with a marriage bargain struck. Since few could write, marriage brokers proliferated. In the south-east you can see the track of a glacier's retreat: a patchwork of lakes between rock-strewn flats west and east of Corrofin. There are ancient graves and medieval abbeys and castles in a romantic state of ruin and, to the southwest, the dizzying screen of the Cliffs of Moher with its breeding sea-birds. On the eastern side of Slieve Elva is the Polnagollum complex, thought to be the longest cave system in western Europe. Ailwee cave is open for visitors. There are relatively few roads but plenty of tracks and miles of stone wall, cattle, sheep, goats.

All the same it is the plants which star here. In late spring and early summer, botanists proliferate almost as much as maidenhair fern, though nothing like as coyly. Insects, naturally, are present in huge numbers, not least the moths whose males are tricked by the patterns and smells of certain orchids into thinking that they are landing on females of their own species. Beetles – the most successful of all forms of life in the world – are proportionately active, and do their bit for plant pollination. But to experience the most familiar pleasures of the Burren, stop on some rough pavement in this limestone moonscape, peer into the surrounding grikes and hollows and marvel at the extent and variety and buoyancy of species which, against all apparent odds, make the area a paradise of flowers.

BEFORE YOU GO
Maps: OSI Discovery Series, map Nos 51 and 52.
Guide-books: *The Book of the Burren* (Tír Eolas); *The Burren, a Companion to the Wildflowers* by Charles Nelson and Wendy Walsh (The College of Psychic Studies, 1999).

GETTING THERE
By car: from Galway take the road out to Oranmore and then follow the N18 (south) to Kilcolgan. The N67 leads on to Kinvarra, Ballyvaghan and down to Lisdoonvarna. The R477 runs along the coast from Ballyvaghan to Lisdoonvarna and the R478 from Doolin to the Cliffs of Moher.
By rail: trains run from Dublin (Heuston) to Galway 5 times a day, T: (01) 836 6222.
By bus: buses from Galway and Limerick stop at Lisdoonvarna and Doolin; summer services also stop at the Cliffs of Moher, T: (091) 562000 (Galway) or (061) 313333 (Limerick).

WHERE TO STAY
Hotels: try the 19th-century family-run Kincora House in

The tiniest crack or dip in the limestone pavement north of Doolin provides a niche for bloody cranesbill and other Burren flowers to flourish, screened from the ocean winds.

The spring gentian is one of those alpine plants whose presence in the Burren still causes debate. It is found also in a small area of north England. Apart from that, its nearest occurrence is in the Jura.

Bloody cranesbill (right), a geranium with bright red flowers, hoary rockrose (centre) with its shining yellow petals, and close-packed clusters of white mountain avens (far right) are among the myriad decorations of the Burren's limestone slabs in early summer.

Lisdoonvarna, T: (065) 707 4300.

B&Bs: there are plenty in Doolin including Mrs Cullinan, T: (065) 707 4154, and Mrs Hughes, T (065) 707 4826.

Youth hostels: the independent Corofin Hostel also has camping available, T: (065) 683 7683, Paddy's Doolin Hostel is in Doolin, T: (065) 707 4006, www.kingsway.ie/doolinhostel.

Outdoor living: at Doolin is O'Connor's Riverside CCP, T: (065) 707 4314, and Nagles Doolin CCP, T: (065) 707 4458, both open Apr–Sept.

ACTIVITIES

Walking: there are plenty of scenic walks around the Burren. The 22-mile (35-km) Burren Way runs south from Ballyvaghan on the coast of Galway Bay across the lower slopes of Slieve Elva. Reaching the coast at Doolin, it clings to the top of the Cliffs of Moher, then turns east with the coast to finish near Lahinch.

Cycling: bikes can be hired from Burke's Garage in Lisdoonvarna, T: (065) 707 4022. The Burren provides relatively easy cycling and amazing sea views.

Climbing: there are good climbing routes between Severe and E5 grades on the limestone sea cliffs of the Burren.

Caving: there are several miles of caves around Lisdoonvarna, but they can be dangerous so take precautions and go in an organized group. Thurlough Outdoor Centre, T: (065) 707 8066, organizes walking, caving, canoeing and climbing holidays.

FURTHER INFORMATION

Tourist office: the BF office at the Cliffs of Moher, T: (065) 708 1171, is seasonal. Offices in Ennis, T: (065) 682 8366, and Galway, T: (091) 563081, are open all year.

Ecology: the Burren Centre at Kilfenora has a museum and video display explaining the nature of the region, T: (065) 708 8030. The centre also has guide-books for sale.

Coole Lough

A park, in east County Clare, of powerful literary associations, with a landscape of lakes and woods interesting for flora, fauna and limestone formations, and an imaginative interpretative centre

I cannot imagine that when families consider where to go for their annual holiday – a decision made in most cases around New Year, amid a litter of Sunday-paper travel supplements – they pass remarks like 'I've always wanted to get my teeth into the geology of Norway' or 'the plant life of Portugal', or 'Sicilian sea-birds' or whatever it might be. Some, yes; but not, surely, most.

Yet the Irish Tourist Board and the Northern Ireland Tourist Board have put a huge investment into programmes of digestible education to be enjoyed by tourists. All down the west coast and in many other parts of Ireland you can call in at regional centres and watch films, look at displays and hear lectures about local ecology, history and geography. I can almost foresee the time when tourists will appear before examiners and take away diplomas or academic robes in recognition of the knowledge they have acquired during their stay. Though standards vary from centre to centre, you can certainly acquire an awful lot.

The best centre for learning about the surrounding district is at Coole Park, a place of interest on many counts. It was the home for centuries of a family of Anglo-Irish imperial administrators, the last survivor of whom was a great literary patron and important collector of local folklore, Augusta, Lady Gregory. The poet Yeats was a close friend and stayed here often. So did almost everyone of literary eminence in the early part of the 20th century. Yeats loved the lake, with its fifty-nine swans, and the woods where he once actually brushed against a badger. After Lady Gregory's death the house was allowed to decay and was finally pulled down in 1941 by the Forestry Department, which had bought the estate, now run as a nature reserve.

A converted stableyard occupies part of the site, and a film and a clever visual display show the unusual nature of the landscape round about and the abounding wildlife. This district is an extension of the higher limestone landscapes of the Burren, a few miles west. Here water is elusive. Rivers come and then go underground, to reappear a mile or several miles further on. Lakes are of the special kind known as turloughs (meaning dry lakes, a habitat unique to Ireland within Western Europe), scooped out of the prevailing limestone by the movements of ice or formed by solution hollows. The water in them also comes and goes.

The trees are in their autumn beauty,
  The woodland paths are dry,
Under the October twilight the water
  Mirrors a still sky;
Upon the brimming water among the stones
  Are nine-and-fifty swans.

W. B. Yeats, 'The Wild Swans at Coole'

Where it survives the summer it might be at a level 30 feet (9 metres) below the winter high. The furtive behaviour of water here is due to its action on the limestone, eating away the softer rock to make caves, swallowholes and subterranean channels. While some water enters and runs out of the turloughs in the form of streams, a lot of it simply sinks and rises within the natural porosity of the limestone. This provides plants with an important benefit, for the rising water brings with it fresh quantities of dissolved lime, a natural fertilizer.

The variations challenge the birds and plants which have settled here. Turloughs often hold large numbers of waterfowl in winter, although in early summer breeding waders can be in trouble if water suddenly appears. Many plants have to survive submergence through the winter and prolonged dryness in the summer. Their adaptations illustrate the ingenuity of evolution. The violet family, for instance, is represented on the turlough's sides by heath dog violet (*Viola canina*) at one level, common dog violet (*V. riviniana*) higher up, and the rare fen violet (*V. persicifolia*) close to the highest attained edge. Nature, of course, is crowded with such multiple adaptations. The Centre's film shows how each member of the tit family, all of which live in the woods, has evolved a beak ideally fitted for specialist problems such as coping with conifer needles or with deep or shallow fissures in different nuts.

You can walk through the thick woods of the demesne to Coole Lough, a turlough which always retains a good deal of water. Bewick's, whooper and mute swans are present in winter, along with a number of ducks and waders and the ringed plover. There are pine martens and red squirrels in the woods.

The river which tops up Coole Lough flows through the town of Gort from Lough Cutra, which lies within a grand demesne whose ownership has ricocheted between the noble and military families of Gort and Gough – Lord Gough having defeated both Chinese and Sikhs in days when you were rewarded for doing so. Between Lough Cutra and Gort, signposted just off the Ennis road, is a deep dank tree-girt depression into which the river flows from the underground channel in which it has been confined. The scene is the very model of an 19th-century romantic print. The river stays visible as far as Coole. Thereafter it reappears as a turlough in Garryland, surrounded by a fine old native wood once part of the Coole estate. It then returns to its tunnel and stays mostly submerged till its passage into the sea at Kinvarra.

BEFORE YOU GO
Maps: OSI Discovery Series, map No. 52.

GETTING THERE
By car: from Galway, take the N18 south to Gort, which is within a mile of Coole Lough.
By rail: services run from Dublin (Heuston) to Galway 5 times a day, T: (01) 836 6222.
By bus: Bus Eireann services from Ballina stop at Galway, Gort, Limerick and Cork, T: (096) 71800.

WHERE TO STAY
Hotels & B&Bs: there is 1 hotel, Sullivan's Royal, T: (091) 31401, and a few B&Bs in Gort, including the Glynns' Country Inn on Bridge Street, T: (091) 631047.
Youth hostels: in Kinvara are the independent Johnston's, T: (091) 637164, and the An Oige Doonis House, T: (091) 637512. There are hostels in and campsites near Galway.

ACTIVITIES
Walking: marked trails run through the nature reserve near Coole Lough.
Cycling: BF recommends a route that goes past Coole Lough and through Gort.

FURTHER INFORMATION
Tourist offices: the nearest BF offices in Ennis, T: (065) 682 8366, and Galway, T: (091) 563081, are both open all year.
Ecology: audio-visual displays are available at the visitor centre in the nature reserve at Coole Park, T: (091) 631804.

THE BURREN WAY

OSI Discovery Series, map Nos 51 and 57;1:35,200 map of the Burren by Tim Robinson (T. D. Robinson, 1977)

The Burren Way takes in the most dramatic scenery of west Clare. It starts at Ballyvaghan and after a short coastal stretch plunges south and then south-west through the Burren heartland, mostly at a height which offers good views of the Aran Islands, the ocean and the south coast of Galway. It regains the coast at the music-rich fishing village of Doolin, and stays with it along the tops of the Cliffs of Moher, one of Ireland's more breathtaking features. The last few miles are eastward, still along the coast, which here overlooks a sometimes storm-wracked bay noted for the multitude of ships it has dragged to the bottom. Ballinalackan and Doolin are good places for a more or less central break.

Before you go *Guide-book: The Burren Way Map Guide* (Shannon Development).
Getting there *By car:* head south from Galway on the N18, then take the N67 to Ballyvaghan. For Liscannor either continue along the N67; or follow the R477 and the R478 along the coast. Ballinalackan is just where the R477 meets the R479. *By rail:* the closest stations are Ennis and Galway, T: (091) 561 444. *By bus:* summer Bus Eireann services from Killarney, Galway and Doolin stop at Ballyvaghan. The summer service between Killarney and Galway stops at Ballyvaghan, Lisdoonvarna and Liscannor, T: (091) 562000.
Where to stay *Hotels and B&Bs:* in Ballyvaghan, the Hyland's Hotel, T: (065) 707 7037, e-mail: hylands@tinet.ie, or the cheaper McGann's, T: (065) 707 7083; in Liscannor the 4-star Gregans Castle, T: (065) 707 7005, www.gregans.ie.
Youth hostels: 4 independent hostels in Doolin are the Rainbow, T: (065) 707 4415, and Flanagan's, T: (065) 707 4564, both open all year; Paddy's, T: (065) 707 4006, shut only at Christmas; and the Aille River Hostel, T: (065) 707 4260, www.iol.ie/ailleriver, open Mar–Dec.
Outdoor living: Nagles Doolin Camping Park, Doolin, open Apr–Sept, T: (065) 707 4458.
Activities *Walking:* the 22-mile (35-km) Burren Way is split into 2 sections: Ballyvaghan to Ballinalachen (13 miles/20 km) and Ballinalachen to Liscannor (9.5 miles/15 km).

This consists of one entire rock with here and there a little surface of Earth, which raiseth earlier Beef and Mutton, though they allow no hay, than any land in this Kingdom, and much sweeter by reason of the sweet herbs intermixed and distributed everywhere.

Journal of Thomas Dineley, on the Burren (17th century)

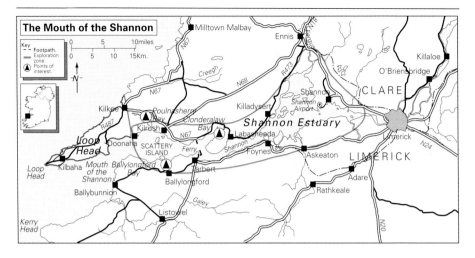

The Mouth of the Shannon

Loop Head

A long spearhead of land jutting out into the Atlantic, lined along part of its north coast with steep cliffs and rock stacks, summer home of thousands of sea-birds

The west coast of County Clare from Kilkee north-eastwards to Lahinch is fine and dandy but dedicated to the family holiday, evoking the bucket and spade more than the chough and lordly raven. South-west of Kilkee the scene is more cliffy, wilder, less peopled. But there are people, and there are farms and villages. At Loop Head itself there is a walled-off working lighthouse. The wildness rating could at best be middling. Worth seeing, to overquote the great doctor, but not worth going to see.

Kilkee, hugging its broad sandy bay, lives for tourists. Trading – or over-trading – on distinct scenic advantages, it has, in building all it imagines tourists may want, considerably uglified itself. All that stops at

its boundaries, however, and after a minute or two of climbing the sights are of chunks of cliff seemingly broken and floated from the mainland to make clearly striated islands, rimmed with foam: cliffs, ravines, tapering or top-heavy stacks. Back from the sea is a seemingly simple ecology of grass, thrift, buttercups, rabbits, wheatears springing from every wall and post, hooded crows, rock pipits, and a fine herd of feral goats, most white, some dark with spectacularly black faces, black beards and their elegant twin plumes of horn.

Ten miles from Kilkee the coast has become a giants' tip of mighty slabs, once piled like sheets, now bent, toppled, folded and broken by underlying settlement and the corrosive action of waves. These are the shales and flagstones which lie underneath the carboniferous limestone that forms the surface of so much of middle Ireland. Sea water has tunnelled through and gurgles into pits and swallow-holes. Nevertheless nature has neatly created two broad arched bridges – the bridges of Ross – whose bent

slabs have broken to look like the slabs human builders would have used. It is a freak construct amid stormy deconstruction.

Inland, where the rock has neither been broken nor its inner strata exposed, the country is dull: a flat, treeless landscape of unadorned villages and rough pasture. A field thick with buttercups is the biggest treat. Along the coast the discordant ballet of rock shapes and movements continues to Loop Head, where electrified wire ensures that you do not stray from the cliff-side. (It is a peculiarly pugnacious thing, electric wire: the threat of physical pain imposed by some absent landowner, another lapse in conventional Irish friendliness.) Twenty or so feet from the cliff a huge, elongated vertical stack is drawn up like a petrified liner riding at anchor. Through the dividing ravine water wars and storms its way through in waves of cobalt, turquoise, aquamarine and white. Aeronaut fulmars and smart dark-booted kittiwakes nest on the stacks. Fleets of guillemot and razorbill float on the sea, and lesser black-backed gulls

91

dive with uttered menace at intruders (but always turn aside well in time). You can lie on a bed of pink thrift, look down at this crowded world and wonder, if you are like me, at the wagtail or swallow that flies six feet above you and an instant later a hundred feet above the sea without appearing to register any difference. Eskimos are said to have twenty words for snow. I cannot imagine swallows have even one word for vertigo.

Before you go *Maps:* OSI Discovery Series, map No. 63.

Getting there *By car:* from Kilkee, the R487 runs south-west to Loop Head at the end of the peninsula.

By rail: Ennis is the nearest station with 2 trains daily from Limerick. The Dublin–Limerick service has 10 trains a day, T: (01) 836 6222.

By bus: Bus Eireann services from Ennis to the coast are infrequent. Contact Ennis bus station, T: (065) 624177.

Where to stay *Hotels and B&Bs:* Halpin's Hotel, T: (065) 905 6032, www.greenbook.ie/halpins, Mrs Fitzpatrick, T: (065) 905 6244, and Westcliff House, T: (065) 905 6108, are all in Kilkee. *Youth hostel:* the independent Kilkee Hostel, Kilkee, T: (065) 905 6209.

Outdoor living: in Kilkee, Cunningham's Holiday Park, T: (065) 905 7011, e-mail: cunninghams@tinet.ie; in Doonaha, Green Acres CCP, T: (065) 905 7011; in Kilrush, Aylevarroo CCP, T: (065) 905 1102, e-mail: aylevarroo@njogorman.ie.

Activities *Cycling:* in Kilrush bikes can be hired from Gleeson Wholesale, T: (065) 905 1127, and from the Korner Shop, T: (065) 905 1037.

Further information *Tourist offices:* seasonal BF offices in Kilrush, T: (065) 51577, and Kilkee, T: (065) 905 6112.

Shannon Estuary

A broad inroad of ocean, much used by man, but hiding sanctuaries of wilderness to north and south

Like the Severn, which is also the longest river in the countries it flows through, the Shannon debouches in a huge and important estuary on the west coast. The works and influence of man are never far away. Long before it begins to broaden at O'Briensbridge, ten miles above Limerick, the bulk of its water has been snatched from its channel, forced to walk the plank of a canal, and dropped 100 ft (30 m) at Ardnacrusha to furnish vast quantities of electricity. The scheme, completed in 1929, created a huge reservoir between O'Briensbridge and Killaloe, drowning villages whose steeples and gables continued to appear, at low water, for years afterwards.

Canals and river channel are reunited above Limerick, a town of some 65,000 inhabitants, whose industrial and domestic effluents can hardly enhance the nature of the water. Here and there along the estuary banks are lesser towns, docks, industries, power stations and what was once the country's principal airport. The dimensions and illuminations of some of these make them conspicuous for miles. The amazing thing is that it is all absorbed. Along the 50 miles (80 km) from Limerick to the sea there is a rich range of concealed bays, islands great and small, marshes, mud-flats, a wildlife and waterfowl population to match and every opportunity to imagine that

man has not trodden here before.

The sensible means of exploration would be a sailing-boat or dinghy. Half a century back this was no problem. Shannon Airport was not thought about, boats were readily available from Foynes, Tarbert and elsewhere, and steamers regularly plied between those two towns and Kilrush and Limerick. In fact, the further back we look the more important sea travel was. Roads, forests and freebooters made land travel impossible or dangerous. Trade, buoyant smuggling and war used ocean routes. Today you would be lucky to make some private arrangement. Although there is a frequent car ferry from Killimer on the Clare coast to Tarbert in Kerry, and a regular summer boat service between Kilrush and the monastic island of Scattery, the only dependable option is to go by road.

Limestone flanks both sides of the eastern half of the estuary, and the broad mouth of the River Fergus, which joins it on the Clare side. The rich pastures here have created the elegant demesnes of County Limerick, and to a lesser extent, of the opposite bank. Grand Ascendancy houses, some intact, some ruinous, most of them picturesque, recall the old landlord days. In the western sectors they thin out as the old overlay of shales, slate and coal reduces the quality of the soil. On the south side the mud-flats of Tarbert and the coast west of it support huge numbers of duck (mainly wigeon, teal and mallard) and waders. Ballylongford Bay is a good place to watch them. But the main interest and the more indented and islanded shore is on the north side – the Fergus estuary and west. Lanes and tracks lead from the

Killadysert–Labasheeda–
Kilrush road to the water,
sometimes across old causeways
or dykes, and at Killadysert to a
harbour newly spruced at
Europe's expense. Two bays,
each a couple of miles long,
hold thousands of waders in
winter. Clonderalaw Bay is also
noted for its pintail duck and
Poulnasherry Bay supports
brent geese, wigeon and other
ducks. Both are easily accessible
from the road.

The tides wash out the
estuary every day, but in spite of
that the water is seldom clear.
The temptation to bathe is not
great, not with the clear blue of
Kilkee or the Dingle to right
and left of the Shannon's
mouth. But a boat would be
good. You would probably have
all the world –– that you could
see, at least –– to yourself.

Before you go *Map:* OSI Discovery Series, map No. 63.

Getting there *By sea:* boats run
during the summer from Cappa
pier to Scattery Island, T: (061)
451327. A car ferry crosses the
Shannon estuary between Killimer and Tarbert, Apr–Sept,
T: (065) 53124/53126.

By car: the N68 runs direct
from Ennis to Kilrush. Alternatively take the R473, R486 and
N67 to Kilrush along the north
bank of the River Shannon.

By rail: Ennis is the nearest station with 2 trains daily from
Limerick. The Dublin–
Limerick service has 10 trains a
day, T: (01) 836 6222.

By bus: the Dublin–Kilkee Bus
Eireann service goes via Limerick, Shannon and Ennis. A
summer-only Galway–Cork
service stops at Kilkee and Kilrush; local services also run to
Kilbaha. Contact the bus station at Ennis, T: (065) 24177.

Where to stay *Hotels:* Halpin's
Hotel, Kilkee, T: (065) 905
6032, www.greenbook.ie/
halpins; Tubridy House,
Coovaclare Village, Kilrush, T:

(065) 905 9033.

B&Bs: Mrs O'Loughlin, off
Quin Road, Ennis, T: (065) 682
9363; Westcliff House, on the
seafront, Kilkee, T: (065) 905
6108; Mrs O'Neill, Kilrush, T:
(065) 905 9059, e-mail: old-
parochial @webheads.ie.

Youth hostel: the Katie O'Connor's hostel is in Kilrush, T:
(065) 905 1133.

Outdoor living: the Aylevarroo
CCP in Kilrush is open May–
Sept, T: (065) 905 1102, e-mail:
aylevarroo @njogorman.ie.

Activities *Walking:* bracing
walks can be had around Loop
Head, Co. Clare's southernmost point, with views north to
the Aran Islands and south to
the Dingle peninsula. Long
hikes also run along the cliffs to
Kilkee.

Cycling: bikes can be hired
from Gleeson Wholesale in Kilrush, T: (065) 51127. BF can
provide details of a route that
runs right along the Shannon
Estuary from Ennis.

Riding: hacks are available
from the Clare Equestrian Centre, Doora, T: (065) 40136, and
Cahirgel Riding, near Newmar-

ket-on-Fergus, T: (061) 368358,
www.cahirgelridingcentre.ie.

Fishing: Allard Fisheries in
Ennis hires out equipment and
provides licences, T: (065) 682
4369.

Watersports: Kilkee is a well-
known diving area. Shore dives
are from Duggerna Rocks and
boat dives from Black Rocks.
Kilkee Diving Centre, on the
harbour, hires out equipment
and air bottles, T: (065) 905
6707. The Kilrush Creek
Adventure Centre, Kilrush,
T: (065) 905 2595, offers sailing
instruction and hires out
wind-surfing and canoeing
equipment.

Bird-watching: the estuary
mud-flats attract large numbers
of waders and wildfowl, but the
colonies are widely scattered.
The best viewing is at the Fergus estuary.

Further information *Tourist offices: there are* summer-only BF
offices in Kilrush, T: (065)
51577, and Kilkee, T: (065) 905
6112. All-year offices are in
Ennis, T: (065) 682 8366, and at
Shannon Airport, T: (061)
471664.

The pine marten, on the decrease but still found in some central and
western counties, has a sweet clean look but is a ruthless killer of small
birds and insects.

Kerry and Cork

Most easterly, landward approaches to the south-west of Ireland lead you up, over the watershed, and then pleasurably down, as if this region of long, bony red sandstone fingers pointing westward into the sea is a reward for uphill toil. Some say its attractions are fatal. Many of Killarney's beauties are defaced by an excess of tourists, and lesser-known parts are getting better known by the year. Really, it's no matter. The place is big enough to retain its wilderness and secrets. Standard tourists stick to celebrated routes and prescribed areas, many preferring an audio-visual presentation of the Skelligs on the mainland to a rough, ten-mile sea crossing and a wet strenuous climb when you get to them. These four peninsulas, and the smattering of islands round about them, have grandeur, drama, wildness and stirring beauty. Small wonder that the great and good who want escape from crowds and recognition – General de Gaulle, Benjamin Britten, Françoise Sagan, Charlie Chaplin and many more – had or have holiday homes in the area. Numbers of young Irish and English people, in search of some kind of alternative nirvana, have settled here, too. You can still, in most of the area, imagine yourself a thousand miles from people.

Each ridge-backed promontory has its own character, and the biggest and best-known is the Iveragh ('Eve-raw' comes close to the pronunciation). The coast road of this promontory is called for obscure reasons the Ring of Kerry.

Sunset brings a golden haze to the smoothly rounded mountains of the Iveragh peninsula, seen here from the Beara peninsula, across the 5-mile (8-km) width of the Kenmare River.

With Killarney at one end, the Skellig Rocks at the other and the Mac-Gillicuddy's Reeks (a mountain range of great beauty containing Ireland's highest peaks) in between, it is perhaps the most spectacular. Other peninsulas have more exotic, even alien, appeal. Indeed, the foreign character and connections of this part of Ireland are deep and legion. Spanish and French traders have come and gone for 2,000 years or more. Fleets from France and Spain, Barbary privateers, German U-boats have raided. As long ago as Neolithic times the Atlantic here was one of the great communicating waterways of Europe. From Dingle, there are plausible reasons to believe, the first Europeans to find America set off. And on the hills and mountains are long-settled plants that have arrived, by uncertain means, from more familiar quarters in Spain, Portugal and America. According to legend, the King of the World once did County Kerry the honour of invading it (he was repelled after much slaughter). From here, it was thought, a boat could take you over the water to the Land of Eternal Youth. It is a mistake to think, as many have and do, that in coming here you are approaching the limits of the civilized world.

The Dingle, north of the Ring of Kerry, is the peninsula most pervaded by the taste and feel of other countries and climates. Dark hair and Spanish looks are sometimes remarked upon, and there is talk, less dependable maybe, of an elusive monster from the Amazon in one of the mountain lakes. I think it is the people from whom the alien impression comes. On a dark wet day, I have to say, Dingle looks as darkly, wetly Irish as anywhere else, and on a fine day under a clear blue sky its sweeps of green and purple mountain, its rocky bays, broad sandy beaches and

enchanting islands with their ghost-dwellings are utterly Irish too.

South of Iveragh lies the Beara peninsula. It too has bays, beaches, mountains, lagoons, bog, moorland, off-shore islands, sea-birds, rare plants – but these are no more than the local currency. The character that marks it off from Iveragh to its north and Mizen to its south is harder to name or define. A little wilder, I should call it, rather rougher textured, agreeably short on tourist amenities, though by no means without them. (There is even a ski-lift for getting over to Dursey Island, situated at its western tip.) Many resident tradespeople are trying to sharpen Beara's tourist appeal, which at its extreme means, I suppose, Killarnefying. Before they succeed, if they ever do, I for one shall return and return.

The southernmost peninsula is double-pronged, with the mighty natural ramparts of Mizen Head at its southwestern end and much rough and indeterminate landscape on the way to it. It is in the southern edge that its main appeal lies, in its curlicued coastline and dazzling views over an archipelago of islands – the lone and no-longer-manned lighthouse of Fastnet solid and upright in the distance. Of the two islands served by regular ferries, Cape Clear is famous for its resident and, even more, its migratory birds. It was here forty years or so ago that systematic scanning, with the benefit of improved optical technology, began to disclose the astonishing wealth of sea-bird life on Ireland's coasts. In comparison, Sherkin Island is not at first sight spectacular, but a recent survey shows a plant count far in excess of that previously accepted.

Baltimore is one of the ferry ports: a pleasant town, with a new restaurant added every time you turn your back (as seems to be the way in these parts), it was once a fishing depot, where agents from Britain and continental Europe waited to bid for incoming catches. The foreign link here is a bloody one. In 1631 Algerian pirates, who often prowled this coastline, landed, slaughtered a large number of townspeople and took away more as slaves. The bay here is spattered with rocks and islets, and the neighbouring land not so much undulating as bumpy or choppy. Round the corner, at the beginning of the ravels of County Cork's south coast, a first pretty inlet narrows to a tidal channel which feeds Lough Ine, a rarity in that it is an inland lake made up of salt water. Its richness in marine fauna and flora – a richness which extends out to sea but is more easily studied within these confines – is only one of the natural wonders in this south-west corner of Ireland. Mile after mile of lane is edged with fuchsia and escallonia. Rarities like the strawberry tree flourish in certain locations. Only a few miles off-shore lie Ireland's largest gannetry and the largest breeding colonies of storm petrels in the world.

GETTING THERE

By air: British Airways fly from UK airports to Cork and Shannon, T: (0845) 722 2111, www.britishairways.com; so do Aer Lingus, T: (0845) 973 7747, www.aerlingus.ie; and Jersey European, T: (0870) 567 6676, www.jerseyeuropean.co.uk. (All UK numbers.) There are flights to Shannon from Atlanta, Boston, Chicago, Los Angeles, Miami, New York and major European cities; and to Cork from Amsterdam, Frankfurt and Paris. Both airports have useful web-sites: www.cork-air port.com and www.shannon airport.com. The airport in Co. Kerry is at Farranfore, a 15-min drive from Killarney. Ryanair operate flights from London (Stansted) to Kerry, T: (01) 609 7999, www.ryan air.com, and Aer Lingus from Dublin. Further information is available from Kerry airport, T: (066) 976 4644.

By sea: Swansea Cork Ferries sail to Cork from Swansea 4 days a week in the off-peak season and 6 times a week in summer (including an overnight crossing), T: (01792) 456116 (UK), www.swansea-cork.ie.

By rail: the Dublin–Cork service runs 8 times a day all week; 5 trains a day run from Dublin to Killarney and Tralee,

and a regular service runs from Cork to Killarney, T: (01) 836 6222, www.irishrail.ie.

By bus: regular Bus Eireann services run from Dublin, Waterford and Galway to Cork, Killarney and Tralee, T: (01) 836 6111, www.buseireann.ie.

WHERE TO STAY

The area is well provided with self-catering (vacation-home) accommodation, hotels, B&Bs, hostels and camp-sites, although Killarney can get overcrowded in summer. Bord Fáilte publishes guides to approved places to stay.

ACTIVITIES

Walking: there are 5 way-marked walks in the region. The longest is the 134-mile (215-km) Kerry Way which loops round the Iveragh peninsula passing through Caherciveen, Waterville, Caherdaniel, Kenmare and Kilgarvan. It often follows old drovers' roads and offers an opportunity to explore the spectacular uplands and MacGillicuddy's Reeks. The 95-mile (153-km) Dingle Way circles the mountainous Dingle peninsula. Starting from Tralee Bay the trail follows the coast, taking walkers past Dunquin and Slea Head, commanding views of Europe's most westerly islands - the Blaskets (see p103). The 120-mile (196-km) Beara Way (see p118) and the 56-mile (90-km) Sheep's Head Way offer more gentle coastal walking, but amid impressive mountain scenery. Lastly, the Blackwater Way stretches 118 miles (188 km) from Muckross in MacGillicuddy's Reeks to Clogheen, nestled in the Knockmealdowns, passing through the handsome Boggeragh and Nagles Mountains. Maps and guides are essential for all these walks, and are available from BF. *A Guide to the Sheep's Head Way*, published by the Sheep's Head Way Development Committee, has useful maps. Walking holiday agencies include: South West Walks Ireland, Tralee, T: (066) 712 8733/(087) 250 2434, e-mail: swwi@iol.ie; Wild Ireland Tours, Glencar, T: (066) 976 0211/(087) 268 1535, www.wildireland.com; and Into the Wilderness Walking Tours, Glencar, T: (066) 976 0101/(087) 265 7534, e-mail: climbers@iol.ie.

Cycling: for serious climbs head for the lakes, rivers and coast of west Cork. The Ring of Kerry offers a 129-mile (206-km) route, while the Dingle peninsula takes cyclists along-

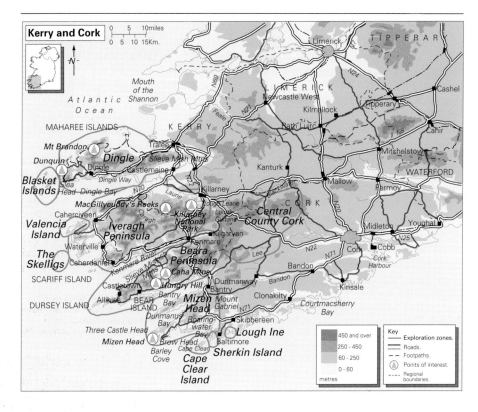

side monuments to Ireland's early-Christian history. Cycle Ireland, in Killarney, T: (064) 32536, e-mail: cycleire@iol.ie, and Go Ireland in Killorglin, T: (066) 976 2094, e-mail: goireland@fexco.ie, can provide bikes and accommodation.

Riding: trail rides and residential packages round the Dingle peninsula are organized by El Rancho Farmhouse, Ballyard, Tralee, T: (066) 721840, e-mail: elrancho@iol.ie. Rocklands Stables in Killarney, e-mail: rocklands@tinet.ie, offer riding instruction at all levels and offer 2- and 3-hr treks in the Old Oak Wood, part of the Kenmare Estate now owned by the Forest Service, T: (064) 32592.

Climbing: Kerry and west Cork offer the finest climbing country in Ireland. MacGillicuddy's

Reeks provide exciting ridge walking. Carrantuohill is Ireland's highest peak at 3,414 ft (1,024 m). The Iveragh peninsula also has Mullaghanattin and Knocknagantee with their complex of combes, corries and lakes. On the Dingle peninsula there are challenging climbs at Dun Sion and at the Three Sisters; for details contact the Mountain Man Outdoor Shop in Dingle, T: (066) 915 2400. The Cappanalea Outdoor Education Centre, near Killarney, organizes rock-climbing trips in Kerry, T: (066) 976 9244, www.oec.ie/cappanalea.

Fishing: the Upper Caragh, the Laune, the Sheen and the Cummeragh rivers all have salmon. The River Laune also has brown trout. Lakes with brown trout include Lough Leane, Lough Barfinnihy and Lough

Guitane. For information contact the South Western Regional Fisheries Board, 1 Nevilles Terrace, Masseytown, Macroom, Co. Cork, T: (026) 41221.

Watersports: the Irish Sailing Association can provide full details of sailing clubs in the Cork and Kerry area, T: (01) 280 0239. The International Sailing Centre in Cobh, T: (021) 811237, offers tuition for all levels. The Dingle Marina Centre offers diving and sailing courses, T: (066) 915 2422.

FURTHER INFORMATION
Tourist offices: BF in Killarney, T: (064) 31633, and Tralee, T: (066) 21288, are open all year. There are seasonal offices in Dingle, T: (066) 915 1188, Kenmare, T: (064) 41233, and Waterville, T: (066) 917 4646.

Dingle

Northernmost of the long mountain-spined promontories of Kerry and Cork, stretching into the Atlantic

Early Christian monks chose wonderful wild places in which to live and pray: Meteora, Iona, Sinai, Mount Athos, the Grande Chartreuse. Mount Brandon, Ireland's second-highest mountain, and the six-mile (ten-kilometre) range that almost blocks off the western quarter of the Dingle peninsula equal any of these sites. The mountains' spiny ridge, hanging above a series of ice-carved cirques and ice-cold corries, commands Olympian views of Connemara to the north, MacGillicuddy's Reeks to the south-east, and the Atlantic to the north, south and west. But the view that makes magic of this place is the blazing golden turmoil far out over the water when a bright sun sinks below the horizon.

I saw Mount Brandon first when, as a student, I spent a holiday month at Anascaul, on the south side of the peninsula. Here, for the first time I read about my namesake St Brendan and climbed the mountain to see the spot where, in the early 6th century AD, he built an oratory and gazed on perhaps a hundred such sunsets. Brendan saw within that golden submersion visions of blessed and immortal lands, and resolved to go in search of them. Back in my lodgings, eating Mrs Kennedy's beefsteak (whose excellence owed something to her being the butcher's sister), I quickly forgot the climb and that inspiring view as my landlady told me of a walk she had arranged for me with two village girls and a visit the following week in other company to Puck Fair at Killorglin. Both occasions were delicious, as were most encounters with the courteous, subtle, weathered residents of the Dingle, with their lilting tones and sweet assentings. But that mountain-top vision returned. In time I read virtually all that had been written about the sailor saint; about his preparations, his setting off with a crew of monks in a coracle of cowhide, and the many miracles he encoun-

tered on the sea – at Easter an obliging whale docked beside the coracle so that mass could be held on its broad back – before discovering a land that many since have identified as America. (Though a 19th-century sceptic recognized in all the saint's landfalls features distributed around Galway Bay.) In due course I fell in love with Celtic Ireland and wrote a book about Brendan and his contemporaries.

The Dingle peninsula is 30 miles (48 kilometres) long and varies from five miles (eight kilometres) to 12 miles (19 kilometres) across. It is the northernmost of the long bony fingers which Kerry and Cork point into the Atlantic. It is the most westerly land in Europe, a spit of old red sandstone raised, like the other promontories, from its archaic sea-bed by the east–west folding and faulting,

Black-headed gulls – a small, noisy, boisterous, scavenging species with a distinguishing dark brown hood – fish and play above Inch Strand, a long sandy spit protruding from the southern coast of the Dingle peninsula.

squeezing and cracking that took place during the so-called Armorican orogeny nearly 300 million years ago – long before the Himalayas were formed. For most of its length the central (and broken) mountain chain rises – from flat, sand-fringed coastlands – steeply, cut by threads of falling water on the north side, but with more gentle gradients in the south. Three-quarters of the way along, the ridge turns sharply northward, to rise in turn to the Dingle's most spectacular pinnacles, Brandon Peak and Mount Brandon, this latter being (at 3,127 feet/938 metres) the second-highest mountain in Ireland.

The peninsula thrusts on westward for ten miles or so to the curved and foamy ceramics of Slea Head, pounded by waves blown in from America, with views of the humpy Blasket Islands (page 103) and their abandoned habitations. The cliffs at this extreme of the promontory and along its northern flank are among Ireland's most dramatic: Sybil Head, the Three Sisters, Ballydavid Head and Brandon Head. Up to 1,000 ft (304 metres) high, they are the haunts of chough, raven and the elusive Manx shearwater, and more often than not assaulted by sheets of spume. Yet alongside such gothic pandemonium the Dingle offers mile upon mile of uninterrupted, flat and tranquil sand. Stradbally, within Brandon Bay on the north side, is Ireland's longest beach. It runs a full 12 miles (19 kilometres). There are long strands (the Irish word) at Smerwick and Ventry. And far from the Atlantic thunderings of the west lies the three-mile (five-

kilometre) sandspit of Inch, protecting the extensive mud-flats of Castlemaine harbour.

This area, tucked between the Dingle and Iveragh promontories, contains a rare colony of Kerry toads (*Bufo calamitas*, known in its few British sites as the natterjack), distinguished from the common variety by its smaller size, a yellow line running down its back, and a much moister skin. Here and nowhere outside the county, it wallows, swims, spawns, hunts. Occasionally seen at night on the sands, it spends most of its days cooling damply underneath.

There are other natural rarities. The dull but well-camouflaged Sandhill rustic moth (*Luperina nickerlii* ssp. *knilli*) occurs among Dingle dunes, on the Aran Islands, and nowhere else. The feral goat is sometimes, not quite reliably, reported in the west, though it has the talents of the abominable snowman for eluding humans. In recent years a bottlenosed dolphin has commonly turned up to play with all comers in Dingle harbour.

The great wealth of the area is its birds. On either side of the base of the peninsula, Castlemaine harbour and Tralee Bay afford the brent goose one of its main winter homes in Ireland. Several thousand are present on each site, along with strong populations of sea-ducks. Some winters, Inch accommodates the red-throated diver (loon); more often seen is the great northern diver, whose call, rising from a co-ordinated babble and then falling sadly away, is to my mind one of the most poignant sounds in nature. Lough Gill, on the Maharees promontory, and Akeragh Lough, a series of duney lagoons on the east coast of Tralee Bay, receive large winter populations with a rich record of rarities.

Dingle has changed since my stay at Mrs Kennedy's. Then the vehicles parked outside the church at mass were almost all pony and trap. Cottages were thatched and traditional – no such thing as a Spanish bungalow. Bank-notes were deposited more under mattresses than in banks. The old talked Gaelic until on the approach of an Englishman they courteously switched to English; the young forgot Irish the moment they could and emigrated for work. There were scarcely any tourists, hotels or restaurants to keep

The shoveler duck is mainly a winter visitor to the lakes, rivers and estuaries of Ireland, though it does breed in the midlands and at various coastal points.

them even seasonally busy. Nobody wasted effort climbing mountains or rocks and the only thing people went to sea for was fish. Smiling Killarney, to the south, was left to net all the tourists. The Dingle was magnificently private, gruff and magical, as it must have seemed to St Brendan and those hardy anchorites who sheltered in the cramped helmet-shaped stone huts which survive in relict townships along the way.

The tourist is accommodated now. Bungalows sprout, signs shout, caffs and B&Bs and souvenir emporia proliferate. Dingle has a new pier. Daily ferries run to the Blaskets. Paths and mountain ascents are waymarked, and the tarmacked roads, financed by EU-money, grow broader and smoother by the year. During the holiday season, walkers following the official waymarked Dingle Way, a round trip starting and finishing at Tralee, will find that others have been funnelled into the same routes, particularly the easier stretches.

Yet they will frequently lose the world of modernity as they climb to the heights of the Slieve Mish and later, on the return leg (and if weather allows), ascend and explore the Brandon complex and its purlieus. These include the west coast of Brandon Bay and the broad and daunting blanket bog that stretches westward from it, the cluster of corrie lakes below Slievanea, the raven-priested isolation of the pass of Mullachveal, and the valley of the Owenmore, falling away from Brandon Peak. A waymark sign does not mean there is anybody up there. Brandon's ascent offers a continuous disclosure of new hills and valleys, slits of sea and distant blue mountain ranges, besides the powerful views close-to, of lakes suspended under towering bays of rock, and the tweedy colour-subtleties of the pervasive blanket bog. It used to be a common pilgrimage, second in status only to Croagh Patrick in County Mayo. Less difficult from Tiduff on the west than from Cloghane on the precipitous east, it always calls for the usual precautions for dangerous ascents.

BEFORE YOU GO

Maps: OSI Discovery Series, map Nos 70 and 71; *Dingle and District Walking Map* by Laurence Jones (Learscaileanna an Daingin, 1998).

Guide-books: *Walking in Ireland* (Lonely Planet, 1999) has good accounts of the Beara Way, the Kerry Way, the Dingle Way and several others. *Walk Cork and Kerry* by David Perrott and Joss Lynam (Bartholomew's, 1994) includes walks on Dingle. Also very useful is the *Dingle Way Map Guide* (Menasha Ridge Press, 1992). *The Dingle Peninsula* by Steve MacDonogh (Brandon Book Publishers, 2000) is highly informative about the place and its history, nature, climbs, culture, language and archaeology.

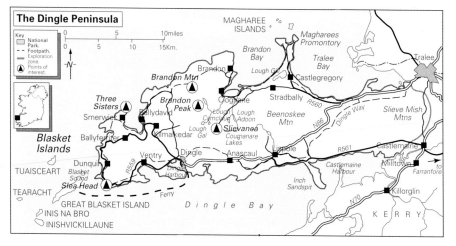

CHAPTER 3: KERRY AND CORK

GETTING THERE

By car: from Tralee follow the N86 towards Dingle, the main town on the peninsula. The R559 describes a circle round the tip of the peninsula, passing close to Slea Head and Smerwick harbour. Tralee can be by-passed by those coming on the N22 from Cork and Killarney by taking the R561 at Farranfore.

By rail: the nearest station is Tralee, with trains to and from Mallow, where there are connections with Cork, Dublin, Limerick and Rosslare, T: (01) 836 6222.

By bus: Bus Eireann run regular services to Tralee from Dublin, Cork, Galway, Limerick and Rosslare. There are 4 buses a day from Tralee to Dingle and an additional summer service from Tralee, via Dingle, to Slea Head, which takes you along the south coast of the peninsula, T: (066) 712 3566.

WHERE TO STAY

Hotels and B&Bs: there are lots of places on the Dingle. The homely O'Connor's Guesthouse is at Cloghane, T: (066) 713 8113. In Dingle itself is Captains House, T: (066) 915 1531, e-mail: captigh@tinet.ie, and on the shore of Dingle Bay, Heaton's Guesthouse, T: (066) 915 2288.

Youth hostels: in Dingle try the Ballingart House Hostel and Equestrian Centre, which also has camping available, T: (066) 915 1454, e-mail: btaggart@iol.ie. Seacrest, T: (066) 915 1390, and Fuchsia Lodge, T: (066) 915 7150, are in Anascaul; the Bog View Hostel, in Inch, T: (066) 915 8125; Tigh an Phoist, in Ballydavid, T: (066) 915 5109; and the Connor Pass Hostel, in Stradbally, T: (066) 913 9179. Dunquin has an An Oige hostel, T: (066) 915 6121.

Outdoor living: there are lots of camp-sites around the peninsula, including the Seaside CCP near Tralee, T: (066) 713 0161; Anchor CCP, Castlegregory, T: (066) 713 9157; and Oratory House CCP, Dingle, T: (066) 915 5143.

ACTIVITIES

Walking: the Dingle Way is a 95-mile (153-km) circular way-marked route that loops round the Dingle peninsula. It takes 5 to 6 days to walk, passing towns and villages and offering unrivalled views, Celtic remains, Gaelic speakers and colourful myths. A map or guide is essential; contact BF in Dingle, Killarney or Tralee for further information.

Cycling: bikes can be hired from The Bicycle Shop, Dykegate Street, Dingle, T: (066) 915 2311.

Riding: Dingle Horse Riding, Ballinaboula, Dingle, T: (066) 915 2199/915 2018, e-mail: dinglehorseriding@tinet.ie, organizes riding on the peninsula. Their rates are hourly, daily or weekly.

Climbing: there is excellent sea-cliff climbing for the experienced at Dun Sion, near Dingle, and at the Three Sisters, near Ballyferriter. Contact the Mountain Man Outdoor Shop in Dingle, T: (066) 915 2400, e-mail: irasc@tinet.ie.

Fishing: good sea-trout fishing is available near Castlegregory and Dingle. Contact Mr O' Connor, T: (066) 915 9947, to arrange fishing trips.

Watersports: in Tralee Bay Jamie Knox, T: (066) 713 9411, hires out surfing and wind-surfing equipment; for diving contact Ronnie Fitzgibbon, T: (066) 712 5803. In Dingle, Michael and Becky O'Connor arrange sailing activities, T: (066) 915 9882. The Dingle Bay Sailing Club is run by Margaret Holdereid, T: (066) 915 1469.

Bird-watching: Kerry is the favoured first landfall of more than half the birds that migrate to or through Europe from Iceland, Greenland and northern Canada. In spite of the relative shortage of nature reserves in Ireland, there are 3 on the Dingle peninsula, and others within in a few miles. At Castlemaine harbour, *Zostera marina*, a plant whose seeds can be ground into good flour, grows in abundance and, along with natural shelter and spacious mud-flats and salt-marsh, induces thousands of wildfowl to winter here. Brent geese, wigeon and pintail occur by the thousand, shoveler and common scoter by the hundred. There is good viewing from various points along and below the road from Castlemaine to Anascaul. With similar inducements to those of Castlemaine harbour, Tralee Bay attracts huge winter colonies of brent geese, wigeon and common scoter. Lough Gill, on the promontory leading to the Magharee Islands, attracts, along with 3 species of swan, many kinds of duck, including gadwall, teal and shoveler. Up the coast, among the lagoons of Akeragh Lough, migrating waders, flocking in from northern Europe and Greenland, add substantially to the bird count. Killarney BF can supply useful guides to these spots, including information on access.

Viewpoints: the R561 and the N86 loop the Slieve Mish and Beenoskee mountains. The Conor Pass, north-east of Dingle, affords wonderful views of the corrie-pocked east side of the mountains.

FURTHER INFORMATION

Tourist offices: the BF office in Dingle is open Apr–Oct, T: (066) 915 1188/915 1241. The offices in Tralee, T: (066) 712 1288, and Killarney, T: (064) 31633, are both open all year.

Blasket Islands

*Group of islands off the west end of the
Dingle peninsula, virtually uninhabited since
1953 and rich in bird life*

Ireland is full of the Ozymandias effect:
greatness gone by, gathering dust, its
meaning forgotten. It inspires the great
Celtic gloom, known from the Hebrides to
Portugal, a weeping for a lost culture, a lost
language, lost loves, the wild ducks and the
wild geese flown away. The Blasket Islands, a
stone's throw beyond the end of the Dingle
peninsula, are the site of a great loss recent
enough not to be quite forgotten, but slip-
ping away through the hourglass as those
old enough to remember disperse or die, and
memory is formalized in remnant writings.
They say that careful observation could pick
out former inhabitants of the Blaskets in
Dunquin and Dingle, the mainland towns to
which they were finally transplanted in 1953.
A lifetime of rowing curraghs in all weathers
had made the men's neck sinews stand out
hard and strong; walking along sheep-walks
had predisposed them to proceed in single
file. There is less, if any, point looking for
these characteristics now.

It would scarcely matter if the Blaskets
were not so beautiful, and if the several
written accounts of the life lived there were
not powerfully beautiful too. Geologically
the islands are a continuation of the peninsula, heavily folded seams of stripped sandstone and slate on which the sea has
encroached and, in doing so, changed everything. The humps of the Great Blasket, the
biggest of the islands, rising to 1,000 feet
(300 metres) on the north edge, begin hardly
more than a mile from Dunmore Head. It is
three and a half miles (six kilometres) long.
Beyond it, to the left, is Inishvickillaune
(privately owned by Charles Haughey,
former *taoiseach* or prime minister), with an
erratic history of occupation, and Inis na
Bro, with Tearacht hidden behind the big
island. Over to the north looms the sharp-
toothed silhouette of Inishtooskert, rather

like a miniature Skellig Michael. Much closer in lies the plain of Beginish, overlooked
by the ruined village of the Great Blasket.

From the mainland, using field-glasses,
you can see the ruins of Great Blasket, and
the sheep that have been left to graze by
those who own or have inherited land. One
or two of the houses have been restored for
basic habitation. Tourists go over on day-
trips and some people camp. For years after
the abandonment, the islands were visited
by Americans who had migrated as children
when a hundred or more people still lived
there. They were often shocked, quite unpre-
pared for the desolation, the short brutish
work that nature had made of their childhood world.

Nature had never been a dependable ally,
and the islanders had suffered its buffets. To
pay for their clothes and tobacco, they had

Guillemot, razorbill and kittiwake (anti-clockwise from
left) are three common sea-birds which during the
breeding season often occupy the same sheer,
ledged, coastal cliffs. The first two are auks: brilliant
fishers and underwater swimmers. The kittiwake is
particularly attractive and very graceful in flight.

taken what they could from it: fish from the sea, lobsters, seals, birds and eggs from their nests, rabbits from their warrens. They hunted thrushes and lifted unsuspecting puffins from their roosting holes. It was not Arcadia. But there was a wholeness, a harmony, a need each for the other, poetry, music, dance, deep humour, wry irony. They knew the land like their hands and read the sea like a blind man braille, telling its mood and motions by feel and touch through the taut skins of their air-light curraghs. And for all the hardship they could still wonder at the sunsets and seas and mists and the changing colours of the mainland mountains, and celebrate it all in ancient ritual dances. More than one ambitious young man crossed the sea in search of fortune, disembarked at Dunquin, climbed the pass below Mount Eagle and seeing for the first time little Ventry and its two hundred houses ahead, turned about and returned home, deciding the world was too impossibly crowded for comfort.

It was the decline of the herring shoals that did for the islanders in the end, though Richard Mersey in his book *The Hills of Cork and Kerry* points to something else. For Maurice O'Sullivan, one of the trio of native authors whose sublime books will continue to keep some memories of the islands alive, the neon sign of the Capitol Cinema in Dublin represented civilization's peak. The lure of modernity had been draining humans off the islands for years before the final break. We who revere the old ways never lived the life. The sinews in my neck are quite hidden.

That will not stop us going. The birds have not left. The outer islands in particular are home to many sea-birds: guillemots, razorbills, fulmars and various gulls, all of which are easily seen by day. Another species, which comes in and leaves by night, is more likely to be seen as shadows or heard as coos and shrieks. These are the Manx shearwaters, present in their thousands during the breeding season, and storm petrels, which appear in their tens of thousands. The female shearwaters lay one egg each, and the newly emerged chick would be vulnerable to gulls if it did not remain within a hillside burrow. Intensely security-conscious, the foraging parent birds – most of whose life is spent on the open ocean – float near the land as darkness comes and fly in only when they gauge it safe. On brightly moonlit nights they do not come at all, and the young must go hungry. This influx of birds, scarcely seen, hauntingly heard, almost touched, is one of the eeriest things in nature.

BEFORE YOU GO
Maps: OSI Discovery Series, map No. 70.
Guide-books: *The Blasket Islands* by J. and R. Stagles (O'Brien Press, 1980), *Twenty Years A-Growing* by M. O'Sullivan (OUP, 1983).

GETTING THERE
By sea: weather permitting (and it often fails to), a passenger ferry operates from Dunquin to Great Blasket, Apr–Oct, T: (066) 915 6422. The first boat leaves the mainland at 10 am and the last boat leaves the Blaskets at 5 or 6 pm.
By bus: summer Bus Eireann services from Killarney and Tralee stop at Dunquin twice a day, as do those from Dingle and Slea Head, T: (066) 712 3566.

WHERE TO STAY
Hotels and B&Bs: Kruger's, T: (066) 915 6127, is in Dunquin; Mrs Firtear, T: (066) 915 6120, and Mrs Long, T: (066) 915 9822, at Slea Head. Overlooking Ventry Bay are Mrs Murphy, T: (066) 915 9072, Mrs O'Connor, T: (066) 915 9947, and Mrs T. O'Shea, T: (066) 915 9050.
Youth hostels: Dunquin has an An Oige hostel, T: (066) 915 6121. A small private hostel on Great Blasket opens in summer. For details contact BF.
Outdoor living: camping is permitted free on most parts of Great Blasket.

ACTIVITIES
Walking: there are some good, but unmarked, walks along the length of Great Blasket. The Dingle Way passes through Dunquin and Slea Head.
Bird-watching: the islands are a good place to see many varieties of sea-bird in season, including guillemot, razorbill, fulmar, storm petrel and Manx shearwater.
Sightseeing: the Blasket Centre in Dunquin records the islanders' history, T: (066) 915 6444/915 6371.

FURTHER INFORMATION
Tourist offices: the BF office in Dingle is open in summer, T: (066) 915 1188; in Tralee all year round, T: (066) 712 1288.

Iveragh Peninsula

Largest of the great promontories and home to Ireland's highest mountain, Carrantuohill; includes Killarney National Park

A hundred years ago they called the railway round the Iveragh peninsula, opened in 1893, the 'Grand Atlantic Coast Route'. Roads have replaced the railway track now and people speak of the 'Ring of Kerry'. It is not, in point of fact, a ring nor does it encircle Kerry. The Dingle, part of the Beara, much of the Shannon estuary and all inland Kerry fall outside it.

The Iveragh lies between some of the finest sights in the world: the Skellig rocks ten miles (16 kilometres) out to sea to the west, and to the east, Killarney, which remains, if you can find or imagine it without tourists and the carnivorous end of the tourist trade (say on a sunny weekday morning in January), the equal of Eden. Most of the peninsula's approximately 40 by 17 miles (64 by 27 kilometres) is occupied by mountains, of which there are four main ranges: the Glenbeigh horseshoe in the north, with the outlying Knocknadobar to its west; the Dunkerrons running close to

the south coast; the Mangerton range overlapping them and continuing eastward; and MacGillicuddy's Reeks, north of Mangerton and west of Lough Leane.

Among all these stands the highest mountain in Ireland, Carrantuohill, one of the Reeks (3,404 feet/1,038 metres). There are five more mountains over 3,000 feet (in other words, 'Munros', a tiresome distinction which has people who cannot tackle their mountain-climbing in a way more in tune with the landscape notching up peaks as others do railway-engine numbers), and a total of 63 over 2,000 feet (610 metres). Among so many peaks, rainfall is high, reaching 140 inches (350 centimetres) a year in certain parts. That and the relative warmth make mist a frequent obstacle and danger to climbers.

Not that obstacles and dangers put climbers off – for many they are among the main attractions. The real draw, however, must be the sights of that removed vertiginous world, suspended behind its excluding wall of rock, unpeopled, unbuilt, close to that cardinal rawness in which the earth's heavings and convulsions and contractions left it millions of years ago, sharing its plane of existence only with the sky. It is a world of peaks and dips, of neat sharp cones and long lolloping sprawls of mountain, shimmering wet curtains of solid stone, lake cavities ladled out of the rock by retreating ice, water

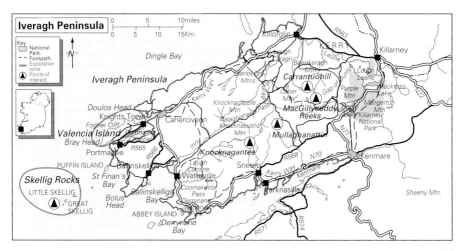

Along with fuchsia and estallonia, gorse – seen here beside a weed-cracked road west of Kenmare on the Iveragh peninsula – is one of the pervading glories of the early Irish summer.

as lake, water as stream, water as thin white cataract, bouncing off rock stairs in a precipitous plummet, water – rarefied – as the air you breathe and the mist that blinds you, as the cloud coiling up the valley below you, water as the contents of the corrie that offers the hot and sticky climber the shock and bliss of cold immersion. There are cols and aiguilles and saddlebacks and steps and chimneys and nunataks and sugar loaves and soggy bogs.

Each of these ranges provide fine climbs. Richard Mersey, author of *The Hills of Cork and Kerry*, who has been up them all, says the 2,539-foot (774-metre) Mullaghanattin is 'Kerry's finest peak ... the Matterhorn of Ireland'. It rises towards the eastern end of the Dunkerrons, above the lower valley of the River Caragh, being only a few miles from the Reeks, the Mangerton range and the Glenbeigh horseshoe. Taken from its northern side it presents you with toils and

thrills and wonderful views, unlike the long steep and steady slope of the southern access: 'monotonous and ghastly', according to Mersey. Not far from Mullaghanattin's summit is a memorial to a climber of world class and experience who died on a stretch many might treat too lightly. Indeed most writers emphasize the treachery of apparently easy climbs. The large numbers of people climbing Carrantuohill, often in guided groups, becoming for an instant the highest people on Irish soil, give an impression that the enterprise is simple. It is, in truth, not very difficult, but there are real dangers. There are more accidents on this one mountain than on all the others in the county put together. Most arise from the over-confidence of the inexperienced.

The blessing for cyclist and driver is that roads cross these ranges of mountains, and tracks take you to an impressive array of views. There is a wonderful picture of Mullaghanattin from the pass called Ballaghisheen, on the westward road to

A dramatic cloudscape heralds the dusk near Sneem on the Kenmare river.

Waterville between the lesser peaks of Knocknacusha and Knocknagapple. Ballaghisheen means the road of Oisin, poet, warrior, one of the great figures of Irish myth, son of the hero Finn. Oisin was here on this pass, when the goddess Niamh of the golden hair carried him off to the land of promise (beyond the sea to the west) to live in perpetual youth and bliss provided he never touched his native land again.

Eastward, across the main body of the Reeks, the Gap of Dunloe, with its river and string of lakes, cuts through from north to south, isolating the final eastern peaks of Shehy and the Purple Mountains. The Gap marks, roughly, the western end of the district of lakes, mountains, waterfalls, cliffs, islands, castles and other visual delights known collectively after the little town of Killarney. This loveliness is adulterated for much of the time by the massive presence of people and their traces. (The traces extend a few miles west to Carrantuohill's summit, which supports not only a large steel cross but a tide of sweet and cigarette papers, cans and other jetsam.) Guides and boatmen and jarvies with their jaunting cars open their mouths along geological faults to produce smiles that have coaxed money out of the unwary for years and will for years more. But it is not too difficult to evade them and to enjoy the three principal lakes (Lough Leane, Muckross Lake and Upper Lake), the caves and cascades, and the rocks that thrilled Queen Victoria, drawing a poem out of Tennyson and a serenade from Britten. Ladies' View, just above the Upper Lake on the road from Kenmare, is as good a place as any from which to survey the scene with no more effort, if you are in a car, than turning the head. More dramatic panoramas are offered from the peaks of Torc mountain and Mangerton to the east, and Purple mountain, accessible from the Gap of Dunloe, to the west.

As always, you need only stir a few yards from the tourist beat to find lesser-known beauties and curiosities. There are the queer rock sculptures made by water eating away the carboniferous limestone around Lough Leane and Muckross (the district divides neatly between carboniferous rock in the north and old red sandstone in the south, which as in all these south-western peninsulas, erupted through the limestone to create the main heights). There is also the wide variety of plants, many of them unexpected in these islands, flourishing on lime or the more acid sandstone, on the rain and moisture-laden air, and normally benign temperatures. Snow, on its rare visits, stays high on the mountains, and even frost is not a common sight.

Ancient woodlands survive in Killarney National Park. From the lake-side limestone of Muckross rise sizeable stands of yew. Oak and, to a lesser extent, birch and holly and hazel make up the largest area of native woodland in the country. Among smaller, shrubby plants, the strawberry tree (*Arbutus unedo*) thrives in the wild, while thorn-apples (*Datura stramonium*), tree-ferns (family *Cyatheaceae*), numerous bamboos (genus *Bambusa*), mesembryanthemums and others proliferate in those gardens which fulfil their soil requirements. Two saxifrages, and the insect-eating greater butterwort, are among the colonists from the Iberian peninsula.

During the tourist season, the Ring of Kerry can seem crowded – in contrast to the Beara and other southern peninsulas. They will afford you a beach to yourself in June and September if not in August. The Ring of Kerry will assuredly not. The southern sections of road and coast west from Kenmare are relatively dull. At Parknasilla the prettiness is like pictures in frames: not wild, not quite real. (Shaw stayed in the Great Southern Hotel here to write parts of *Saint Joan*.) At Derrynane, however, things are much better. Derrynane Abbey, once the home of Daniel O'Connell, cleverest and most cunning of the prophets and campaigners of Irish nationalism, stands restored at the head of Derrynane Bay. There is also a superb sandy beach, with access at low tide to Abbey Island.

Scariff Island, a few miles further west, is a bigger affair, about a mile from end to end with formidable coastal cliffs. The wildlife here includes the petrels, shearwaters and puffins which frequent and nest on so many islands around these coasts. For a week or two a year, the Marquess of Waterford and his sons are dropped in without victuals but with guns in order to acquire them, in the form of seals, seagulls and rabbits. Their home is a wonderful Vanbrugh house in a beautiful demesne in east Waterford. I suppose they own this too. Somebody I know owns a small island not far from here. I think an aged relation left it to him. On his next visit to these parts he hurried down to the shore, from which he had been given to understand it would be easily seen. It was not. A local man explained: 'You'd have to be waiting for the tide to go out for the island to emerge from the water.'

This western end of the Iveragh is delectable. From the pass of Coomakesta (north of Derrynane and providing a first distant view of the pointed Skellig rocks), the Atlantic, innumerable islands, inland mountains, the grand profiles of Dingle and Beara, crescent strands and tumbling cliffs are constantly reshuffled into new panoramas. The prospects from the road along the south of Lough Currane are beautiful, and the area affords a good starting point for climbs in the western Dunkerrons. The next road right leads along the rising Inny valley

to the Reeks and the meeting point of all the Iveragh ranges. But keeping to the coast takes you round the sweep of Ballinskelligs Bay, and uphill to overlook St Finan's Bay, a wilder affair exposed to everything wind and ocean can throw at it. Puffin Island, rich in bird life but not (for that reason) open to the public, forms the north end of the bay. Northward and below is Valencia Island.

The northern section of the Ring is a wonderful land to explore, both on the seaward and landward sides. It boasts an abundance of walks among climbable hills, little lakes, pretty bays and rocks, with the continual presence to the north of the Dingle's bumpy silhouettes. Before Glenbeigh, a comfortable resort, the pinnacled wall of the Glenbeigh horseshoe curves round its clutch of corries. Out of town, a right turn leads for three or more miles past Lough Caragh, where a boat may be hired, to an unlikely refreshment of woods (mainly oak) and grassy glades, with streams purling under stone bridges and down gentle slopes. It was once a spot favoured for shooting, and the lake still draws fishermen. Above, the brotherhood of MacGillicuddy's Reeks continue their timeless conclave.

BEFORE YOU GO

Maps: OSI Discovery Series, map Nos 78, 83, 84; OSI Explorer series, Killarney National Park, 1:25,000.
Guide-books: *Walk Guide Southwest* by Seán O'Suilleabháin (Gill & Macmillan, 1997); *The Hills of Cork and Kerry* by Richard Mersey (Alan Sutton and Gill & Macmillan, 1987); *The Kerry Way Map Guide* (Cork Kerry Tourism, 1992).

GETTING THERE

By car: to reach the Iveragh peninsula and the Ring of Kerry from Killarney, follow the R562 (north-west) to Killorglin, then join the N70 towards Caherciveen, which runs right round the edge of the peninsula.
By rail: the nearest station is

Killarney. There are 4 services daily from Cork and 5 from Dublin (Heuston), T: (066) 712 3522.
By bus: Bus Eireann provide regular services from most major towns to Killarney. The Mon–Sat service from Killarney to Waterville goes to Caherciveen. A summer bus runs from Tralee to Killarney and then round the Ring of Kerry, terminating back in Tralee. Contact Tralee Bus Station for full timetable details, T: (066) 712 3566.

WHERE TO STAY

Hotels: the 4-star Caragh Lodge, T: (066) 976 9115, e-mail: caraghl@iol.ie, and the 3-star Glendalough House, T: (066) 976 9156, e-mail: deskerry@iol.ie, are on the shores of

Lough Caragh. The 18th-century Glencar House is at the foot of MacGillicuddy's Reeks, T: (066) 976 0102, e-mail: country@iol.ie.
B&Bs: try Mrs O'Leary, Killarney, T: (064) 33351; Mrs O'Sullivan, Sneem, T: (064) 45181; or Mrs O'Connor, Kenmare, T: (064) 41682, e-mail: bruachan@iol.ie.
Youth hostels: there are 3 independent hostels in Killarney: the Park, T: (064) 32119; Killarney Railway Hostel, T: (064) 35299; and Neptune's Town Hostel, T: (064) 35255, e-mail: neptune@tinet.ie. Just outside Killarney are the Fossa Holiday Hostel, Fossa, T: (064) 31497; the Peacock Farm Hostel, Muckross, T: (064) 33557; and Donash Lodge, Longfield, T: (066) 64554. Sive Hostel is at

Caherciveen, T: (066) 947 2717.
At Caherdaniel there is the Village Hostel, T: (066) 947 5277,
e-mail: skelliga@iol.ie, and the
Carrigbeg Country Hostel,
T: (066) 947 5229. An Oige hostels are at Killarney (the Killarney International Hostel, just
to the west of the town), T:
(064) 31240; Ballinskelligs, T:
(066) 947 9229, and Beaufort,
T: (064) 34712.

Outdoor living: there is a good
choice of camp-sites on the
Iveragh peninsula, including
Mannix Point CCP, Caherciveen, T: (066) 947 2806;
West's Holiday Park near Killorglin, T: (066) 976 1240; and
at Waterville, T: (066) 947 4191.
At Killarney are the Beech
Grove CCP, T: (064) 31727,
and Flesk CCP, T: (064) 31704.
White Villa Farm Caravan and
Camping Site, T: (064) 32456,
and Fossa CCP, T: (064) 31497,
are closest to Killarney National Park.

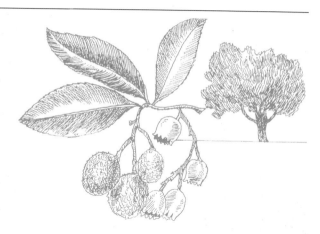

The strawberry tree has pretty white pendant bell-flowers and a red fruit that looks like a strawberry but is in fact quite inedible. A native of Spain that has found its way to Ireland without human agency and settled successfully, it abounds in the Killarney area.

ACTIVITIES
Walking: the Kerry Way is a
134-mile (215-km) waymarked
route, which starts and ends in
Killarney, running right round
the Iveragh peninsula. It is divided into 9 sections: 1, Killarney to Black Valley (13
miles/20 km); 2, Gearhameen
to Glencar (13 miles/20 km); 3,
Glencar to Glenbeigh (11
miles/17 km); 4, Glenbeigh to
Foilmore (13 miles/20 km); 5,
Foilmore to Dromod (11
miles/17 km); 6, Dromod to
Castlecove (11 miles/17 km); 7,
Castlecove to Tahilla (14
miles/22 km); 8, Tahilla to Kenmare (13 miles/20 km); 9, Kenmare to Killarney (15 miles/24
km). MacGillicuddy's Reeks

The cloud-capped line of the
Slieve Miskish, on the Beara, is
visible across the Kenmare river in
this night-view from Caherdaniel,
on the Iveragh peninsula.

provide exciting ridge walking
with lovely views. Carrantuohill
is best approached from either
the head of Black Valley
(south) or from Hag's Glen
(north). A traverse of the entire
range from the Gap of Dunloe
to Beenkeragh or Caher is a
long, strenuous but highly rewarding walk. Classic Tours, T:
(064) 34677, can provide further information and organize
walking tours.
Cycling: it is possible to cycle
right round the Iveragh peninsula, along the Kerry Way.
Bikes can be hired in Killarney
from O'Sullivan's, T: (064)
31282; O'Neill's, T: (064)
319700; and Killarney Rent-A-Bike, T: (064) 32578.
Riding: contact Cois Linne
Riding Stables, Caherciveen, T:
(087) 236 4533. Killarney Riding Stables in Ballydowney
arrange rides through Killarney
National Park, T: (064) 31686,
e-mail: krs@tinet.ie.
Fishing: the whole of this region offers excellent lake and
river fishing. Lough Currane is
particularly good for trout;
Lough Leane and some of the

smaller lakes are good for
brown trout. There is no coarse
fishing in the area, but contact
Michael Fenton in Castlecove
for sea-angling, T: (066) 947
5305. Permits, licences and information are available from
O'Neill's in Killarney, T: (064)
31970.
Watersports: contact
Ballinskelligs Watersports, T:
(066) 947 9182, and Skelligs
Aquatics Ltd in Caherdaniel,
T: (066) 947 5277.
Sightseeing: there are quite a
few important archaeological
sites on the peninsula. For
more information see BF's *Ring
of Kerry Guide* or *The Iveragh
Peninsula: An Archaeological
Survey of South Kerry* edited by
J. Sheehan and A. O'Sullivan
(Cork University Press, 1996).

FURTHER INFORMATION
Tourist offices: there are seasonal BF offices in Caherciveen, T: (066) 72589, and
Kenmare, T: (064) 41233. The
office in Killarney is open all
year, T: (064) 31633.
Park office: Killarney National
Park, T: (064) 31440.

111

Valencia Island

An island off the north-west corner of the Iveragh peninsula, with fine, bird-thronged cliffs. Terminal, from 1865, of the first transatlantic cable

A bridge at Portmagee takes traffic to Valencia, given its name by the Spanish merchants who frequented it. (There is much said and written about the dark Iberian looks encountered on these western coasts as far up as Galway.) The island's capital, Knights Town, is at its eastern end. It basks in old glories: a fine harbour, the old seat – now sold and sold again – of the Knights of Kerry, descendants of one of three brothers supposedly given uniquely hereditary knighthoods by Edward III after a hard-fought battle in Scotland. From 1866 well into the 20th century Knights Town was the eastern

terminal of the Atlantic telegraph cable which gave it the handsome sea-facing terraces where employees once lived. Now history has abandoned it. The bridge to link Valencia to the mainland was sited, to the dismay of many, beside Portmagee. The manufacture of billiard tables from the slate quarries under Geokaun (888 ft/270 m) virtually died out a hundred years ago. Knights Town sleeps on with a smile on its lips. It has a renowned diving centre, where visitors may explore underwater life, along with boats, decent food, nice places to stay, and the rich subtropical flora of the garden of Glanleam, the Knights' old home. It is a quiet and underpopulated island, with dramatic outcrops in the Fogher cliffs west of Geokaun and at Bray Head, at its extreme west.

Before you go *Maps:* OSI Discovery Series, map No. 83.

Getting there *By car:* from Tralee follow the N70 to Caherciveen. A mile down the road,

take the R565 to Knights Town. *By rail:* the nearest station is Killarney. There are 4 services daily from Dublin (Heuston) and Cork, T: (066) 712 3522. *By bus:* a daily service from Tralee and Killarney stops at Caherciveen and Waterville, with additional buses in summer, T: (066) 712 3566.

Where to stay *B&Bs:* on Valencia Island try Shealane House, T: (066) 947 6354. *Youth hostels:* apart from an An Oige Hostel, T: (066) 947 6141, there are 2 independents: the Ring Lyne, T: (066) 947 6103, and the Royal Pier, T: (066) 947 6144.

Activities *Cycling:* bikes can be hired from Curran's, T: (066) 947 6247. *Fishing:* for sea-angling trips, contact Dan Mc-Crohan, T: (066) 947 6142. *Watersports:* Valencia Island is a popular scuba-diving centre. Contact Des Lavelle, T: (066) 947 6124. *Bird-watching:* Des Lavelle also organizes day trips from Valencia to Puffin Island.

Further information: from the seasonal Heritage Centre in Caherciveen, T: (066) 947 2589.

The Skelligs

Two steep sea rocks famous for their breeding birds, monastic remains and isolated grandeur

In the great medieval best-seller *The Voyage of St Brendan*, the intrepid and godly sailor and his crew come upon an island on which is a very large tree. Not a leaf of this tree is visible for its branches are covered with large white birds: one flies down – his wings tinkling like little bells – to explain that they are the spirits of those who fell from heaven with Lucifer, and now spend holy days and festivals singing the Creator's praises from dawn to dusk in penance.

It seems impossible that this description could have been inspired by any bird other than the gannet, which lives and breeds not in trees but on a few isolated rocks pitched in the seas round Britain and Ireland. The biggest Irish colony is settled on the Lesser Skellig rock, eight or so miles to the west of the Iveragh peninsula. There seems to be no particular reason for gannets representing the spirits of sinners, but that they should be thought of as glorifying God seems wholly appropriate.

You get to the Skelligs by boat from Portmagee, Knights Town or Ballinskelligs, weather permitting. The journey may take three-quarters of an hour each way, and a curious process takes place in its course. On the mainland, it goes without saying, humans call the tune. Birds, when you see them, are peripheral, glosses on the margin.

Slowly, as the boat chops through the waves, you move into a bird world. Increasing numbers fly near or over, carrying fish or grass for nests, or engaged in some less patent purpose. Almost from the start there are individuals afloat or diving, but as the miles go by they become groups and then whole fleets of puffin, gannet, guillemot or gull. They take no notice of you, expecting no harm. You are the gloss now, moving through their space as if invisible. They fly, cry, dive, plunge or ride the waves as indifferent to your existence as you were to that of sparrows back on land.

The lesser of the two Skellig rocks grows as you approach it, in silhouette a tableau of sharp crags. It seems to be a dull, yellow-white colour, which does not square with your knowledge that both rocks, like so many of these south-western promontories and islands, consist of red sandstone and slate. The steady level of noise, too, comes out to meet you: an unrelieved crescendo of baying, braying, cawing and shrieking. An acrid whiff of guano hangs in the air. There are birds above and all around you, reminiscent of a beehive in alarm, except that this is routine pandemonium, not panic, and you are not regarded as either danger or voyeur. You are not regarded at all.

The yellowy-white is simply solid gannet. Their heads and necks are yellow, and their wings end in a triangle of black, and everything else is snow-white. You can infer the shape of the rock from the shape the gannets collectively make, filling every available niche, ledge and cranny, sitting, preening, standing, wing-flapping, waving their necks in display, disgorging or accepting fish, flying off or alighting, and all the time maintaining a raucous babble. There are over 20,000 nesting pairs at peak season.

The boat chugs slowly into a narrow channel, vertical black rock rising high on each side. No gannets here – they clearly prefer the open air and the panorama. This confined space is a kittiwake tenement, tier after tier of these neatly pretty gulls sitting on eggs in rock-based nests composed, like swallows' nests, of miscellaneous materials assembled and glued together.

Boat trips follow a standard route. There

The gannet's headlong dive into the sea, the closing of its wings just before entry, and its re-emergence with the fish it spotted a hundred feet up, can be seen up to fifty miles away from whichever raucous rocky colony the search for prey has brought it. There are half a dozen colonies round the Irish coast, some with over 20,000 breeding pairs.

is no landing allowed on the Lesser Skellig, and you move on a mile or more to the Greater, where you can disembark and climb about five hundred rock-hewn steps to the restored remains of an early-Christian monastery, and a couple of hundred feet more to the peak. On the way up, you will – at the right time of year – find yourself walking feet away from nesting guillemots and razorbills and an arm's length from kittiwakes. Higher up, if you could stay till they return at the end of the day, you would have to wait for puffins to waddle out of your way on the steps. The burrows in which they nest often riddle the earth on either side of these ancient steps.

The monastery provokes thoughts of men prepared to endure a punishing wilderness for the sake of their god, a tradition imparted by the desert hermits of Sinai, received and continued with uncanny enthusiasm by the Irish. They even adopted the word desert – it survives to this day on the sites of many monasteries, however green and lush and wet their setting. No written records survive the monastic occupation of Skellig Michael, which lasted from the 7th to the 10th century perhaps. Everything we know about the monks' way of life involves guess-work,

113

The south-western corner of Ireland breaks up into innumerable splintered fragments, headlands with off-shore rocks and islands, among them Lamb's Head, last in a line of hilly promontories running west from Castlecove on the Iveragh coast.

though given the climate, it is certain they were cut off in these narrow confines, above sheer precipices, often in dense mist or rain or violent gale, for weeks on end. They must have fished. Probably they grew vegetables (as 19th-century lighthouse keepers did). Perhaps they had grain to grind and bake. The water they drank must have been rain, caught in hollowed-out stone or rock basins. The rabbits that thrive here now were not brought in, it is thought, until the 19th century. A faith that may not be conceivable in our times must have driven them. An insecurity with which we are becoming more and more familiar finally did for them. Vikings, it seems, raided the island, and in the end made continued residence impossible.

Nothing in Ireland makes more impression on me – and on many others – than these two sequestered, sea-whipped rocks. They stand as a testament to the faith of man in a world beyond this one, and to man's trust in nature, when he keeps in check his talents for killing, maiming and despoiling, and regards the wonders of the world with seemly awe.

BEFORE YOU GO
Maps: OSI Discovery Series, map No. 83.

GETTING THERE
By sea: Sean Feehan runs boats from Ballinskelligs on the mainland, T: (066) 947 9182. He also offers diving and sea-angling. Brendan Casey, T: (066) 947 2437, and Patrick Murphy, T: (066) 947 7156, cross from Portmagee, Des and Pat Lavelle from Valencia Island, T: (066) 947 6124.

WHERE TO STAY
B&Bs: Bay House is at Derrynane, on the mainland, T: (066) 947 5404, e-mail: derrynanebay

house@tinet.ie; Mrs Curran is near Cahirciveen, T: (066) 947 2844.
Youth hostels: in Caherdaniel is the Village Hostel, T: (066) 947 5277, and the Carrigbeg Country Hostel, T: (066) 947 5229.
Outdoor living: there are campsites in Waterville, T: (066) 947 4191, e-mail: waterville caravans@tinet.ie, and in Caherdaniel, the Wave Crest Caravan Park, T: (066) 947 5188.

ACCESS
Landing on the Lesser Skellig is not permitted.

ACTIVITIES
Climbing: scrambling enthusi-

asts will enjoy the climb up the 712-ft (217-m) jagged rock of Skellig Michael.
Bird-watching: both islands are home to a large variety of seabirds including storm petrels, kittiwakes and puffins. The Lesser Skellig supports a large gannet colony. Viewing can be had off-shore. Des Lavell organizes trips, T: (066) 947 6124, or contact Bird Watch Ireland, T: (01) 280 4322, www.bird watchireland.ie.

FURTHER INFORMATION
Tourist office: Caherciveen BF is open all year, T: (064) 31633; Waterville, T: (066) 917 4646, is open May–Sept.

Beara Peninsula

One of the great south-western promontories, between the Kenmare river and Bantry Bay, containing the Caha mountain range

West Cork and west Kerry contain between them the wildest parts of Ireland, mostly made up of rather secretive mountain groups or chains with many peaks over 2,000 feet (600 metres). Formed of red sandstone with slate fringes, raised, tipped, fissured and faulted by the Armorican upheaval of 300 million years ago, these ranges take a roughly east-to-west direction, narrowing down to the promontories that are now (because of their appeal to outsiders) the pride and joy of the region. Each one ends with an afterthought of islands.

Mountains, precipitous coast and scattered islands are the three land-forms that are most likely to be ignored by farmers. Nevertheless, most of the islands were pastured at one time, and some still are, while the lower slopes of the mountains were covered by oak forest until the end of the 16th century, when it was thoroughly cropped for iron-smelting and ship-building. Despite these qualifications, wildness, in the rare but real sense of land virtually unaffected by man, is present here to a degree not found elsewhere in Ireland.

The heights of the Caha mountains, with their almost universally steep sides, narrow serpentine valleys, cliffs and corries, occupy the centre of the peninsula, falling to the long inlets of sea that lie both north and south: respectively the Kenmare river and Bantry Bay. Westward, the range narrows to the caudal spine of the Slieve Miskish, its mostly steep and high cliffs deeply indented by the work of the sea. This process has created several natural harbours, including the well-protected anchorage of Bear Haven, an important Royal Naval base while Britain and Ireland were united (and for nearly twenty years afterwards). In spite of this kind of activity the Beara has kept to itself down the centuries. The clan of O'Sullivan, whose name easily outnumbers all others in these parts, has not always been quick to welcome outsiders. During the Tudor conquests their resistance had cruel and disastrous consequences, bringing English landlords, copper mines and the naval garrison.

Beara's essential isolation survived up to a generation ago when there were only 65 tourist beds in the whole peninsula. (One English town, Blackpool, to go to the other extreme, has 120,000 tourist beds.) Things have changed. The population is drastically reduced: no more than half what it was a hundred years ago. Fishing, which in 1891 kept a thousand men in work, died out in the 20th century but has since returned, and Castletownbere is a big centre for trawlers and fish-processing. There are plenty of places offering food, accommodation and a warm welcome. But nowhere in Beara has tourism developed to the same extent as in the two peninsulas to the north. Which makes it in some ways my own favourite.

A road goes round the margin of the peninsula, though often enough, keeping a straighter course than the shoreline, it leaves access to the sea to little diverging lanes. These can lead along quiet foothills to lovely bays, creeks and harbours. On the south coast, the further west, the quieter. Towards the east, frost-free Glengarriff and its neighbours are overdeveloped, too groomed and cosy, swathed in rhododendron, fuchsia, Chilean myrtle (*Clethra arborea*) and the so-called strawberry tree (*Arbutus unedo*), which, flourishing here and in south-western

France and Spain, but not in between, belongs to those several expatriates known as the Lusitanian flora.

West of Castletownbere, with one exception, the artifice has gone. There are wild cliffs, wild rocks, castle-capped headlands, broad bays, palely alluring strands – especially, these last, on the north coast. The exception is down a lane to the left a couple of miles west of Castletownbere. Almost immediately there is a bridge and a pretty inlet of the sea, hemmed by rhododendrons and other shrubs and trees. Among all this is a story-book gothic gate-lodge consisting of a compact cluster of towers, crenellations, round walls, slit windows, turrets. You pay your fee into an honesty box and walk (or drive) into a grand park, with the broadening inlet on the left and the huge shambling ruins of a 19th-century Anglo-Irish family extravaganza on the right. Further on again come the sparse remains of the medieval O'Sullivan Beare castle, beautifully set among yews and other trees, beside the straits that divide the mainland from Bear Island.

This western end of the Beara is a place where the wild and the tamed come together, and where some of the main themes of the peninsula's story are united. The O'Sullivans sided with the Spanish in their attempts – towards the end of Queen Elizabeth's reign – to settle in Ireland with a view to ousting the English. The Battle of Kinsale, at the end of 1601, utterly dashed Spanish aspirations, but the O'Sullivans held out against the English, here at Dunboy, for a further six months. Two massacres ended their resistance: the one on Dursey Island, the other, after two more weeks, here. The Irish chief, Donal O'Sullivan Beare, who had escaped the siege, led a tragic but heroic march of survivors to sanctuary in the north of Ireland, from where many were shipped to permanent exile in Spain. The castle was destroyed by the victors.

By the 18th century, the Dunboy demesne and much of the peninsula belonged to an Anglo-Irish family with mining interests in Cornwall, the Puxleys. They seem to have been mercenary, mean, mostly absentee and punitive, but for many years they engaged in the important local industry of smuggling and got on well with others, notably the remaining O'Sullivans, doing so. But the real Puxley allegiance was to the crown in London, while the O'Sullivans preferred to serve the interests of the Spanish or Austrians and supply their armies with disgruntled Irishmen. Differences deepened. In 1757 a Puxley was murdered. In due course the responsible O'Sullivan was besieged in his house and shot dead as he emerged in a bid to escape.

When copper ore was discovered in the mountains behind Allihies, the Puxleys grew fat on the profits. Nobody else did. When mineworkers' tools were worn by use, and consequently weighed less, appropriate deductions were made from their wage packets. The grandiose pile whose substantial ruin was passed on the way to the old castle was erected in the mid-19th century. Inside and out, it was a lump of gross ostentation. But eventually copper ore ran thin, income slumped, and the Puxley family returned for the most part to Cornwall. In their absence in 1921 the old IRA, which used the grounds for manoeuvres, set fire to the house. As many have pointed out, being a ruin suits it better.

The themes of Beara thread out east and west, to mountains and coast. O'Sullivans are everywhere still. Puxleys are nowhere, but their story is told in Daphne du Maurier's novel *Hungry Hill*, which cloaks all the characters in pseudonyms. There is a Hungry Hill, a steep and imposing peak overhanging the road and good for climbs a few miles east of Castletownbere, but it is not – as the book makes it out to be – the site of the copper mines. These mines are located above Allihies, facing the Atlantic at the west end of Slieve Miskish.

The gloom of Dursey Island, at the peninsula's tip, is said to have come down in part from the fearful massacres of 1602 (though there has, in truth, been much to depress it in between). Another novel, *Two Chiefs of Dunboy*, stirringly recounts the 18th-century feud between Puxleys and O'Sullivans. It was written by the historian J. A. Froude, while staying at Derreen, Irish home of Lord Lansdowne, overlooking Kilmakillogue

harbour on the north coast, ten miles west of Kenmare. A 17th-century ancestor of Lansdowne, Sir William Petty, was granted huge estates hereabouts. It was a wild territory then, no doubt, though not as wild as another historian, Macaulay, with the misunderstanding of an alien culture common among colonizers, painted it: the haunt of wolves, and 'half-naked savages, who could not speak a word of English, made themselves burrows in the mud and lived on roots and sour milk'. Petty, like his first patron Cromwell, tackled tasks thoroughly, opening ironworks (for which he felled oak forests), lead mines and sea fisheries. He also put forward a plan for solving the Irish problem: convey 20,000 marriageable Irish girls to England, and 20,000 English to Ireland. The latter's children would be brought up as Protestants loyal to England. A tough but ingenious policy, and more humane than straightforward annihilation of the natives, as practised in America north and south.

You see the beauty of this part of Beara as you come over the Healy Pass on the long hairpin haul from the south side to the north, with its vista of lakes, fields, woods, the compact symmetry of Knockatee, the sea beyond, and the patrician profile of the Iveragh peninsula beyond that: a promised-land vision. For the climber, the best of the region is to the right and left of the pass itself – the varied delights of walking in the Caha range. There is a lake far below the pass to the north-west, called Glanmore. A considerable climb starts from the horseshoe valley to its west, up the mountain called Tooth mountain on the half-inch map. In *The Hills of Cork and Kerry* Richard Mersey (a descendant of Petty and the Petty-Fitzmaurices of Derreen) brings these mountains to vivid life with detailed description, entertaining anecdote and the kind of knowledge only experience gives. He warns against collapsing walls, for instance, but insists that farmers make them purposely that way. A sheep will easily get over a firm wall, but will keep well away from one that a quick test shows might fall on it. Mersey calls that climb from Glanmore 'the crown of climbs'.

BEFORE YOU GO

Maps: OSI Discovery Series, map No. 84.

Guide-books: *Best Walks in Ireland* by David Marshall (Constable, 1996) includes walks from Allihies to Beara; *Walk Guide Southwest of Ireland* by Sean O'Sulleabhaín (Gill & Macmillan, 1997); *The Beara and Mizen Head Peninsulas* by Barry Keane (The Collins Press, 1997); and *The Beara Way Map Guide* (Cork Kerry Tourism).

GETTING THERE

By car: from Killarney take the N71 south through Kenmare to Glengarriff. To circle the Beara peninsula, follow the R572 to Cahermore, then the R575 and the R571 back to Kenmare.

By rail: there are 4 trains daily to Killarney from Cork and 5 from Dublin, T: (01) 836 6222.

By bus: Bus Eireann, T: (021) 506066, run daily services from Cork to Bantry and Glengarriff, with 3 buses a week to Castletownbere. Berehaven Buses, T: (027) 70007, run a Mon–Sat service between Bantry and Castletownbere.

WHERE TO STAY

Hotels and B&Bs: there is a good selection on the peninsula. In Glengarriff, Mrs Guerin's is on the waterfront, T: (027) 63079. Mrs McGurn's is in Castletownbere, T: (027) 70508. Mrs O'Sullivan's is on the Castletownberehaven Coast Road at Ardgroom Inward, T: (027) 74369; and Muxnaw Lodge in Kenmare overlooks the bay, T: (064) 41252.

Youth hostels: the independent hostels on the peninsula are the Village Hostel at Allihies, T: (027) 73107; Murphy's Village Hostel, Glengarriff, T: (027) 63555; and the Fáilte Hostel, Kenmare, T: (064) 42333. An Oige hostels are at Cahermeelabo, outside Allihies, T: (027) 73014, and at Lauragh, T: (064) 83181.

Outdoor living: choose between Dowlings CCP, Glengarriff, T: (027) 63154; Creveen Lodge CCP, Lauragh, T: (064) 83131; Berehaven Camper & Amenity Park, Castletownbere, T: (027) 70700.

ACTIVITIES

Walking: the Caha Mountains form the backbone of the entire peninsula. The Sugar Loaf and Hungry Hill peaks offer well-marked short walks, and the long valleys are worth exploring. A traverse of the range, starting at Glengarriff, offers a good 2-day trek, the night spent at or near the Healy Pass. The 120-mile (196-km) Beara Way is a circular waymarked route starting from Glengarriff.

It is split into 9 stages: stage 1, Glengarriff to Adrigole (10 miles/16 km); 2, Adrigole to Castletownbere (14 miles/22 km); 3, circuit of Bere Island (13 miles/21 km); 4, Castletownbere to Allihies (8 miles/13 km); 5, Allihies to Dursey Sound (12 miles/19 km) with an additional 9-mile (15-km) section on Dursey Island itself; 6, Allihies to Ardgroom (14 miles/22 km); 7, Ardgroom to Tuosist (13 miles/21 km); 8, Tuosist to Kenmare, via Dowres (6 miles/10 km); 9, Kenmare to Glengarriff (15 miles/24 km).
Cycling: bikes can be hired from Raleigh Rent-A-Bike, T: (027) 70520, in Castletownbere. There is a good route round the coastline of the Beara peninsula; contact Cork Kerry Tourism for details.
Fishing: there is a brown trout lake just outside Glengarriff. Fishing-rights fees are payable

at the Maple Leaf pub.

FURTHER INFORMATION
Tourist offices: the nearest Cork Kerry Tourism offices are in Glengarriff, T: (027) 63084, open July–Aug, and Kenmare, T: (064) 41233, open Apr–Oct. Killarney, T: (064) 31633, is open all year. In summer, tourist information is available from a small shed next to the fire station in Castletownbere.
Ecology: Glengarriff woods are home to the speckled Kerry slug, which is found only on the peninsula and in other small areas of Kerry.

The large-flowered butterwort has been called the most beautiful of Irish flowering plants, its dainty violet flower swaying on a delicate stem over the broad rosette of green, sticky leves at its base: sticky for the purpose of trapping insects which are then digested by means of secreted chemicals.

The peaks and valleys of the Caha range on the Beara peninsula afford some of the finest mountain formations and scenery in Ireland.

Dursey

Island with a handful of inhabited cottages and with imposing cliffs at the west end of the Beara peninsula

I was alone, swaying in a windowed wooden box maybe ten feet by five, which shook and rumbled high above a swirling sea and margins of sharp rock, and slowly progressed from east to west. On the wall, the text of psalm 91: 'a thousand may fall dead beside you, ten thousand all round you, but you will not be harmed'. Beside it, in a bottle modelled into a statue of the Blessed Virgin, holy water. The flow of water in the strait below was reported to be the fastest on Ireland's periphery: too often too perilous for a reliable ferry. This was why the county council, 25 years before, had approved the installation of a cable car to convey passengers from the end of the Beara peninsula to Dursey Island, and why I was now winging down to the island's landing place. The journey – say 150 yards or metres – took five minutes.

Dursey is unfriendly, treeless, lacking all facilities to sustain or help the visitor and, in spite of cattle and sheep pasturing in wired fields, wild. *Farouche* might be the better word. If you walk – you have no other option – towards the west end, the first mile may suggest to you, as it did to me, life after a holocaust. There are cottages that look blasted, their slates grouted with cement; a young mother smoking and answering my greeting with an uncharming, unmusical note; a car the weather has vandalized;

a tractor that might have been reclaimed from the sea. Hardly more than seven or eight houses seem inhabited.

Others have commented on the surliness, the aloof independence of a population reduced from hundreds, cut off (till the cable car came) for weeks at a time by a treacherous flood, a people who have lost even their language in a couple of generations – perhaps, it occurs to me, for want of talking. It may have to do with the only recorded drama of their history, when in 1602 the English piked, impaled, shot and drowned three hundred men, women and children, and left the castle and church the ruins they remain, down by the harbour.

Beauty and interest are found here and there: grassy banks sliding away to sheer, 300-foot (91-m) drops into the liquid blue, hemmed by staves of yellow-lichened rock. Further west, approaching the terminal cliffs, are carpets of orchids, and the continual cautionary barrage in summer of meadow pipit, robin, stonechat and wheatear. It is a good place to see migrating sea-birds, but what have caused most surprise in recent years are sightings of smaller perching birds: warblers or finches blown wildly off course by Atlantic gales.

Naturally, the views are beautiful on fine days: long peninsulas to the north and south, bony headlands resting their chins on the sea, a scattering of islands. There are three islands of jutting rock out in the Atlantic beyond Dursey's tip: the Bull Rock three miles off, The Cow two, and The Calf one. The names refer to their relative sizes rather than their shapes. Gannets breed on the Bull Rock, taking the overflow,

perhaps, from the Skelligs to the north. The inimitable gannet, diving, plunging and emerging moustached by a large fish, is one of the most entrancing sights in this whole region.

There is nowhere to stay on Dursey, but permission to camp would be readily given. I myself preferred to run again the gauntlet of the cheerless straggle of houses known in some quarters as a village, and churn across the swirling strait without further delay.

Before you go: OSI Discovery Series, map No. 84.

Getting there *By car:* from Kenmare take the R571 and R575 (west) to Cahermore, then the R572 to the cable-car terminus – the only cable car in Ireland – which connects the island to the mainland, weather permitting. Services run 9–11 am, 2.30–4.30 pm, and sometimes 7–8 pm, although cattle may get precedence over humans, T: (027) 73017.

Where to stay *Outdoor living:* there is no accommodation on the island, but it is easy to find somewhere to camp, with permission.

Activities *Walking:* the Beara Way includes a 9-mile (15-km) section on Dursey Island. Although there are no other marked trails on the island, it is small enough for the average walker to make short work of; and the treeless landscape offers decent walking along the coast.

Bird-watching: the sometimes spectacular migration of sea-birds can be witnessed from Dursey. You can also, if you are lucky, have some interesting sightings of smaller birds, blown off course.

Further information *Tourist offices:* the nearest BF offices are in Kenmare, T: (064) 41233, and Bantry, T: (027) 50229, open June–Sept.

Mizen Head

Southernmost of the great south-western promontories, between Dunmanus Bay and Roaringwater Bay, with a south coast known for its coves and harbours

In some ways the south-west of Ireland has always kept up to the minute. In the 19th century passengers on ships from America would toss messages into boats bound for Clear Island, where they could be telegraphed all over Europe. In this way the islanders learned the news of the American Civil War long before anybody in Britain or on the Continent. For the best part of a century transatlantic telegraph cables ran from Valencia Island, off the Iveragh peninsula. Here on the Mizen promontory an aircraft-tracking station is marked by two gleaming futuristic domes atop Mount Gabriel, making it seem from a distance that Martians have landed. But beside and under and around, older ways persist. This ancient, gnarled finger of old red sandstone pointing out to the Atlantic carries a bounty of natural delights, many having nothing at all to do with human agency.

The sand of the sandstone was washed away, reddened by rich quantities of oxidized iron, by rivers and tides to be dried, toasted, compacted and folded in the Armorican upheaval, caused by tectonic collision some 300 million years ago. In the previous geological era limestone-forming shells had drifted down through the warm sea which then covered the country. After the ruptures much of it remained on the surface, sandwiched between strata of sandstone, but in time, being of weaker consistency, the limestone eroded faster than the sandstone, and the result is the row of high, west-directed, old red sandstone peninsulas along the coasts of Cork and Kerry, divided by deep inlets, loughs or rias. You might think these long lines of land would be difficult to distinguish the one from the other, but nothing could be further from the truth. Dingle and the Iveragh (or Ring of Kerry)

get most of the limelight, but I am not sure that Mizen and the Beara are not my favourites.

The sea, of course, is what makes them: the stretched coastline with its bays and estuaries, islands near and far, distant views of isolated rocks, the natural fortress of Fastnet, like a formidable square keep, supporting its lighthouse. Schull, half-way along the south coast, has a pretty, rock-strewn harbour with a daily ferry to Cape Clear (also reached from Baltimore). You can fill a basket here with your dinner of mussels. The town is attractive, its houses painted many colours (as they tend to be from Macroom westward) and with the sort of shops not common in many parts of Ireland: antique shops, second-hand bookshops, pastry shops, delicatessens and a range of restaurants.

There is no need to be specific. You can turn off the road at a dozen points to enter a little world of steamily burgeoning plants beside sand, rock or rock-pool. You look around at the ingredients of one particular brew of Irish magic: the bay, the headlands, ruined castle, cove, beach, aquamarine sea. Treasure Island has to be somewhere beyond. Thrush, robin, wren, and blackbird

---

The stonechat is encountered on rough grassland and heath all over Ireland: a bold and conspicuous bird whose male is a dandy with black head, buff to orange chest and white collar (which does not go round the bird's back).

Glenbeg Lough, easily reached from Ardgroom, on the north coast of the Beara peninsula, is a 2-mile by ½-mile valley of water edged north and south by sheer walls of cliff. Unmoved by this grandeur, sheep graze on the lake's edge.

repeatedly announce their presence; when they flag, the tuneful willow warbler – possibly the rarer garden warbler – takes over the midday watch.

Richest of all is the rocky sward on which you are standing: a pattern of flowers which for some reason – light, clarity of air, freedom from pollutants – are more brightly coloured than their counterparts elsewhere in Europe. Out of a bed of mosses and grey or orange lichens or white-flowered stonecrop (*Sedum anglicum*) rise taller flowers in placements and confluences never achieved by any gardener in the world's history, though they are mainly common cranesbill, bird's foot trefoil, melilot, oxeye daisy, plantain and dandelion, thrift, sea campion. How dainty and delicate the wild can be. And always in these parts there are orchids: mainly the common spotted orchid (*Dactylorhiza fuchsii*) and the early marsh orchid (*Dactylorhiza incarnata*). If I were to advise someone beginning to learn the identification of plants where to start, I might say come to one of these unpeopled backwaters on a sunny day, bring book, strong and middling lenses, and notebook; and be prepared to work hard and with concentration. But I should be wrong, of course. The attention of all but the toughest would stray.

Further west come crescendos of scenery (whose only significant drawback is that people know about them). There are three high headlands at the end: Three Castle Head, Mizen Head and Brow Head, the last two divided by the broad expanse of Barley Cove, where gannets plunge into the clear blue waters and skim the large expanses of sand. Inland is a large, sandy shallow lake, Lissagriffin, where a few whooper and Bewick's swans, along with some teal and wigeon, pass the winter, while mute swan and mallard may be present at any time of the year. You might if you are lucky see a peregrine or a chough hereabouts.

Mizen Head dramatically shows off its angular cliffs of clearly striated sandstone, the lines going along and down, curving like race-tracks or stacked like shelves of deckle-edged paper. Guillemots and fulmars nest on any available niche in the cliff faces, the latter displaying their customary mastery of the air in incredibly long glides without benefit of wing-beat, or by hovering motionless on air-currents like ping-pong balls on invisible jets of water. In the spring and autumn many of the untold thousands of seabirds which cross Cape Clear, a few miles just south of east across Roaringwater Bay, cross here too: the various species of shearwater, auks, kittiwakes, skuas and others. Rarities occur here, but I have no wish to encourage the twitchers who transport their huge and expensive lenses by car, rail or plane when some enfeebled creature, blown off course and possibly starving, is reported to them. The rarer the bird, the more certain it is that, when they have had their way of it, patted themselves on their backs and added its name proudly to their 'life-lists', it will do the only thing left for it – die.

BEFORE YOU GO

Maps: OSI Discovery Series, map No. 88.

GETTING THERE

By car: from Skibbereen follow the N71 to Ballydehob, on the coast of Roaringwater Bay. The R592 and R591 (west) lead to Crookhaven, near the end of the peninsula.

By rail: the nearest stations are Killarney and Cork, with 4 services to and from Dublin daily, T: (01) 836 6222.

By bus: Bus Eireann operate a frequent daily service from Cork to Goleen, stopping at Schull and Ballydehob, T: (021) 506066.

WHERE TO STAY

Hotels: Bantry House is in Bantry, T: (027) 50047, e-mail: bantry@hidden-ireland.com; the Manor House in Ballylickey, T: (027) 50071; the Blairs Cove House in Durrus, T: (027) 61127; and the family-run East End Hotel in Schull, T: (028) 28101.

B&Bs: try Reendonegan House in Bantry, T: (027) 51455; The Heron's Cove in Goleen, T: (028) 35225; or Mrs Brosnan in Schull, T: (028) 28425.

Youth hostels: there are 2 independent hostels: the Bantry Independent Hostel, T: (027) 51050, and the Schull Backpackers' Lodge, T: (028) 28681.

An Oige run a hostel in Allihies, T: (027) 73014.

Outdoor living: the Barleycove CCP is near Crookhaven, T: (028) 35302; and the Dunbeacon CCP is on the road to Durrus from Bantry, T: (027) 61246.

Orchids still survive in Ireland, sometimes abundantly and mostly in the west; these are not the large and exotic tropical species, but smaller, daintier blooms, including (from left): marsh orchids, which flower in early summer and are sometimes prolific in wet grasslands; the bee orchid, which attracts certain male bees for pollination purposes by looking and smelling like a female bee, and keeps to dry sites; the pink-flowered pyramidal orchid, a lover of sand-dunes; and the lesser butterfly orchid, happy in damp heathland and pastures.

ACTIVITIES
Cycling: bikes can be hired at Freewheelin in Schull, T: (028) 28165.
Watersports: Schull Watersports Centre rents out dinghies, wind-surfing and diving equipment, T: (028)

28554/28351. Fastnet Manne Centre runs sailing courses, T: (028) 28315.
Bird-watching: Roaringwater Bay is a home to many seabirds, including shearwaters, auks, kittiwakes and skuas. Inland there are many breeds of

duck. Occassionally peregrines and choughs can be sighted.

FURTHER INFORMATION
Tourist office: the BF in Bantry is seasonal, T: (027) 50229, and in Skibbereen open all year, T: (028) 27766.

Cape Clear Island

Inhabited island with enterprising fish-farm and wind-power. Site of an important bird observatory

If you are a native of Clear Island and your name is not O'Driscoll it will probably be Cadogan. But it is much more likely to be O'Driscoll. That sort of thing is often the way with islands. The last time I was there I stayed at Mary O'Driscoll's guest-house, though I could equally have stayed at Eleanor O'Driscoll's. I had no cause to regret the choice.

I spent the day tramping the island, and came near to being, and but for idleness would have been, the most southerly person on Irish soil, for Fastnet is the only Irish territory more southerly than Cape Clear, and it is no longer manned. I talked, looked at birds on the western and southern cliffs, and watched fishing boats hauling in lobster pots out at sea. Without success I scanned the blue for a sight of the minke whales which are quite often seen, or the turtles which had been seen a week or so before. I watched children who had come to learn Irish – for O'Driscolls and their fellow islanders are resilient Irish-speakers, and people of all ages come from the corners of Ireland to learn from them. The children were taking their afternoon exercise of canoeing, swimming and sailing in the warm blue southern harbour of the cape.

I had some surprises. There is a lake in the west from which a narrow stream leads towards the cliffs and, as I walked along it, I saw the laws of gravity confounded by a perpetual upward spray of water ahead of me,

as if when it reached the end of its channel the water ascended into the air instead of dropping into the sea below. Well, it did, for the reason I now saw: a powerful and consistent current of air, rising beside the cliff – the same which birds delighted to use as elevator and support – was catching the water and transporting it several yards in a powerful upward shower. The other surprise was the spotting of a rare bird. It was big and heavy and a field or two away. I peered through binoculars. It was something like a guinea fowl. And here was another, its mate. They were indeed guinea fowls, but there was no call for excitement. An islander, it turned out, had brought them in to breed.

Mary and Ciaran O'Driscoll have a large room for the use of their guests. Along two sides there are tables at which to eat (or write or talk). The rest is a couple of feet lower with a fireplace and sofas, books and magazines. The differing levels of the floor make it easy for people to see each other and talk if they so wish. There is a nice unforced intimacy, and Mary O'Driscoll, a native of Schull over the water – she was born a Molloy – is a good and bright conductor of conversation. A young Swiss couple – she an air hostess – were staying, and two women and a boy from the mainland. An older islander called and stayed an hour, and young Alan Dalton of the bird observatory with his huge knowledge and not so easy nasal Dublin accent came in for a while. An awful lot was talked of, a great deal told.

No, said Mary to the Swiss girl, no, she did not feel out of touch on Cape Clear. So much went on here, it was a good place to live, and it was sometimes said that Cape Clear was the hub, and Ireland the off-shore island. Not that things were ideal. Some of the vanished past was to be regretted. Vegetables and most other provisions came over from the mainland now; few if any grew their own. With 25 island boats and 8 men to each, fishing had once provided 200 men with jobs: more than the present total population. The fishery now is part of a mainland co-operative – far the best arrangement for the times, but at a cost of enterprise and control over decisions. The efficient and graceful wind-propellers set up by a German company to generate energy some years ago would lose pride of place when electricity was piped in off the national grid for the first time. Worst, Mary's two sons, now at the island's excellent primary school, would have to proceed to school on the mainland (where they would board except at weekends), there to be educated beyond any job the island could offer. There was no other option. A kind of progress nobody much wanted would prevent an island, which all hoped to prosper, from prospering.

Some people, said the old man, claimed the Capers were pure descendants of the Milesians, a prehistoric race from whom the Irish have always been prone to trace their descent. He thought there was little truth to it, and remembered hearing as a child that soldiers landed and stayed during Napoleonic times, took local wives and bred families. That kind of dilution, he thought, had gone on all down history. Indeed it was said that many Aran islanders had the blood of Cromwell's soldiers running in their veins.

What was beyond dispute was the hardness of the lives islanders used to lead. There were no mills on the island, and all grain was ground with a hand quern. Selling fish never presented a problem: both Irish and English dealers in Baltimore were ready to buy every last mackerel, but there had been times when the fish went away and hauls were scant for years on end. Now, of course, the state took care of everything and the young did not know what it was to be without food or money. Nor had they any idea about sailing, or the skills, hazards and salty joys of their forefathers. I asked Alan about the island's bird life. It had occurred to me that keeping a check on birds was a little like taking the world's ecological temperature. Birds are international, deeply sensitive to changes in farming methods and patterns, desperately vulnerable to pollution from the Arctic to the Antarctic. Being considerate of arctic terns in Ireland or nightingales in England – not that we necessarily are – did not ensure their well-being. Obligations do not stop with national boundaries. They must, nevertheless, start in our own gardens. We berate farmers whose silage-making slowly wipes out the corncrake, or the French or Italians who shoot larks and thrushes so as to clear the whole firmament of birds; but do we not seal our own attic and neatly net our thatch-roofs and lofts against bats and swallows? Do we not cut weeds in which warblers may nest, or poison slugs and snails a thrush might catch and eat?

On Cape Clear pollution is minimal. What the records reveal is the astonishing legacy and responsibility that the Irish and the rest of us inherit. Cape Clear well illustrates the global significance of Ireland's sea-birds. An acid-soil island, dowsed with salt water on up to 200 days in the year can host a very limited number of plant species. Desperately short of trees, Cape Clear is little use for nest building birds unless, like some thrushes (song and mistle), blackbirds, wrens and robins, they have learned to build in holes in rock walls. For sea-birds, of course, island status and surpluses of rain are no handicap. Sea presents no barrier. On the contrary, it is the source of densely packed fish. Hence the rich turn-out and variety on, beside and above the Cape Clear cliffs. There are times when the air of Cape Clear is alive with the beat of wings. Over a small part of these 741 acres (300 hectares) of rock and heath and marsh there fly, during periods of migration, thousand upon thousand of various species of sea-bird. Counting birds in flight takes skill and experience. Alan has both, and can affirm that at certain times in late July and August up to 30,000 Manx shearwaters are passing overhead every hour. Other shearwaters – sooty and great – along with great and arctic skuas, guillemots, razorbills and kittiwakes, swell their ranks. All sorts of other birds occur in lesser numbers, and over 280 species common and rare – two-thirds of the number for all Ireland – have been recorded here.

BEFORE YOU GO
Maps: OSI Discovery Series, map No. 88.
Guide-books: *The Walkers' Guide* (available from the tourist office on the island) and Sharrock's *The Natural History of Cape Clear Island* (London, 1973), available from libraries.

GETTING THERE
By sea: boats leave from Baltimore, at the end of the R595 from Skibbereen. They take 45 mins to reach the island. Contact the tourist office in Baltimore (see below), or telephone the boat office direct, T: (028) 39119. Cape Clear & Sherkin Cruises run passenger ferries from Schull, T: (028) 28278.

WHERE TO STAY
B&Bs: on the island are Mrs C. O'Driscoll (who also has self-catering accommodation), T: (028) 39153, and Mrs E. O' Driscoll, T: (028) 39135. The Krugers rent out a stone farmhouse, T: (028) 39157, e-mail: ckstory@indigo.ie.
Youth hostels: there is an An Oige hostel on the island, T: (028) 39198. The bird observatory provides some accommodation; contact the warden, T: (028) 39181.
Outdoor living: camping is available on the island, T: (028) 39136. If you get no answer, call the Co-op (see below).

ACTIVITIES
Walking: there is a marked walk that runs right round the coast of the island and takes around 3 hrs.
Bird-watching: the bird observatory on the North Harbour is open all year. Advance booking is essential. The observatory offers bird-watching courses for beginners, T: (028) 39181.

FURTHER INFORMATION
Tourist offices: the Cape Clear Co-op office is open all year, T: (028) 39119, as is another privately run office in Baltimore, T: (028) 20441.

Lough Ine

A lake-like sea inlet with a nature reserve and marine biology station

I should like to own Lough Ine and its surrounds, live in the big white house that sits on a grassy bank at its north-east corner, close the roads that now give me and the rest of the public access to its northern and western shores, and enjoy in selfish seclusion this rough rectangle of salt-water lake. I should relish its curious and abundant natural life, its islands, the castle ruin, the thin rocky channel which the tide in its motions turns into rapids, the curlicued coast beyond – a labyrinth of inlets and islands – and the hills furred with forest trees that rise on all sides. Last time I was there I even envied the cows that lay chewing and mooning below the house and the rhododendrons, for not having to leave.

An inland lough consisting of salt water is a rarity in itself, but the slow comings and goings of the tides and the great depth of the lake – up to 164 feet (50 metres) in parts – mean a slow rate of change, allowing time for the fresh water coming down from the hills to dilute it to a weaker salinity than the sea itself. Its consistency is thus unusual. So are its inhabitants, for it contains a wide variety of habitats.

A small building beside the rapids is used as a research base by the Cork University team, who keep an eye on life on and under the surface. The rest of us have to take things on trust. There is fishing. Swimmers must take the greatest care not to put their feet on the lough bed for fear of stepping on a common sea urchin or its very bristly cousin the purple sea urchin. A walk along the side will present arm's-length dogfish to view. Others of the 60 species of fish recorded may be more elusive. It is a remarkable tally, which includes goldsinny wrasse, tompot blenny, pipe-fish, butter-fish, sometimes the subtropical trigger fish, and the red-mouthed goby, seldom found anywhere else in north-west Europe.

Reading the lists of the lough's inhabitants made me pine for an aqualung or a glass-bottomed boat, but the sea-gooseberry or comb jellyfish, the variegated scallop, snakelocks anemone, sea hare (a marine slug), common and spiny starfish, sea scorpion, sea cucumber, sea butterfly, fifteen-spined stickleback, mussel, prawn, brittlestar, velvet fiddler-crab or bristleworm *Sabella*, which brought the young Julian Huxley here early in the 20th century for thesis research, will be seen, if at all, only through luck during a walk along the accessible parts of the rim. Plankton – the sea soup of embryonic life, an infinity of minute plants and the eggs and larvae of fish, shellfish, starfish, worms and thousands of other creatures – require a microscope to be seen at all. The nearest we can come to awareness of them is by means of some helpful illustrations, diagrams and texts placed on boards beside one of the parking places. But a visit is not wasted. You can drive or walk to watch the four-times daily passage of the tide, or visit Bullock Island Bay, from which fishermen carry their lobster pots out to sea. This is one of those many places on the Irish coast where I wish my car would, in good weather anyway, turn into a sailing dinghy.

Before you go: OSI Discovery Series, map No. 89.

Getting there *By car:* from Cork follow the N71 (south-west) to Skibbereen, then the R595 to Baltimore. Signposted lanes off the R595 lead south to Lough Ine.

By bus: a Bus Eireann Expressway summer-only service between Cork and Killarney stops at Skibbereen, as does a daily Expressway service between Cork and Goleen. There are 2 buses daily between Skibbereen and Baltimore, T: (021) 508188. **Where to stay:** several B&Bs and 1 hotel, the Beacon Park, T: (028) 20143, and 1 hostel, Rolf's Hostel, T: (028) 20289, in Baltimore; more in Skibbereen.

Activities *Walking:* can be enjoyed in the small nature reserve just above Lough Ine. *Cycling:* bikes can be hired from Roycroft Cycles, T: (028) 21235, in Skibbereen. *Riding:* pony-trekking is available at the Limbo Trekking and Riding Centre, near Lough Ine, T: (028) 21683, e-mail: barthyscully@eircom.net. *Watersports:* Baltimore is a popular sailing centre.

Further information *Tourist office:* BF office open all year in Skibbereen, T: (028) 21766.

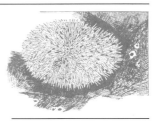

The purple sea urchin, whose greenish globular shell, or test, is about 2 in (4 cm) across and covered with a dense nap of purple spines, is essentially a Mediterranean animal, but is commonly found off the south and west coasts of Ireland and the south-west coast of England.

Sherkin Island

Inhabited island with rich flora close to Baltimore in south-west Cork. Site of an important private marine-research station

Sherkin is easily reached from the pretty little harbour town of Baltimore. The ferry comes and goes all day. On the island there is nothing you could call a town or village. Near the quay is an old abbey, built by 15th-century O'Driscolls and sacked fifty years later, recently much restored. Nearby there are ruins of a castle and a large Becher family house, and off to the north, overlooking Hare Island, the ghost of a settlement where boats were built a hundred years ago. For the rest, habitations are spaced well apart, in the Irish manner.

The most dynamic enterprise on the island is the marine-research centre started and run by Matt Murphy. It is not open to the public, but used to be. There was an aquarium and an informative exhibition. People crossed from the mainland and began the mile and a half walk but almost all succumbed to the lure of warm blue sea or to fatigue and the wish to go home long before they reached their destination. So it closed to the public. Its work continues, based on Matt Murphy's desire to expose the hidden life of the sea about him: something nobody – not even, to their shame, coastal universities like Galway – had thought of doing before he and his late wife settled here 25 years ago. Young scientists – drawn here by love, not money – carry out continuous marine-research programmes. They have good facilities and an excellent library. The world they explore, though not the complexities of their work, is disclosed in a wonderful book of underwater photographs published by the centre, suggestive far more of life in tropical or subtropical waters than in these northerly latitudes. Yet a multiplicity of colourful and exquisitely intricate starfish and jellyfish and sea urchins and squirts and scorpions and bristleworts and polymorphous plankton are resident hereabouts, all valid denizens of Ireland's wilderness.

Matt Murphy says he knows no science, only how to push those who do in the right directions. His primary concern is practicable conservation. He wants better awareness, use and protection of Ireland's natural resources, and to further these ends produces an authoritative, deeply interesting, often rather cross, slightly impatient quarterly review called *Sherkin Comment*. In this publication he is as likely to sound off at airy ecologists – Greenpeace and others have been carpeted – as at greedy farmers or totalitarian civil servants. What seems to me of most value about him and his paper is his constant attempt to focus on truth, the simpler the better, without regard to received or lazy opinion or widespread prejudice. He clearly approves of fish-farming. It does not improve the look of coastal bays and it has introduced new problems related to fish disease. Matt Murphy swipes equally at those who sentimentally deplore the whole business and those who try to gloss over the complications. His paper made it suddenly plain to me that fish-farming has only just started to do for fishing what agriculture did for hunting five or six thousand years ago; that it is here to stay and that, in spite of detractors, it can bring enormous benefits. It could turn out to be the most effective way of allowing ravaged ocean stocks to heal and revive.

Sherkin offers more than theory. The north coast is a succession of bays and rocky or sandy coves, generous reward for the walk needed to get to them. Off-season, in migration times, waves of duck and wader settle along the shore, either for a respite of a few days, or to stay for the winter while ice and snow put their northerly haunts out of bounds. Advancing summer sees a dense, rich and varied growth in vegetation. Trees and shrubs burgeon with blossom in the lanes and hedges. Like the other islands which crowd Roaringwater Bay, Sherkin has a dense mosaic of plant habitats: marsh, rock, sand-dune, pebbles, heath and caves. There is not, as in many parts of Ireland, an altogether excessive sheep population (subsidized by a grant from Europe) to hoover the variety of plants into a bland uniformity. But nobody had given much thought to Sherkin's flora until, a few years ago, Matt Murphy brought in Dr John Akeroyd to supervise a detailed survey. It took five years' work by resident botanists and has resulted in a book; what this tells us is that no equivalent area in the whole of Ireland has such a rich variety of plants. Sherkin supports some 540 species, vastly more than anyone previously suspected.

Apart from native plants there are species introduced by settlers – including some 17th-century Algerian pirates, and also the Normans, whose castle precincts are always likely to yield rarities. A new spotlight has been turned on the flora of this part of Ireland by the survey, and it would be rash for anyone interested to go to Sherkin without identification book and lens.

BEFORE YOU GO
Maps: OSI Discovery Series, map No. 88.

GETTING THERE
By sea: there are regular and frequent boat services to the island from Baltimore, T: (028) 20125, and in the summer from Schull, T: (028) 28278.
By car: from Skibbereen follow the R595 to Baltimore, the mainland village nearest to the island.
By bus: Bus Eireann run ser-

vices to Skibbereen from Cork, and from Killarney in summer. A connecting bus to Baltimore operates Mon–Fri, and Sat in the summer, T: (021) 506066.

WHERE TO STAY
B&Bs: try Murphy's Bar, T: (028) 20384; Island House, T: (028) 20314; and the Horseshoe, T: (028) 20598.
Outdoor living: you can camp in many parts of the island, having sought permission from the farmer.

ACTIVITIES
Walking: there are plenty of walks on the island, including one taking in the ruined 15th-century abbey.

FURTHER INFORMATION
Tourist offices: information is available from the community centre on Sherkin Island, T: (028) 20336, www.indigo.ie/sherkin/, the BF office in Baltimore, T: (028) 20441, or the Cork Kerry office in Skibbereen, T: (028) 21766.

Central County Cork

Mountain country lying between the scenic valleys of the lake-rich Lee and the Blackwater, offering quiet surprises

Measure for measure, this country is not the equal of that ravishing region to its west, comprising Killarney, Iveragh and the other promontories of Cork and Kerry. Between the Rivers Lee and Blackwater, with Mangerton mountain and Lough Guitane as a western boundary, rise two ranges of old red sandstone mountains, the Derrynasaggart and the Boggeragh. They are largely cultivated, in part grazed, in part drearily afforested. Though the action of ice is evident in their forms, they lack for the most part the lake-filled corries that bejewel so many other Irish ranges. Why, then, mention them?

Three reasons. Firstly, they possess a few stunning features. There is Gouganebarra Lough, with the forest park rising westward and the lovely River Coomhola just over the hill, descending to Bantry Bay beside the good walking country around Lough Nambrackderg, Knockboy and Priest's Leap. At Gouganebarra Lough itself the island is sacred to St Finbarr (from whom the place-name derives), a 6th-century evangelist with some nice Celtic attributes: he founded an oratory here, overcame a murderous monster, drowned it and crossed the sea to Scotland, for missionary work, on horseback. When he died, the sun shone continuously for a fortnight. He is the sort of saint I for one find it delightful to summon as company on local walks and climbs. Nothing would have got him down.

The withdrawn and commanding ridge of Sheehy mountain a few miles south of the Lee is another site which appeals. Still more impressive are the Paps, twin bosoms of the goddess Anu, according to legend, consisting of sandstone and rising to 2,273 ft (693 m) and 2,283 ft (696 m). They break the local rule and hide two deep and steeply flanked lakes among their upper reaches. The valley of the Lee from Gouganebarra to Macroom is another star of this region, winding broad (the best part of a mile in some stretches) and narrow, among picturesque bluffs of rock, many topped or propped by castle ruins with dramas to relate. Carrignacurra and Carrignamurk can be seen on one cliff, and Carrigrohane on another, while Carrigadrohid, where the English hanged a stubborn bishop three centuries ago, protrudes into the river three miles or so below Macroom. Another castle, Carrigaphouca, five miles west of Macroom on the Killarney road, is built on one of those rotund relics of the Ice Ages, a *roche moutonnée*, or rock carved by ice action into the shape, very roughly, of a sheep. The castle's name is cognate with that of Puck the fairy, and is said to mark the presence of little people, or leprechauns, in the area.

Just above Macroom the river widens, as a result of damming for hydro-electric purposes, into a three-mile stretch of marsh, water and riverine woodland known as the Gearagh. In the winter this becomes a great centre for whooper and Bewick's swans, and various geese and ducks, most commonly wigeon and teal.

The second reason for staying hereabouts rather than further west is that the region derives some benefits from being second best. It is with certain exceptions less known, less crowded in season, less exploitative; it prepares you for the climax of the west. Or – and this is the third reason – it acts as an alternative to the west, offering here and there serendipitous discoveries of lush glen, mountain stream and remote valley, meetings with the kind of amiable country people whom, further west, too much tourism has made prone to turn on their rustic charm to order, and off again if it seems to be going nowhere.

Before you go: OSI Discovery Series, map Nos 79 and 80.

Getting there *By car:* from Killarney, the N22 passes through the Derrynasaggart Mountains on its way to Macroom. From Macroom the R584 goes west along the River Lee, passing Gougane Barra before reaching Bantry.

By rail: Killarney and Cork are the closest stations. Contact Irish Rail, T: (01) 836 6222.

By bus: frequent Bus Eireann services run each day between Cork and Killarney stopping at Macroom and Ballvourney, in the Derrynasaggart Mountains, T: (021) 506066.

Where to stay *Hotels:* Coolcower House is in Macroom, T: (026) 41695; Creedon's Hotel in Inchigeela, T: (026) 49012; and the lovely Bridelands Country House is in Crookstown, T: (021) 336566.

Activities *Walking:* a walk to the summit of Bealick mountain behind Gougane Barra affords good views, and there are signposted trails through the Gougane Barra Forest Park.

Further information *Tourist offices:* Lee Valley Tourism has an office in Macroom, T: (026) 41848. Nearest all-year BF is in Cork, T: (021) 273251.

CHAPTER 4

Lakeland and the Central Plain

Wild Ireland – wilderness, wildlife, landscape left by humans to itself – exists inland as well as along the coast. It is quieter, more discreet, less extensive, but in its way just as beautiful and fascinating as seaboard wildness. It is rich in bird life, plants, animals and insects, rich in diversity of greens and variety of landforms.

The sea is absent; water decidedly not. Chains of linked lakes make large parts of Counties Cavan, Monaghan, Fermanagh, Leitrim, Roscommon and Longford more water than land. By many the region is known as Lakeland. Among these counties and on to the south, the River Shannon runs its eventful course. It takes in the tributaries that vein the 4,553 square miles (7,285 square kilometres) of its catchment area, and here and there opens out into lakes which are among the largest in the country and look at times very much like inland seas. For almost all its length the river is navigable. So too are the lake link-waters. In fact, Lough Gowna, down in County Longford, is the source of the River Erne and from it you can take a small boat through both Upper and Lower Lough Erne to Belleek – one of Ireland's longest navigable stretches.

The Shannon is Ireland's central artery, draining in the course of its 230 miles (370 kilometres) almost every sort of terrain the country possesses. It

Deep blue trout-rich waters, densely wooded islands and forest and parkland hems give Lough Key its pretty, pampered look.

starts among high mountains close to the national border, implying disdain for the Six Counties by turning immediately to the south. Its official source, in County Cavan, is a bubbling spring known as the Shannon Pot on the lower slopes of Cuilcagh mountain. Other early supplies come from the mountains Slieve Anieran and Arigna, and from the hills of south Sligo and north Roscommon. The infant river drops into Lough Allen, a fall of 300 feet (90 metres) in ten miles (16 kilometres). The next hundred miles or so will lower it only 40 feet (12 metres) more. From Lough Allen the river emerges to wind through bog-lands and overgrown, intriguing little towns – Drumshanbo, Leitrim, Jamestown, Drumsna (second syllable stressed: Drumsnah), Roosky – that a generation ago seemed to be dying of neglect and that owe their survival to the recovery of holiday river traffic.

Below Carrick-on-Shannon, dusted by willow and ash, the Shannon side-tracks into reed-beds like Carnadoe water and the western parts of Lough Boderg. These are much patronized by water-birds. Broad Lough Ree opens out beyond, rich in fish, islands, history and sanctity, and not many miles later there will be Lough Derg, equally well stocked with fauna and associations. Between the two, south of Athlone, where the Shannon meets the Grand Canal and passes some mighty buildings associated with the short-lived flowering of waterborne transport, it coils through a quietly charmed area of flat pasture, ancient monasteries and the callows. These are low-lying riverside pastures which are flooded regularly and for long periods in winter and so afford dependable sanctuary to thousands of geese, swans, ducks and waders, well out of the reach of predators. The callows occur beside the Little

Brosna, which joins the Shannon at Meelick, and beside various stretches of the Shannon itself between Meelick and Clonmacnoise. In summer some of these latter fields still sustain the corncrake, a bird so common and well-known (from its grating, nocturnal call) a generation ago and so rare and precarious now that it stands as a symbol of our age's ecological calamities.

Underwater, naturally, Lakeland seethes with fish. To angling people, the region is famous. The Cavan, Westmeath and Longford lakes are known for their coarse fish; Loughs Ree and Derg for trout. Salmon come to breed in streams running into Lough Derg. Along stretches of water popular with game fishermen, much attention is paid at the appropriate time of the year to a fly with a knobbly head, outstretched wings and a long, gracefully curved three-strand tail. The iridescence of its wing panels resembles some stained-glass ornament of subtle colours made by Tiffany's in the 1920s. The mayfly's main hatch is likely to take place long after Easter, in late May or early June. It is of the order *Ephemeroptera*, and its existence is indeed ephemeral. The two sexes mate and the female lays its eggs into the water within hours of emerging. Many fail even in this respect and simply breast the air, exert themselves in a mighty bid for height, slip, fall and moments later struggle for their lives on the water's surface. Many are blown together and rotate in eddies, flapping wildly and ineffectually as if the surface were of syrup. A fish – likely as not a trout – sees the disturbance, checks the colour-code, and snaps. Or a swallow or sand-martin scoops up the flies in a surface skim. The brief life of the mayfly, the culmination of up to three years spent as egg and nymph among the mud and stones, is generally over in an hour.

The luckier among them will survive a day or two. During that time they eat nothing. The most they can achieve is that others will come after them and repeat a seemingly joyless curriculum. The first mayflies are noticed by locals with practised eyes. Some varieties do, in fact, appear earlier than May, such as the March Brown, which rises out of fast-flowing rivers. Observers pass on the news. People hear for miles around. Messages are sent on the telephone to Dublin. Once upon a time the lines hummed with telegrams to London. Straight away, or the weekend following, city-weary anglers begin their migration. The mayfly is arrived, trout are biting, and local hotels and guest-houses rapidly filling.

Lough Derg is deeply indented with bays and coves of great variety, gnawed into the bordering limestone. They may be wooded, built round, or lapping pasture or rougher patchworks of heather, gorse and bracken. Like Ree, Lough Derg is seasonal home to wildfowl which, when danger threatens in one bay, like to be able to fly to another nearby. In the south the lough narrows between highlands of rumpled sedimentary rock, and at Killaloe returns to river dimensions for its final windings, through Limerick, to the estuary.

A few miles east of Lough Derg, as the Shannon approaches the end of its journey, three famous Irish rivers begin theirs, the River Nore and the River Barrow on the slopes of Slieve Bloom and the River Suir a few miles south, continuing south or south-east until they reunite and enter the sea as one at Waterford harbour. The Slieve Bloom is the most substantial protrusion from Ireland's limestone heartland. Not mountain-high (it is well below 2,000 feet/600 metres at its highest), it is all the same a world apart from the hurly-burly of people and houses below: a land of smoothly rolling carpet bog, huge baize spreads of conifer, good farmland on its lower levels, cracked at intervals by the deep glens where, because they are not susceptible to human exploitation, plants and animals of interest survive. None of these features, alone or collectively, quite conveys the air of abstraction, of antiquity, of remoteness that shrouds you as you wander among old trees and old paths and boisterous young head-waters which in their maturity, far below, will irrigate the farmlands of the South-East.

GETTING THERE
By air: Dublin is the principal international airport in the area with direct flights from major European cities and North America. For further information contact Dublin International Airport, T: (01) 814 1111, www.dublinairport.com. In addition Aer Lingus fly from Birmingham and London to Shannon, T: (0645) 737747/(020) 8899 4747 (UK). British Airways, T: (0345) 222111 (UK), Ryanair, T: (0541) 569569 (UK), and Aer Lingus also fly to Knock, Co. Mayo.
By sea: Stena Line, T: (0990) 707070, www.stenaline.co.uk, and Irish Ferries, T: (0990) 171717, www.irishferries.ie, operate from Holyhead to Dublin and Dun Laoghaire. Irish Ferries also operate from Cherbourg and Roscoff to Rosslare, T: (01) 638 3333 (Dublin).
By rail: Boyle and Carrick-on-Shannon on the Dublin (Connolly)–Sligo line are good bases for exploring the Bricklieve Mountains and Lough Allen.

For Lough Ree, regular trains from Dublin (Heuston) stop at Athlone. Two services a day from Dublin (Heuston) also stop at Portlaoise and Nenagh, close to the Slieve Bloom Mountains and Lough Derg, T: (01) 836 6222, www.irishrail.ie.
By bus: frequent Bus Eireann services run from Dublin to most major towns in the region, T: (01) 836 6111; www.buseireann.ie.

WHERE TO STAY
Bord Fáilte publish guides to

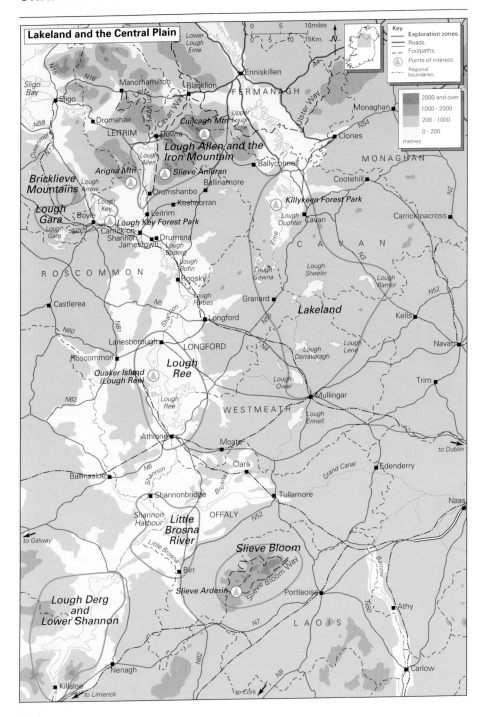

Lakeland and the Central Plain

Key
— Exploration zones.
— Roads.
-- Footpaths.
(A) Points of interest.
-·- Regional boundaries.

2000 and over
1000 - 2000
200 - 1000
0 - 200
metres

Lower Lough Erne
Sligo Bay
Sligo
Manorhamilton
Blacklion
Enniskillen
FERMANAGH
Dromahair
Culcagh Mtn
Upper Lough Erne
Monaghan
LEITRIM
Dowra
Clones
Lough Allen and the Iron Mountain
MONAGHAN
Arigna Mtn
Lough Allen
Slieve Anieran
Ballyconnell
Bricklieve Mountains
Lough Arrow
Ballinamore
Cootehill
Drumshanbo
Killykeen Forest Park
Keshcorran
Lough Gara
Lough Key
Boyle
Leitrim
Lough Oughter
Cavan
Carrickmacross
Lough Key Forest Park
Carrick-on-Shannon
Drumsna
Jamestown
Lough Boderg
Erne
C A V A N
Lough Bofin
Lough Gowna
Lough Sheelin
Lough Ramor
Roosky
R O S C O M M O N
Lough Forbes
Granard
Lakeland
Castlerea
Longford
Kells
Lanesborough
LONGFORD
Lough Derravaragh
Lough Lene
Navan
Roscommon
Lough Ree
Quaker Island (Lough Ree)
Lough Owel
Trim
Lough Ree
WESTMEATH
Mullingar
Athlone
Lough Ennell
to Dublin
Moate
Clara
Grand Canal
Edenderry
Ballinasloe
Shannon
Brosna
Tullamore
Naas
Shannonbridge
Shannon Harbour
Little Brosna River
OFFALY
to Galway
Little Brosna
Slieve Bloom
Barrow
Birr
Slieve Bloom Way
Lough Derg and Lower Shannon
Slieve Arderin
Portlaoise
Athy
L A O I S
Nenagh
Carlow
Killaloe
to Limerick
to Cork

approved places to stay, although many good establishments are not BF-recommended. For hostels contact An Oige, the Irish Youth Hostel Association, T: (01) 830 4555, www.irelandyha.org; or the Independent Holiday Hostels of Ireland, T: (01) 836 4700, www.hostels-ireland.com. Hidden Ireland recommends hotels, B&Bs and properties for rent in unspoilt places, 37 Lower Baggot Street, Dublin 2, T: (01) 662 7166, www.hidden-ireland.com.

ACTIVITIES

Walking: the Slieve Bloom Way is unfamiliar to many Irish people, but this 48-mile (77-km) circular route is well worth trying as it displays some of the best scenery in the area. Elsewhere, country lanes and trails in Killykeen Forest Park or by Lough Key offer good walking. The canal tow-paths near Kildare are ideal for those who do not fancy hill-walking.
Cycling: this is one of the best

ways to explore the Lakeland region. The routes are generally less strenuous than in the more hilly coastal regions. Athlone is a good base for the 160-mile (258-km) Lough Ree and Shannon route. To the north of Mullingar, it is possible to follow a Bord Fáilte 200-mile (320-km) approved route which winds around the lakes and little hills of Counties Cavan, Longford and Monaghan. There is also a Slieve Bloom mountain route which climbs to a height of 1,476 ft (450 m). Bikes can be rented from Mr Hardiman, Athlone, T: (0902) 78669; Brendan Sheerin, Boyle, T: (079) 62010; Eugene Clerkin, Market Street, Monaghan, and from the Lough Key CCP in the Lough Key Forest Park, T: (079) 62212/62363.
Riding: in Co. Westmeath, Mullingar Equestrian Centre provides instruction and accommodation, T: (044) 48331/40569, e-mail: horsehol@iol.ie. The Killykeen Equestrian Centre offers cross-

country courses in Killykeen Forest Park, T: (049) 436 1707, e-mail: killykeenequ@tinet.ie.
Climbing: the Slieve Bloom Mountains have moorland tops, but these drop away into a series of radiating wooded valleys. Arderin is the main peak at 1,734 ft (529 m).
Fishing: the River Shannon and the lakes of Monaghan, Cavan and Roscommon provide excellent coarse fishing and attract anglers from all over the world. Pike, roach, rudd, brown trout and tench are all to be found. Restrictions apply when fishing for pike. Contact the Shannon Regional Fisheries Board, Thomond Weir, Limerick, T: (061) 455171.

FURTHER INFORMATION

Tourist offices: there are BF offices in Mullingar, T: (044) 48650; Athlone, T: (0902) 94630; Birr, T: (0509) 20110; Roscommon, T: (0903) 26342; Boyle, T: (079) 62145; Cavan, T: (049) 433 1942; and Monaghan, T: (047) 81122.

Lough Allen and the Iron Mountain

Bleak, forbidding iron country and source of the River Shannon

There was a time when I used to drive quite often between Dublin and Sligo. Sometimes I took a turn round pretty Lough Key and got a look at the battery of mountains to the north-east: Arigna, and beyond it the solid and intractable furniture of Slieve Anieran, the Iron Mountain, with Cuilcagh backing it up. I knew perfectly well what was on the other side of Anieran – the top tip of County Cavan and then the national border and Fermanagh with its lakes – but something in the disposition of the mountains made me forget that. Anieran,

rising above Lough Allen, looked like a climactic and terminal barrier, world-ending, impenetrable, mysterious. I dare say Mount Everest, with out-of-bounds Tibet beyond, gives out similar signals. It is not the only time that I've had such feelings. There is a valley across the water in Somerset which I always think of as the approach to Castle Perilous, it so well matches the inner picture inspired by Malory's *Morte d'Arthur*. What it leads to has nothing Arthurian about it, but the expectation never fails.

There is, in fact, something final about Anieran. It brings the flat lakeland of southern County Leitrim to a grand, majestic end and ushers in the northern highlands. Crossing the border to Northern Ireland is, in fact, just as easy a matter here as anywhere else. Indeed, reconditioning of the old Erne–Shannon canal through Ballinamore and Ballyconnell now makes the transit possible in a boat. No, much of Anierin's end-

135

of-the-world quality is a figment of its shape and lie. It does, however, add zest to climbs and explorations.

There used to be a lot of coal near the surface of the mountains round Lough Allen but it has been worn away to thin and local patches. In most places extraction is hardly economic, though Arigna's coal was until recently used to fuel a power station. The coal dates back to the time when a warm sea flooded much of northern Europe 375 million years ago. Coral and other calcareous matter floated to the bottom and gradually created the carboniferous limestone bed which underlies much of inland Ireland. In time, rivers brought down sands and clays from the highlands still jutting above the sea; millions more years of pressure changed these into sandstone and shale. As the sea subsided, plants, both herbaceous and woody, grew, died, rotted and were pressed by layers of later debris into what became coal.

Slieve Anieran means 'mountain of iron'. Iron was worked here and at various places southward as far as Lough Ree, and the woods of oak and ash which covered large parts of the country were felled for the work of smelting. There are furnaces and remains of other ironworks on the mountain, but Anieran now is mainly a mass of heather-covered turf. Its 1,927-foot (587-metre) peak offers wonderful views over Lough Allen, Arigna, the Curlews and Bricklieve Mountains to the west, and the lake-studded peneplain to the south, but there are better walks and climbs to be had along its edges and in the smaller mountains to the north.

Low on Cuilcagh's west side is the Shannon Pot, officially but not in technical fact the river's source (since a source – for what it matters – is taken to be the waterway of highest origin, and the Owenmore is higher). This spring, billowing out from an underground river flowing through buried strata of limestone, is overhung with willows and has been favoured with Tourist Board treatment, preluded by a gravel path, car park and picnic area. Cuilcagh and the mountain known for obscure reasons as the Playground, show to advantage the drumlins of the Owenmore valley between them. The smooth oval shapes, densely packed in parts, make me think of this as buttocky country.

The fox, attracting by its intelligent face and cunning survival methods, and repelling by its pointless massacres of captive poultry, is found all over Ireland. It has fearlessly expanded its range from country to town to live off dumps, rubbish heaps and dustbins.

BEFORE YOU GO
Maps: OSI Discovery Series, map No. 26.
Guide-books: *The Leitrim Way* (Leitrim County Council, 1993).

GETTING THERE
By car: from Dublin take the N4 to Carrick-on-Shannon. From there take the R280 north, and go straight on to the R207, which runs along the east side of Lough Allen and gives access to Slieve Anieran on the right.
By rail: services to Carrick-on-Shannon from Sligo and Dublin (Connolly) run 3 times a day, T: (01) 836 6222.
By bus: Bus Eireann services from Dublin and Sligo run 3 times a day to Carrick-on-Shannon. A Fri and Sat service between Sligo and Carrigallen

stops at Drumshanbo, at the south end of Lough Allen, T: (071) 60066.

WHERE TO STAY

Hotels and B&Bs: there is plenty of choice in Carrick-on-Shannon, Drumshanbo and Ballinamore. Mrs Curran runs a B&B at Fenagh, south of Ballinamore, T: (078) 44089; the 19th-century Glebe House is at Mohill, T: (078) 31086, e-mail: glebe@iol.ie.

Youth hostels: the Town Clock Hostel is in Carrick-on-Shannon, T: (078) 20068, and the Holiday Hostel is at Ballinamore, T: (078) 44955.

Outdoor living: free camping is available on the banks of the river at Carrick-on-Shannon. Otherwise find an agreeable spot and ask the farmer's permission to camp there.

ACTIVITIES

Walking: the Leitrim Way, a 30-mile/48-km waymarked route, starts in Drumshanbo and runs along the east coast of Lough Allen. There are 2 stages: 1, Drumshanbo to Dowra (10 miles/16 km); 2, Dowra to Manorhamilton (20 miles/32 km). The 16-mile (26-km) Cavan Way starts in Dowra and passes north of the Cuilcagh Mountains. For details contact Leitrim County Council, T: (078) 20005, and Cavan County Council, T: (049) 433 1799.

Cycling: bikes can be hired at Geraghty's in Carrick at any time during the summer and at other times of year by appointment, T: (078) 21316.

Riding: the Drumcoura City Ranch in Ballinamore organizes horse-riding treks and

provides accommodation, T: (078) 44676/(071) 77507.

Fishing: there is good fishing to be had in the clean lakes of Co. Leitrim. Lough Allen is home to pike, bream, perch, rudd, tench and trout. Geraghty's in Carrick-on-Shannon, T: (078) 21316, hires out tackle. Drumshanbo at the southern tip of the lough is an angling centre. Further information is available from the Shannon Regional Fisheries Board, T: (061) 455171.

FURTHER INFORMATION

Tourist offices: the seasonal BF centre in Carrick-on-Shannon is at the Old Barrel Store, T: (078) 20170, www.leitrim-tourism.com. The region's head office in Sligo is open all year, T: (071) 61207, www.ireland. northwest.travel.ie.

Bricklieve Mountains

Mountains with megalithic tombs and rewarding views over Lough Arrow

In Boyle, a small town sloping down on both sides to the river of the same name, I had been directed to the shoe shop; not to buy stout shoes for walking, though that would certainly have been possible, but to get advice from the proprietor Maurice Corrigan, who has walked everywhere worth walking hereabouts. His colleagues Adrian and Patsy joined in the discussion. Adrian drew a map of the Bricklieve Mountains, beyond the Curlews to the north of the town, in order to show me what he believed to be 'the best walk in Ireland'.

'I'd do anything to be going with you, but I've work ...' Maurice said to me. 'Now, see, I'll tell him to put in north. He can't tell his north from his back door. Put in north and south, Adrian.'

Adrian, to Maurice's chagrin, got it right. Later they wrote their names down for me. 'Go on Maurice,' said Adrian, 'M-A-U-R.' The twitting was still going on when I left. A day or two later my car, having sprung an oil leak, was lastingly repaired by a fitter, his son and grandson who happened to live close by. After the hour it took, I had the sight of three generations vehemently refusing any payment. 'Sure it wasn't your fault it broke down.' These are scenes which it is easy but wrong to imagine do not occur in the new Ireland. By the new Ireland I mean a country at pains, much of the time at least, to show itself different from other countries (above all England) and at the same time modern, progressive, European and viable. It has been very successful in its efforts. Sadly, and too often, a high price is paid: the reduction of some agreeable customs and attitudes – among them talk and kindness to strangers – that take up too much time for today's hectic pace. Other countries threw them away years ago. This makes it doubly nice to find them in pockets here and there, surviving and even thriving.

137

From different points in the distance the Bricklieves take on protean forms: various kinds of hat, upturned pudding basins, earthbound ships, but most of all those cakes from whose sides, in my childhood, you peeled strips of fringed paper, and whose summits swelled with icing. Walls of grey limestone are what the removed paper discloses, and the icing is green and brown or purple, the colours of grass and heather. The decoration consists of massive cairns of rough, sharp stones, piled between four and five thousand years ago on Stone Age passage graves which have been excavated and are in some cases kept open to view. This is the sprawling megalithic graveyard of Carrowkeel. I was told that, to excavate some of the cairns, archaeologists early in the 20th century cleared the stones away with dynamite: not recommended.

Otherwise the summits are tussocky, dell-strewn, cave-pricked sheep-land plateaux: grass, heather, reed and crowberry (*Empetrum nigrum*) with little corners of richer vegetation. Here and there a dwarf hawthorn has almost grafted itself into a rock to take cover from winds of Atlantic or Arctic provenance; in small sheltered cuts and corners you can find golden saxifrage (*Chrysosplenium oppositifolium*), appealingly small primroses (*Primula vulgaris*), wood-sorrel (*Oxalis acetosella*), white stonecrop (*Sedum album*) and several different ferns and mosses. Not far from the summit are patches of orchid. Ravens wheel, dive and croak overhead. At irregular intervals there are old peat workings, jigsaw pieces of turf five or six feet (up to a couple of metres) high where village diggers have come to a resistant seam – of bog oak or pine maybe, hardened by three or four thousand years of soaking – and swerved.

We know little of those who made and inhabited the Stone Age tombs of these summits save that they liked to be buried with bone pins, pottery and stone bric-a-brac, and to face the north. It seems a reasonable aspiration, for the world offers few better views. Below are the short limestone ravines, with ivy drapes and precariously sprouting ash and birch. Down to the right Lough Arrow

Lough Derravaragh, its waters and banks teeming with life, sees the sun sink beyond the boggy plain to its west.

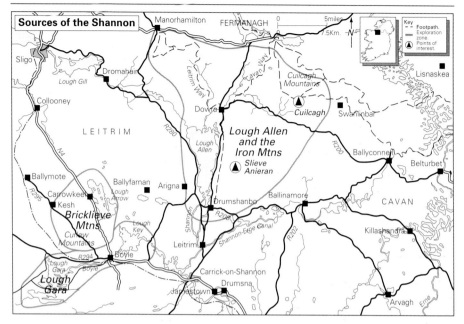

sparkles with emerald islands. In the foreground is a playground of wavy green, cut by hedges and stone walls, dappled with yellow gorse, bright white houses and little occasional lakes. Toy country, fairy country, Yeats country: Sligo – a county quite unlike any other in its land-forms and emporium of folklore. Far ahead lies Ben Bulben (see page 36), as evocative a figure as any in Ireland, the long slant of the Ox Mountains, Sligo Bay and the great hunched Slieve League headland beyond. The ascent of the Bricklieve presents little challenge, except perhaps in keeping to the correct route, and the rewards for the climb are quite out of proportion to the effort involved.

BEFORE YOU GO
Maps: OSI Discovery Series, map Nos 26, 32 and 33.

GETTING THERE
By car: from Carrick-on-Shannon follow the N4 (west) to Boyle, and continue north on the same road towards Sligo. Just beyond Boyle the road passes east of the Bricklieve Mountains.
By rail: three services run each day from Dublin (Connolly) and Sligo to Boyle and Ballymote, T: (01) 836 6222.
By bus: the Bus Eireann Expressway from Dublin to Sligo stops at Boyle. A Mon–Sat local service between Sligo and Athlone stops at Ballymote and Boyle, T: (071) 60066.

WHERE TO STAY
Hotels and B&Bs: the Abbey House, T: (079) 62385, and the Royal Hotel, T: (079) 62016, are both in Boyle. Mrs Mullin's B&B, T: (071) 83449, and the Temple House, T: (071) 83329, e-mail: accom@templehouse.ie, are in Ballymote. In Tobercurry try Mrs Kelly, T: (071) 85235, or Crawley's, T: (071) 85025.

ACTIVITIES
Walking: part of the Miner's Way & Historical Trail crosses the Bricklieve Mountains, running close to the many megalithic burial mounds in the area. *The Miner's Way & Historical Trail Map Guides* (East-West Mapping, 1999) contains maps and useful information.
Cycling: Brendan Sheerin's in Boyle, T: (079) 62010, hires bikes.
Fishing: boating and fishing are available at Coopershill House, Riverstown, near Carrowkeel, T: (071) 65108, e-mail: ohara@coopershill.com. Fishing is also available at Lough Arrow.

FURTHER INFORMATION
Tourist offices: the BF tourist office in Boyle is open May to late Sept, T: (079) 62145.

REMAINS IN THE WILD

Ireland is full of discarded ruins, some of them dating back 4,000 and even 5,000 years. They occur everywhere and anywhere. Certain of them fit into categories.

Dolmen. Neolithic tomb dating from 2000–3000 BC, consisting of vertical flagstones on which rests an often huge capstone, the whole formerly covered with earth. May be rectangular or wedge-shaped. Mainly found in the northern half of Ireland.

Court cairn. An open courtyard surrounded by one or more covered burial chambers. Mainly found in the northern half of Ireland, many in Mayo and Leitrim.

Passage graves. Neolithic burial chambers approached by stone-walled passages and covered in circular mounds of earth; constructed about 4,500 years ago. The finest examples in Europe are beside the Boyne. Others can be found in Carrowmore and Carrowkeel (in north and south County Sligo respectively), and elsewhere in the northern half of Ireland.

Stone circles. Circles of free-standing megaliths dating back about 4,000 years, probably used for religious rituals, mainly found in Cork and Kerry.

Standing stones. Also around 4,000 years old (late Stone Age, early Bronze Age), these can be of enormous size, reaching up to 20 ft (6 m) in height. Probably constructed for ritual use, they occur all over Ireland. From the Iron Age, a century or two BC, there survive huge shaped stones carved with Celtic patterns. Pillarstones of rectangular section, found in south-west Ireland, date from about AD 300–600 and often have a series of notches cut down one corner. These notches are ogham script, used generally for commemorative purposes, and recording personal names.

Iron Age forts. Comprising rings of concentric stone walls, these date from about 2,000 years ago. The most impressive is Dun Aengus, built on a perilous cliff-top on the largest of the Aran Islands.

Clochain. Beehive huts of rough stones, built by corbelling. Often round outside and square in, they were in many cases used by religious hermits. Situated mainly on the Dingle peninsula, they date back to about AD 450-700.

Round towers. Tall, thin stone towers which are in some cases over 100 ft (30 m) in height and capped by stone cones. Numbering 120, they date from between the mid-10th and mid-13th centuries. Built within monasteries, they were almost certainly bell-towers that doubled as defensive sanctuaries.

High crosses. Constructed between the 9th and 12th centuries, these massive stone Celtic crosses (with the uprights and cross-pieces joined by a circle of stone) were usually deeply carved with abstract patterns and representations of religious scenes.

Ring-forts, or raths. A series of alternating circular earthen ramparts and ditches, these were no doubt the defences surrounding individual homes or settlements. They may be anything from 1,000 to 3,000 years old. There are said to be 30,000 extant.

Crannog. Artificial island in a lake or marsh, hemmed in by stakes or stones and connected to the mainland by a (submerged) causeway. Used for defensive purposes between 1000 BC and AD 1000.

Modern structures. Crosses, with or without a figure of Christ, shrines to the Blessed Virgin Mary, cairns – piles of stones – and other artefacts have often been placed on mountain tops in recent years.

Lough Gara

Popular angling lake 6 miles (10 km) west of Boyle, surrounded by moist, warm, peaty mire

It is a small-time site, a lake that came to prominence in the 1950s when draining exposed numbers of lake dwellings, or crannogs, dating from two to three thousand years ago. The Lung river and other streams feed it, and the Boyle river takes its waters on through Lough Key to the Shannon.

Greenland white-fronted geese, whooper swans and various duck spend the winter on it. It is crossed east to west by a causeway carrying a road from which at various points you can walk down on to a peaty mire. You may sink in up to your knees, unless you keep to stones or reedy tussocks which are likely to have some firmness underneath. Like most lakes, it is popular with anglers.

I like Lough Gara. I like the certain ordinariness it has about it. I like to sit in the heat, when there is some, and insinuate myself into the pleasures of concentration and empathy. From woods of willow and blackthorn comes a commotion of bird-song: warblers, chaffinch, wren, thrush and that incompetent tenor the blackbird, while snipe sometimes burble or bubble from ground level, and swallows flit, too busy for static recitals. Kingcup, buttercup, yellow flag, bog asphodel, orchids and cotton grass burgeon in the moist warmth. It is this protean natural ferment, this glory of colour, hum and buzz for which I have always treasured this part of Ireland.

The lane along the north-east side of the lough allows you closer to the water. Swans, terns and gulls pattern the view with ballets of white. From here you can walk, or better canoe, into the town of Boyle. Church ruins, a mixed Catholic and Church of Ireland graveyard, crumpled stone walls and empty windows along the way would toll endless death and decay were it not for the irrepressible tangle of vegetation that uses them as life-support. It all comprises a recurring summer festival.
Before you go *Maps:* OSI Discovery Series, map Nos 32 and 33.
Getting there *By car:* from Carrick-on-Shannon follow the N4 (west) to Boyle. The R294 from Boyle (west) passes close to the north end of Lough Gara.
By rail: services from Dublin (Connolly) and Sligo stop at Boyle, T: (01) 836 6222.
By bus: Bus Eireann services from Dublin, Sligo and

Athlone stop at Boyle, T: (071) 60066.
Where to stay *Hotels and B&Bs:* there is a good choice of B&Bs in Boyle, including Mrs Eileen Kelly, T: (079) 62227, and Mrs Taylor, T: (079) 66075. The Royal Hotel is on the river, T: (079) 62016.
Outdoor living: the closest camp-site to the lough is the Lough Key CCP near Boyle, open Apr–Sept, T: (079) 62212/62363.
Activities *Cycling:* bikes can be hired from Brendan Sheerin's in Boyle, T: (079) 62010.
Fishing: contact the Boyle and District Angling Association, T: (079) 62455. Fishing tackle is available from Tooman's, T: (078) 21872/(087) 560220, in Carrick-on-Shannon. Lough Key is a particularly good pike and brown-trout lake.
Watersports: wind-surfing and sailing equipment are available for hire on Lough Key. Contact the Lough Key Forest Park for details.
Further information *Tourist office:* the BF office in Boyle is open May–late Sept, T: (079) 62145.
Park office: Lough Key Forest Park, T: (079) 62363.
Ecology: the park office organizes guided nature walks.

Lakeland

Mass of lakes on a bed of slate; an angler's paradise

A woman I loved long ago banned the word 'boring' from her vocabulary. I think she adopted the principle from her mother. She certainly tries – with mixed success – to pass it on to her own children. Everything is interesting, she says, provided you look at it in the right way. What bores is in the eye of the beholder.

On much the same grounds I try to avoid the cliché 'See one and you've seen them all'. It is glib and it demeans the subjects. But the lakes of Counties Cavan, Longford and Westmeath test my resolution. They would not try an angler in the same way. He would distinguish the lakes like the books in a library: different larvae, different flies, different currents and pools and temperatures, different shades from different trees, different shores and access, different – amazingly different – fish. They list them on local signposts, white on brown: Rudd this way,

---

LAW OF THE COUNTRYSIDE

Fox-hunting, which takes place all over Ireland, is restricted to the months November to March.

Fishing regulations are subject to local variation and should always be checked. Salmon fishing opens at the beginning of January and ends in September. Brown-trout fishing opens in February and ends in October. The sea-trout season runs from May, June or July to September or October, depending on the fishery. Coarse fishing has no closed season. Sea-fishing takes place throughout the year.

Shooting seasons, and the species which may be taken, are regulated by the National Parks and Wildlife Service (address on page 216).

Perch that, Bream, Pike the other. It often strikes me as a strange alliance of sportsman and bureaucrat, this matching of location and species. But I am not, it may seem superfluous to add, a fisherman. To me one lake is much like another. But they are not dull, not as long as the wild processes on which fishermen depend continue.

To those of us not dedicated to the condition of suspended animation known as fishing, the mayfly, the staple bait of the fly-fisherman, and its companions offer interest too. On warm afternoons they rise in swarms for the mating flight. The females drop their eggs when the sun has set. Other forms may gather for a while in warm, sunny or sheltered corners of the lake: stoneflies, including the angler's favoured yellow sally (*Isoperia grammatica*); needleflies (*Leuctra* spp.), gathering their wings tightly about them; the water boatman (*Notonecta* spp.), buoyed by a bubble of air, game to attack tadpoles, small fish and the occasional human finger; whirligig beetles (*Gyrinus natator*), using their legs as oars to dart towards ditched flies or floating corpses, half an eye (literally) above and half below the water's surface, receding from severed wings or hollow head-cases, turning curves and circles on the glistening rink, or congregating in huge herds. Such scenes wait at the end of every lake path leading from the road.

As to the sameness of the lakes, it is half inevitable and half untrue. Inevitable because a mass of lakes distributed across a bed of slate that dips and lifts within narrow limits are likely to have much in common; untrue in that the greater waters of this central lakeland are palpably distinct.

Lough Oughter is a huge watery labyrinth, a baffling area of lake sliced and broken by countless insertions of land and islands. It follows on, after a break, from the similar maze of Upper Lough Erne. Lough Sheelin, on the River Inny, a tributary of the Shannon, is a large lake (4 by 2 miles/7 by 3 kilometres maximum) nicely fringed with woods, some of them of a stately demesne elegance. Lough Ramor, on the Boyne, lying in the pretty country of south-east Cavan, sparkles with islands and trees. Lough Derravaragh is set in a heartland of history and myth, its eastern side well bounded with commanding hills. Running through this vast expanse of lakes, Ireland's longest river, the Shannon, creates yet more lakes of great variety – Boderg, Bofin, Forbes, Ree – by its expansions and contractions.

Before you go *Maps:* OSI Discovery Series, map Nos 34, 35, 41 and 42.

Getting there *By car:* from Mullingar, the N4 to Longford runs past Lough Owel and the R394 (north) goes past Lough Derravaragh and, after Finea, alongside Lough Sheelin. The R395 (south-east) from Castlepollard passes Lough Lene. Lough Gowna can be reached by heading north out of Granard. Lough Oughter and Killykeen National Park lie northwest of Cavan.

By rail: Mullingar, Edgeworthstown and Longford are on the Dublin (Connolly)–Sligo line, with 3 trains daily to and from Dublin, T: (01) 836 6222.

By bus: Bus Eireann services from Dublin, Ballina, Sligo and Athlone stop in Longford and Mullingar. An Expressway service between Athlone and Cavan stops at Granard and a local service between Dublin and Granard stops at Castle-

pollard. Services go to Cavan from all over Ireland, T: (049) 31353/32533.

Where to stay *Hotels and B&Bs:* there is a good selection in and around Mullingar and Cavan. The Crover House Hotel on Lough Sheelin also hires out fishing boats, T: (049) 854 0206.

Youth hostels: the Holiday Hostel, at Ballinamore, T: (078) 44955, and the Town Clock Hostel in Carrick-on-Shannon, T: (078) 20068.

Activities *Walking:* there are some fine walks and nature

At any given time particles of domesticated Ireland are returning to a wild state: here a cottage, bodily discarded in favour of a bungalow.

trails in Killykeen Forest Park.
Cycling: bikes can be hired in the summer from Abbey Set Printers in Cavan, T: (049) 433 1932. For details of the Kingfisher Cycle Trail see Cycle Ireland's web-site: www.cycle ireland.com.
Riding: hacks are available at The Killykeen Equestrian Centre, T: (049) 436 1707, e-mail: killykeenequ@tinet.ie.
Fishing: the lakes around Cavan are known throughout the world for their excellent coarse fishing, primarily for pike, bream, perch and roach;

game angling for trout is available in Lough Sheelin. Trout fishing on Lough Owel, Lough Lene and Lough Derravaragh runs from Mar to mid-Oct. All these lakes, apart from Lough Lene, are controlled by the Shannon Regional Fisheries Board, T: (061) 455171. For tackle contact Sam Smith, T: (044) 40430, or O'Malley's, T: (044) 48300, in Mullingar. For information on Lough Derravaragh, contact Mr Newman,

T: (044) 71206; for fishing on the lough call Oliver Daly, T: (044) 71220. Mrs Dooran rents out boats and operates gillie services on Lough Owel, T: (044) 42085.
Further information *Tourist offices:* the BF office in Cavan, T: (049) 433 1942, is open all year and in Mullingar June–Sept, T: (044) 48650, e-mail: midlandseasttourism@tinet.ie.
Park office: Killykeen Forest Park, T: (049) 433 2541.

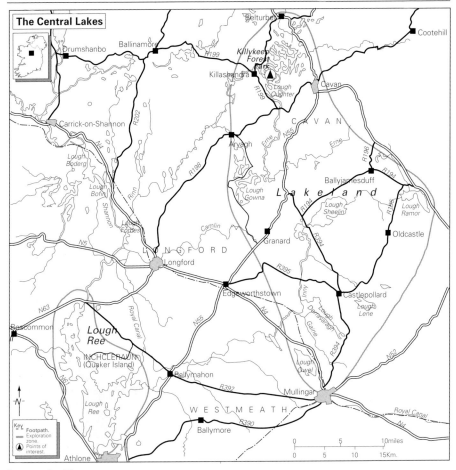

The Central Lakes

Lough Ree

Fourth largest lake in Ireland; breeding ground of the endangered common scoter

On the Ordnance Survey map many more place-names are shown around the southern borders of Lough Ree than the northern. John O'Donovan, whose admirable survey of the country is still the basis of these maps, is said to have been courting at the time of this

work a farmer's daughter whose home was close to the southernmost tip of the lake. He spun out his time to remain close to her, and the effect on the survey reappears with each new edition.

Whatever their romantic charms, the purlieus of Lough Ree are very flat. The tremolo undulations of Counties Longford, Westmeath and Roscommon hardly figure in the view from the lake. It has none of the picturesque appeal of Lough Derg. The Athlone–Galway railway, which runs up the west side, and an extensive acreage of

reed and mud at the edges, make it difficult, often, to get to the water. The best way to see Lough Ree is from a boat.

Fifteen miles (24 km) long and at most seven (11 km) wide, it occupies 39 square miles (62 square km) and is the fourth largest lake in Ireland. Many of its innumerable islands possess remains of great interest, including castles and monastic buildings. On one of them, Inchcleraun or Quaker Island, are a number of ruined churches, one of which was pulled down by a 19th-century Quaker in order to build a home. The sacrilege led to a curse and his removal from the island. Rather less fortunate was Queen Maeve, whose desire to possess the Brown Bull of Cooley led her to ravage the kingdom of Ulster. While bathing from this island, the legend goes, she was killed by an Ulster prince with a stone from his sling.

Birds are present in modest numbers, possibly more than have been recorded given the difficulty of seeing them. In winter, there are diving and dabbling ducks – over a thousand tufted ducks in the north-east sector. Common terns and black-headed gulls come in spring to breed, along with a small number of common scoters, now an endangered species in Ireland. You can see them from lanes that bring you to the water's edge, but it is extraordinary how much is obscured by nearby vegetation and headlands. Again a boat is the best viewpoint, but if I were in a boat I should be off to Lough Derg or the entrancing coils of the Shannon that lie between the two lakes.

Before you go *Maps:* OSI Discovery Series, map Nos 40 and 47. **Getting there** *By car:* from Dublin take N6 to Athlone, then N61 (north) to Roscommon, up the west side of Lough Ree. *By rail:* services from Dublin (Heuston) to Galway, Westport and Ballina stop at Athlone. Westport and Ballina trains also stop at Roscommon, T: (0902) 73300. *By bus:* Bus Eireann services stop at Athlone and Roscommon. A Mon–Sat Longford–Galway service stops at Lanesborough, T: (091) 562000. **Where to stay** *Hotels:* try Abbey Hotel in Roscommon, T: (0903) 26240, or Castle Ffrench at Ballinamore Bridge, near Athlone, T: (0903) 22288. *Outdoor living:* Gailey Bay CCP near Roscommon, on the west shore of Lough Ree, T: (0903) 61058, open Apr–Oct, and Hodson Bay CCP near Athlone, T: (0902) 92448, open May–Sept. **Activities** *Cycling:* Hardiman's in Athlone hire bikes, T: (0902) 78669. *Fishing:* the lough is well stocked with trout. *Birdwatching:* in summer common terns, black-headed gulls and common scoter. **Further information:** the Athlone BF is open all year, T: (0902) 94630.

THE CAVAN WAY

OSI Discovery Series, map No. 26

The 16-mile (26-km) Cavan Way is a fairly straightforward walk across the extreme west of the county. Dowra, at the south-western end, stands on the border of Cavan and Leitrim, at the head of Lough Allen, and the first half of the Way is along the final ascent of the Shannon valley. The river ends at the Shannon Pot, fenced, spruced and footpathed for the delectation of tourists. The second half of the walk, north-east to Blacklion on the Northern Ireland border, goes through hilly country very rich in megalithic remains: ring-forts, chamber-tombs, gallery graves and so on. There are also several sweat-house ruins, where once a draining heat-session was followed by a plunge into the nearest water. Some walkers regret the demise of this institution. From Blacklion, at the end of the walk, the Ulster Way takes over, leading north towards Donegal and south-east to Upper Lough Erne.

Before you go *Guide-books:* Cavan Way Map Guide (Cavan County Council). **Getting there** *By car:* to reach Blacklion follow the A4 (west) from Enniskillen. To reach Dowra and Lough Allen, take the R207 (south) after Blacklion. *By bus:* the Mon–Sat Bus Eireann Expressway between Westport and Enniskillen stops at Blacklion once a day. The Sligo–Enniskillen bus stops at Blacklion twice a day, T: (071) 60066. **Where to stay** *Hotels and B&Bs:* Lough Macnean House, T: (072) 53022, and The Olive Grove, T: (072) 53443, are in Blacklion. In Enniskillen, try the First Lodge Hotel, T: (028) 6632 3275, the Killyhevlin Hotel, T: (028) 6632 3481, e-mail: rodney@easynet.co.uk, and many more. *Youth hostels:* the nearest are at Ballinamore, T: (078) 44955, and Sandville House, just south of Ballyconnell, T: (049) 952 6297. **Further information** *Tourist office:* the nearest to Blacklion is the Fermanagh Tourist Information Centre in Enniskillen, open all year, T: (028) 6632 3110/6632 5050 (Northern Ireland). The Library Service, Cavan County Council, Cavan Town, Co. Cavan, T: (049) 31799, can provide a map and guide for the Cavan Way.

Little Brosna River

Flooded meadows on the river are home to Ireland's last surviving corncrake population

Some places are wild in season. The flat-lands bordering the central Shannon between Loughs Ree and Derg are a magical area of peat bog, containing the remnants of human enterprises from the Stone Age to the boom-time of canals, from the pagan to the Christian. The landscape is punctuated by those serpentine sweepings of the glaciers known as eskers, curved ridges of grass-topped gravel and sand brought down by melt-waters from the mountains and deposited in deep escape channels in the glacial ice. Along the rivers there are rich pastures on alluvial soils, and footpaths for fishermen. No summer visitor could call any of this wild.

The rains come in autumn, in quantities to flood the meadows. By November these are underwater. The river is an inland sea. Then the birds arrive from the north for the worst of the winter. There are wigeon, mallard, teal, pintail, shoveler, Greenland white-fronted goose, three kinds of swan, black-tailed godwit, dunlin, greenshank and also breeding populations of curlew, lapwing, redshank and snipe. Wigeon can be numbered in thousands, as can the black-tailed godwits and other waders; swans, geese and various ducks come in hundreds. Numbers peak in February and March. In a normal year the waters recede soon after. The birds depart for Iceland and the Arctic. The callows, as these floodable meadows are called, are tame again.

In spring and summer the callows are home to most of the remaining population of Ireland's corncrakes. They survive here because grass grows more slowly on the callows and because hay or, increasingly, big-bale silage is cut later here than elsewhere in the country. The corncrake is an odd bird, with a gawky flight – it wisely prefers to run for cover – and a rather dumpy figure. At most times round the clock, but particularly for an hour or two after midnight, the males make a curious noise variously represented as a 'crake', from which comes the bird's English name, or as *Crex crex*, which is its Latin name, or as an electronic purr, or as the sound of a comb being grated. A generation or so ago everybody in rural Ireland (and a great many in rural Britain) was familiar with the characteristic nightly crakes or crexes during the breeding season. They took them for granted and never bothered to mention them. Then farmers adopted the practice of making silage. This happens earlier in the season than hay-making, at a time when the female corncrake and her chicks are in among the grass. Whereas scything in times gone by gave the birds plenty of time to get out of the way, the modern mechanical cutter is difficult to escape; more so as it tends to be steered round the field from the outside to the middle, enclosing its victims in a diminishing space until it hacks them to bits at the centre.

Another disturbing ritual is carried out by some farmers on the rich farmlands of the midlands and the East at about the same time. This is the shearing of hedges by mechanical cutter. Nests are sliced or toppled and bird populations fall further. Though rather an eccentric bird, with its shy habits and curious night-calls, the corncrake has come to be a symbol of persecuted wildlife. Every year it is reported to be losing numbers or to have disappeared from places – such as Inishbofin off the Galway coast – where it has hitherto managed to hold out. It remains on the flood plains of the Shannon, but there are experts who think it cannot last for long.

Before you go *Maps:* OSI Discovery Series, map Nos 47 and 53.

Getting there *By car:* from Athlone take the N62 south to Cloghan, then the R356 and R456 to Banagher. Minor roads lead down to the river. *By rail:* services stop at Roscrea twice a day from Dublin and Limerick. Daily services from Dublin (Heuston) to the West stop at Tullamore, T: (01) 836 6222. *By bus:* Bus Eireann services from Dublin, Portumna, Cork and Athlone stop at Birr, T: (01) 836 6111. Kern's Coaches, T: (0509) 20124, run from Tullamore to Galway, also stopping at Birr.

Where to stay *Hotels and B&Bs:* in Birr are County Arms Hotel, T: (0509) 20791; Maltings Guesthouse, T: (0509) 21345; Mrs Spain, T: (0509) 20256; Tullanisk Dower House, T: (0509) 20572, e-mail: tnisk@indigo.ie. In Cloghan, Mrs Finneran, T: (0902) 57355, and in Banagher, Brosna Lodge Hotel, T: (0509) 51350.

Activities *Cycling:* bikes can be hired from P. L. Dolan and Sons in Birr, T: (0509) 20006.

Further information *Tourist offices:* the BF office in Birr is open May–Sept, T: (0509) 20110, and in Athlone all year, T: (0902) 94630.

Lough Derg and the Lower Shannon

This geologically puzzling section of river and lake provides good boating and isolated walks

Lough Derg is like an inland sea: a miniature Mediterranean with counties for countries, and rather less climatic and cultural variation. County Clare to the west is the O'Brien fief: rough and rocky, poor and mountainous. To the south, County Limerick takes the outflow of the Shannon (of which the lough is really a mightily swollen section) and, at a place called Ardnacrusha, in a huge man-made hydro-electric water-

Twenty years ago and more the corncrake was well-known all over Ireland; not by sight, for it is shy, but for its sound: an absurd grating noise uttered in the middle of the night. It is scarce now, reduced to half a dozen or so localities in the whole country where the hay is cut late.

Reeds are blown aslant under a scowling sky on Lough Oughter, in the watery Killykeen Forest Park.

fall, drops much of it a hundred feet. County Tipperary to the east, traditional Butler territory, is a place of rich pasture and small towns and modest mountain ranges, of which the Arra comes close to the lough shore. Flat, green, damp and stony on the north-western bank, County Galway here gives no indication of the highland dramas it packs into its Atlantic half. Each county, through its soil, contours and climate, has worked its will on the porous and erodible limestone of the lake's bed to produce the variant shapes and sizes of bays, headlands and islands, the changing nature of coastal vegetation, the orientation of fields and woods. There are occasional unique features: the Irish fleabane (*Inula salicina*), which is not unlike a small sunflower, is found nowhere else in these islands. It is by no means common here. Far more than bland Lough Ree to the north, Lough Derg is busy, lively and a pretty filigree of detail.

The course taken by the lake's outflow at its southern end presents geologists with a puzzle. The mountains which edge its southern flanks are of old red sandstone with an inner core of quartzite. They are much harder than the limestone that makes up the rest of the lake's bed and, since the eruptions that threw them up 300 million years ago, they have formed three huge islands in the limestone. Instead of leaving the lake by one of the channels between these mountains, the water seems to have carved a way through the southernmost of them, giving itself a great deal of unnecessary trouble. Of course there must be an explanation, and Frank Mitchell, doyen of Irish geologists, finds it in the movement of ice from the north. Coming against the mountain wall, it divided and flowed east and west, except for a central thrust of ice which, finding a valley, forged ahead, deepened it, and eventually gouged out the gorge which now conveys the outflow.

From end to end of Lough Derg, the points at which the River Shannon respectively expands from and retracts into sensible river dimensions are 22 miles (35 kilometres) apart. Its width is not so easily given because so many deep bays have been bitten out of its edge. At its widest, from the west end of Scarriff Bay to the east of Youghal Bay (the name denotes yew woods, no longer there), it reaches eight miles (13 kilometres), though for most of its length it is less than three (five kilometres). Border lands are rich in woods and copses and stately lone trees, and there is an uneven spattering of islands, from a mile (1.5 kilometres) to a few feet across. Many have shrubs and trees, a few of them cottages or castles, and one, Holy Island, a mile or so south of Mountshannon, preserves among its lazy sprawl of grass and bushes the remains of a 7th-century abbey with a 10th-century round tower 70 feet (21 metres) high. Some islands have a pretty green symmetry, like upturned powder puffs of tree foliage. There are grand lake-side demesnes, their mature parklands handed down from the days of the Ascendancy to an age which is doing nothing to maintain their beauty and grandeur.

Twenty years ago the tourist authorities, touting for custom, could truly claim that the density of boats on the Shannon was one one-hundred-and-eightieth of the density on England's Norfolk Broads. Today, the disparity is still dramatic but distinctly reduced. Killaloe, Mountshannon, Garrykennedy, Dromineer and other towns and villages with quays buzz with activity in season. Ancillary shops – chandlers, provision stores and restaurants – have burgeoned, along with places to stay.

In the early 1970s I cruised down the river. There was a night at Garrykennedy, a little harbour village as wily about water and its ways as can be and, while not used to tourists, consummate in hospitality towards them. We were brought to the pub. As I remember, it was a grim succession of cells whose low ceilings and walls were stained dull yellow from decades of cigarette and pipe smoke. We sat on metal barrels and talked of twenty-pound salmon, of the pike that fought like Attila, of rough waters and the storm that years before sank a Guinness tanker, from the wreck of which barrels of stout were being hauled ashore for months afterwards. We bought each other pint after pint, we sang, and there were strong men exhibiting that strange, tense, sweaty resolve to hit the right note, or something near it, and continue it to its end, despite the attempts of alcohol and gravity to reduce them to snoring piles on the floor. I zigzagged back to the cruiser well after tea and, under the spindly ruins of the old castle, contrived to lower my feet on to the boat rather than the water, and got to bed.

I do not want such Viking sessions now, and I am not sure that they are to be had. A new class of nautical amateurs has replaced the gnarled old crewmen. They wear protective clothes of many colours, talk gung-ho among themselves and never greet strangers; they comport themselves on their motor cruisers as if they were skippering schooners; their pubs are clean and bright and comfortable. No matter. The lough is big enough to absorb them (I have wished it would). It is big enough for the fishermen who sit in motionless, miserable threes in rowing boats for six hours at a stretch. It is big enough for you or me to walk without a human in sight among the lake-side grasses and occasional orchids, watch the circular ripples set in motion by a trout snapping at a mayfly, or climb to the prehistoric graves of the Leinster Men on the slopes of Tountinna, to survey the entire scene.

BEFORE YOU GO
Maps: OSI Discovery Series, map Nos 52, 53, 58 and 59.

GETTING THERE
By car: from Galway take N6 (east) to Loughrea, and after continuing 3 miles on the eastward N6 take N65 to Portumna at the north end of Lough Derg. There is a good road system round the lake.
By rail: the nearest stations are at Nenagh and Birdhill with services from Dublin and Limerick, T: (061) 315555.
By bus: a Bus Eireann service runs every day between Dublin and Portumna. The Galway–Eyrecourt service runs Mon–Fri (not Thurs) and stops at Portumna. The regular Dublin–Limerick Expressway service stops at Nenagh, T: (01) 836 6111.

WHERE TO STAY
Hotels and B&Bs: options include Mrs Brennan, Killaloe, T: (061) 376704; Waterman's Lodge, T: (061) 376333; Mrs Delaney, Nenagh, T: (067) 32053; and Ashley Park House on the shore of the lake, T: (061) 38223, e-mail: david_mackenzie@compuserve.com. In Portumna try the Dolans, T: (0509) 41269, or Mrs Ryan, T: (0509) 41138.
Youth hostels: the independent Galway Shannonside Schoolhouse hostel is in Portumna, T: (0509) 41032.
Outdoor living: the Lough Derg Caravan and Camping Holiday Park at Killaloe is open May–Sept, T: (061) 376329, and the Lakeside Camping and Caravan Park at Mountshannon is open May–Oct, T: (061) 927225.

ACTIVITIES
Walking: *The Lough Derg Way* leaflet has a map and notes on historical sites. It is available from local BF offices (see below).
Fishing: there is plenty of coarse fishing in the area. Lough Derg is known for its brown-trout, salmon, pike and rudd fishing.
Watersports: for sailing and wind-surfing contact Karen Weeks at the Killaloe Activity Centre, Co. Clare, T: (061) 376622.

FURTHER INFORMATION
Tourist offices: BF offices are in Killaloe, open June–Sept, T: (061) 376866; and Limerick, open all year, T: (061) 317522. In summer, information is also available from Mr Clasby in Portumna, T: (0905) 76201. Shannon Erne has a web-site, www.shannon.erne.ie.

Mayflies are common on and near lakes and rivers where water quality is good, the females laying their eggs during the few days of their adult existence. Fishermen use artificial flies as bait for trout and other fish.

Slieve Bloom

A scenic bulge in the central plain; unspoilt mountain bog and glens

Ireland's protuberant navel, a big bulge above the prosperous, peaty midlands, the pride of locals, perfectly accessible from numerous towns and endowed with the largest area of mountain bog in the country (bigger even than Wicklow's) is mercifully less visited than such a central, substantial and agreeable feature might be. Wildness persists, despite the efforts of desk-bound bureaucrats, who have dubbed the Slieve Bloom (which means the mountains of Bladh – a hero of ancient myth) an Environment Park. If we were faithful to the old meanings of words, this would quite misleadingly signify a park on the outskirts of the Bloom Mountains – and how inept to try to catch this massive billow of ancient rock, which could conceal all the people of Ireland within its glens, in a suburban tag: park. Thankfully, the range remains relatively unspoilt.

There is a lot to spoil. North to south the range stretches 12 miles (22 kilometres), and east to west it is 14 miles (23 kilometres) long. Almost all the overlying rock is old red sandstone, laid down as marine sediment around 400 million years ago. Underneath it lay older, Silurian rocks, which had been bunched together into tall mountains by that clash of tectonic plates known as the Caledonian orogeny and then greatly reduced by weathering. There are areas either side of the Slieve Bloom ridge where subsequent erosion has allowed this older rock (older, that is, than the 'old' red sandstone) to break through, as has happened in bigger ranges to the south-west, similarly formed. Streams and waterfalls in the many glens have also exposed earlier deposits. But for the most part no rock is visible, being covered with several feet of peat or soil.

The Slieve Bloom is not dramatic. It gets no higher than 1,734 feet (529 metres) and the shapes that make it up are so gently

curved that you can often look about you and imagine you are on the plain. The name of its highest point – Arderin, or the Height of Ireland – sounds pretentious until you see the astounding views. On the other hand, it is greatly different from what lies about it, which actually is the plain, the endless, boggy (or formerly boggy) flat-lands of central Ireland. Really the Slieve Bloom is a sort of dry-run island, as distinctive as an island in its shapes, constituent materials, growth, outlook and activity from its surroundings. The people who occupy its villages and scattered farmsteads are hill people, grazing their cattle on grassy slopes and hilltops, among copses of oak and beech and riots of bramble and thorn. They and their dogs are used to humping uphill and striding out

---

THE IRISH SKY

Someone was praising the quality of Irish air to Jonathan Swift, the mordant champion of the Irish against English greed and exploitation. 'Hold your peace, sir,' he replied, 'lest the English should tax it.' People talk of the balminess of Irish air, cleansed by its ocean journey (it usually comes from the south-west, often enough bringing rain). Then again, Irish rain is not like that of other countries. 'The rain here,' the German novelist Heinrich Böll wrote from Ireland, 'is absolute, magnificent and frightening. To call this rain bad weather is to call scorching sunshine fine weather.' It would be silly to claim that there are no miserably sodden, dark days during which nothing feels dry, indoors or out. But summer rain can be short and refreshing, its wetness soon blown away by the same light, sweet breeze that brought it.

Clouds are another ocean import, and it is worth keeping an eye on the sky just for the scenic bonus of towering cirrocumulus, infinite mackerel patterns, darkening storm-skirts or Old Testament clouds impaled on shafts of golden sunlight. It was such a vision, appearing over the western sea, that stirred St Brendan the Navigator to sail away in his curragh and discover America.

downhill. The area's history is one of ancient myth, a record rich with tales of outlaws and highwaymen and the search for sanctuary, as well as the universal Irish themes of war, confiscation, strain and struggle between landlord and tenant, famine and emigration. There are the remains of many mines and quarries, too. On the south side is what is called a famine field, made up of the ridges and ditches used for the planting of potatoes in 1848, a year of devastating famine. The succession of long mounds appropriately suggests an uncannily packed and orderly graveyard.

Some of the finest slopes are alongside the numerous waters that ripple down Slieve Bloom's glens. Here begin three of Ireland's principal rivers, the Nore, Barrow and Suir. The pity is that, 50 and more years ago, most of these glens were planted with forestry trees which gradually blotted out plants that had recurred for thousands of years. (Three hundred years before, a different human activity, the smelting of iron, a process requiring oak charcoal, had caused the uprooting of thousands of acres of oak on the south and west slopes of the range.) The Silver river is the notable exception. To ensure it remains so, it has been acquired by the council and made an official reserve complete with nature trail. Its name comes from the minute particles of silver found in its upper rocks and also, from time to time, in the water, in worthless quantities. More interesting are the layered walls of old red sandstone alternating with silts which border the current in parts, forming here and there a fairly complete geological record. Oak and birch woods still survive here, as do those lesser plants which share a fondness for acid and sandstone and root themselves often enough in cracks in the vertical rock or in boulders standing up from the water: ferns, mosses, liverworts, lichens. The walk upstream from Cadamstown is wonderfully varied as the glen's character changes. Glenbarrow is another glen where the layered rock structure is clearly visible. Some hold it to be the most beautiful glen, too – it is one of the best known. Also popular is Glendine, its east divided from its west by the Glendine Gap, which rises close to Arderin,

offering wonderful views.

The broad sweeps of blanket bog-land – distinct in character and origin from the raised bogs of the central plain – are probably Slieve Bloom's most natural and authentic terrain. They are there to walk, and it is a good experience (some say particularly good for joints) to feel the spring offered by the dominant heather (*Calluna vulgaris*) and the underlying peat. The botanist Robert Lloyd Praeger, without initially intending to, once walked from Mountrath to Kinnitty and back by a different route 'in mists and sheets of rain', a total of 37 miles (59 kilometres). 'It was nothing much', he wrote. But then 'a modest twenty to twenty-five miles per day, spread over twelve hours to allow plenty of time for botanizing, and continued for as many days as necessary' – 'done', he added, 'on a toothbrush and a collar' – was probably so routine for him that he sometimes did it in his sleep. The region is not known for its plant rarities. However, Praeger on his walk was pleased to

The path down to any of the Lakeland waters – in this case Lough Derravaragh – is, in season at least, most often trodden by anglers.

151

find the Welsh poppy (*Meconopsis cambrica*) and filmy fern (*Hymenophyllum tunbridgense*) in a gully by the Glendine Gap. There are also bog cotton (*Eriophorum spp.*) and deer sedge (*Trichophorum caespitosum*), both of which thrive after fire, and other standard bog plants. What may be the rarest, as well as the most beautiful, of the plants of the area, according to the polymath geologist John Feehan, is the mountain pansy (*Viola lutea*). Usually yellow, as its Latin name implies, it is here, in the one occurrence known to Feehan, 'a most marvellous blue violet'. It grows on a grassy bank of stone facing south-west.

Animals abound in the area. Fallow deer, badgers and foxes are sometimes seen, pine martens and otters only very occasionally. They have all been here since time immemorial. Others used to be. In the 5th century, according to monastic texts, St Ciaran made a friend of a wild boar in this vicinity. When the good man wanted materials for building a cell, the boar severed the necessary branches and reeds with his teeth. Soon a fox, badger, wolf and stag were added to his coterie. But such liaisons were familiar stuff in those magical times. For want of a yet-to-be-invented alarm clock, St Mochua's mouse licked his ear each morning to wake him. And when he paused from the reciting of psalms, a devoted fly stood at the point of the text he had reached, to keep his place.

A VOCABULARY OF IRISH ENGLISH

Irish (Gaelic) and English are the joint official languages of Ireland, but throughout most of the island it is English which is spoken. Not always, however, with the same meaning as it has in England. Here are examples of essentially Irish meanings of English words (with a few common Irish usages added).

avenue, *drive (the approach to a house)*
barney, *fight or fuss*
booley, *transhumance; farming system in which cattle are moved to the highlands each summer*
callows, *river-banks flooded widely and regularly*
cess, *evil (literally, a tax)*
cod, *cheat*
crack, *enjoyment*
crane, *heron*
crow, *rook, crow, jackdaw*
Dail, *lower house of Irish parliament*
demesne, *estate attached to a large house*
destroyed, *appalled or hurt*
ditch, *bank*
evening, *afternoon or evening*
fadge (in Ulster), *potato bread*
fir, *men*
garda, *policeman*
gas, *fun*
gentry, *fairies*
gombeen, *extortionate money-lender*
haggard, *stack yard*
he did *not, (form of agreement)*
hunting, *shooting*
jarvey, *driver of a jaunting car*
johneen, *Irishman who has assumed smart English ways*

lawn, *park*
moin, mona, *peat*
mna, *women*
pampooties, *leather sandals*
pan (of bread), *loaf*
pioneer, *member of a temperance society*
porter, *dark beer, stout*
powerful, *extraordinary*
press, *cupboard*
rere, *rear*
roach, *rudd*
Saherda, *Saturday*
shebeen, *unlicensed pub selling poteen*
sib, *sibling*
soft, *rainy*
stocious, *drunk*
strand, *beach*
strong, *possessing a large farm (of farmer, usually English or Protestant)*
Taoiseach, *prime minister*
this day week, *a week ago today, or a week from today*
town, *small settlement (as few as 20 houses)*
turf, *peat*
whisht, *shhh, be quiet*
will I?, *would you like me to?*
would you be able for?, *can you?*
your man, *the man in question*
youse (in Dublin), *you*

BEFORE YOU GO
Maps: OSI Discovery Series, map No. 54.
Guide-books: *The Slieve Bloom Way* (Bord Fáilte) contains information for hikers. Also consult *The Slieve Bloom Way Map Guide* (EastWest Mapping, 1996); *The Way-Marked Trails of Ireland* by Michael Fewer (Gill & Macmillan, 1997); the *Slieve Bloom Environment Park* brochure (Laois & Offaly County Council); the *Slieve Bloom Environment Park Map* (An Foras Forbatha, 1986); and *Landscape of the Slieve Bloom* by John Feehan (Blackwater Press, 1979).

GETTING THERE
By car: from Portlaoise the N7 (west) to Mountrath and the R440 (north) to Birr run right through the Slieve Bloom Mountains.
By rail: regular services run each day from Cork, Dublin and Limerick to Portlaoise, T: (01) 836 6222.
By bus: the Bus Eireann Expressway between Dublin and Limerick stops at Portlaoise, Mountrath and Borris-in-Ossory. Daily services from Dublin stop at Birr and Mountmellick, T: (01) 836 6111. O'Connell's run buses between Dublin, via Portlaoise, to Mountmellick, T: (0502) 24416. J. J. Kavanagh's run a service between Limerick and Dublin stopping at Roscrea, Mountrath and Portlaoise, T: (087) 262 1389.

WHERE TO STAY
B&Bs: there are several within the Slieve Bloom area; try Noreen Laighin (see Walking below); Mary Lalor, Kinnitty, T: (.0509) 37029; Ardmore House, Kinnitty, T: (0509) 37009; and Janet Dooley, Coolrain, near Portlaoise, T: (0502) 35013.
Youth hostel: the nearest are Farren House in Ballacolla, T:

(0502) 34032, and the Crank House Hostel at Banagher, T: (0509) 51458/(0902) 57561.The Birr Outdoor Education Centre provides accommodation for groups, T: (0509) 20029.
Outdoor living: try the Streamstown CCP in Roscrea, open Apr–Nov, T: (0505) 21519; or Kirwan's CCP in Portlaoise, open Apr–Oct, T: (0502) 21688.

ACTIVITIES
Walking: there are some good walks in the area including the geologically interesting Silver River Nature Trail from Cadamstown and hikes to the summit of Arderin mountain from where it is possible to see the highest points of all 4 of the ancient provinces of Ireland. The waymarked Slieve Bloom Way (48 miles/77 km long) makes a complete circle of the mountains, taking in most major points of interest. It is split into 5 stages: 1, Glenbarrow to Monickew (7 miles/12 km); 2, Monickew to Glendine East (7 miles/12 km); 3, Glen-

dine East to Forelacka (8 miles/17 km); 4, Forelacka to Glenkeen (12 miles/19 km), and 5, Gleenkeen to Glenbarrow (10 miles/16 km). Mrs Noreen Laighin provides route information to walkers and has a B&B at the foot of the mountains, just off the R440 and open all year, T: (0502) 32727, e-mail: conlanhouse@ oceanfree.net. Dooley's Hotel in Birr, T: (059) 20032, organizes walking tours and Siultoiri Cluain na Sli, T: (0502) 28197/28082, organizes guided bus and walking tours through the mountains.
Cycling: Slieve Bloom Bike Hire at the Village Inn in Coolrain, T: (0502) 35126/35277, rents out bikes and can arrange accommodation.

FURTHER INFORMATION
Tourist offices: there are BF offices in Portlaoise, T/F: (0502) 21178, open all year; Birr, T: (0509) 20110, open May–Sept; and Tullamore, T: (0506) 52617, open June–Sept.

The Irish hare is a sub-species of the blue or Arctic hare. It occurs all over the country, wherever the lie of the land provides cover and shelter. The brown or common hare is found only in lowlands in the north-west of Ireland.

CHAPTER 5

The South-East

Wexford has a world-famous opera festival but most foreigners arriving in Ireland think of Rosslare, New Ross, Wexford, Waterford and Clonmel as towns to get through or by as rapidly as possible on their way to the West. The local coast hardly gets a thought, and the nearby mountains are neither required nor expected to be anything but a nice background for the drive. Considering that County Wexford is a few hours from the Welsh coast (nearer than England is), it is surprising how undiscovered it remains. People have said this for years and it makes little difference. Yet the South-East is an area of astonishing variety and attraction. Moreover, if wildness is confined to places too high, too rocky, too wet or too sandy to cultivate, the region is surprisingly rich in wildness. Especially with regard to sand. For while northwest Ireland consists of sheer, stark bastions of rock resisting the Atlantic battery, the surface rim of the South-East is for the most part a low, duney tousle, in which the works of man are slowly worn, gnawed, nibbled, felled and buried by the combined forces of tide and sand.

The most remarkable thing about this stretch of the country is its unheralded diversity. Only a few miles inland from the unending strands, gravel beds, dunes and lagoons of the coast, the country is all green hills, woods and pastures, not unlike the Kentish Weald. (When weighing east against west it is fair to remember another Kentish analogy: rain is half as much on the east as on the

A stunning view opens out from the northern ridge of the horseshoe of rock containing Lough Coumshingaun, in the Comeragh Mountains.

west, and sunshine almost double. June sees an average eight hours of sunshine a day; even September manages six.)

Deep broad rivers like the Suir, Barrow, Nore and Slaney cut across the land in valleys rich in trees, broken now and again by ancient, elegant market towns, crumbling castles and monastery ruins. This is a lush, fertile, gracious national garden. Beyond – again only by a few miles – the wavy lowlands bubble up into mountains: the Blackstairs range dividing Counties Wexford and Carlow, the Comeraghs, Monavullaghs and Knockmealdowns rising in County Waterford, and the Galtees enhancing Tipperary with their bouncy east–west squiggle of a silhouette. The Comeraghs and Galtees in particular offer all kinds of walking and climbing, up and down gradual gradients or sheer rock-faces, among beguiling and evocative contours, with icy lakes, mountain birds, moorland plants and occasional broad views across endless plains or out to sea. From the Comeraghs the Saltee Islands can be visible on a clear day.

Islands on this coast are few. Indeed the north, east and south coasts of Ireland, in sharp contrast to the west and its sprinkled archipelagos, have scarcely more than half a dozen islands each, and only one or two of those possess life or landscape worthy of note. The Saltees, five miles (eight kilometres) out from the coast of Wexford, have character and to spare. Great Saltee is a crucial bird reserve, whose winged population at the end of the breeding season approaches 100,000. These consist mainly of those sea-birds familiar on inaccessible Irish cliffs and islands. There is besides, on cliffs at the south end of the island, a multiplying colony of gannets. Several hundred shags breed here, but not their similar and close cousins the cormorants. These are found on Little

Saltee, in one of their biggest breeding accumulations in the whole of Ireland.

Inhabited and farmed during the 19th century, the two islands, like many off the west coast, lost their populations during the first half of the 20th. When the present owner, the self-styled Prince Michael of the Saltees, bought them for a few pounds in 1943, the wild was inexorably returning. In fact, the islands provide a tiny glimpse of the nature of wildness, its course and force and drive to repossess what has once been taken from it in one particular habitat. Embryonic wilderness in such a setting takes the form of wild flowers in hedge and pasture, slowly giving way to bramble and suffocating bracken. More noticeably, it gives way to rabbits. Such were their numbers back in the 1930s that as they moved the land itself seemed to be in motion.

There were rats too. They could be killed in their hundreds by tempting them with bait under a propped-up door and letting it drop on them. During the Second World War rabbits were trapped for meat, but afterwards their value fell away, especially when their grubbing and burrowing ended an expensive afforestation project. Destroying them proved a problem. Imported ferrets died in their first winter. Foxes settled but none of their offspring survived infancy. Forty-six cats were let loose. They killed rats, which was thought fine, and puffins, which caused outrage. The cats died, or charmed and went home with picnicking visitors, while rabbits continued to thrive. It was myxomatosis, introduced in 1962 and recurring every few years since, which has controlled rabbit numbers. There are rats, too, but some sort of balance seems to have been established.

Out beyond Carnsore Point the sometimes-visible turbulence is due to the meeting of two currents, the Gulf Stream coming in from the Atlantic and the southward flow from St George's Channel. The collision ensures a rich mix of plankton. It brings fish, birds, seals and shark to feed off it or off each other. It creates currents which can here and there make bathing dangerous. More insidiously, over decades and centuries, it has amassed long, hidden reefs of sand which have dragged down untold numbers of ships. For millions of years it has pulverized the ancient rocks of the region into sand. This destructive process has nevertheless created sand-dunes where plants thrive that thrive nowhere else, sand-hemmed lakes and lagoons where several kinds of birds breed in relative safety, and miles and miles of white strands. Where it has buried or half-buried stone keeps, churches, walls, even whole villages – places where history was made by invasion, the signing of treaties or dynastic marriages – it evokes a desolation as pungent as the pyramids, and a suggestion that the final winner in the old struggle for dominance between humans and wild nature will always, in the end, be nature.

GETTING THERE

By air: all flights into Waterford airport, T: (051) 875589, are from the UK. British Airways fly from London (Gatwick) and in the summer from Manchester, T: (0845) 722 2111; Scot Airways fly from Luton, T: (01223) 293393. Dublin is the Republic's main international airport, T: (01) 814 1111, www.dublin airport.com, with direct flights from the UK, major European cities and North America.

By sea: Stena Line run 2 services from Fishguard to Rosslare, a Lynx Fastcraft 99-min crossing or a 3-hr 30-min ferry service, T: (0870) 570 7070 (UK), www.stenaline.co.uk; Irish Ferries have a 4-hr crossing from Pembroke to Rosslare, T: (0870) 517 1717 (UK), and services from Cherbourg and Roscoff to Rosslare, T: (01) 638 3333 (Dublin), www.irish ferries.ie.

WHERE TO STAY

Tipperary, Waterford and Wexford have a huge range of accommodation. The countryside is dotted with B&Bs and campsites. The local Bord Fáilte offices provide accommodation booking services.

ACTIVITIES

Walking: the Wexford Coast Path stretches 125 miles (200 km) from Kilmichael Point to Ballyhack in Waterford harbour and offers some spectacular sea views. Wexford County Council, T: (053) 42211, produce a leaflet on the path, also available from BF. The 43-mile (70-km) East Munster Way connects with the South Leinster, Wicklow and Blackwater Ways and is split into 3 stages: 1, Carrick-on-Suir to Clonmel (18 miles/26 km); 2, Clonmel to Newcastle (11 miles/16 km); and 3, Newcastle to the Vee (11 miles/16 km). The Suir towpath, the Comeragh foothills, the Nire valley and the broad, boggy Knockmealdowns make for fine walking. The uplands offer magnificent views across the plains of Tipperary, or over to the swelling silhouettes of the Galtees. There is a particularly good hike up Mount Leinster along the 62-mile (100-km) South Leinster Way, which is split into 5 stages: 1, Kildavin to Borris (12.5 miles/20 km); 2, Borris to Graiguenamanagh (8 miles/13 km); 3, Graiguenamanagh to Inistioge (8 miles/13 km); 4, Inistioge to Mullinavat (12.5 miles/20 km); and 5, Mullinavat to Carrick-on-Suir (14 miles/22.5 km). Much of the route is rich in rural scenery: the heathery Blackstairs Mountains, a few miles of old towpath beside the River Barrow, the rich pastoral undulations of County Kilkenny and, finally, the River Suir itself.

Cycling: with the exception of the Knockmealdown and Comeragh Mountains, the South-East offers relatively easy cycling. Celtic Cycling organizes tours in the area, T: (0503) 75282, www.celticcycling.com.

Riding: the arable farmland of the area offers pleasant riding, and the sandy beaches exhilarating gallops. The 5-Star Tipperary Trail is organized by John and Rosetta Ann Paxman, T: (067) 21129, who also offer residential courses. Nire Valley Equestrian Trail-Riding and Trekking is near Clonmel, T: (052) 36147. The Horetown Equestrian Centre in Foulksmills, Co. Wexford, is run by the Young family from their 18th-century home, T: (051) 565771; e-mail: poloxirl@iol.ie.

Fishing: there is good fishing on the River Barrow at Carlow Town and Graiguenamanagh. A popular angling festival is held on the river in May. For

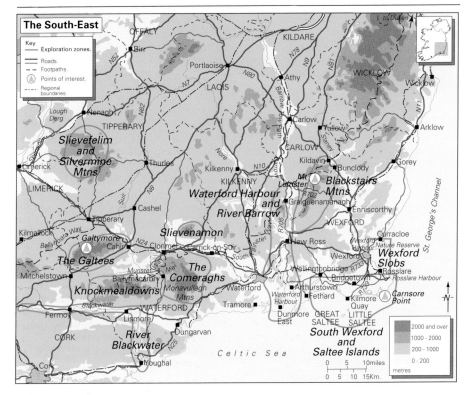

The South-East

Key
- Exploration zones.
- Roads.
- Footpaths.
- Points of interest.
- Regional boundaries.

OFFALY · Birr · Portlaoise · KILDARE · N78 · N9 · N81 · to Dublin · WICKLOW · Wicklow · N7 · N80 · Athy · Barrow Farm · LAOIS · Carlow · Arklow · Lough Derg · Nenagh · TIPPERARY · Thurles · Kilkenny · N10 · Kildavin · Bunclody · Gorey · Slievefelim and Silvermine Mtns · Mt Leinster · Blackstairs Mtns · Limerick · LIMERICK · Cashel · Waterford Harbour and River Barrow · Graiguenamanagh · Enniscorthy · WEXFORD · Tipperary · Suir · Kilmallock · Ballyhoura Way · Galtymore · Slievenamon · N24 · Clonmel · Carrick-on-Suir · New Ross · Wexford Harbour · Curracloe · Nature Reserve · St. George's Channel · The Galtees · Cahir · Mitchelstown · Ballymacarbry · Munster · The Comeraghs · Knockmealdowns · Monavullagh Mtns · Waterford · Wellingtonbridge · Bridgetown · Rosslare · Rosslare Harbour · Wexford Slobs · Blackwater · WATERFORD · Tramore · Arthurstown · Fethard · Kilmore Quay · Carnsore Point · Fermoy · Lismore · Dunmore East · GREAT SALTEE · LITTLE SALTEE · CORK · River Blackwater · Dungarvan · N25 · Celtic Sea · South Wexford and Saltee Islands · Cork · Youghal

2000 and over
1000 - 2000
200 - 1000
0 - 200
metres

0   5   10miles
0   5   10 15Km.

-N-

---

details contact the Southern Regional Fisheries Board, T: (052) 23624. Waterford's sea-angling service, T: (058) 41514, can arrange deep-sea fishing. The Clonanav Fly Fishing Centre and School, Ballymacarbry, Waterford, offers angling tuition and activities for the non-angler such as walking, horse-riding and golf, T: (052) 36141, www.flyfishingireland.com. South East Tourism's *Angling Guide* covers all the region's angling.

FURTHER INFORMATION
Tourist offices: there are year-round BF offices in Wexford, T: (053) 23111, Waterford, T: (051) 875823, and Tipperary, T: (067) 31610. The ones in Clonmel, T: (052) 22960, and Cahir, T: (052) 41453, are open in the summer only.

POTEEN

Traditionally, poteen is a potato spirit, illicitly distilled. It used to be served mixed with goat's milk in little shops called shebeens, distinguished by clods of turf hanging on their doors. The goat's milk and shebeens have gone but poteen continues to be made all over the place. One reason for its survival is that avoiding duties was a gesture of defiance against the occupying English and gained a respectability which has not entirely faded, even 80 years after the English left. The word means a little pot.

Grain of one kind or another is often used to make poteen instead of potatoes. It does not too much matter, since the motive of drinkers is more tipsifactory than epicurean. Poteen can be procured in most parts of Ireland through discreet inquiry. One strong argument against it is that the quality is sometimes very bad and even dangerous – there are tales of painful deaths. Whether this is propaganda put about by the authorities is hard to say. Some poteen is undoubtedly delicious and without bad effect. It should be. The Irish are practised distillers. They invented whiskey (as they generally spell the word), and it was an Irishman, Aeneas Coffey, who took his patent method to Scotland and started the process there.

Slievefelim and the Silvermine Mountains

Rolling highlands with isolated valleys and little lanes and waterways, dominated by Mauherslieve, the Mother Mountain

From the rich pasture of the Suir valley in County Tipperary the land rises to a spread of smooth-backed mountains contoured like a school of porpoises. This is a clutch of highlands of which the Slieve Kimalta, or Keeper Hill, in the north-west, rises to 2,278 feet (694 metres), Slievefelim to 1,411 feet (423 metres) and most of the rest – Knockastanna, Ring Hill, Knockalough and the substantial centre-piece of Mauherslieve or Mother Mountain – to altitudes in between. Around 300 million years ago, because of tectonic pressure from the south as the plate on which Africa rests slowly closed with that underlying Europe, subterranean quartzite, edged by sandstone, broke through the limestone layers laid down by an invasive sea 50 million years previously.

The resultant ranges are not grand or dramatic – more animal and interesting, with deeply incised little valleys providing routes for an abundance of lanes and waterways. Unregenerate, too, for somehow the new Europe's golden touch does not seem to have penetrated here. An old, sometimes tumbledown mellowness hangs about farm buildings and fences, and roads are more than normally pocked and cratered. Hard-skinned farmers wave in courteous astonishment in the lanes. Reeds and cuckoo flowers (*Cardamine pratensis*) and other marsh plants clog the undrained boggy pastures of the lower slopes. You could walk almost anywhere and see, at the risk of a bootful of marsh water, an old-style wealth of butterflies, birds, ichneumons, sawflies and others – except, that is, among the conifers of various ages which cover parts of Mauherslieve and elsewhere like drilling regiments on the parade ground. Higher up come friendly workaday plants found all over Ireland and Britain: gorse, primrose, violet, bedstraw, bugle, more cuckoo flower, with much bracken and moss, and hedges of thorn, elder, honeysuckle and some box, shaded at times by a benison of beech or ash. In the face of nature's variety, houses are reticent, beige-painted or grey-pebbled, as against the shining whiteness of the new bungalow. Every so often an enclosed vista contains stone ruins engulfed by ivy, melancholy and beautiful though beyond function, set among sympathetic trees that nod overhead. Here and there the wildness turns to a Wild West variety, exemplifying that careless human disdain for rural beauty which daubs a wood mill, its clutter and refuse, or a huge wire-fenced motor-works, its spilt oil and prowling Dobermanns, across unoffending valleys or water meadows.

There is, too, the uglier face of old Ireland. A mangy, skin-and-bone cat and a scrawny mule put me in mind of the hobbled cattle seen not so many years ago on the western peninsulas, and tinkers' horses lame and pus-ulcered by the roadside. There are the informal refuse tips – a kind of hypermarket excrement voided into Arcadia. It seems you are never far from one of these (and, oddly, a charge is made for garbage taken to the proper tip).

There is also that almost stage-Irish inconsistency which can make you smile or smoulder according to your mood. Without warning the road deteriorates to battle-site unevenness. A car limps as if two of its wheels had been mined away. The hazards are passed. The road is fine again. Looking back through your rear window you see all of three notices unfairly favouring the traveller in the opposite direction with full warnings. What matter if the words used, SLOW, ROAD WORKS AHEAD, are somewhat fictional.

The region has not been neglected by the tourist authorities. Little is. There is the 'Keeper Hill Drive' and the 'Slievefelim Way' and 'Sarsfield's Ride', commemorating a dash by the Jacobite general Patrick Sarsfield to ambush an artillery train of the invader King William III. There are many viewpoints, not to mention 'Community Alert Areas' – all of them scrupulously signposted, at times indigestibly. They all have merits. My own preference is for the Silver-mine Mountains and, given the energy, Keeper Hill. There are wonderful views: to the north-west the Arra Mountains, with Tountinna and the southern tip of Lough Derg; to the east a mountainous play-ground, a succession of nature's peaks and trampoline dips stretching far away and out of sight.

BEFORE YOU GO
Maps: OSI Discovery Series, map Nos 58 and 59.

GETTING THERE
By car: from Nenagh take the R497 (south) to the R503 and follow this (west) towards Lim-erick. This route will take you through the middle of the Sil-vermine Mountains and past Slievefelim.
By rail: there are 2 services each day to Nenagh from Dublin (Heuston) and Limerick, T: (01) 836 6222.
By bus: Bus Eireann run Ex-pressway services to Nenagh from Dublin and Limerick. A summer bus between Limerick and Nenagh stops at Silver-mines, T: (01) 836 6111. Toohey's Coaches run a daily service between Dublin and Limerick, via Nenagh, T: (067) 26266.

WHERE TO STAY
Hotels and B&Bs: there are a couple of hotels and quite a se-lection of B&Bs in Nenagh, in-cluding Mrs Delaney, T: (067) 32053; Mrs Devine, T: (067) 31118, e-mail: williamsferry @tinet.ie; and Ashley Park House, T: (067) 38223. Hotels in Tipperary include the Bally-glass Country Hotel, T: (062) 52104, and the Royal, T: (062) 33244, e-mail: royalhtl@iol.ie.

ACTIVITIES
Walking: there are trails through the forests surrounding the Silvermine Mountains and Slievefelim.
Cycling: bikes can be hired from J. Moynan in Nenagh, T: (067) 31293.

FURTHER INFORMATION
Tourist offices: the BF office in Nenagh is open May–Sept, T: (067) 31610.

The Galtees

A roller-coaster single-ridge range offering tough walks past desolate lakes and corries

There is something pampered and comfortable about the south riding of Tipperary, with the fertile greenery, bulging hedges and velvet woodlands of its broad, loamy valleys: those of the Suir river, the Glen of Aherlow and the Golden Vale. This snugness is made more obvious by the contrast of the dark bog-covered mountains hemming all sides of the lowlands: the Slievefelim, Slievenamon, the Comeraghs, Knockmealdown, Kilworth and the Galtees. Of these, the Comeraghs stand flat plateau-topped, in quiet and rarefied dignity, in the region's south-east. The Galtees are a grand but more animated affair to the north-west, easily reached from any direction, with an outline seen from north and south that suggests the course of a bouncing pingpong ball. They are made up of a single ridge, rising at intervals to conical peaks, one of which, the more or less central Galtymore, is at 3,018 ft (905 m) the third-highest mountain in the south of Ireland.

For the walker and climber the options are not so numerous as in the Comeraghs, but wonderful scenery and views reward any ascent in fine weather. Essentially you choose to walk from end to end – the Cahir end to the Mitchelstown end or vice versa – or over the top between the northern and southern valleys. In either case it is desirable to have two cars or a non-participant driver of one car who will drop you at the start and pick you up at the end. Of course, there are plenty of round walks, but a linear route from one side or end to the other shows you a good deal more of Ireland and best suits the ridge form.

Of the starting points, Cahir is a pretty and historic town, but the Cahir to Mitchelstown road along the south of the mountains is straight, fast and nasty. On the north, the leafy lane among the forestry plantations, meadows and hamlets of the Glen of Aherlow is a prettier, quieter approach, and gives good and tantalizing views of the scree-scrapes, massy buttresses, grooves and groins on the north faces. Higher up, too, the north has the advantage, with the most dramatic scenery of the Galtees – several mountain lakes – ranged along that side of Galtymore and Greenane. While all of these have character, each has an individual personality. Lough Muskry and Lough Curra are big and generous, Curra being easily got at and with a formidable 1,000-foot (300-metre) curtain of rock as backdrop. Of Lough Diheen,

The hen harrier may be seen in any part of Ireland, but in decreasing numbers, hunting low over moor, heath, marsh or estuary.

on the other hand, lying between them, Robert Lloyd Praeger, while admitting he saw it on a dull and windless day, says, 'I think I never saw a more lifeless or gloomier place in Ireland'.

A mile south of the Cahir to Mitchelstown road and not far to the west of its mid-point are the Mitchelstown caves. It was Praeger who did the original mapping of this complex underground system, which is privately owned. Regular guided tours are conducted along a large section of the system. It is worth seeing, though similar systems can be seen elsewhere and many more must exist unexplored. Rain, with carbon dioxide superadded from the air, exploits faults in the limestone beds that form so much of Ireland's foundations. They burrow through joints and excavate pipes until the water finds the prevailing water table.

The process has carved out a subterranean Gruyère, with huge hollow caverns, slowly dripping stalactites and slowly rising stalagmites, as well as water coursing through the channels it has most recently carved out. All this is illuminated and shown to advantage.
Before you go *Maps:* OSI Discovery Series, map Nos 66 and 74.
Guide-books: Ballyhoura Way Map Guide (Ballyhoura Country Holidays); and *Mountains of Ireland* by Paddy Dillon (Cicerone, 1992).
Getting there *By car:* to reach the Galtee Mountains, take the N24 from Clonmel to Cahir and then either the N8 (west) or the N24 (north-west). To reach the Mitchelstown caves follow the N8 from Cahir towards Mitchelstown and after 9 miles (14 km) turn left following the signs to the caves.
By rail: there is 1 daily service from Rosslare to Cahir and Limerick Junction (near Tipperary). Trains run frequently from Cork, Limerick and Dublin to Limerick Junction, T: (01) 836 6222.
By bus: Bus Eireann operate regular services from Dublin, Kilkenny, Cork, Limerick and Waterford to Clonmel; and from Cork, Limerick and Kilkenny to both Cahir and Mitchelstown. The Waterford Expressway also stops at Cahir, and the daily Clonmel-Mitchelstown bus stops at Clogheen, T: (01) 836 6111.
Where to stay *Hotels and B&Bs:* there is a good choice in Cahir, such as Carrigeen Castle, T: (052) 41370, and Castle Court Hotel, T: (052) 41210. In Bansha, B&B is available at the Castle, T: (062) 54187, Lismacue House, T: (062) 54106, e-mail: lismac@indigo.ie.
Youth hostels: An Oige hostels in the area include the Ballydavid Wood House at Bansha,

T: (062) 54148, and the Mountain Lodge at Burncourt, Cahir, T: (052) 67277. There is also one independent hostel: the Lisakyle Hostel, Church Street, Cahir, T: (052) 41963.
Outdoor living: the Apple CCP, Cahir, T: (052) 41459, opens 1 May–30 Sept, as does The Powers the Pot CCP, at Clonmel, T: (052) 23085. Parson's Green CCP, near Clogheen, is open all year, T: (052) 65290.
Activities *Walking:* the main summit of the Galtee range, Galtymore, is the third highest peak in Eire. The approach from the south is easy, dry and grass-covered, while the north side is covered in crags and scree, though there are tracks among them. The traverse along the main ridge from the north of Mitchelstown to Cahir is well worth the effort. Part of the Ballyhoura Way stretches through the Glen of Aherlow and over the Slievenamuck ridge. There are shorter, easier waymarked walks on the lower slopes of the Galtee Mountains. Enthusiasts may be interested in the annual Ballyhoura International Walking Festival, held in May. Local guides organize a variety of routes for hundreds of walkers on the mountains and in the Glen of Aherlow. For more information, guides and maps, contact BF. Galty Vee Valley, Clogheen, T: (052) 62258, offers year-round guided walks and pony-trekking in the mountains.
Cycling: a circular route from Cahir Castle, passing through Ballyporeen, Burncourt and Clogheen, also takes in the

Heavy rain (*overleaf*) shrouds the broad, reedy, islanded expanse of the River Blackwater at Villierstown jetty, 10 miles (16 km) upstream from its estuary at Youghal.

Mitchelstown caves. For details see South East Tourism's *South East Walking & Cycling* guide-book.

Riding: for treks in the Galtee Mountains contact Bansha House Stables, Bansha, T: (062) 54194; or the Hillcrest Equestrian Centre, Gabally, T: (062) 37915, e-mail: hillcrestcentre @tinet.ie.

Fishing: coarse and salmon fishing are available on the River Suir. Contact the Southern Regional Fisheries Board in Clonmel, T: (052) 23624.

Sightseeing: the Mitchelstown caves are open all year, 10 am– 6 pm, T: (052) 67246. The system has about 1 mile (1.6 km) of passages and some spectacular chambers.

Further information *Tourist offices:* the BF office in Cahir is open May–Sept, T: (052) 41453. Clonmel is open June –Sept, T: (052) 22960, and the office in Tipperary is open all year, T: (062) 51457.

Knockmealdowns

A graceful 15-mile (24-kilometre) old red sandstone range north of Lismore

For most who pass this way, the Knockmealdowns *are* the Vee Gap, more or less, and the Vee Gap is the Knockmealdowns. The Vee itself is a hairpin bend – V-shaped – in the main road crossing the mountains between Lismore in County Waterford and Clogheen in County Tipperary. Close to it a track leads down to a lovely, ice-cold mountain lake, Bay Lough, the result of a lens of ice, formed from compacted snow and with rocks embedded in it, scouring a cavity out of the rock. In early summer the slopes rising steeply behind the lake are splashed with the

vibrant mauve of the rhododendron – a colour people seem to have become increasingly sniffy about, though it still seems pretty to me. On the other hand, the plant's spread in many parts of Ireland, especially the West, has choked out so many other species that it is considered and treated as a pest.

From a distance the Knockmealdowns, a range of old red sandstone stretching some 15 miles (24 km) east to west, form a graceful outline of bosomy heights, mostly not as high as the Comeraghs to the east or the roller-coaster range of the Galtees to the north, but rising to the respectable 2,608 ft (782 m) of Knockmealdown mountain itself. Much of the area, but not the peaks, is under cultivation, and besides the usual forestry plantations there are some thick concentrations of oak, beech, birch, alder (on the wetter ground), shrubby hazel, holly, yew and other natives and broadleaves in the cuts and valleys on the north and south sides. From these there is the usual progression to heathery heights, broken by shoals of anaemic grasses and splashes of bare or lichened rock.

In open competition the Knockmealdowns score somewhat lower than their mountain neighbours. Apart from Bay Lough and tiny Lake Moylan to the south-east of Sugarloaf Hill, there are no picturesque mountain corries – rather a severe aesthetic lack by Irish standards – and no great crags or precipices. But the mountains provide wonderful outward views and make the southern half of County Tipperary, which is what you see to the north, seem as broad and unending as a continent. On the south side you can see County Waterford to the east,

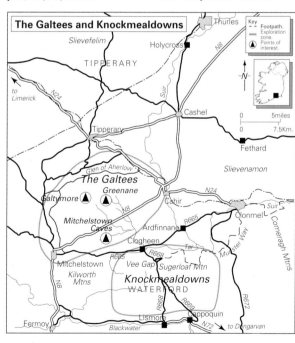

The Galtees and Knockmealdowns

Slievefelim
Thurles
Holycross
TIPPERARY
to Limerick
Tipperary
Cashel
Fethard
Glen of Aherlow
Slievenamon
The Galtees
Greenane
Galtymore
Cahir
Clonmel
Mitchelstown Caves
Ardfinnan
Comeragh Mtns
Clogheen
Mitchelstown
Vee Gap
Sugerloaf Mtn
Kilworth Mtns
Knockmealdowns
WATERFORD
Fermoy
Lismore
Cappoquin
Blackwater
to Dungarvan
Munster Way
Suir

Key
Footpath.
Exploration zone.
Points of interest.
-N-
0   5miles
0   7.5Km.

County Cork to the west and in the distance the sea. It is not difficult to be at the summit of the Knockmealdowns and bathing in the sea with only a two-hour (or less, if you step on it) interval. Above the Vee is the stone beehive grave of a certain Samuel Grubb, one who certainly appreciated the view, and had himself buried upright to be able to see his former Tipperary estates. He may have taken his cue from the 18th-century local landowner Henry Eeles, to whom, long before Benjamin Franklin, the sight of lightning on these mountains suggested a connection with electricity. He, too, had himself buried, along with his horse and dog, at the summit of Knockmealdown, but all trace of the grave has since gone.

The range is not noted for natural rarities, but many of the familiar birds and plants of the blanket bog may be seen. Ravens and peregrines visit Bay Lough. Claims have been made that the last killing of an Irish wolf took place here in 1770. (Rival claims are made for other regions.) The gap would have been a wilder spot then, with the harridan Petticoat Loose haunting Bay Lough, the ever-present hazard of highwaymen, and nothing but a mud track to carry carriages between north and south.

Before you go *Maps:* OSI Discovery Series, map No. 74.

Guide-books: Exploring the South of Ireland by Paddy Dillon (Cassell, 1999); *Knockmealdown Walks* (Galty Vee Valley Tourism)*,* and *The Galty, Knockmealdown and Comeragh Mountains* by Barry Keane (The Collins Press, 1998).

Getting there *By car:* from Dungarvan follow the R672 (north-west) to the N72, then take this road to Cappoquin. The R669 and R668, between Cappoquin and Clogheen, cut through the mountains. *By bus:* the Tallow-Waterford bus stops at Cappoquin every day. Services run daily to Clogheen from Mitchelstown and Clonmel, T: (051) 879000. There is no bus between Clogheen and Cappoquin.

Where to stay *B&Bs:* in Cappoquin try Richmond House, T: (058) 54278, or Hanoras Cottage, T: (052) 36134. Mrs Moore's B&B is just outside Ballymacarbry on the R672, T: (052) 36217, e-mail: richiem@tinet.ie, and Mrs Power, T: (058) 54273, is in Lismore. *Outdoor living:* Parson's Green CCP is at Clogheen, T: (052) 65292.

Activities *Walking:* Glenshane Park has forest walks and there are some good walks in the mountains, the best taking in Knockmealdown and the Sugarloaf peaks, neither hard to reach from the Vee Gap road, the R668. Helen McGrath, T: (052) 36359, arranges guided walks in the Knockmealdowns on Sun, leaving Newcastle at 12 pm. Contact BF for information on routes. *Fishing:* the Blackwater river, near Cappoquin, provides excellent fishing for brown trout and salmon. Mrs Ryan, Clonanav Farm Guesthouse, Ballymacarbry, T: (052) 36141, can provide fishing permits.

Further information *Tourist offices:* the BF office in Clonmel, T: (052) 22960, is open June–Sept, and in Lismore, T: (058) 54975, Apr–Oct.

River Blackwater

Following an unlikely course, the River Blackwater passes wooded gorges and haunted houses into a tidal estuary rich with bird life

In the early 19th century the Smyths of Ballynatray, a heavy, handsome, Hanoverian house on a bend of the Blackwater a few miles from the river's mouth, had the good sense to take over the captain's barge from a Napoleonic man-of-war wrecked along the nearby coast. They decked it with velvet hangings, put musicians aboard and kept it as their state barge, floating up and down the broad wooded river with the sounds of trumpet and drum echoing off the rocky defiles. Later in the century paddle-steamers with German bands on board took tourists upstream from Youghal, advertising the river as Ireland's Rhine. Cargo craft were plentiful. Nowadays if you want to see the river by boat you paddle your own canoe, or beg or borrow a rowing boat or launch. Otherwise you come at the water wherever the road or other access allows.

It is not the likeliest target for travellers in search of the wild. This is a valley of rich land and one old Ascendancy estate after another. Castles and mansions alternate down the bank like lamp-posts in a lane. Salmon are netted in the tidal reaches and fly-fished upstream by – for the most part – persons of means, paying high prices. (One lawsuit over netting rights continued for several centuries.) At the river's mouth is a town,

Youghal, with a rich past, present and future, and there are substantial towns every few miles along its 75-mile (120-kilometre) length. You might be forgiven for asking if there are any grounds at all for calling the River Blackwater wild.

Ten miles (16 kilometres) above the estuary there stands on the east bank a handsome, haunted house called Dromana, whose supporting walls drop sheer into the river. Opposite, a tributary, the River Owbeg, debouches. Three miles (five kilometres) downstream another tributary, the Bride, flows into the Blackwater River. These meetings take place amid spreading marsh, liable to flood when the rivers are in spate. They attract waders. There are autumn evenings when the curlews' falling cries make the air pregnant with Celtic melancholy. A mile or two up the Bride is one of the county's heronries. On spring evenings the air around the swaying, aerial tenements is thick with fishwife screeches, essential, it seems, for the coexistence of close-packed heron families. But the most varied bird life is seen around the tidal estuary. Various ducks and waders, including black-tailed godwit, coot and moorhen, some hen harriers and short-eared owls are to be found on the mud-flats and flooded fields occurring riverward of Kinsalebeg on the east bank and between the river-bridge and Youghal on the west. They also congregate on the reed-beds and marsh a mile or so south of the town, where the main road turns inland.

The route taken by the river in its last 15 miles (24 kilometres), from Cappoquin to the sea, has puzzled geologists. As is seen clearly by anyone travelling the south-west of Ireland, the great Armorican earth movements (sometimes known as Hercynide, after the Latin name for the Harz Mountains, which were formed at the same time) squashed the surface of the land from the south and caused several sandstone ranges to rise in an east-west direction. The Atlantic promontories of Cork and Kerry are among them. Rivers, naturally, tended to follow the limestone valleys in between, flowing west to east because of the general tilt of the land. But the four principal rivers, the Bandon, Lee, Blackwater and Suir, having followed this rule almost up to the last minute, suddenly disregard it entirely, and turn wilfully southward, cutting through the raised sandstone in what seems a far more difficult course than carrying on eastward. No river illustrates this more clearly than the Blackwater, whose obvious outlet would seem from both map and land to be Dungarvan harbour. We must not, of course, attribute conscious decisions to rivers. The flowing waters followed the easiest route. The problem is why this lay in a southward direction.

The facts have been explained in different ways, based on the pattern of the land before the upheaval, in which the general orientation of contours was north–south. The main reason may be that, after the upheaval, rain was falling and rivers forming their channels on a thick covering of accumulated limestone. Routes were determined by climate and by the surface conditions of the limestone more than by the shapes of the underlying rock. When eventually the upland limestone was eroded and the rivers were thus lowered on to the newly revealed beds of sandstone, they dug channels corresponding to their previous routes. Had they started to form on the sandstone they would no doubt have followed much more closely its trends and features.

What this southward cutting means today is a valley much more picturesque than it would otherwise have been, with rising bluffs and rocks, woods and rapids, for the kingfisher and anyone in possession of a rowing tub or bedizened state barge to enjoy.

BEFORE YOU GO
Maps: OSI Discovery Series, map No. 74.

GETTING THERE
By car: from Cork follow the N8 and N25 (east) to Youghal.

A couple of miles north of Youghal the river is broad, tidal and without bridges, but lanes approach it and run alongside here and there. From Cappoquin, the N72 to Lismore, the R666 to Fermoy, then the N72 to Mallow and Rathmore all run close to the river though the road is seldom contiguous.
By rail: the nearest stations are Cork and Mallow, with 12 trains a day from Dublin (Heuston), T: (01) 836 6222.

By bus: the Expressway between Rosslare and Tralee, via Waterford and Cork, stops in Youghal 3 times daily. There are other services to Fermoy and Mallow from Cork, Dublin and Limerick, T: (01) 836 6111.

WHERE TO STAY

Hotels and B&Bs: in Youghal try Mrs Gaine, T: (024) 92617; Aherne's, T: (024) 92424, e-mail: ahernes@tinet.ie; or the more up-market Devonshire Arms, T: (024) 92827. Ballyvolane House is in Castlelyons, T: (025) 36349, and Glenlohane House is near Ballyclough, T: (029) 50014. Mrs O'Leary is in Fermoy, T: (025) 31386, or try Mrs Walsh, T: (022) 42761, in Mallow.

Youth hostels: the nearest independent is the Kilworth Village Hostel, T: (025) 27565, just

north of Fermoy.

Outdoor living: the Summerfield CCP is just west of Youghal, T: (024) 93537.

ACTIVITIES

Cycling: Frank Murphy, Main Street, Dungarvan, T: (058) 41376, hires out bikes.

Fishing: excellent salmon and trout fishing is available on the River Blackwater. There is a 2-week fishing festival in May–June in Fermoy and deep-sea angling can be done from Youghal. Angling guides to Counties Cork and Waterford are available from local tourist offices.

Bird-watching: many varieties of birds can be seen on the mud-flats at Youghal.

FURTHER INFORMATION

Tourist offices: there are BF offices in Youghal, T: (024) 92390, open Apr–Oct; Fermoy, T: (025) 31811, open all year; Mallow, T: (022) 42222, open May–Sept; and Lismore, T: (058) 54975, open Apr–Oct.

Its cap recently restored, the round tower at Ardmore, on the coast of County Waterford, is one of the country's finest. It dates probably from the 10th century.

Strong winds clear the clouds, revealing a glimpse of Lough Coumshingaun from the middle of the horseshoe ridge in the Comeragh Mountains.

The Comeraghs

Ghostly mountain mists often shroud this gaunt range

I had been minding a house for its absent owners. A 19th-century occupant, who was an amateur archaeologist, had brought back mummies from Egypt and, although these had later been given to the National Museum, a chill aura hung or seemed to hang around the place where they had been displayed. As a consequence, I suppose, ancient Egypt was on my mind.

One day I was driving from Dungarvan to Clonmel, along the east side of the Comeragh Mountains. A gaunt, strong, dignified, timeless range, commanding the central south of Ireland, they form the zenith of the east–west protrusion of old red sandstone and carboniferous limestone squeezed up by the great convulsions of the Devonian period 300 million years ago. Much of their surface is a desolate central plateau, seen from some angles as tamely flat. But their ice-gnawed edges are anything but tame: deep, steep slopes often pivoting to precipice angles and plunging to lonely tarns held in by palisades of moraine.

Some of these cliffs are visible from the road. In particular the site of the corrie of Coomshingaun is recognizable from the two protruding buttresses which enfold it. Probably because I had been sharing midnights with Egyptian ghosts in an ancient house, these two massive bolsters made me think of the knees of the statue of the pharaoh Rameses II at Abu Simbel. The lake would have been contained in his lap, and his body and head rising into the mists that so often crown the range. My feelings of awe for the Comeraghs intensified.

Next time I climbed to Coomshingaun this impression was very much on my mind. The climb itself is simple; I am tempted to say you follow the trail of cigarette butts and chewing-gum papers which smear so many upland Irish tracks. It was a sultry June day. The mist was thick, and the sound of traffic

was soon behind me. Here and there a sheep bleated. The mist closed in to a distance of yards, but the way among the scattered rocks (another legacy of the ice) and gorse and bracken and fairy lights of honeysuckle was still not in doubt. The only thing I did not know was how far I had come – there was no question of overshooting, but I kept anticipating a cooling of air from that desolate glacial tarn.

Mountain mists are alive, I have never had any doubt of that. Not organically alive but certainly alive in having moods and the power of wilful motion. They approach and come no nearer, recede and go no further away. They are sweetly innocent, trailing their wispy pleated skirts towards you, lifting a little to show a distant line of green lowlands. Then they settle and condense, and exclude you from your world, puff cold air and spit at you with drops of moisture, encircle you and close. Ghostly? They are for sure the mother and father of all ghosts. Things I don't, of course, believe in, so that any fear I felt was self-induced. And it was not fear so much as a sensitive apprehension. Really, I was enjoying myself. And then the one thing happened that caused me to miss one heartbeat before returning to normal. Rameses shook his knee.

I shall not try to convince you that this movement took place, because you will not trust me. But the consequence is beyond doubt. The air rippled. Like a cloud of flies the mist cleared from the left knee, which now took form, rounded, firm and sheer-sided, looming above me on my right. He had shaken off an irritation, and the thinned tassels of mist remained distant enough for me to walk through the chill air down to the water's edge. I could dimly descry the vertical wall of rock that forms the opposite bank of the tarn, feeling more than ordinary respect for a handsomely horned ram that watched me from a cottage-sized erratic boulder. I returned to the knee, from where I walked back to the road, and thence drove to centres of population that could have been a million miles from the solitude, from the glacier track in a wall of mountain raised by the clash of the tectonic plates on which Europe and Africa float, from the hauntings

168

of Celtic gods and the possibly spurious overlay of an ancient Egyptian pharaoh.

The tougher climb was out of the question that day. In clearer weather you can turn left where I stopped, cross to the other buttress, ascend, as it were, the right thigh and, having reached the plateau, cross over to complete the circuit of Coomshingaun. A small detour on this route takes in Fascoum, which at 2,597 feet (789 metres) is the highest point of the Comeraghs – though you have to look for it across the bog as it is not much higher than the surrounding levels. There are some quite tough slopes, loose scree and cliff-drops on this journey.

The Comeraghs and the Monavullaghs, which are for most purposes part of the same range, together with their various outliers, are rich in good climbs, both easy and challenging. Almost all of them offer

PRECAUTIONS FOR HILL-WALKERS

The only way to remain safe from outdoor hazards is to stay at home and risk indoor ones. Still, people die on Irish mountains and it is foolhardy to leave everything to luck when walking or climbing. Whatever the conditions before you set off, you may soon be on steep, rough ground and much colder, wetter and blown about than you were at the start. You or one of your companions may be immobilized by injury sustained in a fall. Depending on circumstances, any of the following precautions and prescriptions can help, to the point of saving life.

Before you go:
Weather can be the great enemy. It could be up to ten degrees colder 3,000 ft up, since temperature drops two or three degrees centigrade every thousand feet (300 m). The breeze down below becomes a strong wind up above. Thick mists can float in unannounced, cutting visibility to a matter of feet. Consult a local weather forecast, and assume that the weather will get colder and wetter while you are out.

Pack a map, compass, whistle, torch and first-aid kit, some chocolate or glucose and perhaps a hot drink. Wear strong clothing and boots that protect and support the ankles. Maintain a healthy suspicion of the accuracy of all maps, especially on the heights and where cliffs are concerned. The old half-inch Ordnance Survey of Ireland series has many inaccuracies. Published walk and climb descriptions can be misleadingly ambiguous, and it is worth checking map and text together to avoid confusion on the spot. Arrange to walk or climb with at least three other people in the party and be sure there is

time to go up and come down, allowing for delays and pauses, well before dark. Discounting extended stops and difficult ground, but allowing for short breaks, reckon on covering a distance of 2 miles (4 km) or an ascent of 1,300 ft (400 m) an hour. Leave a note of your planned route at your hotel or guest-house, or with a friend, or in the car if you drive to the starting point.

On the walk or climb:
Remember that in a mist, within only a few minutes, you may double back on your track when you think you have gone in a straight line. Keep consulting your map and compass. When visibility is poor keep as clear as possible of cliffs, especially in high wind.

Be aware that turning signposts and waymarks to point in the wrong direction is a national sport.

Take extra care on the way down hills and mountains when, due to tiredness, most accidents occur.

In trouble:
The official mountain distress signal is six whistle blasts over a minute followed by a pause of a minute, indefinitely repeated; or six torch flashes and a pause of similar timing, also repeated. An acknowledging response is a series of three blasts or flashes repeated with intervals.

If a companion is injured and help is needed, and if signals bring no response, make him or her as comfortable and warm as possible, and try to establish your exact location. When you come on a telephone dial 999 and ask for Mountain Rescue. If there is any difficulty consult the local garda station.

Sky and land almost converge as the sun goes down over the Comeragh Mountains, but from here, at a vantage point beneath the west face of Knocknaree peak, it is still possible to see the ridge of Laghtnafrankee mountain in the distance.

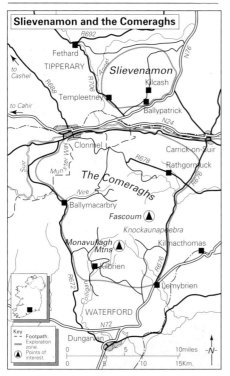

spectacular views over the surrounding countryside. North of Coomshingaun is the eponymous rock from which the highwayman William Crotty could survey half Ireland to his north while keeping watch for redcoats ascending the slopes immediately below. They got him at last and hanged him in Waterford in 1742. His faithful widow, to escape the law, jumped to her death from this same rock. Other bandits took his place. In the 19th century, lawlessness took on a political flavour, threatening the Anglo-Irish Ascendancy at home and at sport. Those who hunted over the Beresford lands to the east put about false information on the whereabouts of their meets, to avoid ambushes, and carried loaded pistols in holsters on their saddles. (Nothing would have forced them to cancel hunting. These were the days when a gentry devotee might have himself buried in a fox's lair, while a Beresford lady had a tiara, necklace and brooch made of foxes' teeth.)

Equally wild are the Mahon falls, thin white lines of plummeting water in a broad bay of a valley under the cone of Knockaunapeebra, just south of Coomshingaun. They reduce to a trickle in a dry summer. Not far south is Seefin (2,387 feet/716 metres), one of the Monavullagh Mountains which offer firmer, less boggy high plateaux than the Comeraghs. The Araglin valley, rising from Kilbrien to the west, affords with

Seefin a lovely circuit for serious walking. Another is around the Nier valley on the western slopes of the Comeraghs opposite Coomshingaun.

Feral goats are a common sight on the mountain slopes, and ravens and peregrines and sparrowhawks above them. In the breeding season, stonechats, hooded crows, jackdaws, meadow pipits and skylarks keep up a fairly perpetual chorus. Trout are present in some lakes, and so are char (*Salvelinus alpinus*), a colourful member of the same salmon family. This species seems to have gradually withdrawn northwards in the post-glacial period, leaving colonies in the chillier and remoter highlands of these islands. A Comeraghs plant of unusual distribution is the St Patrick's cabbage (*Saxifraga spathularis*), a saxifrage with pretty red-spotted white flowers and a long thin stem over a spray of leaves. It is easily confused with its close relation London pride, although, outside Ireland, it is mostly found in southern Europe.

GAELTACHT

The old Irish, or Gaelic, language, already long declining, all but disappeared during and after the 1840s famines when hundreds of thousands of Irish speakers died or emigrated. Local conditions kept it going in a few places, mostly in the far west. Newly independent Ireland in the 1920s took steps to safeguard its survival. Irish was named first of the two official state languages, and although in practice the use of English far outweighs that of Irish, the native tongue is aired a good deal in schools, on radio and television, in the Dail, the civil service and many homes. The Government also declared those areas where Irish had hung on as first language to comprise the official Gaeltacht, subject to certain rules and concessions designed to encourage the inhabitants to keep their language alive.

BEFORE YOU GO

Maps: OSI Discovery Series, map No. 82.

Guide-books: *The Galty, Knockmealdown and Comeragh Mountains* by Barry Keane (The Collins Press, 1998).

GETTING THERE

By car: from Clonmel take the R678 (east) to just past Rathgormuck, then the R676 (south) towards Lemybrien. Alternatively, take the R671 (west) from Clonmel and bend south with it. There is access to the mountains from all these roads.

By rail: the nearest station is Clonmel, where direct trains between Rosslare Harbour and Limerick Junction stop once a day, T: (053) 33114.

By bus: regular Bus Eireann services from Waterford, Cork, Limerick and Kilkenny stop at Clonmel, T: (051) 879000. Prince's Coaches operate between Clonmel and Dublin, T: (052) 31389.

WHERE TO STAY

Hotels and B&Bs: in Clonmel try Fennessy's Hotel, T: (052) 23680, or the family-run Brighton House, T: (052) 23665, e-mail: brighton@iol.ie. Mrs Creighton's B&B is in the village of Marlfield, just outside Clonmel, T: (052) 21089.

Outdoor living: the nearest camp-site to the Comeraghs is The Powers the Pot CCP at Clonmel, T: (052) 23085, open 1 May–30 Sept. Carrick-on-Suir also has a CCP, T: (051) 640461, e-mail: coscamping@tinet.ie.

ACTIVITIES

Walking: there are some good trails among these sandstone mountains.. For further information contact Galtymore Adventure Holidays in Cahir, who offer guided walks of the mountains for groups and individuals, T: (052) 41314/41047. BF offices in Clonmel and Dungarvan supply useful guides and maps.

Cycling: bikes can be hired from Worldwide Cycles, Market Street, Clonmel, T: (052) 21146.

Riding: hacks and treks in the Comeraghs are organized by Melody's Riding Stables, Ballymacarbry, T: (052) 36147, open 17 Mar–2 Nov.

Fishing: there is good trout fishing on the Rivers Nier, Anner and Tar, and salmon fishing on the River Suir. Contact the Southern Regional Fisheries Board, Anglesea Street, Clonmel, T: (052) 23971.

FURTHER INFORMATION

Tourist offices: the BF office in Clonmel is open June–Sept, T: (052) 22960, and all year in Dungarvan, T: (058) 41741.

Slievenamon

The home of the legendary Finn McCool provides an easy climb and spectacular views

Before the invention of electric guitars young maidens fell collectively in love with handsome youths who hunted wild boar and formed armies to raid other armies in pursuit of blood feuds, lands, princesses with prospects and so on. No young man was quite so appealing in these and other respects as Fionn Mac Cumhail, or Finn McCool as his name is usually presented in English, doughty warrior and unrivalled hero of the Fenian cycle of legends, giant of the Giant's Causeway and Fingal of the famous cave on Hebridean Staffa. Finn came from Slievenamon and was here hounded by bevies of desirous young women. The wise King Cormac Mac Art of Tara, whose somewhat cynical remarks about women have come down to us ('arrogant when called on, lewd when neglected, silly ... greedy ... hating ... tedious' and so on) devised a plan. All the women who wanted Finn should race up the mountain's side; Finn would be the winner's prize. Slievenamon means, in fact, mountain of the women. Being in love with Cormac's daughter Grainne, Finn tipped her news of a short-cut. She won, though she quickly regretted it and eloped – fatally, as it turned out – with the younger Diarmuid. The lovers are commemorated in place-names all over Ireland.

I doubt if my way up the mountain is in Grainne's footsteps. It is not the shortest route but it is easy because the road above Kilcash, which is unlikely to have existed in her day, gives you a good start. A track to the summit is signposted from this road. I like on the way to go and glimpse the old Butler castle of Kilcash – this was a Roman Catholic branch of the powerful clan – a mile below the village, festering handsomely under ivy in a private field beside its ruined church.

Slievenamon has little in common with Everest apart from the fact that, in Mallory's phrase, it is there. It is a domed quartzite peak rising to 2,368 ft (719 m), splendidly isolated, rich in myth, a bit spoiled by flanking forestry and a television mast near the top. The ascent is too much of a doddle for anyone to climb it for the sense of physical achievement. You go up for the view, which is spectacular: to the north the plains and hills of Tipperary and Kilkenny, the Galtees to the west, and the marvellously enticing, smooth silhouette of the Comeraghs, over the Suir in County Waterford. Down below is the Suir valley, a long cushion of fertility and ancient demesnes on either side of the pretty river. Not all it used to be, I suppose it goes without saying. The main road, which used to induce a leisurely pace in drivers, is now wide enough for serious speed but too narrow for safety, and you can see some of the factories that have been allowed to take their ugly places on either side. There has also been a progressive prairifying of the landscape as hedges continue to be ripped out, making big fields for big-money crops. There are shocking industrial gashes among the green. But if you do not look too close, you can still see Arcadia smiling up sunnily.

The hooded crow, whose head plumage can make it resemble a bewigged judge, is common in all parts of Ireland; a familiar, raucous omnivore, it is very closely related to the British carrion crow (they are both sub-species of the same species).

Before you go *Maps:* OSI Discovery Series, map Nos 67 and 75. *Guide-books: Mountains of Ireland* by Paddy Dillon (Cicerone, 1992).

Getting there *By car:* from Clonmel follow the N24 and N76 (east). The N76 passes to the east of Slievenamon. *By rail:* trains from Rosslare Harbour to Limerick Junction stop at Clonmel once a day, T: (053) 33114. *By bus:* regular Bus Eireann services from Waterford, Cork, Limerick and Kilkenny stop at Clonmel. Prince's Coaches operate between Dublin and Clonmel, T: (052) 31389.

Where to stay *Hotels:* try the Farrenwick Country House in Clonmel, T: (052) 35130, or the Oak Hill Lodge, at Kilcash, just outside the town, T: (052) 33503. The Grand Inn is at Carrick-on-Suir, T: (051) 647035. *Outdoor living:* try the Carrick-on-Suir CCP, T: (051) 640461, e-mail: coscamping@tinet.ie, or the Powers the Pot CCP at Clonmel, T: (052) 23085.

Activities *Walking:* Slievenamon is easy to climb. A route to the top is signposted from Kilcash and there also a circular walk round the mountain.

Further information *Tourist office:* there is a seasonal office in Clonmel, T: (052) 22960.

Blackstairs Mountains

A 15-mile (24-kilometre) range with broad views from Mount Leinster

The relatively uncomplicated ridge which takes in Mount Leinster and the Blackstairs Mountains is a kind of Sunday-afternoon extension of the Wicklows. Geologically they are parts of the same thing: a core of Caledonide granite rising above shoulders of quartzite and other hard, metamorphosed rocks, though these – in the case of the western edge of the Blackstairs – have been hidden under the widespread sedimentary limestone of the central plain. A 15-mile, north–south silhouette (tipped a little clockwise) of long gentle slopes, cones and curves, it rises to 2,610 ft (783 m) at the summit of Mount Leinster in the north and 2,409 ft (723 m) at that of Blackstairs mountain in the south. And it fills what would otherwise be a gap in the almost continuous line of highlands which occupies Ireland's south-east periphery. Actually it leaves County Wexford, whose boundary with County Carlow it forms, on the outside of the rim – the reason, perhaps, why richly agricultural Wexford has been noted in the past for both a rather British feel to the landscape, and a fiery Irish patriotism.

The ridge provides a natural archive of startling panoramas, requiring very little exertion to be enjoyed. Robert Lloyd Praeger, who probably knew better than anyone, said that the road crossing the northern shoulder of Mount Leinster commanded a wider view than could be seen from a car almost anywhere else in the country. He also thought that walking the range from end to end made a good day's outing. It undoubtedly did, but taking in the distance, all the ups and downs, some squishy bog and punishing scree, would require a body in the kind of trim and training which seems to have been his for over eighty years and few others' for a quarter as long. For most it is probably more satisfactory to take a round walk from road to peak (Leinster or Blackstairs) and back. These do not have to be tame. The writer David Herman's suggestions in the *New Irish Walk Guides: East and South* all involve climbing to 2,000 ft (600 m) or more, and occupy four or five hours of steady and just occasionally strenuous going. Mount Leinster, north of the Scullogue Gap (the only road that takes traffic across the range), is gentler than Blackstairs to the south, which is sprayed thinly with boulders and granite outcrops. The time could be prolonged in early summer by picking bilberries (*Vaccinium myrtillus*), common among the heather on the upper slopes, and one of Ireland's neglected wild harvests.

Before you go *Maps:* OSI Discovery Series, map No. 68. *Guide-books: Exploring the South of Ireland* by Paddy Dillon (Ward Lock, 1999).

Getting there *By car:* from Enniscorthy to Borris, the R702 runs right through the middle of the mountains.

By rail: services between Rosslare Harbour and Dublin stop at Enniscorthy 3 times a day, T: (01) 836 6222. *By bus:* a Bus Eireann Waterford–Dublin service stops at Bunclody and Enniscorthy, T: (051) 879000.

Where to stay *Hotels and B&Bs:* Ms Kinsella, Bunclody, T: (054) 76226/ 77459; and the Murphy-Floods Hotel at Enniscorthy, T: (054) 33413, e-mail: mfhotel m@indigo.ie. *Youth hostels:* the independent Bunclody Holiday Hostel is in Bunclody, T: (054) 76076.

Activities *Walking:* the Wicklow Way passes to the north. Mount Leinster makes a good hike with good views. Blackstairs is a bit tougher.

Further information *Tourist office:* the nearest BF office is in Enniscorthy, T: (054) 34699/35926, open June–Aug.

Waterford Harbour and River Barrow

An estuary teeming with bird life; the great auk was last seen here

For the most part the south-east of Ireland consists of the basins of four big rivers, their drainage areas like four segments of a sliced-through orange, centring roughly on Carnsore Point. The Slaney rises in the Wicklow Mountains and flows through the pastoral undulations of central Wexford to merge with the sea at Wexford harbour. The other three unite in their final reaches and come to the sea as one. The Barrow runs 120 miles (190 km) north to south, dividing (roughly) Counties Laois from Kildare and Kilkenny from Carlow. Just above New Ross it is enlarged by the waters of the Nore,

whose 90-odd miles (140 km) have brought it south-eastward from the slopes of the Slieve Bloom. A few miles below New Ross both are joined by the Suir (pronounced just about as the word 'sure' is) which, having risen not much more than a stone's throw from the Nore's source, has incorporated a big southerly bulge in its 115 or so miles (185 km). Together, they now make Waterford harbour their estuary.

Each river negotiates most of its vertical descent within a few miles of its source, and from then on coils lazily through valleys of rich farmland and woods based on the carboniferous limestone that covers much of the Irish interior. There are some grasslands that flood and provide wintering grounds for waterfowl: greylag geese on the Suir between Carrick-on-Shannon and Coolfin; and others on the lower Barrow floodplain. It is lush green countryside, this, interspersed with big old estates, recognizable – if the big house is hidden or gone – by the grandeur of perimeter walls and park trees. Such estates have bred and nourished some of the world's finest racehorses and are often enhanced by a backdrop of mountain – Comeraghs or Blackstairs or an extended

---

Bog cotton and other acid-dependent plants colonize the slopes of the Blackstairs Mountains, overlooking Carlow's farm lands.

frieze of Wicklows. Wild is not the word this area brings to mind, but there are thin threads of a kind of wildness and the best of these runs up through the harbour, parts of which in summer evenings lose their human associations and become – through sight and sound – a twilight kingdom of touchy, raucous, gradually settling birds. The threads continue into the Barrow, whose lower section lies, exceptionally, in the foundering granite of the Leinster chain and has carved deep wooded gorges where its pace is quickened by the narrowness of the channel.

Waders are drawn to the west side of Waterford harbour by several miles of mudflats, and over 2,000 regularly winter here, so that you can feel aggrieved if you miss the piping of oystercatchers, the unvarying beep of ringed plover, or the curlew's bubbling dirge. There are redshanks, bar-tailed godwits, a lot of common gulls, some dabbling ducks (mainly wigeon), geese (brent) and grebes (great crested). There are also turnstones, wintering here (and on many Irish and British coasts) after breeding in Greenland and the northern limits of Scandinavia. Seen in poor light or at a distance they are often confused with their plover cousins, grey or ringed, but in flight they display a unique and distinct pied pattern of black and white. Their short bills are slightly *retroussé*, and they twitter, but not helplessly. Ringing has shown they can cover 500 miles (800 kilometres) in a day. They are seen in small groups, often riffling through seaweed for almost anything (they are the least fussy of eaters). To the same end they justify their name by turning over stones. Sometimes several join forces to turn over a big one. A relief sculpture of a turnstone on a house in Dublin's Lower Bagot Street (I think) made me link them for ever with Ireland, and I always feel absurdly cheered by the sight of them.

The Barrow connects Waterford harbour with the Grand Canal extension at Athy (pronounced 'a thigh'), whence a small boat can be got, by canal or navigable river, to any region of Ireland. Commercial traffic still plied the river in the 1950s. Now it is mostly converted barges, launches, rowing boats and canoes. The Barrow is tidal as far as St Mullins and thereafter the river is often accompanied by a tow-path. Although many of the interesting and pretty sights along this walk are man-made – houses, locks, lock-keepers' cottages, bridges and towns of mellowed prosperity – nature plays the lead. When the view is clear, Mount Leinster and the Blackstairs show to the east and the graceful line of Brandon Hill (1,703 ft/511 m) to the west. Trees and shrubs support the homelier birds; a streak of blue may signify a kingfisher. The malefactor mink makes appearances. In the water itself there are rudd, perch, bream, pike and trout, and on the bank, at appropriate times, the raptor man spreads the green umbrella which thinking fish probably take to be his wings, and casts his barbed enticements.

BEFORE YOU GO

Maps: OSI Discovery Series, map Nos 67, 68 and 76.

GETTING THERE

By car: from Waterford, follow the N25 (north-east) towards New Ross, in the Barrow valley. For Waterford harbour, follow the R733 (south) to Arthurstown. To reach Graiguenamanagh, take the R700/R705 (north) from New Ross.

By bus: Bus Eireann services from all over Ireland stop in Waterford, and many at New Ross, T: (051) 879000. Suirway operate a Waterford–Dunmore East service, T: (051) 382209.

WHERE TO STAY

Hotels and B&Bs: there is plenty of choice in Waterford and New Ross, with a handful in Arthurstown, Fethard-on-Sea, Dunmore East and scattered rural locations.

Youth hostels: there is an An Oige hostel in Arthurstown, T: (051) 389411, and the independent Dunmore Harbour House is in Dunmore East, T: (051) 83218. There are 2 other hostels in Waterford, the Waterford, T: (051) 850163, and the Barnacles Viking House, T: (051) 853827, e-mail: viking@barnacles.iol.ie.

Outdoor living: Nore Valley CCP is at Bennettsbridge, T: (056) 27229, open 1 Mar–31 Oct; Newtown Cove CCP at Tramore, T: (051) 381121, open 2 Apr–26 Sept; and Ocean Island CCP at Fethard-on-Sea, T: (051) 397148, open Apr–Sept.

ACTIVITIES
Walking: the South Leinster Way runs through Graiguenamanagh. Contact BF.
Cycling: bikes can be hired in Wexford from Hayes, T: (053) 22462, and the Bike Shop, T: (053) 22514.
Riding: contact Callaghane Riding Centre, Waterford, T: (051) 382154.

FURTHER INFORMATION
Tourist offices: the BF offices in Waterford, T: (051) 875788, and Kilkenny, T: (056) 51500, are open all year; the office in New Ross, T: (051) 421857, opens June–Aug.

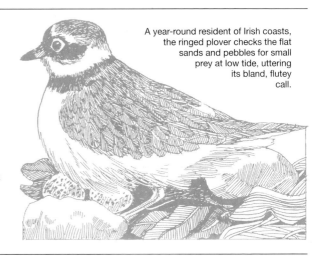

A year-round resident of Irish coasts, the ringed plover checks the flat sands and pebbles for small prey at low tide, uttering its bland, flutey call.

South Wexford and Saltee Islands

A fertile loamy county whose exhilarating outliers provide a bird-breeding success story

Unlike the high rock-dramas of the north-east, north-west and south-west corners of Ireland, the South-East ends in a whimper of sand and boulder clay. The coast is mostly low and soft, and, out to sea, a *cheval de frise* of sand reefs lies in wait for incautious shipping. ('If a ship grounds,' Praeger tells us dispassionately, 'the tide digs a deep hole on the downstream side, into which the vessel topples, and in a surprisingly short time disappears completely.') There are miles of dunes, sometimes sheltering lagoons and inland lakes. An air of haunting ghostliness can hang over the sites of sunken causeways, townships and buildings buried or half-buried by sand. There are sandy bays and banks of wiry marram, broad quiet estuaries and, of course, there are birds. The case for calling Wexford the most important county in Ireland for birds is a strong one. Where there are visible rocks – and there are, in fact, plenty of black granite rock capes

and islets – they lie low, as if undermined by their age, for they are among the oldest rocks in the country.

The area is dotted with ruins. This is the coast that was captured by Normans from Wales, the first toehold in the fateful colonization by Ireland's eastern neighbour. Cromwell was here, too, his divine angel inspiring him to horrors of what he saw as just retribution. The 1798 rebellion was as determined and bloody in County Wexford as anywhere in Ireland. Yet, in many ways, Wexford is the most English-seeming of Irish counties: green, wooded and pastoral with a loamy fertility like the English shires. There was a time when the Wexford gentry went to Bristol and London sooner than to Dublin for special shopping. Perhaps some still do.

This southern coastal strip is an exception on any score. Beyond Carnsore Point, where the tide-race and reefs have always dragged down the unwary, the confluence of currents makes for rich fishing. The Saltee Islands, biggest in the region, have their own royal family; the owner refers to himself as Prince Michael, and had himself crowned on a throne of limestone. The islands also have heady populations of birds on passage.

Generally speaking, this southern Wexford coastline is made up of two crescent bays. The larger, westerly bay curves from Hook Head to Crossfarnoge or Forlorn

RIGHTS OF WAY

In Northern Ireland (as in England and Wales) most rights of way are marked on Ordnance Survey maps, and in some cases signposted. Public libraries have comprehensive and up-to-date maps. In the Republic the legal right to cross land is in the main confined to national parks and long-distance walks.

Restrictions on walking rights have not been a problem in the past. Irish landowners both north and south have been sublimely tolerant of walkers crossing their land. The advice has always been to seek a farmer's permission, which will almost always be charmingly given, if you think you are close to him or his house. The Irish are proud of these gentle conventions, and it is a great pity that they have begun to wear thin. On popular tracks and sites litter-leaving tourists and landowners' fears about legal claims for compensation if people hurt themselves have

brought about a reduction in this Irish charm quotient and an increase in the use of electric wire and impenetrable fences. These fences, with a strand of sharply barbed wire along the top, are subsidized by the EC, and may also result from the sub-division of land previously held as commonage on mountains. They are not always successful at containing the movements of sheep and have substantially reduced the national acreage available to walkers. On recent walks I have had to pass uncomfortably close to electric wire at Loop Head, the Bridges of Ross and elsewhere. I have torn my trousers on wire on Rathlin Island; found that walks described in detail in a book on Sligo had been disallowed by angry landlords; been snarled at by bright red 'Keep Out' notices in the Suir valley; and time and time again been prevented by fences from going where I was free to go only a few years ago.

Point, whose rock, after dipping underwater, re-emerges a few miles south as the Saltees; the easterly bends gently round to Carnsore Point. The one sizeable inlet is Bannow Bay, estuary of the Rivers Owenduff and Corock. For the rest, the inland waters – Lady's Island lake, Tacumshin lake and the Cull behind Ballyteige Bay – are almost entirely bounded by bars of shingle thinly capped by sand. Wind blows the sand back into the lake where it accumulates and continually, though infinitesimally, widens the bar. Wind is not the only unsettling agent. Burrowing rabbits break up the sand further and deeper. In the past, people cut such vegetation as there was for thatching and mattresses. What they removed was marram grass, the most effective answer to these disruptive influences, for its stems and long rhizomes tether and firm the sand into dunes. On this basis, other plants can settle and so, in due course, can the animal life that depends on them and on the sea's resources. Then, cyclically, rabbits arrive and spoil it all again. Some say it was the Normans who introduced rabbits to Ireland, but there is, so far as I know, no proof of this.

An auk with a comically colourful bill, the puffin breeds at a number of coastal and island sites, mainly on the west coast, nesting in disused rabbit burrows and often quite unafraid of human admirers.

There are, all the same, rich and sometimes rare plants here: wild asparagus (*Asparagus officinalis*), sea stock (*Matthiola sinuata*), viper's bugloss (*Echium vulgare*), bee orchid (*Ophrys apifera*) and cottonweed (*Otanthus maritimus*), which is found on only one beach in the south of the county, though common in the west of France and in Portugal. Bird's foot trefoil (*Lotus corniculatus*) and other quite widespread plants like seaside pansy (*Viola tricolor* ssp. *curtisii*) and lady's bedstraw (*Galium verum*) form huge carpets. Colonies of wild thyme (*Thymus drucei*) and eyebright (*Euphrasia nemorosa*) can also be seen as well as that familiar (in the south of Ireland) shrub trio: gorse, fuchsia and escallonia. Butterflies and rabbits are conspicuous by their presence, foxes less so.

Carnsore Point offers the sight of many birds, including some as small as meadow pipits and skylarks, on passage between North Africa and Atlantic destinations such as Iceland and Greenland. Lady's Island lake has several islands, one of which, Inch Island in the southern sector, supports a colony of terns, mainly of the Sandwich variety (*Sterna sandvicensis*) but including some of the increasingly rare roseate terns (*Sterna dougallii*). Several kinds of gull breed on the same island, and elsewhere on and near the lake are seen a wide variety of duck, both dabblers and divers, as well as grebes and many different waders. The movable population of Tacumshin lake is on similar lines but in greater numbers. There are large winter flocks of Bewick's swans, brent geese and numerous ducks. Further west, the long thin inlet known as the Cull has a decent winter population. A certain ingenuity is required of the bird-watcher at Bannow Bay, because the birds' daily movements carry them to pastures and havens miles apart; in addition, they may only come close enough to the shore for a reasonable inspection at high tide, or an hour or two either side of this.

Summer is not the best time for the bird-watcher on the mainland but you are never going to be without some good subject matter. For a change, you can bathe from lovely sandy beaches, turn your attention to plants or butterflies, or take a boat from the pretty fishing village of Kilmore Quay to Great Saltee Island. (Little Saltee, with no cliffs and little cover, is far less rewarding.) May, June and July are the best months, when parts of the island become a frenetic, raucous, avian maternity ward. Thousands of gulls of several kinds nest on the open ground, in fields not farmed in decades, among bramble and bracken, and on the shore. Kittiwakes, guillemots and razorbills, also in their thousands, occupy their customary shelves on vertical cliffs on the western and southern coasts. Puffins nest in burrows above them, along with Manx shearwaters, seen, or more likely only heard, by those who stay overnight.

The extinct great auk, cousin of the guillemot, puffin and razorbill, was last recorded in Ireland not far from here, in Waterford harbour, in 1846. Its disappearance heralded an era of decline for birds which gets more acute each year. More recently the nightingale gave its last Irish recital on the Great Saltee. Now and again, though, a species runs against the current of decrease. Only a few gannets bred here in the early 1930s, but numbers rose over the years, gradually but fairly steadily. Over a thousand pairs breed now, mainly on cliffs at the island's southernmost tip.

BEFORE YOU GO
Maps: OSI Discovery Series, map No. 77.
Guide-books: *Saltees, Islands of Birds and Legends* by Richard Roche and Oscar Merne (O'Brien Press, 1987), and *The Complete Guide to Ireland's Birds* by Dempsey and O'Clery (Gill & Macmillan, 1993).

GETTING THERE
By sea: Saltee Island Cruises, based in Kilmore Quay, go to the Saltee Islands. Contact Declan Bates, T: (053) 29684, or BF in Wexford, T: (053) 23111.
By car: to get to Kilmore Quay, the nearest mainland village to the Saltee Islands, follow the R739 south from Wexford. For Carnsore Point, take the R736 (west) from Rosslare. After Tagoat, take the first lane south, which winds down to the coast. Bannow Bay can be reached by continuing along

the R739 to Carrick, and then taking the road going south to the coast.

By rail: the nearest stations to the south Wexford coast are Bridgetown and Wellington Bridge. Trains between Rosslare Harbour and Waterford stop there twice a day, T: (01) 836 6222.

By bus: the Wed and Sat Bus Eireann service from Wexford to Kilmore Quay, along with the 3 weekly buses between Waterford and Wexford, all stop at Wellington Bridge. Many national services terminate in Rosslare Harbour, T: (051) 879000.

WHERE TO STAY

Hotels and B&Bs: there is no accommodation on the Saltee Islands, but there are a handful of hotels and B&Bs in Kilmore Quay, such as Quay House, T: (053) 29988; and in Rosslare Harbour, Aisla Lodge, T: (053) 33230. The charming 18th-century Churchtown House is in Tagoat, T: (053) 32555.

Youth hostels: the independent Kilturk Hostel is in Kilmore Quay, T: (053) 29883, and there is an An Oige hostel in Rosslare Harbour, T: (053) 33399.

Outdoor living: the Saltee Islands are privately owned so permission must be sought from the owner before pitching your tent. Contact Declan Bates, T: (053) 29684. The Ocean Island CCP is at Fethard-on-Sea, T: (051) 397148, and St Margaret's Beach CCP at Our Lady's Island, T: (053) 31169.

ACCESS
Landing on the Saltees is possible only in fine weather. So is leaving them.

ACTIVITIES
Fishing: for rock and beach fishing, licensed charter boats are available in Kilmore Quay. Contact Paddy Nolan, T: (053) 29967, or Dick Hayes, T: (053) 29704. Angling permits can be got from Mr Masters of Tipperary Flycraft in Raheenroe,

near Fethard (no tel.).

Bird-watching: the Saltee Islands support puffins, guillemots, razorbills, cormorants, shags, kittiwakes and various auks as well as the most accessible of all gannet colonies. The best time to visit is during the spring and early-summer nesting season and the spring and autumn (partial) migrations. The observation tower at The Wexford Wildfowl Reserve is open all year. Contact the warden, T: (053) 23129, or visit Bird Watch Ireland's web-site, www.birdwatchireland.ie. Carnsore Point, south of Rosslare Harbour, sees a wide variety of migratory birds.

FURTHER INFORMATION
Tourist offices: BF offices in Wexford, T: (053) 23111, and in Rosslare Harbour, T: (053) 33622, are open all year.

A pattern of pines looms through fog in Knockaun Forest, on the west side of the Comeragh Mountains.

Wexford Slobs

Home to huge populations of geese, these mud-flats are protected by extensive wildfowl reserves

Now and again the Celtic genius for lilting place-names gives out. Ballyhooly, Tristernagh, Nahanagan and Derravaragh make way for the bog. Or the slobs. Both of which are, if not lyrical, at least onomatopoeic, their sounds hinting at their nature. Slobs are mud-flats, with perhaps admixtures of sand-dunes, inclined to be wet and pliable and, in dry weather, friable. Soppy, perhaps. Or sloppy. Slobs. In this case reclaimed from the sea in the middle of the 19th century and preserved by dykes for use as farmland. Birds use them, too, in colossal numbers. There would be little purpose in anyone not interested in birds visiting these slobs.

Wexford harbour, which is the estuary of the River Slaney, forms a square whose east side is a long thin promontory, which provides the harbour wall, and whose north and south sides bound, respectively, the north and south slobs. The sea along this coast is relatively shallow, streaked with shoals and reefs, submerged sandbanks and the strands of mud which, when the tide is out, emerge to offer their content of burrowing crustaceans and molluscs to the waders which depend on them. Sea movements cause low, flat, sandy islands to come and go. Up to twenty-five years ago Wexford harbour contained the largest colony of terns in Ireland (about 2,500 breeding pairs) but the island they bred on was slowly washed away and they moved elsewhere.

More than half the world's population of Greenland white-fronted geese spend their winter on the slobs. Numbers have reached about ten thousand, but early last century the most numerous species of goose to winter here was the greylag. They were present in Scotland too. After the Second World War Scottish farmers raised their production of root crops, a move which attracted the Irish greylags to join the Scottish. Brent geese, who find the mud-flats more to their liking, moved in. Other changes, notably drainage schemes carried out by farmers who own all the land outside the nucleus belonging to the Irish Wildbird Conservancy and National Parks and Wildlife Service, have seemed more menacing, but in the event numbers remain more or less stable.

There are plenty more birds. Maverick geese of several species get caught up with the huge white-front and brent populations. Several hundred Bewick's swans (named after the great wood-engraver when found to be a species distinct from whoopers) winter here. There are also large numbers of resident mute swans. Among the ducks are large populations of wigeon and mallard (as there are all along the south coast) and a dozen other species. Common scoters float in extensive rafts out at sea in the winter, a few metallic divers and flamboyant grebes in their midst. Waders include several hundred black-tailed godwits and good numbers of lapwing, golden plover and curlew. Amid such rich pickings the presence of birds of prey – hen harriers, peregrines and merlins

The Greenland white-fronted goose has a conspicuous patch which seems to connect the bill with the head. Traditionally a goose of bogs and wet grasslands in the midlands and west, it increasingly chooses intensive farmland during its Irish winters, and the largest flock is based in the Wexford Slobs.

in winter, kestrels and sparrowhawks throughout the year – is not surprising.

Spying from concealment on the huge geese populations resident in winter can be far more exciting than anything in the novels of Le Carré. The little loyal family groups of brent geese muster together and rise, their individual flappings making a huge, collective cloud of shimmering silver, turning black and then silver again as they wheel and turn and slowly descend to a further reach of pasture, or to the sea.

ROADS, MAPS AND SIGNS

Major roads in the Republic were in the past prefixed by the letter T (for Trunk) and minor roads by the letter L (for Local). Major road numbers are now prefixed by the letter N (for National) and minor roads with the letter R (for Regional). The numbers that follow these letters have also changed in most cases. Thus the main road from Galway to Sligo used to be known as the T11 and is now the N17. In many cases an old road number may have have been replaced by up to three new numbers; similarly, one new road number may have superseded several old ones.

The Department of the Environment have replaced all the old T road signs with N signs, but they have not yet finished taking down the old L signs on back roads which are being changed to R numbers. This gradual process means that even recent editions of the OSI *Road Atlas of Ireland* are out of date. The Department advises bemused road users to rely on place-names on signposts more than road numbers. Most road signs are in English only or in English and Gaelic. To confuse matters, OSI maps do not always provide both versions and signs in the Gaeltacht tend to be in Irish only. In this way what appears on most maps as Burtonport (on the Donegal coast) is announced on the road sign as *Ailt an Chorrain*, while Dunglow is *An Clochan Liath*. A driver may not be aware that *Giell Sli* is Irish for the instruction 'Yield' and that 'Danger' is rendered *Dainseas*.

In Northern Ireland road numbers are prefixed by the letters A and B as in the rest of the United Kingdom.

Before you go *Maps:* OSI Discovery Series, map No. 77.
Getting there *By car:* from Wexford, take the R741 (north), then the R742 to reach the Wexford Slobs nature reserve.
By rail: services between Dublin (Connolly) and Rosslare Harbour stop at Wexford 3 times a day, T: (01) 836 6222.
By bus: Bus Eireann operate services to Wexford from all over Ireland. A Mon and Sat bus between Wexford and Gorey stops at Curracloe, about 3 miles (5 km) from the nature reserve, T: (051) 879000.
When to go: a good time to visit the slobs is Oct–Apr when geese and other wintering species are resident.

Where to stay *Hotels and B&Bs:* there is a wide choice in Wexford including Mrs Scallar, T: (053) 21047, and Mrs Whitty, T: (053) 41124. The beautiful Churchtown House, open Mar–Nov, T: (053) 32555, is at Tagoat, near Rosslare. *Youth hostels:* the independent Kirwan House hostel is in Wexford, T: (053) 21208.
Outdoor living: the Ferrybank CCP, open Easter–30 Sept, is at Wexford, T: (053) 42611/42987; Burrow Holiday Park, open 13 Mar–1 Nov, is at Rosslare, T: (053) 32190.
Activities *Cycling:* The Bike Shop, T: (053) 22514, and Hayes, T: (053) 22462, in Wexford, hire out bikes.

Bird-watching: in the north slobs there is a public reception area with a permanent collection of pinioned birds, indoor displays and an observation tower. Well designed and run, it makes an excellent learning centre. The local bird population can be seen all year round; species include Greenland white-fronted, brent, Canada, pink foot and other geese, pintails, Bewick's swans and both varieties of godwit. For details call the Wexford Wildfowl Reserve, T: (053) 23129.
Further information *Tourist offices:* seasonal office in Wexford, T: (053) 23111, and year-round office in Rosslare Harbour, T: (053) 33232.

CHAPTER 6

Wicklow and the East

At the head of broad inlets on the east coast of Ireland, separated by about a hundred miles, stand the two Irish capital cities, Dublin and Belfast, accounting between them for half the island's population. Across the Irish Sea are the coasts of England, Wales and Scotland, and upon the dividing water sails a lot of traffic between Clydeside, Stranraer, Merseyside, Fishguard, Milford Haven and other ports on the British side, and Rosslare, Wexford, Dun Laoghaire, Drogheda, Belfast, Carrickfergus, Larne and others on the Irish. Ireland's east coast is populous and busy. Many of those stretches of it not dedicated to people's work and homes are given over to people's play: resorts, golf courses, marinas and the like. It is not likely ground for that human neglect which permits the survival or development of wildness.

The wild, however, has, if it ever needed to, learned to co-exist with humans. Clinging to the inaccessible edges of human dominion, sea-birds nest on promontories such as Bray Head, Wicklow Head or Howth; or settle to pasture or roost in their thousands beside the golf course on the Bull or peck nourishing molluscs from miles of mud-flat and sandy beach.

Even in the centre of the east coast and within a stone's throw of Dublin, there are a couple of wild places to match the best the West can offer. Ten miles (16 kilometres) north of the capital you can cross three miles (five kilometres) of sea from Rogerstown, near

A winding, rock-lined creek leads down to Lough Tay from Sally Gap, in the heart of the Wicklow Mountains.

Rush (having obtained permission by post from the owner's steward), and visit Lambay, an important bird reserve. The island is all that remains of an extinct volcano and, in marked contrast to the low-lying mainland shore, contains cliffs up to 400 feet (120 metres) in height, obvious home to a full complement of sea-birds. It is rich in igneous and metamorphic rocks, although one former resident would not have held with such data. The 17th-century Archbishop Ussher dated the origin of the universe – the Genesis creation – to the year 4004 BC, a masterfully precise claim widely accepted well into the present century. Ireland's Eye, a little island to the north of the Howth promontory, and so even closer to the city centre and more easy to get to than Lambay, is also rich in sea-birds.

The River Boyne winds through the rich farming and hunting county of Meath. Demesnes of great mansions and castles and ancient royal burial grounds come down to its banks, and beside it, in 1689, a battle decisive in Irish and English history was fought. Every inch of its borders shows the influence of humans. Rivers are still wild, though, and for the most part unseen by humans. None of us can share the trout's view of the shadows he haunts, the pike's view of the trout, eyes peering from tangled roots or dense packs of reeds, the kingfisher skewering his prey, the walk of the dipper or the skimming passage of whirligig and water-beetle across the surface above. Even the patient angler is working on extrapolation and hunch, not knowledge of facts. But we see more than we otherwise would if we sit in a long smooth hollow of wood or fibreglass gliding noiselessly over the surface. A canoe is the discreetest, as well as the most enjoyable, means of spying on the wild.

The best area of wilderness around Dublin is the closest. No other capital city in Europe lives so genially cheek by jowl with a mountain range of great size, variety and beauty. The Wicklow Mountains, taken with the coast beside them, offer examples of almost all that is best of wild Ireland: miles of blanket bog interspersed with monumental peaks and deep, steep-sided mountain corries; waterfalls streaming down rocky defiles to flow into the broad lakes of the big glens; cliffs crammed with nesting birds, good walks, good climbs; pastoral scenery that seems to belong to another age; a rich flora and fauna. An hour or so (much depending on traffic in the city) from the hurly-burly of Georgian squares, Trinity College or the nation's parliament in Leinster House, you can, in a manner of speaking, go wild among features that have changed little in ten thousand years, and almost forget the frenetic pursuit of difference and development continuing without pause a few miles over the hills.

GETTING THERE

By air: Dublin is the republic's major airport, with direct flights from all over the world. Aer Lingus, T: (0845) 973 7747, www.aerlingus.ie, flies from the UK, continental Europe and North America; Ryanair, T: (0870) 156 9569, www.ryanair. com, from the UK, Paris and Brussels; British Midland, T: (0870) 607 0555, www.british midland.com; and British Airways, T: (0845) 722 2111, www.britishairways.com, from the UK (all UK nos). For details of European and North American flights, contact Dublin International Airport, T: (01) 814 1111, www.dublinairport.com. **By sea:** Stena Line, T: (0870) 570 7070, www.stenaline.com, sails from Holyhead, North Wales, to Dun Laoghaire and Dublin Ferryport. Irish Ferries go from Holyhead to Dublin, with a new fast service taking under 2 hrs, T: (0870) 517 1717, www.irishferries.com. Services

to Dublin from the Isle of Man are operated by the Isle of Man Steam Packet Co., T: (0870) 552 3523, www.steam packet.com; and from Liverpool by P&O, T: (0870) 242 4777, and Merchant Ferries, T: (0870) 600 4321, www.merchantferries.com.
By rail: the rail network radiates from Dublin. Stations at Bray and Wicklow are convenient for the Wicklow Mountains, Drogheda for the River Boyne, T: (01) 836 6222, www.irishrail.ie.
By bus: buses from all over Ireland run to Dublin where connections can be made to Wicklow, Rathdrum, Baltinglass and Drogheda, T: (01) 836 6111, www. buseireann.ie.

ACTIVITIES
Walking: the 82-mile (132-km) Wicklow Way stretches from Dublin over the Wicklow Mountains to Clonegal in Co. Carlow. Contact Bord Fáilte or the Wicklow County Council, T: (0404) 67324, for a pamphlet.
Cycling: contact BF for details of routes in the Wicklow Mountains.
Riding: there are many riding centres. See BF's *Equestrian Holidays Ireland* booklet.
Climbing: there are cliffs at Bray Head. Dalkey Quarry, 10 miles (16 km) from Dublin, is a training ground for climbers.
Fishing: Tinnehinch Fly Angling Centre is on the River Dargle, T: (01) 286 8652.
Watersports: Dun Laoghaire Sailing School, T: (01) 230 6654. Fingall Sailing School, T: (01) 845 1979, offers instruction and hires out wind-surfing equipment for the experienced.

FURTHER INFORMATION
Tourist offices: the 3 Dublin BF offices are Suffolk Street, the Airport (for both, freephone 1815 230330) and Baggot Street Bridge, T: (01) 602 4000, www.ireland.travel.ie.

Wicklow Mountains

Extensive, granite range with spectacular walks and views beginning just 12 miles (17 kilometres) from the centre of Dublin; includes Wicklow Mountains National Park

First place in the natural record of the Wicklow Mountains is occupied by a blackbird. St Kevin, a recluse of the early Celtic church, came to a breathtaking gash of a glen, now known as Glendalough, to escape the sinful world. He built a cell, prayed, fasted, ate, slept, studied. One day he sat reading so intently in the cell, with the elbow of his spare arm resting on the window-stone, that he failed to notice a blackbird alight on his open hand. It laid a clutch of eggs. Such was the holy man's Celtic sensitivity and tenderness to nature that he remained quite still until the eggs were hatched. Stories like this abound in the lives of saints. There is always a deep empathy with animals, though not always with other humans, and never with humans having sexual motives. A seductive girl who followed Kevin to the glen was picked up by him and dropped into the lake, where she drowned.

It is not difficult to feel in tune with Glendalough, a deep and lovely valley close to the centre of the Wicklows, holding two lakes (hence its name, two-lake glen) and a cluster of monastic ruins – for, in time, Kevin's cell attracted a large religious settlement. But this is only the most beautiful scene in a galaxy of beauties. The closeness of the range to the capital city is astonishing. The dozen miles that lie between the centre of Dublin and the nearest peaks and valleys – known as the Dublin hills because they fall within the county of that name – can seem like a thousand when you begin to breathe deep draughts of mountain air, look at broad vistas without sight of man, or wait in your car for the lane ahead to be cleared of a herd of cows.

This is not a genteel country park, placed conveniently for the delectation of townspeople, though, of course, townspeople come, in ever-increasing numbers, and some of them leave a great deal of sordid detritus behind them. It is a sizeable range of mountains, the highest reaching 3,039 feet (926 metres), higher than any in Ireland outside County Kerry. It covers an area about 30 miles (48 kilometres) north to south by 15 miles (24 kilometres) east to west, set back from the coast by a strip of lowland farm and parkland, and incorporating the largest spread of surface granite in Ireland or Britain. This rugged wilderness has been a threat as well as a source of recreation to the capital for centuries. Tudor armies were beaten here. Rebels found sanctuary. Native O'Tooles, O'Dwyers and Byrnes periodically provoked the authorities, and there are many relics of nervous government precautions from the 1790s, when the ideas behind the French Revolution were taking seed in Ireland, to blossom, fall and moulder in the agonies of the 1798 rising. The remains of a chain of barracks and other defensive buildings, as well as the Military Road – now in use as one of the main highways – all date from this period.

It was the crust-crushing convulsions of 500 million years before, consequent upon the infinitely slow collision of the American and European tectonic plates, which first created the Wicklows. The newly bunched surface consisted of slates and shales, layers formed from sea sediments compacted by the weight of water during former aeons. The peaks they formed were more than a thousand feet (300 metres) higher than they are now, further raised by the irruption from far below of a mass of molten magma, which cooled into granite. Down the centre of the range, exposure to periods of violent weather slowly eroded the slaty overlay, leaving exposed the long granite core which still forms most of the mountains' heartland. Slate remained on the sides, and here and there it and other sedimentary rocks were metamorphosed by heat and pressure into a harder consistency. The resilient quartzite that makes up the two tall, conical Sugar Loaf mountains near Enniskerry is the most conspicuous result of these processes.

Further weathering and slow corrosion worked by a gentler climate through unimaginable spans of time, made the granite summits big, rounded, and so set, in looks anyway, for eternity. Later the traverses of heavy trains of ice polished this work. The metamorphic slates and schists on either side were more spiky, angular and sharp than the central heights. Ice nevertheless squeezed into and through the several defiles and ravines, leaving them deeper, wider and smoother and sometimes floored with lakes.

But an angularity remains to this day in the short steep glens of the west and the long

– many miles long – broader valleys of the eastern scarp. Ice has left other distinctive features apart from the cones of quartzite at Enniskerry already noted: the sharp features of the Bray Head escarpment, raised riverbeds, waterfalls and several examples of a type of channel caused by the uneven melting of glaciers. As the climate warmed, the highest ice melted quickly. When the process reached the rock valleys and lowlands, the shade and colder ambient temperature greatly slowed things down. At this level the ice became a kind of extension of the lower mountain. Water flowing from the great uplands melt would be checked by its mass and forced to turn to right or left or both. The resultant churning and turning carved out what was to become – and remains – a mountain lake. The escaping overflow, still prevented from descending down the valley by the ice-sheet, excavated a sideways channel, known as a glacial spillway, across the mountain ridge. Here and there – at the Scalp, and Glen of the Downs near Enniskerry, at Piperstown glen below Killakee mountain, and down to the south of the Poulaphuca reservoir above Hollywood – these cross-ridge channels survive, dry, covered by vegetation, and betraying little sign of their icy origins.

Some of the glen rocks contain minerals in quantities once thought worth exploiting. Lead was mined in Glendalough, Glendasan and elsewhere in the 19th century, and there are the ruins of miners' cottages, smelting houses and slag heaps to show it. In the south, on the side of Croghan mountain, there is gold. Somewhere, it seems, there may be quite a lot of gold, in a mother lode buried, perhaps, under hundreds of feet of rock. What has come to light has been in tiny quantities, though enough to set off a couple of gold-rushes – in 1795 and 1935 – and probably to provide the material for large numbers of very beautiful, ancient gold decorative objects, of which many superb examples are in Dublin's National Museum. If you are determined to build your fortune on Irish gold, take your pan to Woodenbridge and progress up Gold Mines river. Or better, catch a leprechaun and squeeze the secret out of him.

There are no surprises among the more accessible fauna. All the birds here are well represented in other parts of Ireland but, if you parcel the adjoining coast with the mountains, there is quite a wide variety. The rocky faces of Wicklow Head and Bray Head provide nesting space for the standard company of Irish sea-birds: guillemots, razorbills, kittiwakes, fulmars, herring gulls, great black-backed gulls, shags. The increasingly rare grey partridge may still occur, though there have been no officially accepted sightings recently. For the ravens and peregrines which nest here, the mountains are hunting grounds, though peregrines may spend a day in Wales, or the North, or the West, for variety. Ravens are quite often seen, scouring the hillside for carrion or prey or simply playing in the winds. They seem to become more common each year, sensitive, perhaps, to the more tolerant feelings of humans, who used to persecute them. They also do extremely well out of the European Union sheep headage subsidy, which has encouraged farmers to run more sheep than the land can nourish. The result is a plentiful supply of carrion.

Ravens are favourites of mine: grand, handsome, with the sinister aura Poe exaggerated, and very clever – they have always been thought that. You may have heard the account of one raven which came on a dead deer on a mountainside. As it began its lone feast a whole flock of ravens appeared and approached. Suddenly the single bird rolled over and lay still, done for, it seemed, by the poison some farmer had put in the carcass. The other birds looked at the meat, strutted over to the body and looked at that, drew their conclusions and flew away. Intelligent, certainly; but ravens can be more intelligent still. As soon as they had gone the original bird got up, shook out his feathers, and resumed his meal.

Wicklow has the usual repertoire of ling (*Calluna vulgaris*), bell heather (*Erica cinerea*) and – on wetter ground – cross-leaved heath (*Erica tetralix*) together with upland grasses found in other acidic Irish ranges. It also has its share of conifer plantations. As they reach maturity the evergreens black out almost all subsidiary life-forms; but here and there are good broadleaf woods, among

A cross-marked standing stone survives from a past age on the west of Tonelagee mountain, in the middle of Wicklow: an ancient waymark, perhaps, on an old pilgrimage route.

them the old oak stands of Glen of the Downs and the Vale of Clara, and the mixed woodlands of Glendalough, Devil's Glen and Shillelagh (which gave its name to the famous Irish oak cudgel), where a lot of small birds breed. Pied flycatchers, which hunt by casting themselves into exquisite aerial loops, breed here, as do monotonously chiffchaffing chiffchaffs, some wood warblers, blackcaps with their lovely choirboy voices and occasional redstarts. On the sparser uplands you might glimpse whinchats, stonechats, linnets, meadow pipits, and those aristocrat assassins the hen harrier, merlin and kestrel – the last being the only true hoverer occurring in these islands, steadily holding its exact position in the air (as you can see if there is a backdrop of hill or tree to check by) with no more than a corrective tremor of its wings.

Deer are present: red (introduced here in 1920, though centuries before in Kerry), fallow (introduced by the Romans, it is thought), sika (escaped from the spectacular gardens of Powerscourt), but mostly sika-red crosses. One October in Wicklow I heard what I took to be a pig grunting but saw no sign of beast or sty or pen or paddock. The noise kept recurring, and then I realized it must have been something I had seldom heard before: a concealed fallow buck, with its deep grunt (what a 32-foot organ pipe would sound like, perhaps, if it were able to belch), soliciting female company and warning rival stags at the beginning of its rut, a season of several weeks during which it does not even feed.

Of other sizeable mammals, badgers are about, and by no means always at night, as is so often claimed. There are foxes, feral goats, rabbits, hedgehogs, pygmy shrews, rats – whose numbers in some years disconcert – mice; and there are Irish mountain hares (*Lepus timidus hibernicus*), a native subspecies of the blue hare (*Lepus timidus*), found in Scotland and other parts of Europe. Unlike blue hares, the Irish animal does not normally turn white in winter. It can be distinguished from the brown hare (*Lepidus capensis*), which is common in Britain, by its shorter ears and pale tail and by its reddish coat, which fades and goes patchy during winter moults – that of the brown hare tends to be dark on top. But 'reddish' will not really do. Hare colours have the rich complexity of a much-used palette, a palette of reds, browns, buffs, chestnut, cinnamon, russet, creams, whites and beiges. It is this, along with their effortless zigzag run and skill at concealment, that has led them to be endowed, in all national myths, with mystical, magic powers. Time and again, a seemingly blameless wife turns out to be a part-time witch, speeding off to covens and other diabolical assignments in hare form, and given away by a graze or bruise in a part of her body corresponding to the wound on a hare the farmer-husband has shot or nearly snared.

If not all things to all men, the Wicklows are quite a lot to quite a few. They are a quick breather, or a day out, for a million Dubliners, a place the visitor landing at Dublin or Rosslare may well take in before heading west, a mighty and magnificent obstacle for midland Irish needing to reach the Wicklow coast and Wicklow coast Irish needing to reach the midlands. For many, they are the site of week-long or longer rambles, hikes and climbs. There is, of course, an ancient picnic tradition, by Loughs Tay or Dan or Luggala or by the Powerscourt waterfall, leading to tales of old-school dons and writers being nasty about each other over Thermos tea and cucumber sandwiches. One Trinity teacher, as Oliver Gogarty records, complained that since a colleague of his had given up preaching sermons he had suffered insomnia in church. And Yeats remarked that the worst thing about a particular compatriot was that when he was not drunk he was sober.

The plurality of Wicklow's roles makes any prescription of route unnecessary. Certainly it would be a pity to miss many of the grandest scenes: the Wicklow Gap, Glendalough, the Sally Gap, the Meeting of the Waters, the Vale of Avoca, the Vale of Clara, Glenmacnass, Glenmalure, Powerscourt and Enniskerry, Roundwood (the highest village in Ireland), the Avondale forestry park, the Glen of Imail. But all the main through-roads, as well as the official long-distance Wicklow Way from Dublin's outskirts to Clonegal, include some of these attractions and most illustrate the varied immensity of the range: the heady rise and fall of the pass-roads, with broad, sweeping valleys narrowing to rock-crimped woody cuts; the accompanying streams or torrents; the stately beauty of the lakes; and a thousand more enclosed and intimate scenes, revealing hill, wood, waterfall, rock feature, gold glinting like good intentions in a stream, bright green hags (as moist enclaves in the bog are called) and that impressive boulder on a hill above the Vale of Avoca, the Motte Stone. Left precariously perched by a receding glacier, the stone is said in the fast-fading local folklore to roll downhill every May Day (a time electric with magic potential) to the Meeting of the Waters for a long draught of water, and thereafter to roll up again.

BEFORE YOU GO

Maps: OSI Discovery Series, map Nos. 50, 56 and 62.
Guide-books: *The Complete Wicklow Way* by J. B. Malone (O'Brien Press, 1997); *The Wicklow Way* by Michael Fewer (Ordnance Survey Ireland, 1998); *Walk Guide East of Ireland* by David Herman, Miriam Joyce McCarthy and Jean Boyell (Gill & Macmillan, 1998); *The Wicklow Way Map Guide* (EastWest Mapping, 1998); *Rock Climbing Guide to Wicklow* by Lyons and Fenlon (Mountaineering Council of Ireland, 1993).

GETTING THERE

By car: from Dublin follow the N82 to Tallaght, the N81 (south) to Hollywood, then the R756 (east) to Laragh. This takes you through the middle of the Wicklow mountains. The R115 from Dublin to Laragh (the old Military Road) is also scenic.
By rail: Bray, on the DART (Dublin Area Rapid Transport), and Rathdrum and Wicklow on the main line, provide good starting points for eastern and southern approaches to the mountains, T: (01) 836 6222.
By bus: there are 8 Bus Eireann services a day from Dublin to Wicklow (Mon–Sat) and 2 to Rathdrum (fewer on Suns). An Expressway between Dublin and Waterford stops at Baltinglass, west of the mountains, T: (01) 836 6111. Bus Eireann and St Kevin's Buses run daily tours to Glendalough, T: (01) 281 8119.

WHERE TO STAY

Hotels and B&Bs: there is a huge selection. The Hunter's Hotel, near Rathnew, is one of Ireland's oldest coaching inns, (0404) 40106, e-mail: reception@hunters.ie; Mrs Cummins' B&Bs is in Enniskerry, (01) 286 0149; Pinewood Lodge at Laragh, Glendalough, T: (0404) 45292; the Enniscree Lodge Hotel in the Glencree Valley, (01) 286 3542; Rathsallagh House at Dunlavin, T: (045) 403112; Mrs Sheehan's in Rathdrum, T: (0404) 46683 /46217; and the Vale View Hotel in Avoca, T: (0402) 35236.
Youth hostels: there are no less than 8 An Oige hostels in the mountains, including those at Glencree, T: (01) 286 4037; Blessington, T: (045) 867266; Glendalough, T: (0404) 45342; and Aughrim, T: (0402) 36366. There are also 4 independents, including Rathdrum, open all year, T: (0404) 46930, e-mail: thehostel@hotmail.com; and The Wicklow Way Hostel, Laragh, Glendalough, T: (0404) 45398/45345.
Outdoor living: Shankill CCP, just south of Dublin, is open all year, T: (01) 282 0011. Nearer to the mountains are the River Valley CCP, Redcross, T: (0404) 41647, open Mar–Sept; Roundwood CCP, T: (01) 281 8163, open Apr–Sept; and Avonmore Riverside CCP, Rathdrum, T: (0404) 46080, open Easter–end-Sept.

ACTIVITIES

Walking: 1,000 square miles of granite domes, including the Wicklow Mountains National Park, offer plenty of scope. Particularly fine walks run from Glendalough, including the hike up Camaderry, which starts at the Upper Lake car park. The Wicklow Way, which is 83 miles (132 km) long, goes from the outskirts of Dublin in the north to Clonegal in the south and offers wonderful views, but some tough walking and, in poor conditions, the danger of getting lost. A compass and map are essential; contact BF for maps and guides. Ballyknocken House at Glenealy, near Ashford,

The red grouse may be seen in uplands in several parts of the country, breaking cover in boglands or heathery moors – the various parts of the heather plant form its favourite food – but its numbers have been steadily declining for some years.

specializes in walking holidays; contact Mary Byrne, T: (0404) 44614/44627.

Riding: Calliaghstown Riding Centre, based in Rathcoole, T: (01) 458 9236, runs trail rides over the mountains.

Climbing: the main centre is Glendalough, with some of the granite peaks rising up to 3,000 ft (900 m). Most climbs are Severe and Very Severe, with some Difficult and Extreme grades. Luggala is another big crag with many fine routes. For a climbing guide contact Joss Lynam, T: (01) 288 4672.

FURTHER INFORMATION
Tourist offices: the BF offices in Wicklow, T: (0404) 69117, and in Dublin on Baggot Street Bridge, T: (01) 602 4000, are open all year.
Park office: the Wicklow Mountains National Park, Glendalough, T: (0404) 45425 /45338 in winter.

Ireland's Eye

Insular nature reserve a few minutes' boat trip from Howth

Islands, islets, sea-girt rocks - even tight-necked peninsulas - are rarities on Ireland's east coast. Lambay, opposite Rush in County Dublin, is the biggest of them. It consists of ancient volcanic and sedimentary rocks, and its cliffs and rock stacks support a good population of sea-birds. It is, however, closed to the public. Dalkey Island, opposite Dalkey at the southern extreme of the capital, is relatively featureless but is an important roost for post-breeding terns in late summer. Other east coast islands include Rockabill, with its lighthouse, which hosts the most important colony of roseate terns in Western Europe, and three low-lying islands, also off Skerries in north County Dublin. The merits of the only other island of substance, Ireland's Eye, are that it is just a mile off the mainland, that boat owners from Howth can usually be hired in summer to take visitors around it, and that it offers a home, particularly on its north-eastern cliffs, to thousands of sea-birds.

There are nearly a thousand nesting kittiwakes, almost as many guillemots and over 150 pairs of razorbill on the Eye, besides fulmars, black guillemots, both great and lesser black-backed gulls, a sprinkling of puffins, and those evil-smelling denizens of guano-spread rock roosts to north, south, east and west of Ireland, the cormorants and shags. Both birds are black almost all over, but the

Map

Wicklow and the East

Key
— Exploration zones.
═ Roads.
- - Footpaths.
Ⓐ Points of interest.
- · - Regional boundaries.

2000 and over
1000 - 2000
200 - 1000
0 - 200
metres

to Castleblaney
CAVAN   Cootehill
Warrenpoint
Kilkeel
Carlingford
Dundalk
Carrickmacross
Dundalk Bay
LOUTH
Ardee
Irish Sea
Kells
Slane
Drogheda
Navan
Julianstown
River Boyne
Balbriggan
Athboy
Skerries
Trim
MEATH
DUBLIN
Rush
Portrane
LAMBAY ISLAND
Kinnegad
Donabate
Malahide
Ireland's Eye
Maynooth
Dublin Airport
Howth
WESTMEATH
Royal Canal
Edenderry
Liffey
Dublin Bay
KILDARE
Dublin
Dun Laoghaire
Grand Canal
Shankill
Naas
Bray
Droichead Nua
Enniskerry
Greystones
Kilcullen
Glen of the Downs
Lough Tay
Lough Dan
Dunlavin
Wicklow Gap
Roundwood
WICKLOW
Glendalough
LAOIS
Wicklow
Athy
Baltinglass
Wicklow Mtns
Rathdrum
Carlow
Vale of Avoca
Woodenbridge
Tullow
Tinahely
Arklow
CARLOW
Gorey

0   5   10miles
0   5   10   15Km.

-N-

cormorant is distinguished by white cheeks and somewhat slower wing-beats. There are also Manx shearwaters nesting in burrows in the ground during the breeding season, uttering shrill, late-night cries. 'Daemonic' is the word often used, but I have heard comparisons with a donkey's bray and a manic mating cat.

And there are gannets, an ornithological success story in an age when there are all too few. None bred here until 1988, but there are well over 50 pairs now, making the usual reeking bedlam of their nesting sites, bickering, posturing, squawking throughout the period of breeding, yet converting on their fishing expeditions into elegantly streamlined aerial torpedoes, plummeting through the air at 30 miles an hour to impale and carry away some unwary mackerel. The founders of this colony came from St Kilda in the Hebrides, far to the north, where 60,000 pairs breed.

Before you go *Maps:* OSI Discovery Series, map No. 50.
Getting there *By sea:* boats can be taken from Howth to Martello Tower, on the island. Contact Lambay Island Trips, T: (01) 831 4200, who run boats every ½ hr during the summer. *By car:* from Dublin city centre, follow the road along the sea-front north-east to Howth, the nearest mainland point to Ireland's Eye. *By rail:* take the DART to Howth, T: (01) 836 6222. *By bus:* Dublin Bus run services to Howth, T: (01) 873 4222, www.dublinbus.ie.
Where to stay *Hotels and B&Bs:* there is a vast choice of accommodation of every kind in Dublin, and some in Howth, including the Baily Court Hotel, T: (01) 832 2691. *Youth hostels:* in Dublin there is the An Oige Dublin International Youth Hostel, T: (01) 830 1766, and 17 independent ones; contact Independent Holiday Hostels of Ireland, T: (01) 836 4700, www.hostels-ireland.com.

Outdoor living: the North Beach Caravan and Camping Site at Rush is open all year, T: (01) 843 7131.
Access: Lambay Island is private property and landing is not allowed without written permission from the owners. Visits to Ireland's Eye are usually restricted to the summer months by the weather. No unauthorized visitors are allowed on Rockabill during the breeding season.
Activities *Fishing:* for sea-angling in Howth contact Dublin Coarse Fishing and Angling, T: (01) 494 6454. *Bird-watching:* Ireland's Eye is a sea-bird sanctuary where visitors can see kittiwakes, razorbills, cormorants, shags and others. For information about Dalkey Island, contact Maurice Bryan, T/F: (01) 493 1877, e-mail: alcedo@indigo.ie.
Further information *Tourist office:* contact the main BF office on Baggot Street Bridge in Dublin, T: (01) 602 4000.

BIRD-WATCHER'S CODE OF CONDUCT

1. The welfare of birds must come first.
2. Habitat must be protected.
3. Keep disturbance to birds and their habitat to a minimum.
4. When you find a rare bird think carefully about whom you should tell.
5. Do not harass rare migrants.
6. Abide by the bird-protection laws at all times.
7. Respect the rights of landowners.
8. Respect the rights of other people in the countryside.
9. Make your records available to the local bird recorder.
10. Behave abroad as you would when bird-watching at home.

Perched on a rock, pole or branch and spreading its wings to dry, or flapping energetically a few feet above the surface of the sea, the cormorant is familiar along the whole of Ireland's coastline; increasingly in recent years it has been found on inland waterways and lakes.

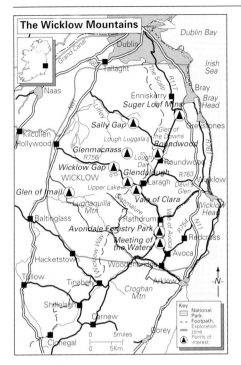

The Wicklow Mountains

River Boyne

A cross-section of County Meath, taking in Navan, Slane, Drogheda and the Boyne estuary

I once canoed down the Boyne from source to sea. My first canoe journey of any length, it was 60 downstream miles (100 kilometres) and could have been done in a day; but I span it out to five, stopping to see Newgrange and the burial mounds in the great, prehistoric royal graveyard of Brugh na Boinne, as well as the site of the battle which finally saw James II off British and Irish soil and marked the end of Roman Catholic monarchy. I watched birds and fish for hours on end. There is no way of intruding so silently on nature as in a canoe (except, I suppose, by balloon). Once a kingfisher almost parked on my head; it panicked about a yard away. Even herons

192

took my arrival calmly and paused to look before making unflustered ascents.

Committing myself, the boat and my possessions packed into two dustbin bags and stowed within the fibreglass prow to each weir as it came, I thought I was worth a medal for valour, though I soon learned it was not me but my almost weightless shiny craft that guided us. Sharp rocks shaved the paint as we careered through the frothing white water, twisting and turning at what seemed (there is the same illusion in surfing) like a hundred miles an hour. Had death come then I should have gone happy. I have loved few experiences in my life as much as those. The only grating thing was an occasional curse or threat from a fisherman who feared, I suppose, that I would foul his line. If I am truthful, something else pained me, but retrospectively. I read later that if the aggregate of an Irish river's dangers is put on a scale of ten, the Boyne's total amounts to one. So much for medals. So much for a glorious death.

Being in a boat on the river is the only way of seeing it all. You and your boat have to be brought to the highest navigable point, of course, which is at the Boyne Aqueduct, carrying the Royal Canal high over the river's channel, and you have to be collected at the mouth, if that is where you finish. The smooth, reedy waters of the elevated canal almost lured me away at the start – it could have taken me to the Shannon, the country's central artery, from which at Leitrim there is now access to Lough Erne by way of the restored Ballinamore and Ballyconnell canal; but I deferred that pleasure till later. The River Blackwater, which slams head-on into the Boyne at Navan, causing it to slew right and north-eastward towards Slane, is another enticing detour. It comes from Lough Ramor in the south of County Cavan.

Best of all, though, is the estuary. You emerge from Drogheda, whose vertiginous quays and hulls impart a pathetically Lilliputian and crushable feel to the toe-high canoeist, into a weird reach of broad river hemmed by 19th-century walls with gaps through which appear bleak, high and seemingly infinite mud-flats. Cormorants stretch their wings to dry on the navigation posts, as if crucified. The tide ripples in, with whatever breeze the eastern seaboard can muster. The atmosphere is surreal. The mud here is rich in mussels, and it is worth seeing the passion with which oystercatchers attack boats loaded with a new cargo of the shellfish. Turnstones may join in. Large flocks of golden plovers and brent geese may be seen from close to. Avocet and little egret are among the many recorded rarities.

The estuary broadens to a width of a mile, then narrows to a neck less than half a mile long and a hundred yards or so wide. I remember my elated arrival here with special warmth. An old man picking cockles from the sand as I paddled by asked where would I be going. To the sea, I said; I just want to finish canoeing the river.

'The whole river?'

'The whole river.'

'Sure, there's madder folk about than I thought there was.'

On my return journey he helped me lift the canoe out and hide it. Halfway through, alarmingly, he called out: 'Amn't I a man as had three heart attacks?' Then he gave me a lift – a rather juddering, halting lift in his small car – to a small hotel a few miles away, talking about local history and his state of health. I approached the beauteous brunette at the desk feeling self-conscious: in shorts, more or less soaked from head to foot, my luggage in two black dustbin bags, sunburnt

Found in or beside – often standing motionless at the edge of – almost all the rivers, lakes, ponds, canals and estuaries in Ireland, the grey heron, often called 'crane' by the Irish, breeds in colonies of flat twiggy nests on the top of tall trees.

skin peeling prolifically. Two ladies, genteelly dressed, and a fully togged priest passed me on their way out.

'Excuse my appearance,' I said to the reception girl.

'You're very welcome,' she said. 'Wouldn't it be a fool would judge a feller by the way he looked?'

And she gave me a heavenly room overlooking beach and sea.

BEFORE YOU GO

Maps: OSI Discovery Series, map Nos. 42, 43 and 49.

GETTING THERE

By car: for the Boyne Aqueduct, take N4 from Dublin to Kinnegad, then R161 to Trim and Navan, from where N51 runs alongside the river to Slane. Continue on the same road to Drogheda.

By rail: the nearest station is Drogheda, with frequent services from Dublin and Belfast, T: (01) 836 6222.

By bus: Bus Eireann run services to Kinnegad, Trim, Navan and Drogheda, T: (01) 836 6111.

WHERE TO STAY

Hotels and B&Bs: Thackeray stayed at Annesbrook, in Duleek, T: (041) 23293. B&Bs include Mrs Finnegan in Trim, T: (046) 31635; Mrs Hevey in Slane, T: (401) 982 4121; Mrs Russell in Navan, T: (046) 23719; and Mrs McDonnell in Drogheda, T: (041) 983 6700.

Youth hostels: Bridge House Tourist Hostel is in Trim, T: (046) 31848.

ACTIVITIES

Cycling: bikes can be hired from Clarke's Sports Den in Navan, T: (046) 21130, during the summer.

Riding: Castlehill and Studd Equestrian Centre is in Julianstown, T: (041) 29430.

Fishing: contact the Eastern Regional Fisheries Board, T: (01) 837 9209.

FURTHER INFORMATION

Tourist offices: the BF offices in Trim, T: (0406) 37111, and Drogheda, T: (041) 983 7070, are open during the summer.

CHAPTER 7

Northern Ireland

Northern Ireland is much misunderstood. People abroad consider it dour, industrial, industrious, fanatic, joyless, gratingly masculine. They think of it as full of tough, Bible-belt fundamentalists calling down the wrath of God on a minority of libertine Catholics. Or vice versa. There are little corners of the North where these ideas have a certain validity. Mostly they are wrong. When I go to the North I expect to be cheered up and almost invariably am. I have wished my life would allow me to live in Belfast, the most buoyantly cheerful, kind, intelligent and alive city I know. I have the greatest difficulty getting people to believe me.

I tell them of the Northern sense of humour, a commodity many think does not exist, of the friendliness and helpfulness you will meet as a traveller – quite as much in the North as in the Republic. People are surprised to hear that outside touchy areas Catholic and Protestant are, and as often as not have been, neighbours, and good neighbours at that. Of course Ulster retains its strong Scottish connection. It would be curious if things were otherwise, for if you look east from the North's east coast, Scotland is the only country you see, as close as 12 miles (19 kilometres) away. The important role played in the history of America by the Scots-Irish of Ulster is often ignored: they provided several presidents and hundreds of thousands of less highly placed immigrants.

Ulster has often led the rest of Ireland, as far back as history takes us. It piloted

---

Slopes of debris running down to the sea skirt the sheer basaltic cliffs of Fair Head, topped by a freshwater lake, at Ireland's north-east corner.

violent bids for independence in the 16th, 17th and 18th centuries, and it has given Ireland many of its heroes, ancient and legendary, modern and real. Not that Ulster and Northern Ireland are quite the same thing. The latter consists of six counties retained within the United Kingdom in 1921 when the rest of the country achieved independence. The ancient province of Ulster comprises these six and a further three – Donegal, Cavan and Monaghan – which, being essentially Catholic, were allowed to go with the South.

The greatest misconception of all is that the North is dull and plain to look at and travel in. For its size it has a variety of scenic beauty that few similar areas can boast. You could walk out of the sea, up the Mourne Mountains, and down to the bird-haunted dunes of the Murlough reserve in an afternoon. An hour's drive in a car could show you the yo-yo undulations of Antrim's east coast; views of Rathlin, the Mull of Kintyre, Islay and the distant Scottish highlands over the water from the dizzying heights of Fair Head; the broad fertile gashes of the Glens; a bleak brown and purple plateau of Antrim moorland and the out-of-kilter architecture of grey basalt hexagons that form the Giant's Causeway.

Not all these items pass as true wilderness. In the North, even more than in the Republic, defining what is wild is difficult. Both countries have cultivated and grazed every inch they can. As in the South, the wild consists in the main of cliffs, sand, rivers, lakes and mountain tops. But here the problem is a little more acute. Because it is richer, because it wants to show off the merits of its system, because it is less content than the Republic to leave things that are doing no great harm as they are, because it has less room,

because it is more provident – for whatever reason, the government of the North tends to look after the external and visible elements of the land better than that of the South.

You notice this at its best and most obvious in the state of road surfaces, the durable solidity of road signs, the neat cleanliness of the houses, castles and other sites open to the public. On the other hand, this dedication to the spick, span and explicit assorts ill with wildness. There are just too many signs, too many nanny hands reaching down to take us along the mountain walk, to the bird-watching hide, or the rocky beach.

There is no need to dwell on this tendency to domesticate, or reduce to human dimensions, because so much of the North is not conducible to this end. The inland lakes – Neagh and Upper and Lower Lough Erne – do little more than nod acknowledgement of the human presence. Neagh, the biggest sheet of water in Ireland, needs getting to know. Its surrounds are mostly flattish and on a grey day it is no more than a wet grey carpet in the plain. Bit by bit it reveals its charms: the Oxford Island bird reserve or the park at Shane's Castle are the obvious points of access, but innumerable little lanes lead to countless little bays in its fish-rich, bird-frequented periphery. The two Lough Ernes are a pattern of islands – 57 in the upper, 96 in the lower – and form part of the longest navigable stretch of water in Ireland. Exploration calls for a boat. Their surrounds are beautiful and they are rich in birds and plant life.

There are two big mountain ranges in the North. Of the two, the Sperrins are the less dramatic: gentle slopes for the most part, and some broad mantles of forestry, but never crowded. The

Mournes, of course, draw the crowds. They are an easy drive from the most populous parts of the province. To my taste, these relatively recent extrusions of granite have made one of the most fetchingly shaped ranges in Ireland. In their roll down to the sea they add another jewel to the North's coastal treasury. The deeply penetrating sea loughs (Belfast, Larne and island-studded Strangford); Antrim's climbs and cliffs; the great flawed Causeway set down for Finn the giant to march to Staffa and the land of Argyll; Sheep Island with its wing-spreading cormorants and Rathlin Island with its avian opera-house and the descendants of the spider that spurred a king to glory – all these are the North. There is nothing dour, dull or humourless about them.

GETTING THERE

By air: British Airways, T: (0845) 722 2111, www.british airways.com, fly direct from London (Heathrow), Paris and Amsterdam to Belfast International. Jersey European, T: (0870) 567 6676, www.jersey european.com, flies from London (Gatwick and Stansted) to Belfast City, and from Toulouse and Paris via Birmingham; easyJet operates a service from Luton, T: (0870) 600 0000, www.easyJet.com; Aer Lingus from New York, T: (0845) 973 7747 (Belfast), www.aerlingus.ie. You can also contact Belfast International Airport, T: (028) 9442 2888.
By sea: crossings to Belfast are operated from Liverpool by Norse Irish Ferries, T: (028) 9077 9090, in 9 hrs 30 mins; from Stranraer, either by Seacat in 90 mins, T: (0870) 552 3523, or by Stena Line in just over 3 hrs, T: (0870) 570 7070. The Isle of Man Steam Packet Co. operates a service from Douglas, T: (0870) 552 3523. (All are UK mainland numbers except those prefixed 028 which are Northern Ireland.)
By car: from the Republic, cross the border only at officially recommended points, marked on road maps.
By rail: there are 4 main lines from Belfast Central, north-west to Derry, north-east to Larne, east to Bangor and south to Dublin. The Dublin–Belfast express takes 2 hrs, with 8 trains Mon–Sat and 5 on Sun. Rail Runabout tickets are available from main stations. Contact Northern Ireland Railways, T: (028) 9089 9411, www.translink.co.uk.
By bus: regular express and local services radiate from Belfast to major towns, most operated by Ulsterbus, T: (028) 9033 3000, www.trans link. co.uk.

WHERE TO STAY

For lists of self-catering (vacation-home) accommodation send an s.a.e. to Northern Ireland Self-Catering Association, Carlton Cottages, Belleek BT93 3FX. For a youth-hostel guide contact Hostelling International Northern Ireland, T: (028) 9032 4733, www.hini.org.uk. Northern Ireland Tourist Board publish an accommodation guide, *Where To Stay In Northern Ireland*, listing hotels, guest-houses, B&Bs, self-catering, hostels and CCPs. NITB has a free-phone credit-card booking service, T: (00800) 6686 6866.

ACTIVITIES

Walking: the Ulster Way is a 560-mile (896-km) circuit of the 6 counties, split into 32 stages.
Riding: NITB lists approved stables.
Climbing: contact Ardelinis Activity Centre, 1 High Street, Cushendall, Co. Antrim BT44 0NB, T: (028) 2177 1340.
Fishing: for information about permit requirements and the kind of fishing available in Northern Ireland, contact the Fisheries Conservancy Board, T: (028) 3833 4666, the Department of Agriculture – Fisheries Division, T: (028) 9052 0100, or The Foyle Fisheries Commission, T: (028) 7134 2100. Licences and permits can be obtained from NITB, T: (028) 9024 6609, and local tackle shops.
Outdoor sports: the Tollymore Mountain Centre in Bryansford, near Newcastle, organizes mountaineering, orienteering, rock-climbing and kayaking courses, T: (028) 4372 2158, www.tollymoreme.com.
Bird-watching: contact Birdwatch Northern Ireland, T: (028) 9069 3232; the National Trust, T: (028) 9751 0721; Royal Society for the Protection of Birds, T: (028) 9049 1547; the Lough Neagh Discovery Centre, T: (028) 3832 2205; and Strangford Lough Tourism, T: (028) 9127 0069.

FURTHER INFORMATION

Tourist offices: the central NITB office is at 59 North Street, Belfast BT1 1NB, T: (028) 9024 6609, www.nitourism.com.

FURTHER READING

The Complete Ulster Way by P. Dillon (O'Brien Press, 1999).

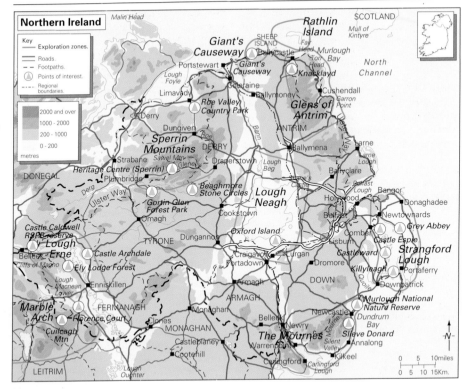

The Mournes

Picturesque mountain range in south-east County Down, rising from the sea between Dundrum Bay and Carlingford Lough

The rewards of climbing Slieve Donard, the highest of the Mourne Mountains, are quite out of proportion to the effort involved. You ascend from the exhilaration of Newcastle's sandy beach to an intoxication of mountain air, and to views over the Mull of Kintyre, the Isle of Man, Lough Neagh and County Down. This is accomplished in a climb of just a couple of hours, yet when you come down you may look back with satisfaction at what is without doubt a serious, steep-sided, cone-shaped mountain that looks as if it would not be out of place in the Alps or the Himalayas. Few other peaks

give such a ready, if only illusory, sense of achievement.

The effect is enhanced if you approach the Mournes from Belfast and the north. Much of the road is through drumlin country, a Lilliput of toy-town hillocks and villages and clean low bungalows. Always ahead is this fine dark silhouette of story-book mountain shapes: up-dome-down, up-cone-down, up-dome-squiggle-dome-down, getting bigger and bigger every mile. That is, of course, on clear days. There are plenty of days on which the peaks fail to emerge at all, as if the weather were affording them beauty treatment: a mudpack of mist, a massage by hail and sleet, a wash of rain, a tonic blow of wind and snow, from which they emerge, a day or week later, in incomparable bright splendour.

The range lies on a diagonal south-west to north-east, but the twelve highest peaks stand close to each other, in a rough circle, at the north-east end. South-east of the mountains the foothills level out for a few miles until they meet the sea or Carlingford Lough. This insulated lowland enclave is known as the Kingdom of Mourne, and consists of good farmland divided by the most impressive dry-stone walls in Ireland. These are constructed not from the slabs or variegated jigsaw blocks of the West, but from balls of stone the diameter of a forearm's length, some of them flattened at the top to make a perfectly level surface. They, and the mountains from which they are sprung, are composed of granite.

It was not a straightforward spew of molten lava that made the Mournes. The main transference was, in fact, contained underground, a mighty displacement caused by the dropping into the earth of a huge volume of shale – all this in the Tertiary epoch, some 65–50 million years ago. A covering of shale remained, so the risen granite was contained within the original outer shell. Since then almost all the shale has been eroded away. Exposed to the range of climates that followed – from tropical to Arctic – the uncovered granite cracked and split into characteristic rectangular blocks. It was these which, weathering and wearing at the corners, became the innumerable rock spheres which still hang around the heights or, having slid to the foothills, have been so skilfully cleared and piled into walls. The last stages of their downward progress were effected by ice, which dragged them along the deep wide valleys carved by its slow movement, whose river names are often repeated in the seaside towns at which they end: Kilkeel, Annalong, Bloody Bridge.

A long periphery of sandy beaches, with water of a green-blue clarity seen less and less in Europe's purlieus, hems the area. To the north, beyond Newcastle, begins a long broad spit of sand-dune, the Murlough National Nature Reserve, rich (and far richer than the mountains) in bird, plant and insect life. South of the Mournes lie the ten miles (16 kilometres) of Carlingford Lough, a varied and islanded sea inlet with the long wall of Carlingford mountain on the far side and wintering brent geese, ducks and waders.

Yet the Mournes are under an hour's drive from the nearly half a million inhabitants of Northern Ireland's capital, Belfast. As resource, natural sanctuary and source of recreation, it is not to be expected that they have been neglected. In high summer they are noisy and crowded and the roads can choke with traffic. Newcastle has more yardage of amusement arcade – 'the machines' – than any town of like size I know. The mountains attract many, but as the air gets thinner the number of people reduces drastically. To throw them off altogether requires great effort and a good deal of luck, and the best hope lies among that exclusive brotherhood of peaks which rise close to Newcastle.

Most of these peaks are linked by a great wall, 22 miles (35 kilometres) long by six feet (two metres) or more high and a yard or so wide. It was built early in the 20th century to enclose the so-called Silent Valley, which was then dammed to create the reservoir which supplies most of the county's, and much of Belfast's, water needs: an artefact, but a beautiful one, reflecting the reeds and shrubs and steep mountain-sides as they slide into its depths. But the finest sights come high on the mountains themselves. There are cliffs and chimneys and natural keeps of broken granite, easy slopes and demanding climbs, including sheer rock faces for those who cannot resist them, and stunning views which change rapidly from seascape to landscape, from rock to pasture, from Scotland to what seems like an unfurled map of all Ireland.

'Men of wisdom love the sea,' said Bertrand Russell; 'men of virtue love the mountains.' With a shore like that of the Murlough reserve nearby, I find my virtue soon crumbles and I am down at sea-level, standing or crouching to look at the flurry of bird life along the beaches and within the dunes. The population changes markedly with every season, for an enormous number of birds, from swans to midget passerines, breed or winter or pause for breath here on long migrations. The regular sandpipers, dunlins, scoters, mallards and others have often seemed to me to share local qualities. Quick, smart, clean-living, hard-working, they flock and bustle over sand and water with what seems like a palpable, Protestant sense of purpose.

THE CATTLE RAID OF COOLEY

The beautiful, red-cloaked and rather martial Maeve was married to King Ailill of Connacht, whose palace was at Rathcroghan in County Roscommon. She and her husband kept separate herds of cattle and one day her famous white-horned bull, unwilling to belong to a mere woman, abandoned Maeve's herd for her husband's. She decided to make good the loss by acquiring the peerless Brown Bull of Cooley (or Cuailgne, now known as Carlingford, in County Louth). She asked the owner for it, offering to sleep with him in return. He turned her down and she went to war. The consequent prolonged invasion was known as the Cattle Raid of Cooley, or *Tain Bo Cuailgne*. It is considered the *Iliad* of Irish myth.

When Maeve's Connacht forces invaded, the men of Ulster were laid low by a mysterious, recurrent sleeping sickness. Only the youthful Cuchulain was fit to fight, but he was remarkable even by heroic standards. To cool his ardour, for instance, three tubs were filled with ice-cold water and he was placed in each consecutively. The first burst asunder. The second boiled. The third got hot. He could contort his face into almost any shape. He could turn around within his skin, so that his feet and hands were behind him and his back and buttocks before him. In the war in question he took up position in strategic places and killed a hundred and more invaders a day. But such efforts took their toll. Even when he was covered with so many wounds that there was not a needlepoint of intact skin left on him, he propped himself up on a pillar-stone, strapped himself to it and fought on. Before the Connacht men killed him the other Ulstermen rallied from their torpor, and took on the fight. The image of Cuchulain dying for freedom remains potent, and was an acknowledged inspiration to those who rose against British rule in 1916.

(028) 4176 2220, and Mrs Mc-Math offers B&B in Annalong, T: (028) 4376 8350. For self-catering (vacation-home) rental at Wyllie Cottage, Newcastle, contact Mrs Maguire, T: (028) 9756 2800, and at Widow's Row, contact Mrs Speedy, T: (028) 4372 2642.

Youth hostels: in Newcastle is the Greenhill YMCA National Centre, T: (028) 4372 3172, and the HINI hostel, T/F: (028) 4372 2133.

Outdoor living: camping and caravan (motor-home) parks include the Annalong Marine Park, open all year, T: (028) 4376 8736, and Shanlieve Cara-van Park, T: (028) 4376 4344.

ACTIVITIES

Walking: abundant options exist at all levels of difficulty. For details of waymarked walks, contact NITB (see below). The Mourne Heritage Trust organize day hikes in the summer, T: (028) 4372 4059.
Riding: the Mourne Trail Rid-ing Centre at Newcastle orga-nizes forest and beach riding for the experienced, T: (028) 4372 4351.
Fishing: for excellent sea and freshwater fishing, contact NITB, T: (028) 3026 8877.
Watersports: the Carlingford Lough Regatta is in Sept; con-tact NITB for details.
Bird-watching: there is good viewing from Dundrum Bay and from Carlingford Lough, a European Special Protection Area (SPA) due chiefly to its winter population of brent geese. Contact the Mourne Heritage Trust rangers' office, T: (028) 4176 9825.

FURTHER INFORMATION
Tourist offices: Mourne Coun-tryside Centre, T: (028) 4372 4059, and the NITB offices in Newcastle, T: (028) 4372 2222, and Newry, T: (028) 3026 8877, are open all year.

BEFORE YOU GO
Maps: OSNI Discoverer Series, map No. 29.

GETTING THERE
By car: take the A24 from Belfast to Clough and then the A2 to Newcastle. To skirt the mountains, follow the coastal route along the A2. To enter the range, drive through Tolly-more Forest Park or Dollard Wood.
By rail: Newry is the nearest station to the Mournes, T: (028) 3026 9271. The Belfast –Newry service runs 5 or 6

times each day, Mon–Sat, and takes 1 hr. Sun services are more limited.
By bus: frequent services run to Newry and Newcastle on week-days, very few on Sun. The journey from Belfast to Newry takes 1 hr 10 mins, and from Belfast to Newcastle, 1 hr 20 mins, T: (028) 3026 3531.

WHERE TO STAY
Hotels and B&Bs: a free book-ing service is available at Newry Tourist Office, T: (028) 3026 6232/3084 8666. The Kilmorey Arms Hotel is in Kilkeel, T:

Lough Neagh

The largest lake in Ireland and the UK, much exploited for private and commercial fishing along its usually low and often marshy banks

Lough Neagh jangles with records and distinctions like a banana-state field-marshal with medals. It is by far the largest lake in Ireland or Britain, about ten miles by six (sixteen kilometres by nine), receives the flow of six major rivers, drains 42 per cent of Northern Ireland's surface. Rich in plants, animals and birds, it provides up to 100,000 wildfowl with winter quarters, and yields 700 tonnes of eel to fishermen every year: the biggest eel-haul in Western Europe. Nearly a third of Northern Ireland's homes get their water from it. The water it contains could fill somewhere in the region of seven million swimming pools.

You may glimpse or come on Lough Neagh from all over the place. A bit east of centre of the province, it adjoins five of the six counties: a huge flat sheet filling the hole left – so the myth says – by the handful of mud Finn McCool, in a rage, grabbed and threw into the sea, to form, as it happened, the Isle of Man. Geology tells a different story. Repeated disgorgements of molten basalt from the depths of Northern Ireland up to about 50 million years ago left huge cavities below. The crust here sagged and slowly sank, in all by some 1,200 feet (350 metres). As it did so the resultant depression was partially filled by clays, sand and plant debris brought in by rivers. Surveys of recent years have shown that much of the plant matter has been converted into lignite, a form of fuel that could be described as peat on its way to coal; consequently the lake is under threat from proposed surface mines and power stations, with the pollution these would involve. The overlying water of the lake is relatively shallow: on average about 30 feet (9 metres) and nowhere deeper than 100 (30 metres).

Lough Neagh scenery is not sensational. There are no picturesque tumbles of mountain or stream down to the waterside. Engaging with the lough always means focussing down from its broad national significance to little intimate encounters. It can be approached from any number of places and almost everywhere, in mild weather, there will be trees, pasture, marsh, reedy shallows, tethered boats and the slap and slop of desultory water toying with the shore. At Shane's Castle in the north-east corner there is a medieval keep and a row of cannon on the terrace over the water. At Gartree to the east is a lone and ancient church, marooned on an airfield. To the west, Ardboe offers a 30-foot (9-metre) rise, pleasant views, and a village of charm. You can swim anywhere.

The true wildness of Lough Neagh is, of course, inaccessibly on or invisibly under the water. A rich growth of algae supports all the teeming life, which in turn feeds a large population of fish. Eel – poor reward for their toiling from the Sargasso – are caught, on autumn nights, on mile-long, thousand-hook lines. Pollan (*Coregonus pollan*), freshwater cousin of the herring, is unique to the lake, while rudd, roach and perch abound, as do pike, those stubborn gourmands that have been seen to swallow fish of their own

A summer visitor from Africa, the common tern breeds in colonies on little islands all round the coast of Ireland, as well as in some inland waters, its excitable screeching belying the exquisite grace of its form and flight.

The massive 22-mile (35-km) dry-stone granite wall bounding the catchment area of the Silent Valley reservoir was built early in the 20th century to keep out animals. Grazed and ungrazed land displays conspicuous differences, despite incursions by some persistent, gap-searching sheep.

size and take three days doing it. A particularly giant variety of greedy pike is found in nearby Lough Beg. But the stars of the lake, as so often in Ireland, are the birds. Oxford Island National Nature Reserve is one of several well placed for sighting great rafts of diving ducks in winter. Abundantly present throughout the year is that flat-capped dandy the great crested grebe, who despite his rakish appearance becomes a dedicated feeder of his family as they grow. Three kinds of swan frequent the lake, and in winter graze on neighbouring pastures. From a distance they can look like flocks of sheep.

BEFORE YOU GO
Maps: OSNI Discoverer Series, map Nos 14, 19 and 20.

GETTING THERE
By car: for the north-east side of the lough, take the M2 from Belfast to Antrim. For Oxford Island and the south-east of the lough take the M1 out of Belfast to junction 10.
By rail: from Belfast Central frequent weekday and reduced Sun services run to Antrim. Trains to Lurgan run regularly all week. Contact NI Railways, T: (028) 9089 9411.
By bus: Goldline Express services run every hr from Belfast to Antrim. Frequent services operate every day between Belfast and Lurgan. Contact Ulsterbus, T: (028) 9033 3000.

WHERE TO STAY
Hotels and B&Bs: there are numerous options in Antrim, Moneymore and Moira.
Outdoor living: lakeside CCPs are at Ballyronan, T: (028) 8676 2205; Oxford Island, T: (028) 3832 7573; and Antrim, T: (028) 9442 8331.

ACTIVITIES
Walking: the shores of Lough Neagh are mostly sedgy and wooded, so park and approach the shore on foot.
Riding: for accommodation and riding try Richill Equestrian Centre, Course Lodge, 38 Annareagh Road, Richill, T: (028) 3887 1258, and Cranfield Equestrian Centre, Randalstown, T: (028) 9447 3716.
Fishing: options include game fishing in rivers, especially for bream and pike; and eels at Toomebridge. Coney Island on the south side of the lough is good for angling and canoeing. The Seagrove Cup fishing festival is held in Nov. Kinnego

Marina is best in May–July for bream, hybrids, perch, roach and rudd. Contact Paddy Preutry, Craigavon Borough Council, T: (028) 3832 7573. **Boating:** boats can be hired at the Lough Neagh Discovery Centre, T: (028) 3832 2205, or contact NITB in Antrim, T: (028) 9446 3113. Master

McGra Cruises organize trips to Oxford Island and Coney Island, Apr–Oct, T: (028) 3832 7573. **Bird-watching:** Lough Beg is good for winter duck and waders, Ballyronan Point for scaup and other ducks in winter, and Oxford Island National Nature Reserve for many other

varieties, T: (028) 3832 2205, www.craigavon.co.uk, open Wed–Sat, Oct–Mar, and daily, Apr–Sept.

FURTHER INFORMATION
Tourist offices: Antrim, T: (028) 9442 8331; Magherafelt, T: (028) 7939 7979; and Cookstown, T: (028) 8676 6727.

Strangford Lough

This sea lough, sprinkled with drumlin islands, is of enormous importance for wildlife both within its waters and along its mostly flat and muddy shoreline

Strangford Lough is a sea lough but, instead of opening into the sea by means of a broad splay of estuary, it is connected by a long and relatively thin neck, some five miles (eight kilometres) long and at one point only 500 yards (460 metres) wide. Twice a day, when the tide has started moving in, the level of water in the sea is higher than that in the lough. Twice a day it is the other way round. Either way the pressure on the water to even up the levels is immense. On its way in it charges through – all 400 million tons of it – and only gradually, as it spreads along the 15 or so miles (24 kilometres) of the lough proper, rounding islands and filling channels and bays, does it settle to serenity. In next to no time it is moving out again.

The wash of water over any particular corner of the lough is likely to be different in force and effect from that in another. That is one of the factors giving Strangford Lough its enormous biological variety. Another is the fact that, although most of its bed and shores are based on carboniferous limestone, the erosion of other kinds of rock, mainly at the northern end, feeds the waters round about with a varied diet of minerals. More comes from the rivers it receives, the Quoile, Comber and Blackwater. In spite of

the million or so people living within a few miles, the lough has not been irredeemably exploited or polluted.

The lough bottom tells much. Unlike the bed of the sea, scraped, grazed and heavily depleted by fishing, it teems with life. Huge carpets of stationary horse mussels provide a firm foundation for other species to settle on, a weird tapestry of things that squirt or sting or squelch: sea anemones, sea squirts, sea gooseberries, scallops, feather stars, sponges, worms, snails, crabs, sand-eels, jelly fish. The intertidal edge is rich in bladderwrack, tangle and other seaweeds. As often, the main and most visible beneficiaries of this abundance are the birds. Like so many of the waters of Ireland, Strangford supports crucial populations of certain species. Most of the world's pale-bellied brent geese pass through Strangford on their way to other coastal sites in Ireland, and the long shoreline and wealth of islands encourage waders and dabblers. The lough is never without great numbers of birds. Not the least conspicuous are the four species of breeding tern: common, sandwich, arctic (the bird world's longest distance migrant, from Arctic to Antarctic) and roseate. With their long wings, split tails and balletic motions – for fishing or display – terns are among the world's most graceful birds, though they leave a different impression when they dive at humans who get too close to their barely concealed eggs, and warn them off with Billingsgate menaces.

Common seals breed on Strangford Lough in large numbers – possibly the largest numbers in Ireland. Grey seals and porpoises are here too. The surrounding countryside is flat and heavily cultivated, but there are fine houses and estates and remains (Castle Stewart, Castleward, Killyeagh, Grey Abbey), and associations with St Patrick at and around Downpatrick. Saul, a mile or two to the east, is held to be the place the saint landed to begin the conversion of Ireland to Christianity in AD 432.

The curlew may be seen – and its plangent call heard – in any part of Ireland, summer and winter. Most of its food is worms, taken from deep in the sand or soil by its extraordinarily long bill.

BEFORE YOU GO
Maps: OSNI Discoverer Series, map Nos 15 and 21.

GETTING THERE
By car: from Belfast take A20 to Newtownards, then continue to Portaferry; or take A22 to Comber and Downpatrick.
By rail: the nearest station is Bangor, T: (028) 9089 9411.
By bus: services run from Belfast to Newtownards and Comber; change at Newtownards for Portaferry; also from Belfast to Downpatrick, T: (028) 9033 3000.

WHERE TO STAY
Hotels and B&Bs: around the lake are numerous B&Bs. In Portaferry try the Portaferry Hotel, T: (028) 4272 8231, e-mail: info@ portaferry hotel.com, or The Narrows, T: (028) 4272 8148. Tyrella House is in Downpatrick, T: (028) 4485 1422; and the Dufferin Arms in Killyleagh, T: (028) 4482 8229.
Youth hostels: there is 1 in Portaferry, T: (028) 4272 9598.

ACTIVITIES
Walking: the 34-mile (55-km) Lecale Trail starts in Downpatrick; contact the Countryside Development Officer, Down District Council, T:(028) 4461 0800. NITB recommend a 7-mile (11-km) walk from Saul village to Ballyalton.
Riding: try Rockfield Equestrian Centre, Comber, on the west shore, T: (028) 9187 2548; or Ardminnan Equestrian Centre, Portaferry, on the east side, T: (028) 4277 1321.
Fishing: contact Des Rogers, T: (028) 4272 8297, or John Murray, T: (028) 4272 8414.
Bird-watching: contact Castle Espie Wildfowl Centre, T: (028) 9187 4146.

FURTHER INFORMATION
Tourist offices: Bangor, T: (028) 9127 0069; Newtownards, T: (028) 9182 6846; Downpatrick, T: (028) 4461 2233.

Glens of Antrim

Series of nine glens cutting seaward and mostly eastward across the high plateau of north-east Antrim, containing several large nature reserves. Linked by a spectacular coast road

Here and there the narrow road rises and falls like a roller-coaster, though to drive as if it were one would be foolish because cars come the other way too. At its highest points the road comes level with the boggy plateau of heather and grass that sprawls over much of north-east Antrim. The dips cross the coastal outlets of glens which have run down, west to east, from plateau to sea. The up-down succession, all the way along the east and north coasts of County Antrim, offers, on a good day, some of the grandest scenery in the world. Scotland, as little as 12 miles (19 kilometres) away, contributes the changing facets of the Mull of Kintyre, the Paps of Jura, the island of Islay and some smaller islets. Off Antrim's north coast, Rathlin Island is another landmark whose aspect changes as you go. Near you, on the mainland, cliffs and slopes jagged like broken glass tumble to a sea that matches sunshine with a rich turquoise smile. At times I feel that at some undiscovered phase of our evolution we were giants with a highly developed frolicsome side, because rolling down the curved hills or pirouetting on the pinnacles or plunging into the blue seems such a desirable and obvious thing to do.

The Scottish connection – the accent, the strong Presbyterian presence (about 50 per cent in this part), the traditional thrift and homely virtues – is a physical presence here. A boat and a breeze would see you in Scotland sooner than a horse and cart could take you to Belfast. Every inch of this territory has a historic or mythical link with Scotland: royal incursions, clan vendettas, marriages, treaties, conquest. As long ago as the Roman withdrawal from Britain the Irish established toeholds in Scotland, as they did in Wales and on Man, set up colonies, and energetically evangelized the local populations.

But that was in the recent past. The first people arrived as soon as the last mile-thick blanket of ice receded and melted. Innumerable remains found at the base of bogs show that Mesolithic hunters were here 12,000 years ago, before the peat even started to form. There is something tremendously ancient and seasoned in this countryside, and every bank, ditch, runnel and tussock may be a clue to some past human activity, the way life was lived, animals killed, habitations built, food prepared.

Ancient is a relative term. Ireland's oldest rocks have been in place 250,000 times longer than the period of human occupation. The rocks of Antrim include the country's youngest but they are also the most varied – possibly the most varied in Europe – and for the geologist as well as the traveller the place is a paradise. The bed-rock of most of the county is basalt (see Giant's Causeway, page 210) but along the coast, and especially in the north-east corner, landslips and settlements have exposed carboniferous sandstones, shales, old red sandstone, broken seams of trias and lias, and chalk. There are curious tree fossils from the Carboniferous period, layers of coal, boulder clay smeared by the ice across the basalt blanket, and flints, contained in the chalk and formed from silica. These were of great use, as innumerable remains show, to our earliest ancestors.

Such rocks underlie also the soils of the glens, with their broad scooped floors and steep hanging sides. Formed first by rivers wearing through surface basalt, these descending valleys were expanded and rounded by the slow and intransigent dynamic of the glacial ice into their present dimensions. Narrow, wooded (sometimes with forestry sitkas) and cut by thin white waterfalls in their upper reaches, they unfurl lower down to provide rich alluvial soils for farmers and to frame rounded views of Scotland beyond the sea. But the glens themselves, for all the attractions of sheep, tufted banks, gurgling rivulets, lichened stone walls and evocative abandoned farmhouses beside their protective groves of pine and beech, are not wild. The wilderness is on the inland heights.

It is unfortunately hard to resist the suspicion that the Garron plateau, some 50 undulating square miles (130 square kilometres) spreading south-west from Garron Point, is the largest area without tracks in Northern Ireland because there is little reason, certainly in the aesthetic line, for crossing it. Wild ponies do, and they are interesting. There are a lot of birds. But these occur elsewhere. Romantics might see a kind of Wuthering Heights appeal in ominous weathers, but even they will recognize that the Antrim uplands tend to be desolate and featureless, hard and soggy by turn, unrewarding. They are seriously upstaged by the dramas of the nearby coast.

Even here, by the sea, there are problems. Indeed, the better the scenery the worse the problem. Murlough Bay is one of the great sights of the north coast, but it is the fate of great sights, especially those consigned to the National Trust, to be tamed to order and predictability. So this steep, bumpy terrain, bristling with rocky outcrops, and falling to a beach in a bay with stony islands, is impaled on a zigzag road which swells into a car park halfway down. The custodian's cottage is suburban-neat. You might have to meet deer and other wildlife by appointment: there is no other way. Individuals and traffic need control. By and large the control is sensible. I am standing aside and moaning for a world gone by.

It is, besides, only in the best-known sites

that the intrusions are seen and felt. Apart from Murlough and Fair Head and the world-famous spectacles to the west of Ballycastle, you can walk the whole coast of Antrim with scarcely more than a signpost to tell you humans have passed this way before. Knocklayd, a mighty if slightly bland mountain south of Ballycastle, is an easy climb with colossal views accumulating as you go. For the bird-watcher the whole daunting stretch of uplands can make walks worthwhile. Curlews nest there, along with a few, a very few, golden plovers, red grouse, black-headed gulls and redshanks. At Fair Head, to match its awesome structures, several birds of prey have bred in recent years: sparrowhawks, kestrels, buzzards, but also the rarer peregrine falcon.

BEFORE YOU GO
Maps: OSNI Discoverer Series, map No. 9.

GETTING THERE
By car: the A2 from Belfast runs along the coast to Ballycastle. Beyond Cushendun the minor coast road passing Torr Head is steep and winding but provides breathtaking views as far as Scotland.
By rail: regular services from Belfast run to Ballymena and Larne. Contact NI Railways, T: (028) 9089 9411.
By bus: regular services go from Belfast to Ballymena but from there, there are only 4 connecting buses a day to Ballycastle (Mon–Sat). The Antrim Coaster runs along the coast between Coleraine and Larne, stopping once a day at Ballycastle, Mon–Sat. Contact Ulsterbus, T: (028) 9033 3000.

WHERE TO STAY
Hotels and B&Bs: there are plenty along the coast and in the glens, including the Thornlea Hotel, Cushendun, T: (028) 2177 1223, and the Londonderry Arms Hotel, Carnlough, T: (028) 2888 5255, e-mail: lda@glensofantrim.com. Ballycastle has a wide selection of B&Bs. Try the Antrim Arms on Castle Street, T: (028) 2076 2284, or the Gortconney Farm

House, T: (028) 2076 2283, open Mar–Sept.
Youth hostels: Ballycastle has The Castle Hostel, T: (028) 2076 2337, the Ballycastle Backpackers, T: (028) 2076 3612, and Sheep Island View, T: (028) 2076 9391, www.sheepisland.hypermart.net. There is a HINI hostel in Cushendall, T: (028) 2177 1344.
Outdoor living: the Silvercliffs CCP, T: (028) 2076 2550, and Maguire Strand CCP, T: (028) 2076 3294, are both in Ballycastle. Camping is also available in Cushendun, T: (028) 2176 61254, and Glenariff Forest Park, T: (028) 2175 8232.

ACTIVITIES
Walking: to walk round Fair Head, park at Murlough car park. A section of the Ulster Way stretches between Ballycastle and Cushendall. For details contact NITB.
Riding: Watertop Trekking Centre, Ballycastle, T: (028) 2076 2576, offers daily treks in July and Aug.
Fishing: there is good sea-angling off the coast. Red Bay Boats, Coast Road, Cushendall, T: (028) 2177 1331, e-mail: info@redbayboats.com, hire boats and tackle.
Bird-watching: at Fair Head there may be buzzard,

A sunset silhouette of muscular oak branches stands out against the lake in Castlewellan Forest Park a few miles north of the Mournes.

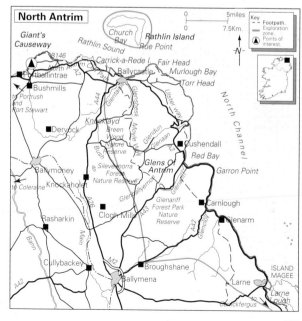

kestrel, peregrine, sparrow-hawk, chough and twite. At Murlough Bay look for eider and fulmar. At Larne Lough/Swan Island there are pale-bellied brent geese in winter and common and sandwich terns in summer, along with red-breasted merganser.

FURTHER INFORMATION
Tourist offices: Ballycastle, T: (028) 2076 2024, and Larne, T: (028) 2826 0088, are open all year; the office in Cushendall is seasonal, T: (028) 2577 1180.
Park office: Glenariff Forest Park, on the A43 Ballymena-Waterfoot road, T: (028) 2175 8232.

Rathlin Island

The shape of an inverted 'L', its cliffs and stacks are important for breeding sea-birds

Crossing to Rathlin you can feel you are within a Gaelic archipelago, with Scotland on the right, Ireland behind and the island ahead. Kintyre, Islay, Jura, and Argyll, kingdom of the eastern Gael, are out of sight to the north. There to your left is the Giant's Causeway, which (in legend at least) carries on submerged to Scotland, where it re-emerges as Fingal's Cave. You hear Scottish accents. And you recall Robert the Bruce, pondering his defeats and exile in a cave in the north-east of the island until the famous imperturbable spider he observed repeatedly trying to spin a web inspires him to go back and fight his English enemies.

I do not know whether arachnologists make pilgrim-ages to the place, or whether Rathlin spiders are otherwise special. There are plenty of caves. There are delightful plants: various of the more common orchids, thyme, broomrape (*Orobanche alba*), and the arum-like fern Adder's tongue (*Ophioglossum vulgatum*). Most of all there are birds: on occasion distinct rarities like golden eagles and sea eagles. Peregrines have bred in recent years. The general run of sea-birds is well represented. Even on the journey across the water (which, by the way, is noted for turbulence, with currents and winds funnelled through the sound) there may be Manx shearwater, and there are certainly common scoter and velvet scoter. Sometimes gannets – another Scottish connection – make a day trip from Ailsa Craig in the Firth of Clyde. The best, however, is yet to come.

Rathlin is a fine, hilly island with a bloody history and interesting remains, including a Neolithic factory for making tools out of porcellanite, a rare mineral of extreme hardness. It is four miles (six km) long and one mile and upwards wide, the shape of a sock, as someone pointed out in Tudor times, with the toe on the east, pointing at Ireland. Most of it is rich pasture, the soil based on the same basalt that covers the mainland opposite, though the underlying chalk is exposed on the south coast, around the harbour. About a hundred people live here. Vast and beautiful views open out to Malin Head (in Donegal), Fair Head, Torr Head and Scotland. The seas yield crayfish and lobsters to the two families that live by them, and a great deal more fish to big trawlers from Killybegs and from Scotland. But you would need to be a keen ornithologist to make the forty-minute crossing from Ballycastle.

In spite of the shearwater and scoter, and the ducks on scattered lakes, nothing is quite as spectacular as the stacks. A five-mile (eight-kilometre) walk or (in summer) bus ride west along the bending, winding road from the harbour brings you close to Bull Point. Here there is a sudden cessation of green field and a plummeting drop to, on one side, a lighthouse, and on the other, what suggests to me an avian opera house in perpetual, chaotic rehearsal for the big night. Far below is this huge, sheer, three-walled natural auditorium facing the sea. Countless sea-birds are tucked into niches, ledges, shelves and hollows, sometimes watching the activity in front of them, sometimes turned to the wall as if to protest at the prima donna. Others are speeding here and there with or without the appearance of a sense of purpose. The composite noise is of a high-decibel level, and much of it comes from what might be seen as the stage, two huge cylinders of black basalt diminishing in girth by stages as they rise from the sea, like tiered wedding-cakes, on which perch and screech and fidget and ovulate and defecate thousand upon thousand of the birds which always make such formations their own: gull, kittiwake, puffin and fulmar but predominantly razorbill (up to 9,000 of them) and not dissimilar guillemot (up to 40,000 in total), whose formal black coats and white waistcoats are very suggestive of a smart but anarchic orchestra. There is no conductor. Nothing seems to begin or end. To me and innumerable others this is, notwithstanding, one of the greatest shows on earth.

Along about two and a half miles (four km) of cliffs stretching north from the stacks (and managed and owned by the RSPB) there are breeding black guillemot, puffin, Manx shearwater, fulmar and five kinds of gull. Eider duck breed in the south-east of the island, and the meadows, marshes and lakes support good populations of characteristic birds.

Before you go *Maps:* OSNI Discoverer Series, map No. 5. *Guide-books: Ordnance Survey Memoirs of Ireland, Volume 24: Co. Antrim IX: North Antrim Coast & Rathlin* by A. Day and P. McWilliams (Institute of Irish Studies, Queen's University Belfast, 1994).

Getting there *By sea:* 2 daily crossings from Ballycastle in the off-peak season, 4 in June–Sept, T: (028) 2076 9299. **Where to stay** *B&Bs:* on Rathlin try the Rathlin Guesthouse, T: (028) 2076 3917, or the Manor House, owned by the National Trust, which can organize nature and bird-watching breaks, T: (028) 2076 3964. *Youth hostel:* there is 1 on the island, Soerneog View, T: (028) 2076 3954. *Outdoor living:* free camping available on the east side of Church Bay; ask landowners for permission.

Activities *Fishing:* conger eels in Church Bay, around the WWI wreck *The Drake*; pollack at Rue Point. Off-shore fishing for cod, haddock and skate. Sharks have been reported north of the island. Deep-sea angling boats can be hired at Ballycastle. Contact Mr McCauley, T: (028) 2076 9521, or Mr Bell, T: (028) 2076 2520. *Bird-watching:* the island's cliffs are home to tens of thousands of sea-birds. The best place to see them is the Kebble Lough Nature Reserve (also known as Rathlin Island Bird Sanctuary) at the west end of the island. Contact Birdwatch Northern Ireland, T: (028) 9069 3232. **Further information** *Tourist office:* 7 Mary Street, Ballycastle, BT54 6QH, T: (028) 2076 2024.

THE IDEA OF THE WILD

Until three centuries ago a publisher would have had what some Ulster Irish call 'a wee bit of a want' to attempt to market books about the wild. Wilderness was the enemy, the abode of the evil, weird and scary. If demons did not get you, highwaymen would. It was the tamed things like gardens that were lovesome. Landscapes painted by Poussin and Claude bathed their mountains and forests in ethereal light and garrisoned them with columned temples and vigilant statues. The Picturesque – an orderly marriage of nature and art – held sway through much of the 18th century. Towards the end, romance and gothicism were moving into art and literature. In stories and painting the appeal of the untamed, the farouche, the unexplained and unamenable continually grew. Thunder, lightning and clouds splashed landscapes; a sea was not a sea if breakers were not hurling ships against rocks. People loved all this. But they tended to love it only within book covers, or in oils and on their drawing-room walls.

The Lake poets – Wordsworth and Coleridge above all – are credited with making the wild physically desirable at the beginning of the 19th century. They actually climbed the Westmorland hills and wrote prose and poetry that reproduced nature's effects in a wholly attractive and appetizing way. Already people were dunking themselves in the sea (albeit from wagon-style bathing machines) for pleasure. The formation of a national police force reduced outdoor risks from cut-throats and robbers. Other aspects of the great outdoors became apparent. The English, leading the movement, discovered the Alps and started inventing things to do on them. They and others penetrated deep into regions of Africa, Asia and America, finding infinite reserves of what seemed to them exotic wilderness, even if to native populations they were just home.

Back in Europe, trains enabled people to get out of grimy cities for therapeutic sojourns on coasts, islands, rivers and mountains. Bicycles have made wild nature more accessible still. Advances in geology and biology added intriguing dimensions to the elements of the wild.

Nowadays things have come full circle. Humanity builds, bombs, lays roads, drains here and floods there, leaves empty cans and cigarette packs on the summit of Carrantuohill, and discards bags, clothes and even corpses on the side of Everest. Instead of our cowering at the thought of the wild, the wild has good reason to fear humanity and its insouciance.

Giant's Causeway

On the north coast of County Antrim, thousands of hexagons, a foot or two across, of columnar basalt, form an uneven floor under tall cliffs
World Heritage Site

This is nature's work; no doubt about that. But wild it is not allowed to be. It is far too grand and strange to be passed by, yet the effect it had on travellers up to fifty years ago and less is not to be had now. The main road you arrive by is so luxuriously tarmacked it feels sprung. By the car park (and thus close to the causeway display centre, the bookshop, the cafeteria, the hotel, the school museum) a National Trust notice pithily spells out your options: 'Starting here, you may choose from four

A trefoil flourishes beside a stream in Glenariff Forest Park, County Antrim. A number of trefoils and other plants have been claimed as shamrock, but since the word simply means clover without identifying a particular species, any could be worn without fear of error on St Patrick's Day.

walks along National Trust paths.' No more, you understand, and no less. There is also a National Trust bus that runs along the National Trust road every ten minutes in season. Here and there, National Trust notices deflect, warn, prohibit, advise. You cannot hope to experience the sense of the sublime our ancestors felt two hundred years ago, once they had overcome the fear of coming here at all. They were thrilled and chilled. They painted pictures which exaggerated the dramas, steepened the cliffs, enlarged the bluffs, puffed up the overhangs, raised the waves, darkened the skies, deepened the sunset, dropped in a shipwreck or two. We go the other way, making so much of the artificial that nature pales into the background, or staying timidly within the frame of a bus or café window.

All the same, more here was made by nature than by the National Trust. The so-called causeway, and the coast to the east of it, round Benbane Head, consist of a series of rocky bays with steep grassy or rocky slopes on the landward side, and, every so often, what seems like an inner skeleton of dark bones showing through. These are more or less vertical clusters of rock piping, each pipe usually of six sides and fitting, as in a honeycomb, tightly against its neighbours. At Benbane Head itself these shafts are fully exposed and rise to the full height of the cliffs. On the seaward side irregular tracts of worn or crushed columns jut out into the water, forming pavements of six-sided flagstones you can walk on. The biggest of these is the Giant's Causeway. The myth says that it was built by Finn McCool, one of the towering heroes of Irish myth, and

continued (and still does, underwater) as far as Fingal's Cave on Staffa, off the Scottish coast, where the columns reappear.

In fact, the causeway is the result of the welling-up of basaltic lava, which overran the prevailing limestone and has in time been eroded, split and stripped by slips and by the relative changes in the levels of land and sea. The hexagon is the form the lava takes on cooling; the slower the cooling, the broader the column. Horizontal stripes of paler rock show that long periods of slow sedimentary rock-building intervened in the build-up of basalt, which lasted in all some 15 million years, coming to an end 50 million years ago.

Before you go *Maps:* OSNI Discoverer Series, map No. 5.
Getting there *By car:* A29 from Coleraine to Portrush, A2 through Bushmills, then B146. *By rail:* Belfast to Coleraine then change for Portrush, T: (028) 3882 2395. *By bus:* services to the Causeway from Ballycastle and Portrush, T: (028) 7034 3334.
Where to stay: Auberge de Seneirl, T: (028) 2074 1536; Peninsula Hotel, Portrush, T: (028) 7082 2293; Bush Caravan Park, Bushmills, T: (028) 2073 1678.
Activities *Walking:* good cliff and coastal paths between Causeway Centre and Ballinatoy. *Riding:* stables at Coleraine, T: (028) 7036 5500. *Fishing:* game fishing in local rivers. *Bird-watching:* buzzard, kestrel, peregrine, sparrowhawk, guillemots, razorbill, eider duck, chough and twite.
Further information: The Causeway Centre, T: (028) 2073 1855; Portrush Countryside Centre, T: (028) 7082 3600; NITB in Portrush, T: (028) 7082 3333, and Coleraine, T: (028) 7034 4723.

Sperrin Mountains

A sprawling mountain range of forest and wild moorland; wooded plains and innumerable streams attract fishermen and gold prospectors

Halfway up the glen, between sea and an endless plateau of moorland, the Glenariff Forest Park is a kingdom of steep, lush and copiously watered woodland.

The Sperrins, in Tyrone, which is probably Ireland's least-known county, are, I suspect, the country's least-known mountain range. The highest peak, Sawel, is at 2,240 feet (670 metres) only two-thirds the height of Ireland's highest, and close to what Lloyd Praeger called, with crisp disparagement, 'the usual Irish height'. There are no spiky cones or vertical rock-sheets or leprous crags or deep dark corries, and hardly any lakes. Mountains have assumed the genteel shape of the open umbrella, more or less. But there are towering views from the heights, and long picturesque rambles (the walkers and writers Wilson and Gilbert offer an 18-mile/29-kilometre route that stays above 1,000 feet/300 metres) and pretty, peripheral wooded glens. Sawel's summit presents you, for the small cost of turning full circle, with the highlands of Donegal, Fermanagh, Cavan, the Mournes, the Antrim plateau and the steep escarpment of the Binevenagh range to the north. There is a great deal of blanket bog, above what might be called the farmhouse line.

The Sperrin Mountains occupy a slightly curved area (swelling southward) about 30 miles (48 kilometres) west to east and 10 (16 kilometres), more or less, north to south. They consist in the main of schists and gneisses, ancient metamorphic rocks blown apart by eruptions of igneous matter which has since eroded away. The River Glenelly, with a good road beside it, forms a rough southern boundary. Neat and kempt and steep-sided, with the odd wooden house, it looks rather Swiss. To the east, between Draperstown and Dungiven, there are dull dark miles of forestry plantation. The western edge slides down to the Mourne river, which runs into Lough Foyle at Derry, and the northern edge is broken by streams and wooded glens. It all makes for a quiet landscape in which to take a quiet pleasure.

The kestrel, hen harrier, peregrine, raven, long-eared owl and low-flying woodcock are sometimes to be seen in the Sperrins, and curlews and a very few golden plovers breed here. Waders winter on the flood plains to the north of Strabane. There is also a plant which occurs nowhere else in Ireland, although it abounds in parts of England, Scotland and Norway: the cloud berry (*Rubus chamaemorus*). Found in a few scattered patches of the high moorland, it is an arctic plant, with a distinctive orange fruit formed like that of its cousin the blackberry. It seems to have thrived during Ice Ages. For some centuries it has survived more by vegetative than sexual reproduction, a sign, perhaps, that it is out of kilter with the climate. The fruit, consequently, is even rarer than the plant.

There is gold in them thaar hills. Not much, and very localized, but there nevertheless, among the head-waters of the Foyle system near Plumbridge. Gold helped to make Ireland rich 2,000 years ago and more. It was made into brooches and other ornaments and exported to Rome and its empire, along with dogs and pottery. Wicklow was the main source (see pages 186–87) but some may have come from Tyrone.

Locals have gone a long way to augment the appeal of their mountains. There are centres with all the usual aids for taking in the nature and culture of the Sperrins and their surrounds; being so out of the way, the area is relatively rich in folklore. Over the years turf-cutting has exposed innumerable remains of Mesolithic and Neolithic inhabitants. At Beaghmore, on the western slopes of Beleevnamore mountain, south of the Glenelly valley, finds have been particularly rich. They include, from the 1930s, a series of seven stone circles, most of the stones being two or three feet tall.

For visitors to the Sperrins, places to stay are plentiful but distant, most of them in the surrounding towns of Dungiven, Draperstown, Cookstown, Strabane and Omagh. In the 1930s, Praeger had to share a five-foot bed with his botanical colleague, both of them over six foot, with their feet sticking out of the window, in the only cottage with rooms to hire. In the morning hens were roosting on their toes.

BEFORE YOU GO

Maps: OSNI Discoverer Series, map Nos 7, 8, 12 and 13.
Guide-books: *The Complete Ulster Way* by Paddy Dillon (O'Brien Press, 1999), *Walking the Ulster Way* by Alan Warner (Appletree Press, 1989) and *Ulster Walk Guide* by Rogers (Gill & Macmillan, 1991).

Other birds try, and up to a point succeed, but the kestrel is the only bird in Ireland that has mastered the art of hovering, while it quarters the ground for prey. It is found year-round in all parts of the country, and is no stranger to towns.

GETTING THERE

By car: take M2 out of Belfast, join A6 and then A31 for Magherafelt. You can drive straight through the mountains on B40 and B47.
By rail: frequent services run from Belfast to Portadown and Ballymena; connecting buses go to the Sperrins, T: (028) 9089 9400.
By bus: buses from Belfast go to Cookstown, Magherafelt, Omagh and Strabane and, Mon–Sat, to Draperstown, T: (028) 9033 3000.

WHERE TO STAY

Hotels and B&Bs: there are places in Cookstown, Omagh, Strabane, Draperstown and the rest of the range's periphery. For self-catering (vacation homes), try Drumcovitt Barn, 704 Feeny Road, Feeny BT47 4SU, T: (028) 7778 1224.
Youth hostels: Flax Mill Hostel is in Dungiven, T: (028) 7774 2655, and the Omagh Hostel in Omagh, T: (028) 8224 1973.
Outdoor living: Gortin Glen Caravan Park is at Gortin, T: (028) 8164 8108, and Drum Manor Forest Park at Cookstown, T: (028) 8676 2774.

WHERE TO GO

Slieve Gallion is worth a detour. It is a beautiful mountain surrounded by hills, collectively known as the Gallion Ring Dyke. Take the B162 from Cookstown and turn right where signed. Slieve Gallion Forest Park is open 9 am–dusk, T: (028) 4173 8284. Sperrin Heritage Centre, Cranagh, where you can pan for gold, is on the B47 towards Plumbridge, T: (028) 8164 8142.

ACTIVITIES

Riding: try Marsh Kyse Riding School, 123 Ballyronan Road, Magherafelt, T: (028) 7941 8860; the Edergole Riding Centre, 70 Moneymore Road, Cookstown, T: (028) 8676 1133.
Fishing: Moyola and Ballinderry rivers are good for trout and salmon, local loughs for brown trout.
Bird-watching: breeding golden plover, peregrine, raven and red grouse can be seen.

FURTHER INFORMATION

Tourist offices: Cookstown, T: (028) 8676 6727, e-mail: econ dev@cookstown.gov.uk; Magherafelt, T: (028) 7939 7979; Omagh, T: (028) 8224 7831; and a seasonal office in Strabane, T: (028) 7188 3735.

Lough Erne

Two lakes formed by massive broadenings of the River Erne, occupying central County Fermanagh and divided by Enniskillen and a narrower section of the river

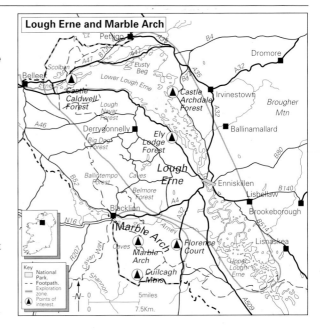

Lough Erne and Marble Arch

Most of the land around Lough Erne is used for farming, as are many of the islands. One island on the upper lough offers bed and organic breakfast. This is smart country, with the prosperous market town of Enniskillen dividing the two lakes. Wildness is usually out of sight or distant, on or in the water. Large numbers of great crested grebe (about 400), mute swan (400) and whooper swan (800) winter on the upper lake. The hundred or so pairs of 'common' scoter which used to make the lower lough the birds' main breeding ground have dwindled to under ten, perhaps due to the introduction of roach (brought primarily as live bait), which disastrously reduced the scoters' food, or perhaps to numbers of mink. There are also regular alignments of human anglers under large green umbrellas. People swim, boat and water ski, for as well as fulfilling other functions the loughs are human playgrounds on the grand scale.

This is an area of great historic interest. Enniskillen was virtually a Protestant frontier town in the 17th century, providing two regiments for the British crown, the Fusiliers and Dragoon Guards, a contribution matched by no other town in Britain or Ireland. The remains of many great Ascendancy estates rim the lakes. Some of these have found modern roles: in particular, Castle Archdale is now a country park, with a National Nature Reserve and arboretum, while Castle Caldwell has a timber forest and RSPB reserve of wooded islands on which a dwindling population of common scoters breeds. Both of these estates are on the lower lake. So are the

The Irish or fastigiate yew, of upright habit, is a variety of the common yew. All Irish yews trace their ancestry to a single, female tree found in the 18th century on a mountain close to Florence Court in County Fermanagh.

cliffs of Magho, dramatically overlooking the north-west corner, and, further along the west coast, Ely Lodge Forest, where fine old woodlands have been allowed to survive. These are in contrast to the miles of conifer plantations on the lake-studded highlands to the west, contained within the bounds of Lower Lough Erne, Lough Melvin and Lough Macnean.

The upper lake is really a dense pattern of islands, like Lough Oughter, from which it is scarcely separated. They used to say that Lough Erne was in Fermanagh except when Fermanagh was in Lough Erne, and before drainage and hydro-electric dams controlled the water levels there was much flooding of the abundant drumlin islands and surrounding coast. It is not always easy for visitors to reach the shores because so much land is private and deterringly

fenced. Great numbers of birds, including the great crested grebe and swans already mentioned and innumerable other winter visitors, have no such problem. Various waders breed in the prolific reed-beds lining the inlets, islands and lagoons. The corncrake – a symbolic victim of new farming methods (see page 146) – is more likely to occur in the marshy lands of this area than elsewhere in Northern Ireland, but even here it is verging on extinction.

Before you go *Maps:* OSNI Discoverer Series, map Nos 17 and 27; OSNI Lough Erne 1:25,000.
Getting there *By car:* M1 from Belfast, then A4 to Enniskillen. *By bus:* 12 Goldline Express buses run from Belfast to Enniskillen Mon–Sat (reduced service on Sun), T: (028) 9033 3000. **Where to stay** *Hotels and B&Bs:* plenty of choice in and

around Enniskillen. Try the Ashberry Hotel on Tempo Road, T: (028) 6632 0333, or the Lough Erne House on Lough Shore Road, T: (028) 6864 1216. The Ortine Hotel is on Main Street, Lisnaskea, T: (028) 6772 1206.
Youth hostels: Castle Archdale Youth Hostel, T: (028) 6862 8118, and the Share Centre, Lisnaskea, T: (028) 6772 2122.
Outdoor living: Castle Island Camp Site (and hostel), Enniskillen, T: (028) 6632 4250; Castle Archdale Caravan Park, Irvinestown, T: (028) 6862 1333; Mullynascarthy Caravan Park, Lisnaskea, T: (028) 6772 1040. **Activities** *Riding:* at Drumhoney Riding Centre,

The Giant's Causeway consists of a series of irregular pavements formed of the tops of basalt columns cooled to hexagonal shape from the molten liquid of ancient volcanic flows.

Drumhoney, Lisnarick, T: (028) 8952 1892. *Fishing:* coarse fishing on Ballinamallard river, pike and roach all through Upper and Lower Lough Erne. Brown and rainbow trout in Coolyermer Lough; brown and sea trout and salmon in Lower Lough Erne, very good at Lusty Beg, Lusty More and Hill's Island. *Boating:* Lough Erne Cruises operate on the lake, T: (028) 6632 2882. *Bird-watching:* large bird populations on Lower Lough Erne: breeding great crested grebes, several species of duck and warbler, including the Irish garden warbler. RSPB reserve at Castlecaldwell in the northwest corner. Contact RSPB Headquarters for more information, T: (028) 9049 1547, www.rspb.org.uk. Upper Lough Erne offers a great variety of habitat and has large winter populations of great crested grebe, mute and whooper swans. **Further information** *Tourist office:* NITB in Fermanagh is on Wellington Road in Enniskillen, open all year, T: (028) 6632 3110.

Marble Arch

Predominantly limestone area of woods, loughs and grand estates containing subterranean waterways, lakes and caves

Cuilcagh (pronounced something like queelca) mountain, whose summit (2,188 ft/798 m) straddles the national border, is divided between Counties Cavan and Fermanagh. Its surface is mainly sandstone with patches of millstone grit above, but the bulk of its body is of limestone. Time, water and the porous nature of lime have caused parts of it to become riddled with holes like a Gruyère cheese.

The mountain offers a good tough climb from the north side, waymarked from the road between Florence Court and Marble Arch. There are other attractions lower down: Lough Macnean Lower, the ash trees of Marble Arch wood, the mixed woods of Spring Grove. Florence Court itself is a grand mid-18th-century mansion, once home of the Earls of Enniskillen and now owned by the National Trust.

In 1780 a nearby farmer found two attractive upright yew trees on his land. He gave one to the Earl. Yews are either one sex or the other and in this case both specimens were female. Breeding true was therefore impossible, but cuttings were taken and the variety spread – always by that means – all over Britain and, in due course, much further afield. Indeed, all the world's fastigiate yews (*Taxus baccata fastigiata*) trace their ancestry from the Florence Court specimen.

A natural freak is found at Marble Arch, west of Florence Court. The arch is a natural, double-arched limestone bridge, and the water moving under it has just emerged from a network of underground channels and caves, through which it has flowed, concealed, down the mountainside. Or mostly concealed: sometimes the ground has given way and a subterranean stream is exposed. From the arch onwards, the water flows above ground to the River Arney. The caves by the arch have now been opened to the public, who can visit various illuminated examples, complete with waterfalls and stalactites. The tour is conducted partly in boats with guides aboard. Higher up the mountain, potholers – who are very unwise to go without local guides – can explore the swallow-holes. Robert Lloyd Praeger, who was among the team which explored and charted the caves in 1907–08, wrote of his experiences in a way that will not induce everyone to venture underground: 'The water is cold and as black as ink, the candle stuck in your hat is inclined to be extinguished if the roof gets too low or if owing to a blunder your head goes under, parts may be too narrow for swimming with the arms, and from the unplumbed bottom knife-edges of limestone may rise ...' But of course it is not candles these days.

Before you go *Maps:* OSNI Discoverer Series, map Nos 17 and 26. **Getting there** *By car:* from Enniskillen take either the A4 to Blacklion or the A32 to Florence Court. *By bus:* there are good Ulsterbus links from Enniskillen to the caves, T: (028) 6632 2633. **Where to stay** *B&Bs:* Belcoo House, Belcoo, T: (028) 6638 6304. For a complete list contact NITB. *Youth hostels:* Castle Archdale Youth Hostel, T: (028) 6862 8118, and the Share Centre, Lisnaskea, T: (028) 6772 2122. *Outdoor living:* Lakeland Canoe Centre, Enniskillen, T: (028) 6632 4250. **Activities** *Sightseeing:* there are tours every day Mar–Sept round the Marble Arch Caves, T: (028) 6634 8855, 10 am–4.30 pm; for the National Trust stately homes of Florence Court and Castle Coole, call T: (028) 6634 8249/6632 2690. **Further information** *Tourist office:* NITB Enniskillen, open all year, T: (028) 6632 3110.

GLOSSARY

An Oige (IYHA), Irish Youth Hostel Association.
B&B, bed and breakfast.
BF, Board Fáilte (Irish Tourist Board). Covers the Republic of Ireland.
Bus Eireann, Irish Bus.
CCP, camping and caravan (motor-home) park.
DART, Dublin Area Rapid Transit, the Dublin suburban rail network.
Eire, Republic of Ireland, T: +353.
Iarnrod Eireann, Irish Rail.
NI, Northern Ireland, the Six Counties that stayed in the UK when the rest of Ireland became independent in 1921, T: +44.
NITB, Northern Ireland Tourist Board.
OSI, Ordnance Survey Ireland.
OSNI, Ordnance Survey of Northern Ireland.
SPA, Special Protection Area. Wildlife designation, established in response to the 1979 EC Birds Directive, covering bird populations of European importance.
UK, United Kingdom of Great Britain and Northern Ireland.
World Heritage Site, listed under the UNESCO Convention Concerning the Protection of the World Cultural and Natural Heritage.

USEFUL ADDRESSES

An Oige, 61 Mountjoy Street, Dublin 7, T: (01) 830 4555, F: (01) 830 5808, e-mail: anoige@iol.ie, www.irelandyha.org.
Bird Watch Ireland, Ruttledge House, 8 Longford Place, Monkstown, Co. Dublin, T: (01) 280 4322, www.birdwatchireland.ie.
Bord Fáilte (BF), Baggot Street Bridge, Dublin 2, T: (01)602 4000, F: (01) 602 4100, e-mail:

user@irishtouristboard.ie, www.ireland.travel.ie.
Bus Eireann, Busaras, Store Street, Dublin 1, T: (01) 836 6111, www.buseireann.ie.
Central Fisheries Board, Mobhi Boreen, Glasnevin, Dublin 9, T: (01) 837 9206, e-mail: paul.bourke@cfb.ie.
Coillte Teoranta (The Irish Forestry Service), Leeson Lane, Dublin 2, T: (01) 661 5666.
Dúchas (The Heritage Service), 51 Stephen's Green, Dublin 2, T: (01) 661 3111, www.heritageireland.ie.
ENFO (Environment Information Service), 17 St Andrew Street, Dublin 2, T: (01) 679 3144, www.enfo.ie.
Environment Heritage Centre, Environmental Protection, Calvert House, 23 Castle Street, Belfast, BT1 1FY, T: (028) 9025 4757.
Fisheries Conservancy Board, 1 Mahon Road, Portadown, BT62 3EE, T: (028) 3833 4666.
Hidden Ireland, 37 Lower Baggot Street, Dublin 2, T: (01) 662 7166, F: (01) 662 7144, www.hidden-ireland.com.
Hostelling International Northern Ireland (HINI), 22 Donegal Road, Belfast, BT12 5JN, T: (028) 9032 4733, www.hini.org.uk.
Iarnrod Eireann, Connolly Station, Dublin 1, T: (01) 836 6222, www.irishrail.ie.
Irish Sailing Association, 3 Park Road, Dun Laoghaire, Co. Dublin, T: (01) 280 0239, www.sailing.org/isa.
Independent Holiday Hostels of Ireland, 57 Lower Gardiner Street, Dublin 1, T/F: (01) 836 4710, e-mail: ihh@iol.ie, www.hostels-ireland.com.
Mountaineering Council of Ireland, House of Sport, Longmile Road, Dublin 12, T: (01) 450 7376, www.mountaineering.ie.
National Coarse Fishing Federation of Ireland, Blaithan, Creighan, Co. Cavan, T: (049)

433 2367.
National Parks and Wildlife Service, 7 Ely Place, Dublin 2, T: (01) 647 8300, www.heritage.ireland.ie.
National Trust Northern Ireland, Rowallane House, Saintfield, Ballynahinch, Co. Down, BT24 7LH, T: (028) 9751 0721, www.nationaltrust.co.uk.
National Waymarked Ways Committee, Dept of Tourism, Sport & Recreation, Frederick Buildings, South Frederick Street, Dublin 2, T: (01) 662 1444, F: (01) 679 9285, e-mail: walsh@entemp.irlgov.ie.
Northern Ireland Forest Service, Department of Agriculture, Dundonald House, Upper Newtownards Road, Belfast, BT4 3SB, T: (028) 9052 4949.
Northern Ireland Railways, Central Station, Belfast, BT1 3PB, T: (028) 9089 9411, www.translink.co.uk.
Northern Ireland Tourist Board (NITB), 59 North Street, Belfast, BT1 1NB, T: (028) 9024 6609, F: (028) 9024 0960, e-mail: info@nitb.com, www.ni-tourism.com.
Ordnance Survey Ireland (OSI), Phoenix Park, Dublin 8, T: (01) 802 5300, www.irlgov.ie/osi.
Ordnance Survey of Northern Ireland (OSNI), Colby House, Stranmills Court, Belfast, BT9 5BJ, T: (028) 9025 5755, www.osni.gov.uk.
Royal Society for the Protection of Birds (RSPB), Belvoir Park Forest, Belfast, BT8 4QT, T: (028) 9049 1547, www.rspb.org.uk.
Sports Council for Northern Ireland, House of Sport, Upper Malone Road, Belfast, BT9 5LA, T: (028) 9066 1222.
Ulsterbus, Europa Bus Station, 12 Glengall Street, Belfast, BT12 5AH, T: (028) 9033 3000, www.translink.co.uk.
Walking/Cycling Ireland, PO Box 5520, Ballsbridge, Dublin 4, T: (01) 668 8278, F: (01) 660 5566, www.kerna.ie/wci.

INDEX

ACKNOWLEDGEMENTS

For much help and kindness,
the author and editors would
like to thank John Lahiffe and
Katrina Flanagan of Bord
Fáilte's London office, and staff
at the London and Belfast
branches of the Northern
Ireland Tourist Office, among
them Joris Minne and Stewart
Hanscombe. Swansea Cork
Ferries generously provided sea
passages between their two
ports, Norse Irish Ferries a
passage from Liverpool to
Belfast and SeaCat a crossing
from Stranraer to Larne.
Eleanor Mayes provided not
only the benefit of her
knowledge as a consultant but
also hospitality. Monica
Duckworth was very generous
with hospitality. Advice and
facts came from innumerable
people all over Ireland and in
Britain: in particular Dr John
Akeroyd, Alan Dalton, John
Feehan, Rosemary FitzGerald
and Matt Murphy.